CURRENT PROBLEMS IN THE PROTECTION OF HUMAN RIGHTS

While the legal systems of the United Kingdom and Germany differ in essential respects, the current process of 'constitutionalisation' is well recognised on both sides of the Channel. 'Constitutionalisation' manifests itself in the evolution of a constitution and the influence of existing constitutional principles on the ordinary law. Human rights law provides one of the best examples of this process, and the aim of this book is to provide a comparative UK-German perspective on recent developments. First, it addresses human rights questions which arise in both jurisdictions in a similar way such as the tension between liberty and security, absolute rights such as human dignity and the prohibition of torture, and the question how conflicts between human rights are to be resolved and conceptualised. A second theme considers the impact of human rights on different areas of law, in particular administrative law, criminal law, labour law and private law generally. Finally, a third theme focuses on the intersection of national, supra- and international human rights law, in particular after the entry into force of the EU Charter on Fundamental Rights. The book thus reveals convergent and divergent answers to similar problems, examines differences in the impact of human rights on the legal systems under consideration, and traces parallel and distinct debates over, and sensitivities about, human rights as well as sensitivities that arise in multi-layer situations in the UK and Germany.

Volume 17: Studies of the Oxford Institute of European and Comparative Law

Studies of the Oxford Institute of European and Comparative Law

Volume 1: The Harmonisation of European Contract Law: Implications for European Private Laws, Business and Legal Practice
Edited by Stefan Vogenauer and Stephen Weatherill

Volume 2: The Public Law/Private Law Divide
Edited by Mark Freedland and Jean-Bernard Auby

Volume 3: Constitutionalism and the Role of Parliaments
Edited by Katja Ziegler, Denis Baranger and AW Bradley

Volume 4: The Regulation of Unfair Commercial Practices under EC Directive 2005/29: New Rules and Techniques
Edited by Stephen Weatherill and Ulf Bernitz

Volume 5: Human Rights and Private Law: Privacy as Autonomy
Edited by Katja Ziegler

Volume 6: Better Regulation
Edited by Stephen Weatherill

Volume 7: Forum Shopping in the European Judicial Area
Edited by Pascal de Vareilles-Sommières

Volume 8: The Reform of Class and Representative Actions in European Legal Systems: A New Framework for Collective Redress in Europe
Christopher Hodges

Volume 9: Reforming the French Law of Obligations: Comparative Reflections on the Avant-projet de réforme du droit des obligations et de la prescription ('the Avant-projet Catala')
Edited by John Cartwright, Stefan Vogenauer and Simon Whittaker

Volume 10: Performance-Oriented Remedies in European Sale of Goods Law
Vanessa Mak

Volume 11: Current Issues in European Financial and Insolvency Law: Perspectives from France and the UK
Edited by Wolf-Georg Ringe, Louise Gullifer and Philippe Thery

Volume 12: Article 82 EC: Reflections on its Recent Evolution
Edited by Ariel Ezrachi

Volume 13: Prohibition of Abuse of Law: A New General Principle of EU Law?
Edited by Rita de la Feria and Stefan Vogenauer

Volume 14: Constitutional Pluralism in the European Union and Beyond
Edited by Matej Avbelj and Jan Komárek

Volume 15: The Protection of Fundamental Rights in the EU After Lisbon
Edited by Sybe de Vries, Ulf Bernitz and Stephen Weatherill

Volume 16: The Involvement of EU Law in Private Law Relationships

Current Problems in the Protection of Human Rights

Perspectives from Germany and the UK

Edited by

Katja S Ziegler and Peter M Huber

·HART·
PUBLISHING
OXFORD AND PORTLAND, OREGON
2013

Published in the United Kingdom by Hart Publishing Ltd
16C Worcester Place, Oxford, OX1 2JW
Telephone: +44 (0)1865 517530
Fax: +44 (0)1865 510710
E-mail: mail@hartpub.co.uk
Website: http://www.hartpub.co.uk

Published in North America (US and Canada) by
Hart Publishing
c/o International Specialized Book Services
920 NE 58th Avenue, Suite 300
Portland, OR 97213-3786
USA
Tel: +1 503 287 3093 or toll-free: (1) 800 944 6190
Fax: +1 503 280 8832
E-mail: orders@isbs.com
Website: http://www.isbs.com

British Library Cataloguing in Publication Data
Data Available

ISBN: 978-1-84946-124-5

Typeset by Hope Services (Abingdon) Ltd
Printed and bound in Great Britain by
Lightning Source UK Ltd

CONTENTS

CONTRIBUTORS

Andrew Ashworth

Vinerian Professor of Law, University of Oxford, and Fellow of All Souls College, Oxford. Publications include *Principles of Criminal Law*, 6th edn (Oxford University Press, 2009); *Sentencing and Criminal Justice*, 5th edn (Cambridge University Press, 2010); *The Criminal Process*, 4th edn (Oxford University Press, 2010, with Mike Redmayne); and *Human Rights and Criminal Justice*, 3rd edn (Sweet & Maxwell, 2012, with B Emmerson and A Macdonald).

Patrick Birkinshaw

Professor of Public Law, University of Hull. Professor Birkinshaw has published many books and articles including *Freedom of Information: The Law, the Practice and the Ideal*, 4th edn (Cambridge University Press, 2010) and *The European Union Legal Order after Lisbon* (Kluwer Law International, 2010, with M Varney). He has acted as a specialist adviser to the House of Commons Public Administration Committee on three separate inquiries and reports and has been a member of the Arts and Humanities Research Council, the Irish Research Council and the Finnish Academy. He is editor of the journal *European Public Law*.

Anthony W Bradley

Research Fellow, Institute of European and Comparative Law, University of Oxford; and barrister, QC (Hon); Emeritus Professor of Constitutional Law, University of Edinburgh; legal adviser to House of Lords, Committee on the Constitution, 2002–05. Publications include *European Human Rights Law – Text and Materials*, 3rd edn (Oxford University Press, 2008, with M Janis and R Kay); 'Relations between Executive, Judiciary and Parliament: an Evolving Saga?' [2008] *Public Law* 470; and *Constitutional and Administrative Law*, 15th edn (Longman, 2010, with KD Ewing).

Anne CL Davies

Fellow and Tutor in Law, Brasenose College, Oxford; Professor of Law and Public Policy, University of Oxford. Publications include *Accountability: A Public Law Analysis of Government by Contract* (Oxford University Press, 2001); *Perspectives on Labour Law*, 2nd edn (Cambridge University Press, 2009); *The Public Law of Government Contracts* (Oxford University Press, 2008); *EU Labour Law* (Edward Elgar, 2012) and articles on public law and labour and employment law topics.

Carsten Herresthal

Professor of German Private Law, Corporate and Commercial Law, European Law and Theory of Law at the University of Regensburg. Professor Herresthal teaches and researches in German private law, European private law, corporate law and the theory of law. Publications include *Rechtsfortbildung im europarechtlichen Bezugsrahmen* ['Progressive Development of Law in a European Framework'] (CH Beck, 2006); 'Consumer Law in the DCFR' in G Wagner (ed), *The Common Frame of Reference: A View from Law & Economics* (European Law Publishers, 2009); and 'Die Regelungsdichte von (vollharmonisierenden) Richtlinien und die Konkretisierungsbefugnis des EuGH' ['The Density of Regulation of Fully Harmonising Directives and the ECJ's Competence of Interpretation'] in B Gsell and C Herresthal (eds), *Vollharmonisierung im Privatrecht – Die Konzeption der Richtlinie am Scheideweg?* (Mohr Siebeck, 2009).

Peter M Huber

Dr iur, Professor of Public Law and Legal Philosophy at the Faculty of Law of the University of Munich; Director of the Research Centre for the Law of European Integration. Professor Huber was Minister of the Interior of the Free State of Thuringia (2009–10). Since November 2010 he has been Judge at the Federal Constitutional Court of Germany [Bundesverfassungsgericht]. He is the author of several books and over 250 articles on constitutional and administrative law, European Union law and human rights, including *Handbuch Ius Publicum Europaeum* 'Handbook Ius Publicum Europaeum'], vol I-V (CF Müller, 2007–2013, with A von Bogdandy, P Cruz Villalón and S Cassese).

Jan Kalbheim

DAAD-Lektor in German Law at Charles University, Prague. He has taught at the Universities of Strathclyde, Bayreuth and Munich and was a visiting lecturer at the Universitas Katolik Parahyangan (Bandung/Indonesia). He teaches public law, EU law, contract law and civil procedure. His main research interests are public law, European law, comparative law, jurisprudence and legal education. Publications include (with R Streinz) 'The Legal Situation for Genetically Engineered Food in Europe' in KJ Keller (ed), *Genetically Engineered Food. Methods and Detection*, 2nd edn (Wiley VCH, 2006).

Sophie-Charlotte Lenski

Dr iur, Interim Professor of Public Law at the Faculty of Law of the University of Konstanz; she teaches and researches in constitutional, administrative and art law. Publications include *Personenbezogene Massenkommunikation als verfassungsrechtliches Problem. Das allgemeine Persönlichkeitsrecht in Konflikt mit Medien, Kunst und Wissenschaft* ['Individual-related Mass Communication as a Problem under Constitutional Law – the Right of Privacy in Conflict with Press, Arts and Sciences'] (Duncker & Humblot, 2007); and *Öffentliches Kulturrecht* ['Public Art and Cultural Property Law'] (Mohr Siebeck, 2012).

Foroud Shirvani

Assistant Professor in Constitutional and Administrative Law, Law Faculty of the University of Munich. From 2009 to 2010 he taught at the Universities of Bayreuth and Freiburg. His research interests are in administrative law, Parliamentary law and environmental law. Publications include *Das Kooperationsprinzip im deutschen und europäischen Umweltrecht* ['The Priniciple of Cooperation in German and European Environmental Law'] (Duncker & Humblot, 2005) and *Das Parteienrecht und der Strukturwandel im Parteiensystem* ['The Law of Political Parties and the Structural Change of the Party System'] (Mohr Siebeck, 2010).

Sebastian Unger

Dr iur, Assistant Professor, Institute of Politics and Public Law, Ludwig Maximilian University, Munich. Sebastian Unger teaches and researches in EU, constitutional, administrative and tax law. Publications include *Das Verfassungsprinzip der Demokratie: Normstruktur und Norminhalt des grundgesetzlichen Demokratieprinzips* ['The Constitutional Principle of Democracy: The Structure and Content of the Principle of Democracy of the Basic Law'] (Mohr Siebeck, 2008); *Die Weiterentwicklung des Risikostrukturausgleichs in der gesetzlichen Krankenversicherung durch das GKV-WSG: Verfassungs-, verwaltungs- und sozialrechtliche Anforderungen* ['The Development of Risk Equalisation in the Public Health Insurance by the GKV-WSG: Requirements from Constitutional, Administrative and Social Law'] (Peter Lang, 2010, with PM Huber); and *Basistexte: Grundrechtstheorie* ['Basic Texts: Theory of Fundamental Rights'] (Nomos UTB, 2012, with Ino Augsberg).

Alison L Young

Fellow in Law, Hertford College, Oxford and Lecturer in Law, University of Oxford. She teaches and researches in constitutional law, constitutional theory, administrative law, European Union law, comparative public law and human rights. Her publications include *Parliamentary Sovereignty and the Human Rights Act* (Hart Publishing, 2009); 'Mapping Horizontal Effect' in D Hoffman (ed), *The Impact of the UK Human Rights Act on Private Law* (Cambridge University Press, 2011) 16; 'Human Rights, Horizontality and the Public/Private Divide: Towards a Holistic Approach' (2009) 2 *UCL Human Rights Law Review* 159; 'Horizontality and the Human Rights Act 1998' in KS Ziegler (ed), *Human Rights and Private Law: Privacy as Autonomy* (Hart Publishing, 2007); and 'Remedial and Substantive Horizontality: the Common law and Douglas v Hello! Ltd' [2002] *Public Law* 232.

Paul Yowell

Fellow and Tutor in Law, Oriel College, Oxford and Lecturer in Law, University of Oxford. He teaches and researches in constitutional law, EU law, and jurisprudence. Publications include 'The Justiciability of the Charter of Fundamental Rights in the Domestic Law of Member States' in P Huber (ed), *The EU and National Constitutional Law* (Richard Boorberg Verlag, 2012); 'Legislation,

Common Law and the Virtue of Clarity' in R Ekins (ed), *Modern Challenges to the Rule of Law* (LexisNexis, 2011); and 'A Critical Examination of Dworkin's Theory of Rights' [2007] 52 *American Journal of Jurisprudence* 93.

Katja S Ziegler

Sir Robert Jennings Professor of International Law and Director of the Centre for European Law and Internationalisation at the School of Law, University of Leicester. Previously, she has been Reader in European and Comparative Law and Erich Brost University Lecturer in the Faculty of Law, University of Oxford, and Fellow in Law and a Fellow of St Hilda's College, Oxford (2007–12); and DAAD Fellow and Deputy Director of the Institute of European and Comparative Law, University of Oxford (2002–07). She teaches and researches in human rights, public international law, EU law and comparative constitutional law. Publications include 'Executive Powers in Foreign Policy: The Decision to Dispatch the Military' in KS Ziegler, D Baranger and AW Bradley (eds), *Constitutionalism and the Role of Parliaments* (Hart Publishing, 2007); *Human Rights and Private Law: Privacy as Autonomy* (Hart Publishing, 2007); and 'International Law and EU Law: Between Asymmetric Constitutionalisation and Fragmentation' in A Orakhelashvili (ed), *Research Handbook on the Theory of International Law* (Edward Elgar, 2011).

Frank Zimmermann

Doctoral candidate and Lecturer/Researcher at the Chair of Professor Dr Helmut Satzger, Professor for German, European, International Criminal Law and Criminal Procedure and Economic Criminal Law, Ludwig Maximilian University, Munich. He teaches and researches in German and European criminal law and criminal procedure. Publications include 'Judicial Assistance and Equality of Arms – to What Extent Can European Cooperation in Penal Matters Serve as a Model for the Reviewed Rome Statute?' in C Burchard, O Triffterer and J Vogel (eds), *The Review Conference and the Future of the International Criminal Court* (Kluwer Law International, 2010) and 'Mutual Recognition and its Implications on the Gathering of Evidence in Criminal Proceedings: a Critical Analysis of the Initiative for a European Investigation Order' (with S Glaser and A Motz) [2011] *European Criminal Law Review* 56.

1

Introduction: Current Problems in the Protection of Human Rights

Perspectives from Germany and the UK

KATJA S ZIEGLER AND PETER M HUBER

This collection of essays comprises the revised papers presented at a joint conference of the Law Faculty of the Ludwig-Maximilians-Universität in Munich and the Institute of European and Comparative Law at the University of Oxford held in 2009. The conference was the first in a series of conferences on challenges of constitutional law in the United Kingdom and Germany from a comparative perspective, generously funded by the Excellence Programme of the German Government.

While the legal systems in the United Kingdom and Germany differ in essential aspects, the current process of constitutionalisation is well recognised on both sides of the Channel. Among the variety of notions attributed to this term, in the present context 'constitutionalisation' refers to the evolution of a constitution on the one hand and the influence of existing constitutional principles on ordinary law on the other hand. Presumably, the best example for this process is the area of human rights. Recent developments include the incorporation of the European Convention on Human Rights (ECHR) into UK law by the Human Rights Act 1998 (HRA) and the impact of the Charter of Fundamental Rights of the European Union, which was given binding effect on 1 December 2009 (Art 6(1) TEU). Protocol No 30 purports to limit the Charter's justiciability in Poland and the UK, but the consequences of this limitation remain doubtful.

This collection includes chapters from three different perspectives. First, the authors contribute perspectives from different jurisdictions on the same sort of human rights questions. Second, the effect of human rights is examined in different areas of law. Third, the law under consideration is not only national but also supra- and international. Such a reflection of different layers and perspectives is increasingly a distinguishing factor of modern legal research. In the light of this overall approach, each of the collection's four parts has a particular focus.

Part One approaches the complex process of constitutionalisation by examining the significance of human rights protection in different areas of law, the first being criminal law and criminal procedure. Against the backdrop of a common assumption about the positive reinforcement of criminal law and criminal justice through human rights and limits imposed by human rights on the criminal law and criminal justice system, *Frank Zimmermann* examines the ambivalent relationship between human rights protection and the substantive criminal law in more general terms. While accepting that human rights may require protection by the criminal law and analysing and comparing the relevant case law of the German Constitutional Court and the European Court of Human Rights ('constitutional minimum'), he also demonstrates and emphasises the 'liberalising' effect of human rights on substantive criminal law. Human rights may limit the application of criminal law, for example by excluding certain forms of punishment or by requiring a balancing act according to the principle of proportionality where other interests protected by human rights are at stake, such as the freedom of speech and the right to privacy ('constitutional maximum'). He concludes that both the proportionality principle and the principle of foreseeability of criminal punishment rooted in the rule of law ought to be activated to further 'constitutionalise' the criminal law, in particular also at the level of the EU.

Andrew Ashworth considers the influence of human rights on the criminal justice system against the background of the structure of the ECHR, taking a critical view on the potentially erosive effect of certain interpretations of human rights on the protection afforded by the criminal justice process. This may be considered to be the result of an already advanced interaction between human rights and the criminal law and criminal justice system as a particularly rights-sensitive subject matter. He critically examines recent trends, pointing to a watering down of the protection traditionally afforded by absolute human rights in the criminal justice system, such as Articles 3 and 5 ECHR. He argues that the European Court of Human Rights still strictly upholds the absolute prohibition of torture in the context of Article 3 ECHR when affirming that a trial that has been vitiated by torture, for example in the way evidence was collected, cannot be considered fair. This approach to torture must be contrasted with case law in regard to the prohibition of 'mere' inhuman and degrading treatment, and, even more so, with regard to violations of the right to private life or the home (Article 8 ECHR) where the structure of the Convention already provides for balancing of interests. He argues that the European Court of Human Rights has not been consistent and is potentially eroding the protections of the Convention by introducing balancing of public interests and proportionality considerations into its examination, which may too easily outweigh the rights protected by Articles 3, 5, 6 or 8 ECHR.

Four chapters then address the process of constitutionalisation in the area of private law from different perspectives. *Anne Davies* deals with the possibilities and problems of constitutionalisation in the area of labour law. In contrast to criminal law, human rights arguments are considered to be a relatively novel feature in UK labour law. *Davies* discusses in particular the tension between the individual and the traditional collective dimensions of UK labour law. For example, an individual common law 'right to work' may conflict with collective labour law rights of closed shop agreements and other expressions of collective bargaining. She argues that concerns that the individual rights dimension may be prioritised over the collective dimension of labour law because of the constitutionalising influence of human rights are currently unwarranted. However, she also points to the limited practical influence of increased use of human rights arguments in the UK and Strasbourg. She identifies a strong policy orientation of the executive and legislature towards employers' interests as one of the reasons. This policy focus influences the approach of the courts, which grant a high degree of deference to other branches of government when it comes to balancing employers' interests and individual (or collective) human rights in labour law. Human rights arguments are made, but only come in as one factor amongst many in the equation, not as an overarching constitutional value. In other words, while the use of human rights arguments reflects the formal constitutionalisation of labour law, this process does not (yet) translate substantively into outcomes or the creation of substantive constitutional values.

The next three chapters deal with the constitutionalisation of private law through human rights and EU law more generally: *Alison Young* considers the impact of the HRA on the horizontal application of human rights in private relationships; *Carsten Herresthal* analyses the impact of human rights on the freedom to contract and autonomy of contracts; and *Peter Huber* considers the evolution and influence of the provisions on non-discrimination in German constitutional and EU law on German law, and in particular private law.

Young examines the meaning and different forms of constitutionalisation of private law through human rights and the HRA 1998, distinguishing between influences on 'manner' and 'content' of private law, the former comprising procedure, procedural rights and institutions as well as the process of adjudication itself. She then reflects on the different forms of horizontal application of human rights and the HRA in particular, concluding that horizontal application of rights is both narrower and wider than the label of constitutionalisation. In analysing the tension and evolution of the relationship between the right to freedom of expression and the right to privacy in English law after the entry into force of the HRA, she demonstrates how the HRA has added legitimacy to the growing process of constitutionalisation not only of English public law but also of English private law. Although the HRA does not give the ECHR direct effect in the UK legal order, she emphasises that the indirect effect and a rather indeterminate and flexible approach taken by the courts may amount to a more effective protection of rights and hence may have to be considered a strength rather than a weakness of the UK's approach to the ECHR.

Herresthal critically reflects on the lack of constitutionalisation of the principle of autonomy in contract law [*Privatautonomie*] as a leading principle of private law, in particular at EU level. He argues that thus far autonomy in contractual relationships has not been reflected and fleshed out sufficiently to make it operable and to give it appropriate weight in balancing it with conflicting interests (such as social standards or consumer protection). He argues that this age-old principle should be strengthened against new challenges posed by human rights and the absence of a clear public–private divide in EU law, for example, by including it explicitly in the EU Charter on Fundamental Rights.

Peter Huber then focuses on the right not to be discriminated against in the light of recent legislative action of the EU. He enquires in his contribution whether anti-discrimination law leads to a shift of paradigm in the protection of human rights more widely. He considers that positive and modernising impulses emanated from the EU in regard to sex discrimination and quotas to promote women where the provisions or interpretations of the *Grundgesetz* [Basic Law] were less forward looking. However, he expresses concern about the influence of EU non-discrimination legislation and case law in regard to age discrimination.

The final chapter of Part One turns to the wide-ranging impulses of the HRA for public law. *Anthony Bradley* examines the impact of the HRA in more detail with regard to administrative law, revealing its strong constitutionalist force in the absence of a single constitutional text in the UK. He distinguishes two aspects of how the HRA influences administrative law: 'internally', concerning the content of administrative law; and 'externally', concerning the delimitation of the jurisdiction of the administrative judge. In regard to the latter, using the example of the right to be heard, he demonstrates how the ECHR (through the HRA) has enabled UK courts to protect this fundamental right where they would not have had jurisdiction under common law. With regard to the internal perspective, he discusses how the addition of human rights as a substantive ground for judicial review by the HRA has been crucial to enable judicial review in immigration cases. However, not all limitations of the common law have been overridden. For example, claims for damages in tort for unlawful administrative decisions (which breach human rights) will not necessarily be successful because the HRA did not create a new tort in English law; hence it would be wrong to conclude that a 'wholesale reform of the common law' has taken place. Nevertheless, as *Bradley* critically observes, the use of jurisprudence of the European Court of Human Rights by UK courts, in particular in deportation and terrorism cases, has triggered a debate about whether the courts go beyond their constitutional role and whether the HRA should be repealed.

Part Two turns away from subject area analyses to the cross-cutting question of how courts technically apply human rights, and more specifically, how they deal with, and have capacity to deal with, balancing between individual rights or rights and other interests. *Sophie-Charlotte Lenski* and *Paul Yowell* reflect on the criteria by which courts determine breaches of human rights from a conceptual and theoretical perspective in the context of balancing rights. While *Lenski* looks more closely at how conflicting rights are balanced in the light of recent case law of the Federal Constitutional Court, *Yowell* examines the practical application of the proportionality principle and the capacity of courts to deal with factual and empirical information when applying it.

Lenski contrasts a new analytical perspective of multipolar fundamental rights situations which can be found in several recent cases of the *Bundesverfassungsgericht* [Federal Constitutional Court] with the more traditional notion of indirect effect of human rights (as expressions of a system of values) in private law. She argues that the concept of multipolar legal relationships facilitates the resolution of conflicts between fundamental rights without having to refer to the objective dimension of fundamental rights. This is so because balancing between conflicting rights through the multipolar approach can take place at the same level as the rights in question, rather than using one right as a starting point, which possibly biases the outcome. While she argues that the concept of multipolar legal relationships is capable of generalisation beyond the specific cases discussed, it remains to be seen whether the Federal Constitutional Court will take this route.

Yowell discusses the relationship between human rights and institutional competence/capacity when engaging in complex fact-finding and risk assessment. He demonstrates how the proportionality principle requires judges to collect and assess empirical evidence by reference to historic and recent case law in the US and Canadian Supreme Courts as well as the *Bundesverfassungsgericht.* In particular he analyses how these courts have considered and used empirical evidence in three high-profile cases: restriction of speech by the prohibition of violent video games (USA), the possible interference with the right to life by the prohibition of private health insurance (Canada), and business and property rights affected by a smoking ban in pubs (Germany). He critically exposes the often haphazard nature of gaining factual information from – at least in this context – doubtful sources (such as Wikipedia) and the lack of scientific training of judges when it comes to interpreting empirical and statistical data. He argues that courts which have the power to decide on the validity of legislation should have access to research services at least similar to those of parliaments.

Part Three considers a specific issue: absolute rights. Whereas the previous parts enquire into the trajectory of constitutionalism at large and the technique of balancing, Part Three focuses on one expression of constitutionalism, that of normative hierarchies and on the accommodation of diversity where national and European constitutionalism conflict. The right to human dignity serves as an example for the divergence and convergence of human rights protection in the United Kingdom and Germany.

Based on Article 1 of both the *Grundgesetz* and the Charter of Fundamental Rights of the European Union, *Sebastian Unger* describes the inviolability of human dignity as a constitutional taboo. After sketching out the interpretation of the meaning of human dignity by the *Bundesverfassungsgericht,* he critically analyses the consequences of an assumption of an absolute legal value. He argues that an inflation of the meaning of human dignity has taken place and that the concept has been applied where reference to ordinary fundamental rights would have been sufficient. Human dignity, therefore, should be reserved for a narrow category of cases.

Jan Kalbheim examines the status of national identity in the EU treaties and case law and considers the impact of EU law on the right to human dignity. He looks at how, in a situation where different layers of law apply (namely EU and national law), a balance is achieved where concerns for a national identity are raised. He uses the *Omega* decision of the European Court of Justice as an example to show how national identity may be protected under EU law when conflicting with a market freedom. By allowing a Member State to legitimately restrict a market freedom on the basis of a specific aspect of its national identity, national identity may be accorded priority, at least in a situation where concepts of dignity diverge vastly between Member States.

Part Four is dedicated to the ambivalent relationship between human rights and security, in particular the restriction of human rights through anti-terrorism measures. *Foroud Shirvani* describes the evolution of anti-terrorist legislation in Germany from the 1970s, when the terrorist activities of the 'Red Army Faction' peaked, to recent days. He then focuses on the anti-terrorist legislation following the 9/11 attack. He discusses the expansion of the possibilities and competences of the authorities in charge of public security to collect and process data in order to combat terrorism. He demonstrates how in two key decisions the *Bundesverfassungsgericht* has taken a restrictive approach towards preventive collection and use of information and police action. He concludes that the 'preventive state' has to accept limits if it intends to retain its self-image as a guarantor of both security and freedom, the suitable constitutional concept being primarily the task of the legislature and only secondarily the task of the courts.

Patrick Birkinshaw's contribution provides a counterpart analysis from a UK perspective. He examines critically the recent legislation and case law concerning various restrictions on access to information in the UK in relation to suspects of terrorist offences, such as secret evidence and the Special Advocates in the Special Immigration Appeals Commission (SIAC), control orders and their successors (civil preventative measures) as well as public interest immunity in criminal cases. He highlights the widespread resort to deference to the executive by UK courts where an actual or perceived security interest of the state is at stake, but also critically points out how the features of secrecy have spilled over into other contexts. He points out that problems of secrecy are likely to continue in the light of the Government's Green Paper on *Justice and Security* published in the autumn of 2011. Nevertheless he stresses the improvement of human rights protection by the HRA and the ECHR.

* * *

A project such as the conference from which this volume draws and the publication of a book would not have been possible without the assistance of a number of people. Particular thanks are due to Sara Dietz at Munich and Jenny Dix at Oxford for their tireless efforts and enthusiasm in organising the conference, to Patrick Luff for his assistance in editing the manuscript, and to Eirik Bjorge for compiling the index. We thank Dagmar Coester-Waltjen for her initial impulse for the series of workshops and for her help in procuring funding.

Thanks are also due to the contributors to this volume and the publishers for their patience with the publication process.

Oxford and Munich, May 2012
Katja S Ziegler
Peter M Huber

Part One

Constitutionalisation by Human Rights in Specific Areas of Law

2

Human Rights and Criminal Law: An Ambivalent Relationship

Perspectives of the German Bundesverfassungsgericht and the European Court of Human Rights

FRANK ZIMMERMANN*

I. Introduction

This volume is dedicated to the 'constitutionalisation' of the British and German legal systems through the influence of human rights. In this respect, criminal law can be seen as a matter of special interest: its close connection with constitutional law is illustrated by the fact that such fundamental principles as *nulla poena sine lege* have their origins in the pre-constitutional era[1] – they were laid down in constitutions after they had been elaborated in a criminal law context. Thus it appears legitimate to say that criminal law has contributed to the genesis of modern constitutional law. However, this contribution will focus on the reverse question of how the modern doctrine of human rights shapes our criminal laws. This influence can be characterised as ambivalent: on the one hand, punishment can serve the protection of the (potential) victims' interests; on the other hand, criminal laws themselves can infringe basic rights. It is the goal of this chapter to compare the approaches of the German Constitutional Court [*Bundesverfassungsgericht*] and the European Court of Human Rights (ECtHR) and to deduce some general parameters from their case-law for the application of criminal law.

Given the necessity to limit the scope of this study, I will concentrate on constitutional issues in the field of substantive criminal law. Both the influence of human

* I am greatly indebted to Ms Johanna Weiß for her assistance with the manuscript.

[1] B Schünemann in B Schünemann (ed), *A Programme for European Criminal Justice* (Munich, CH Beck, 2006) 346.

rights on the law of criminal procedure[2] and the enforcement of criminal sentences deserve a more detailed analysis than can be presented here. The same applies to the very recent case-law regarding the German statutory provisions on preventive detention [*Sicherungsverwahrung*].[3] Furthermore, the perspective will mainly be that of a German criminal lawyer, but as a certain tribute to readers from a common law background, this contribution is based upon selected court decisions.[4]

This chapter proceeds as follows: first, it will examine the necessity of imposing criminal sanctions in order to protect human rights in certain circumstances (section II). It will then assess the risks for individual freedom resulting from an excessive use of criminal law (section III). On this basis it will sketch out a guideline for the moderate use of criminal law as an instrument of human rights protection in a final step (section IV).

II. Criminal Law as a Means for the Protection of Human Rights

The starting point is the assumption that some forms of behaviour are so unacceptable that society needs to react with criminal punishment. This statement is not at all one that can only be found in polemic television discussions or in the tabloid press – there are German as well as European court decisions that point in the same direction.[5]

A. Jurisprudence of the German Constitutional Court

That the legislature can be obliged to criminalise behaviour becomes most visible in two decisions of the German Constitutional Court regarding the criminal punishment of abortion. The debate about this highly political issue, which has lasted for many years and still continues to date, has led to several amendments of these provisions in Germany's criminal law (§§ 218 ff StGB [German Criminal Code, *Strafgesetzbuch*]).

[2] In this regard see R Esser, *Auf dem Weg zu einem europäischen Strafverfahrensrecht* (Berlin, De Gruyter, 2002).

[3] For details see M Pösl and A Dürr, 'Germany's System of Preventive Detention Considered Through the European Court of Human Rights and the German Federal Constitutional Court' (2012) *European Criminal Law Review* 158.

[4] Since most of the court decisions presented herein have been discussed intensely in the past, all references will have to be confined to a minimum. However, two fundamental monographs deserve to be mentioned: I Appel, *Verfassung und Strafe* (Berlin, Duncker & Humblot, 1998); O Lagodny, *Strafrecht vor den Schranken der Grundrechte* (Tübingen, JCB Mohr (Paul Siebeck), 1996).

[5] Also, the development of international criminal law could hardly be imagined without the influence of human rights. The traditional primacy of national sovereignty, which made it impossible to hold heads of state or military leaders accountable for their actions, would probably not have been overcome without the increasing role of human rights.

i. The 1975 Abortion Decision

The first decision of the Constitutional Court dates from 1975,[6] when a new provision (§ 218a StGB) had been inserted into the Criminal Code, exempting abortions from punishment on the principal condition that they took place within the first 12 weeks of a pregnancy. Hence, the Court had to examine whether such an amendment was compatible with the state's obligation to protect the unborn life. Although it stated that this duty could not be outweighed by a woman's constitutional rights,[7] the Court did not directly call for the use of criminal law to prevent abortions. In principle, the legislature should be free to choose the instruments to express society's disapproval of abortions as long as it established the minimum level of protection demanded by the Constitution.[8] In particular, the Court did not require criminal sanctions if a woman could not be expected to carry her child to term because of a serious personal conflict.[9] Yet, it held that the amendment to the German Criminal Code was unconstitutional and annulled it: since the amendment resulted in a complete abolition of criminal punishment for abortions within the first 12 weeks of pregnancy, the Court feared that it might create the *impression that such acts were no longer forbidden.*[10] Furthermore, it argued that the amendment would have allowed a woman to terminate her pregnancy *at will.*[11] According to the Court, these consequences would only have been acceptable if the legislature had compensated the partial decriminalisation with adequate alternatives to protect the unborn life. However, it deemed the requirement of pre-abortion counselling (in the way stipulated by the amendment) insufficient to compensate for the lack of criminal punishment. Under these circumstances the Court concluded that the legislature could not entirely renounce criminal sanctions for abortions within the first 12 weeks of a pregnancy.[12] Whether German constitutional law *always* requires the protection of the unborn life by means of criminal law is a different question, which was not clearly resolved in this first judgment.[13]

ii. The 1993 Abortion Decision

In the aftermath of German reunification, the Federal Republic once again amended its criminal law regarding abortions. Much in the same vein as with the attempt some 20 years previously, criminal punishment was to be abolished if a pregnancy was terminated within the first 12 weeks and if the woman had received

[6] BVerfGE (Reports of Judgments and Decisions of the German Constitutional Court) 39, 1–95 (1975).
[7] Ibid, 42–44 (paras 154–55).
[8] Ibid, 46–47 (para 162).
[9] Ibid, 48–51 (paras 164–68).
[10] Ibid, 53–54 (paras 174–75).
[11] Ibid, 55–56 (para 180).
[12] Ibid, 65 (para 202).
[13] B Jähnke in H-H Jescheck, W Ruß and G Willms (eds), *Leipziger Kommentar zum Strafgesetzbuch*, vol 5, 10th edn (Berlin, De Gruyter, 1988) Vor §218, para 31.

counselling beforehand. As an additional requirement, the procedure had to be carried out by a physician. Under these conditions the amendment explicitly declared that an abortion was 'not unlawful' (and therefore not punishable). One of the considerations for this second attempt to reform the law on abortion was that the old law (enacted after the judgment of 1975) had, according to statistics, failed to reduce the number of abortions, and thus failed to establish a satisfactory level of protection of the unborn life.[14]

When the Constitutional Court decided on the constitutionality of the amendment in 1993,[15] it went beyond its first judgment in one respect. It stated that, *as a general rule, the prohibition of abortions had to be laid down in criminal law* (notwithstanding its *ultima ratio* character).[16] This indicated that the judges regarded criminal punishment as indispensable in order to prevent abortions.

After this rather strong statement one could expect an even clearer rejection of the amendment than in the 1975 Abortion Decision. However, this time the Court's main criticism was not the result – the possibility of terminating a pregnancy without being punished – but merely the formulation of the provision, ie the declaration that abortions were 'not unlawful' if the above conditions were met. The term 'not unlawful' [*nicht rechtswidrig*] is quite common in German criminal law and usually expresses that the respective act is *approved* by society.[17] For example, an act causing bodily harm would be 'not unlawful' (in other words: would be lawful) if justified in self-defence or if it amounted only to a moderate injury covered by the victim's consent. As a consequence, such an act must not only be considered lawful from the point of view of criminal law, but in all fields of law. To declare an abortion 'not unlawful' simply because the woman had received counselling would therefore, according to the Court, have created the impression that such conduct is tolerable. But pursuant to the Basic Law [*Grundgesetz*, the German Constitution], the extinction of life, whether born or unborn, in principle had to be regarded as 'unlawful' – a verdict that could only be overturned under exceptional circumstances (for example imminent danger to the mother's life or health).[18] Thus, the second judgment follows the same line of argumentation as the first one.

Yet, the Court continued that *socially disapproved behaviour did not have to entail criminal sanctions*. Thus, if the legislature wanted to exempt 'unlawful' abortions from punishment under certain conditions, it could do so[19] – as long as 'lawful' and 'unlawful' abortions were not treated equally.[20] This shows a considerable shift away

[14] This argument was used in order to defend the new amendment before the Constitutional Court, see BVerfGE 88, 203, 245 (para 139).

[15] Ibid, 203–366 (1993).

[16] Ibid, 258 (para 177).

[17] Ibid, 273 (para 210).

[18] The Court also lists a (serious) disability of the embryo and the probability that the pregnancy emanated from an act of sexual abuse, ibid, 269 (para 201). These 'indications' had already been inserted in § 218a StGB after the Constitutional Court's first decision from 1975.

[19] BVerfGE 88, 273–74 (paras 209–12).

[20] Ibid, 281 (para 225).

from the 1975 Abortion Judgment because it essentially allows what had then been struck down: the abolition of criminal punishment for abortions within the first 12 weeks of a pregnancy. This second judgment therefore permitted less strict criminal laws in the field of abortion, although the Court had first (apparently) clearly called for criminal sanctions.[21]

In order to comply with the decision, the legislature amended § 218a(1) StGB slightly and limited its scope of application. Now the provision reads that an *abortion shall not constitute an offence* within the first 12 weeks of the pregnancy if it is carried out by a physician after sufficient counselling. As demanded by the Court, the law also distinguishes between abortions that are 'lawful' and others that remain 'unlawful' without being punished: for instance, health insurers only have to pay for 'lawful' abortions (§ 24b(1) of Book V of the German Social Welfare Code [*Sozialgesetzbuch*]).

From the perspective of criminal law, it may be asked whether this distinction is of any importance as the result is the same: a person concerned does not have to fear criminal punishment. In this context, it has to be pointed out that German criminal law distinguishes between different categories of grounds which can exclude a criminal conviction and that each of these categories has a different connotation (and can have different consequences, for example as regards the possibility of punishing accessories to the offence[22]). Maybe this complex way of thinking is typical for legal orders that are based upon written law. The focus in a common law system is (at least traditionally) the *ex post* decision of a single case. In civil law systems (like the German one), by contrast, the legislator has to act *ex ante*, and a legal provision must be appropriate for an unpredictable number of cases. This leads to a high level of abstraction and makes it necessary to develop a coherent concept for the handling of different cases. As a consequence, there may be a need to discuss the theoretical classification of a case even though it has no obvious effect on the result. The ad hoc development of new categories of 'exemption' from criminal punishment by the Constitutional Court is therefore problematic because it risks incoherence of the system of criminal law.[23]

B. Jurisprudence of the European Court of Human Rights

The ECtHR has also stated on several occasions that the protection of human rights can require criminal law provisions. However, the Court in Strasbourg has refrained from making a clear statement on the extent to which the Convention

[21] See also C Roxin, *Allgemeiner Teil des Strafrechts*, vol 1, 4th edn (Munich, CH Beck, 2006) § 2 para 96.

[22] However, it is undisputed that participation in an abortion which is exempted from punishment also must not be punished itself, A Eser in A Schönke and H Schröder (eds), *Strafgesetzbuch*, 28th edn (Munich, CH Beck, 2010) § 218a, para 12.

[23] Also the judgment in question is in parts contradictory – it stigmatises abortions as unlawful, but also obliges the legislature to establish counselling centres and thereby assist in the preparation of such 'unlawful' acts. For details see Eser (n 22) paras 14–16.

requires punishment for the termination of a pregnancy and has left this question to be decided by the states parties.[24] The beginning of life (in the sense of Article 2 ECHR) and its consequential protection must therefore, in principle be determined on the basis of national concepts.[25]

i. The Case of A v The United Kingdom

One judgment illustrates with particular clarity the requirement of criminal sanctions in order to protect human rights. In 1998 the ECtHR had to decide the case of a British boy who had been beaten by his stepfather with a garden cane.[26] In the criminal proceedings, the defence had argued that this constituted a form of 'reasonable chastisement' since the boy 'did not respond to parental or school discipline'. The jury approved this interpretation and acquitted the defendant.

According to the ECtHR, however, the stepfather's actions were 'inhuman or degrading treatment' to which no one shall be subjected, according to Article 3 ECHR. From this provision the Court did not only derive a prohibition against acts of torture or inhuman treatment that are performed by state officials, but also an obligation of the authorities to protect from similar perpetrations by private individuals. Consequently, it regarded the failure to punish the stepfather as a violation of Article 3 ECHR.

Two aspects of this decision deserve criticism. First, it can be doubted whether the behaviour was sufficiently serious to be classified as 'inhuman or degrading treatment'. Although it is convincing that inhuman and degrading treatment in the sense of Article 3 ECHR requires a lower level of severity than torture,[27] it should nevertheless be interpreted in the light of the criteria for torture. Therefore, physical or mental injuries suffered by the victim of inhuman or degrading treatment still have to be of an extraordinary character.[28] This reading is also supported by Article 15 ECHR, which prohibits a derogation of the rights laid down in Article 3 (without distinguishing between the alternatives) even in times of war or public emergency. Yet, the Court mainly relied on the victim's young age in order to affirm that the case reached the level of severity required by Article 3.[29]

The second aspect to which the Court should have paid more attention was the fact that the acts had not been committed by a representative of the state. Although the assumption that the Convention obliges Member States to protect their citizens against torture and inhuman or degrading treatment by private individuals is convincing too, whether the act in question is also of sufficient severity when

[24] An overview of the relevant case-law can be found in *Vo v France* App no 53924/00 Reports 2004-VIII, (2005) 40 EHRR 12, paras 75–80.

[25] Ibid, para 82.

[26] *A v The United Kingdom* App no 25599/94 1998-VI, (1996) 22 EHRR CD 190.

[27] H Satzger, *International and European Criminal Law* (Munich, CH Beck and Oxford, Hart, 2012) § 9 paras 50–51.

[28] See the ECtHR's definitions in *Ireland v United Kingdom* App no 5310/71 Series A no 25 (1978), (1979–80) 2 EHRR 25, para 167.

[29] Ibid, para 21.

committed by a private individual should be assessed with particular care. However, the Court exclusively referred to the special vulnerability of children (it argued the victim's age for a second time) in order to establish that the stepfather's conduct fell within the scope of Article 3.[30]

All this results in the criticism that because of the high value and absolute nature of Article 3 ECHR, the ECtHR should be more careful in finding obligations of states to protect their citizens from inhuman or degrading treatment by means of criminal law. Otherwise Article 3 ECHR could be applied to too many cases in which states leave the infliction of physical or mental harm unpunished, and the exceptional character of the provision could thus be eroded.

ii. The Case of Gäfgen v Germany[31]

The 2010 judgment of the ECtHR's Grand Chamber in the case of *Gäfgen v Germany* illustrates that under different circumstances an obligation to punish breaches of Article 3 ECHR by means of criminal law can be established with less difficulty. In this case, two police officers had threatened the applicant (who was then suspected of having kidnapped a boy and later confessed to having killed him) with torture during an interrogation, thus committing an act of inhuman treatment. A German criminal court had convicted one officer of coercion in an aggravated case (since the offence had been committed by an official in the course of his duties) and the other one of having incited his subordinate. However, it imposed only comparatively moderate fines on the officers – which were even suspended.

Asking whether the breach of Article 3 ECHR had been remedied, the ECtHR also took into account the officers' criminal convictions. It held with remarkable clarity that:

> imposing almost token fines . . . and, furthermore, opting to suspend them, cannot be considered an adequate response to a breach of Article 3 . . . Such punishment, which is manifestly disproportionate to a breach of one of the core rights of the Convention, does not have the necessary deterrent effect in order to prevent further violations of the prohibition of ill-treatment in future difficult situations.[32]

One might argue that the impact of this decision is not quite as strong as that of *A v The United Kingdom* because in the latter the act had not been punished at all, whereas the main question in the *Gäfgen* case had merely been whether the sanction inflicted upon the police officers had been sufficiently severe. Nevertheless this judgment shows that the level of criminal sanctions also can be influenced by obligations under the ECHR.

[30] Ibid, para 22.
[31] *Gäfgen v Germany* App no 22978/05 (2011) 52 EHRR 1.
[32] Ibid, para 124.

iii. The Case of X and Y v The Netherlands

A further case concerned a gap in the Dutch law on sexual abuse.[33] A man had forced a mentally disabled girl to have sexual intercourse with him. The only criminal law provision which was applicable to the case required a complaint by the victim, but the girl was neither in the state of mind to file such a complaint herself, nor did Dutch law allow for a replacement of the girl's complaint by her father's. As a result the perpetrator could not be punished.

Once again the ECtHR derived a duty of the state to adopt 'measures designed to secure respect for private life even in the sphere of the relations of individuals between themselves'[34] from a guarantee laid down in the Convention – the right to respect for privacy, Article 8(1) ECHR. But unlike the decision in *A v The United Kingdom*, this judgment gives less reason for criticism: Article 8 ECHR is not construed as an 'absolute right' like the prohibition of torture and inhuman or degrading punishment. States can derogate from it under the conditions laid down in Article 15 and except from it under the conditions provided by Article 8(2). Furthermore, sexual abuse constitutes a very serious interference with the right to privacy, whilst it is not equally obvious that being hit with a garden cane falls within the scope of Article 3. It would even have been more convincing to deal with the *X and Y* case under Article 3.[35]

An additional aspect of this case which deserves mention is that the ECtHR also took into account potential civil law remedies for sexual abuse, but considered them insufficient to protect the victim's right to privacy effectively.[36] As a result, it held that there had been a violation of Article 8(1) ECHR.

C. Conclusion

It can be concluded from the judgments discussed above that human rights may oblige the legislature to take protective measures and to prohibit and sanction by criminal law activities which affect or could affect human rights. This does not mean that the conduct in question automatically must entail a criminal sanction because the German Constitutional Court as well as the ECtHR concede a broad margin of appreciation to the legislature. But at least a core of legal interests and values (*Rechtsgüter*) are so essential that the level of protection demanded by the Constitution can only be established through criminal punishment.[37] Whereas the German Court has declined to define an absolute 'constitutional minimum' of criminal law provisions, the ECtHR is less vague in this respect. This becomes

[33] *X and Y v The Netherlands* App no 8978/80 Series A no 91 (1985), (1986) 8 EHRR 235.

[34] Ibid, para 23.

[35] The ECtHR did not decide this issue, ibid, para 34. The Commission had rejected a violation of Art 3 because it did not see a 'close and direct link between the gap in the Netherlands law and "the field of protection covered" by the Article'.

[36] Ibid, para 27.

[37] Lagodny (n 4) 262–72 presents several proposals in order to concretise this conclusion.

understandable if one takes into account that in the abortion judgments, the judges had to review the constitutionality of an abstract law, whilst the proceedings before the ECtHR discussed above involved specific cases of human rights violations.

In order to explain the necessity of criminal sanctions, the German Constitutional Court argues that criminal law is the most effective tool to demonstrate what is right and what is wrong.[38] In other words, the existence of criminal laws shall *strengthen the public sense of justice* and thereby help to prevent comparable acts by other potential offenders [*positive Generalprävention*].[39] A similar reasoning is given by the ECtHR. Although it concedes to the states a margin of appreciation as regards the choice of means intended to ensure the respect of human rights, it highlights that in some areas '*effective deterrence* is indispensable . . . and it can be achieved only by criminal-law provisions'.[40]

III. Excessive Use of Criminal Law as a Threat to Human Rights

Criminal law does not only proscribe conduct that leads to an imminent danger for the rights of others. Often it also serves as a general mechanism of law enforcement. Up to this point, however, this chapter has focused on the constitutionally required minimum of criminal law; the case-law discussed so far does not allow any conclusions as to the extent to which a broader use would be acceptable. It can hardly be disputed that criminal sanctions constitute serious interferences with the basic rights of those on whom they are inflicted. Furthermore, the prohibition of an activity always limits personal freedom.[41] For these reasons, it is also worthwhile to reflect upon the 'constitutional maximium' of criminal law.

A. The Jurisprudence of the German Constitutional Court

i. Punishment Itself as an Interference with Human Rights

The first aspect that deserves a closer analysis is the conflict between fundamental rights and the infliction of a criminal sanction itself. At the outset it must be noted that every criminal punishment is by definition intended to restrict the convicted person's rights.[42] But apart from that, two issues deserve a closer consideration:

[38] BVerfGE 39, 1, 57–58 (para 182); BVerfGE 88, 203, 273 (para 210).

[39] BVerfGE 88, 203, 272, 278 (paras 207, 220).

[40] *X and Y v The Netherlands* (n 33) para 27 (emphasis added).

[41] For details on this distinction see K Binding, *Die Normen und ihre Übertretung*, vol 1, 4th edn (Leipzig, Meiner, 1922) 35–45; in the context of human rights see Lagodny (n 4) 79, 88; also see H Satzger, *Die Europäisierung des Strafrechts* (Cologne, Heymanns, 2001) 223–26.

[42] E Schmidhäuser, *Vom Sinn der Strafe*, 2nd reprinted edn (Berlin, Logos, 2004) 40.

a. The 'Stigmatising Effect'[43] of Criminal Sanctions

It is characteristic of criminal sanctions – at least in Germany – that they express a particular social disapproval of an act, combined with a personal reproach against the perpetrator.[44] This blaming – one could even say dishonouring – effect is also addressed by the Constitutional Court when it relies on the need to demonstrate what is right and what is wrong in order to justify the necessity of punishment in the case of an abortion. By imposing a criminal sentence, the society figuratively points at the offender and tells him: 'What you did was wrong!' This becomes visible, for instance, when a sentence is entered in a criminal record. But it is also mirrored in the public perception of a criminal conviction; someone who has been sent to prison is stigmatised and often no longer recognised as part of society. It can hardly be doubted that the fact that the state singles out and exposes one of its citizens in such a way infringes upon this individual's rights.[45] Considering these characteristics of criminal sanctions, one might even raise the question whether and under what conditions such an instrument is necessary and acceptable at all. However, this questions the legitimacy of criminal sanctions and criminal law as a whole. This problem has been discussed for a long time and no more convincing solution has been found thus far than that our societies simply cannot do entirely without criminal law.

b. The Influence of Human Rights on the Spectrum of Criminal Sanctions

Human rights have developed a considerable influence on the spectrum of criminal sanctions insofar as they prohibit certain ways of treating an individual. Probably the most prominent example of this phenomenon is the abolition of the death penalty, as provided by Article 102 of the German Basic Law. But less severe forms of punishment have also been disputed. In 1977 the German Constitutional Court had to decide on the constitutionality of life imprisonment.[46] The case was brought against the background of empirical studies which indicated that long-time prisoners showed massive changes in their personalities. In its reasoning, the Court initially emphasised that every human being is, thanks to his or her dignity, entitled to determine his or her life freely.[47] In the context of criminal law, human dignity precludes cruel, inhuman or degrading punishment and requires that every penalty leaves intact the basic requirements of an individual's existence in the society.[48] According to the Court, this would not be the case if a prisoner had no perspective ever to live in freedom again.[49] If this was the case, the enforcement of the penalty would exclusively serve to deter and to strengthen the public sense

[43] Cf resulting from the expression of social and moral disapproval by society inherent in the penalisation of certain conduct [*sozialethisches Unwerturteil*].

[44] BVerfGE 27, 18, 29, 33 (paras 31, 42); Appel (n 4) 493; Lagodny (n 4) 96–106; Schmidhäuser (n 42) 43.

[45] Appel (n 4) 492; Lagodny (n 4) 287.

[46] BVerfGE 45, 187–271 (1977).

[47] Ibid, 227 (para 144).

[48] Ibid, 228 (para 145).

[49] Ibid, 239 (para 178).

of justice: the convicted person would become a mere object in the prevention of crime by the state. As a result, the Court called for explicit legal regulation of the grant of parole to inmates who are sentenced to life imprisonment. The common practice of pardoning prisoners serving a life sentence was considered to be insufficient because such acts of grace were merely extra-legal decisions, characterised by a broad margin of discretion and a lack of satisfactory judicial review.[50] Yet, the Court pointed out that human dignity does not establish an obligation to release a delinquent who is still dangerous to society.[51] The German legislature responded to this judgment by amending the Criminal Code. New paragraphs (§§ 57a ff) were added which allow the release of a prisoner sentenced to life imprisonment after a minimum of 15 years.

ii. Conflicts between a Criminal Law Prohibition and Human Rights

As mentioned before, not just the punishment as such, but also the prohibition of certain activities – an integral element of every criminal offence – will often conflict with human rights. Therefore, this aspect plays an important role when a 'constitutional maximum' of criminal law is to be defined and various court decisions could exemplify the necessity to restrict the scope of criminal offences.

a. Libellous Statements v Freedom of Speech

A particularly illuminating judgment was delivered by the German Constitutional Court in 1995. It involved the constitutionality of criminal convictions for use of the slogan 'soldiers are murderers'.[52] In its decision, the Court developed guidelines for balancing the freedom of speech against the respect for personal honour. It quashed the convictions and called for new trials because it could not be excluded that the criminal courts would have come to different results if they had respected the following principles.

In the first place, the Court underlined that too broad an interpretation of criminal law provisions could easily have a 'chilling effect' in the sense that even reasonable criticism might not be expressed for fear of punishment.[53] Therefore, any statement that can be interpreted as a contribution to the public debate, prima facie must fall within the scope of the freedom of speech. Even controversial or polemic statements are protected as long as they are not intended to harm other persons (like hate speech).[54] In order to assess whether a statement actually contributes to 'public debate', all relevant circumstances of the case must be taken into account.[55]

However, the Court not only elaborated on the great importance of the freedom of speech in a democratic society, but also assessed the weight of the conflicting

[50] Ibid, 245–46 (paras 192–94).
[51] Ibid, 242 (para 184).
[52] BVerfGE 93, 266–319 (1995).
[53] Ibid, 292 (para 118); see also BVerfGE 43, 130, 136 (para 17).
[54] BVerfGE 93, 266, 293–95, 303–05 (paras 122–23, 144–47).
[55] Ibid, 295 (para 130).

protected interest (the personal honour) in the specific case. In particular, it took into account that not only a single person, but a group of people (soldiers) had been defamed. It supported the prevailing opinion among Germany's criminal lawyers[56] that a libellous statement shall not constitute an offence if it refers to a collective whose members are so numerous that the defamation cannot relate to a single member's misdemeanour or personal traits.[57]

Nevertheless, the conclusion approved by the Constitutional Court appears quite odd: as long as the sentence 'soldiers are murderers' referred to soldiers in general, the addressees would be so numerous that the statement did not aim at a specific victim, and no member of the group could reasonably feel affected in his or her personal honour. The solution would be different, however, if the statement exclusively referred to soldiers of the German *Bundeswehr*. The latter being a collective defined with sufficient clarity, the statement would harm the soldiers' honour and entail criminal punishment.[58] Of course it is desirable to exempt statements from punishment which mainly express (even harsh) criticism of war and not primarily disdain of a single person. But should it not be possible to use similarly drastic words in order to criticise especially the participation of the *Bundeswehr* in a military mission? Therefore, it would have been more consistent to ask whether the statement amounts to hate speech and is mainly intended to defame another person – a possibility indicated earlier in the same judgment.[59] In contrast, the differentiation between soldiers of the *Bundeswehr* and other soldiers seems to be motivated rather by political considerations.

b. Defamation of the State v Freedom of the Arts

Not freedom of speech, but freedom of the arts was the main issue in two further judgments that involved controversial political views.[60] In 1986 a journalist published 'alternative lyrics' for the German national anthem in which he enumerated various aspects of history, culture and everyday life which, in his opinion, were typical of Germany. Since the text was in parts very rude and offensive, he was convicted of 'defamation of the state and its symbols' (§ 90a StGB). The Constitutional Court rejected this interpretation of the provision and criticised that the satirical dimension of the text had not been taken into account at all by the criminal courts. Furthermore, it clarified that the classification of a text as 'art' cannot depend upon its quality[61] – a clear parallel to the right to free speech, which also protects controversial statements and not only such as are commonly approved of.

[56] BGHSt (Decisions of the Federal Court in Criminal Cases) 11, 207; with several restrictions also BGHSt 36, 83, 85–87; T Lenckner and J Eisele in Schönke and Schröder (eds) (n 22) preliminary remarks §§ 185 ff StGB, paras 7a–7c.

[57] BVerfGE 93, 266, 301–02 (para 140).

[58] Ibid, 302 (para 141). However, the criminal courts have to take into account all circumstances in order to establish whether a statement refers to soldiers in general or to soldiers of the *Bundeswehr*.

[59] Ibid, 293–95, 303–05 (paras 122–23, 144–47).

[60] BVerfGE 81, 278–98; BVerfGE 81, 298–309 (1990).

[61] BVerfGE 81, 298, 305 (para 20).

The second, very similar case (decided on the same day) involved the cover of an anti-militaristic book showing a photo-collage with a man urinating on the German flag. On this occasion the Constitutional Court also analysed why national symbols deserve protection by criminal law. It concluded that, although the flag served the citizens' identification with the essential values and the liberal and democratic constitutional order of the Federal Republic,[62] in the particular case the collage was used to transmit a (political) message. Therefore the need to protect this symbol was outweighed by the freedom of the arts. Otherwise, § 90a StGB might be abused in order to 'immunise' the state against criticism.[63]

c. Money Laundering v Free Exercise of One's Profession

A more recent case involved the constitutionality of the German criminal law provision on money laundering (§ 261 StGB).[64] Owing to its broadness (which is in parts due to international obligations[65]) and to the generally low thresholds for the establishment of *mens rea* in German criminal law,[66] a defence lawyer would have committed the offence of money laundering if he accepted payment from an alleged criminal and was at least aware that the money might be derived from illegal activities. Of course it is not at all unlikely that during the preparation of the trial a defence counsel will find out something that hints at this possibility.[67] Consequently the exercise of a defence lawyer's profession would often create a risk of criminal punishment – even if he or she did not know for sure whether they were paid from illegal sources. This is especially problematic if one takes into account that a suspect must have the opportunity to consult a legal expert for his or her defence. But how shall a relationship of mutual trust between suspect and counsel – which can be essential for a successful defence – be maintained if the latter has good reason to mistrust the client in order not to be incriminated himself?[68] For these reasons the Constitutional Court held that the relevant provision infringed the lawyer's freedom of the exercise of his profession (Article 12(1) of the Basic Law). The provision on money laundering must, therefore, be interpreted more narrowly so that defence lawyers can only be held criminally liable if they have positive knowledge of the illegal origin of their payment.[69]

[62] Ibid, 278, 293 (paras 50–51).
[63] Ibid, 294 (para 52).
[64] BVerfGE 110, 226–74 (2004).
[65] See Directive 91/308/EEC [1991] OJ L166/77; replaced by Directive 2005/60/EC [2005] OJ L309/15.
[66] For details see Roxin (n 21) § 12 para 21; H-H Jescheck and Th Weigend, *Lehrbuch des Strafrechts Allgemeiner Teil*, 5th edn (Berlin, Duncker & Humblot, 1996) 299; G Stratenwerth and L Kuhlen, *Strafrecht Allgemeiner Teil I*, 5th edn (Cologne, Heymanns, 2004) § 8 para 117; each with further references.
[67] BVerfGE 110, 226, 255 (para 109).
[68] Ibid, 256–60 (paras 112–23).
[69] Ibid, 265–66 (paras 140–43). In the case which was at the origin of the proceedings before the Constitutional Court, these requirements had already been met.

B. Parallels in the Jurisprudence of the European Court of Human Rights

Not just the German Constitutional Court, but also the European Court of Human Rights has had opportunities to elaborate on the liberalising effect of human rights in the context of criminal law.

i. The Punishment Itself as an Interference with Convention Rights

Comparable to Germany, the abolition of the death penalty is also embedded in the European legal order and explicitly regulated in Article 1 of Protocol No 6 (which still allows capital punishment in times of war) and Article 1 of Protocol No 13 (which abolishes it without any exception) to the Convention. Further examples of the influence of the ECHR on the spectrum of criminal sanctions can be found in the case-law of the ECtHR.

a. Life Imprisonment

The Court in Strasbourg has considered the compatibility of life imprisonment with the Convention in several decisions, and it is not easy to see a clear line there. In most of the cases, the Court dealt with this question under the issue of lawfulness in Article 5(1) ECHR. More specifically, it asked whether the deprivation of liberty was arbitrary. In two rather recent judgments it has pointed out that this shall not be the case as long as either the 'punishment element' of the sentence or other aspects, such as the detainee's dangerousness to society, justify keeping the individual in detention.[70] As regards the prohibition of inhuman or degrading punishment in Article 3 ECHR, the Court equally chooses a rather restrictive approach: the 'anxiety and uncertainty linked to prison life' inherent in every life sentence in principle (that is, in the absence of additional aggravating facts) will not reach the level of severity required by Article 3.[71] Nevertheless, the ECtHR explicitly 'has not ruled out the possibility that *in special circumstances* an irreducible life sentence might also raise an issue under the Convention where there is *no hope of entitlement to a measure such as parole*'.[72] There are obvious parallels to the German Constitutional Court's judgment presented above. In another decision the ECtHR indicated that the perpetrator's age or the particular facts of the committed offence might be such exceptional aspects.[73]

[70] *Léger v France* App no 19324/02, judgment of 11 April 2006, not officially reported, para 74 (this judgment was referred to the Grand Chamber which subsequently, on 30 March 2009, decided to strike the application out of its list of cases since the applicant had died in 2008), see (2009) 49 EHRR 41; *Stafford v The United Kingdom* App no 46295/99, Reports 2002-IV, (2002) 35 EHRR 32, para 80.

[71] *Léger v France* (n 70) para 93.

[72] Ibid, paras 90, 92 (emphasis added) with further references.

[73] *Weeks v The United Kingdom* App no 9787/82 Series A no 114 (1987), (1988) 10 EHRR 293, para 47.

b. Corporal Punishment

In 1978, the ECtHR had to decide the question of whether judicial corporal punishment is contrary to the prohibition of inhuman or degrading punishment as enshrined in Article 3 ECHR.[74] A 15-year-old youth had been sentenced to 'three strokes of the birch' because he had committed an assault occasioning actual bodily harm on an older schoolmate. The punishment, for which the boy had to take down his trousers and underpants, did not cause serious injuries, although it was executed with considerable force (so much so that pieces of the birch broke on the first stroke). The Court came to the conclusion that such a penalty as a form of 'institutionalised violence' makes the convicted person an object in the power of the authorities and hence constitutes a degrading treatment from which Article 3 seeks to protect.[75] To such forms of punishment, the ECtHR underlines, 'it is never permissible to have recourse . . . whatever their deterrent effect may be'.[76]

An additional aspect of that judgment that merits attention is that the Court distinguished between the particular level of humiliation required by Article 3 ECHR and the one inherent in every criminal sanction.[77] Its approach shows a clear parallel with the German conception that criminal punishment is characterised by its 'blaming effect'.

ii. Conflicts of a Prohibition with Convention Rights

a. Criminalisation of Homosexual Acts v Right to Privacy

In the case of *Dudgeon v The United Kingdom*,[78] the ECtHR had to decide about a complaint against the existence of laws in Northern Ireland which had the effect of making certain homosexual acts a criminal offence, even though committed in private and by consenting adults. The main question in the case was whether this interference with the right to respect for private life (Article 8(1) ECHR) could be justified by Article 8(2), which allows, inter alia, measures necessary for the protection of morals. As regards the element of necessity, the Court held that the case concerned 'a most intimate aspect of private life. Accordingly, there must exist particularly serious reasons before interferences on the part of the public authorities can be legitimate.'[79] Notwithstanding the national legislature's margin of appreciation, the ECtHR denied the existence of a 'pressing social need' to criminalise the respective homosexual acts – at least as long as they were conducted in private and by consenting adults. According to the Court, there was 'no sufficient justification provided by the risk of harm to vulnerable sections of society requiring protection or by the effects on the public'.[80] In particular, the fact that parts of

[74] *Tyrer v The United Kingdom* App no 5856/72 Series A no 26 (1975), (1979–80) 2 EHRR 1.
[75] Ibid, para 33.
[76] Ibid, para 31.
[77] Ibid, para 30.
[78] *Dudgeon v The United Kingdom* App no 7525/76 Series A no 45 (1981), (1982) 4 EHRR 149.
[79] Ibid, para 52.
[80] Ibid, para 60.

the population of Northern Ireland would disapprove of the decriminalisation of these acts should not per se legitimise the maintenance of criminal offences in such an intimate field of privacy. Consequently, the Court stated that the mere risk of criminal punishment in this area violated the applicant's right under Article 8(1) ECHR.

This judgment even went beyond the ones of the German Constitutional Court discussed above because it did not simply correct the interpretation of a generally acceptable provision, but actually declared the existence of a criminal offence to be incompatible with the Convention.

b. Prohibited Political Symbols v Freedom of Expression

In the case of *Vajnai v Hungary*,[81] a Hungarian national appealed against his criminal conviction for wearing the communist red star at a legal left-wing demonstration in Budapest. The criminal court had highlighted that this badge – in the light of the Hungarian experiences with the Soviet power – was anti-constitutional. By contrast, the ECtHR argued that the meaning of the emblem was less clear and that the red star could also be seen as a symbol of anti-fascism and of the communist idea as such.[82] Furthermore it underlined that no instance had been reported when such conduct had indeed caused public disorder, the prevention of which the criminal law provision sought to achieve. Since the danger was therefore rather speculative in nature, it could not justify an interference with Convention rights[83] – even less so because of the 'chilling effect' that the prohibition might entail for the exercise of the freedom of expression,[84] 'one of the essential foundations of a democratic society'.[85] The Court therefore concluded that Article 10(1) ECHR had been violated.

c. Protection of Personal Reputation v Freedom of Expression

The same guarantee was also the main point in the case of *Juppala v Finland*.[86] In 2000 a grandmother who had found bruises on the body of her three-year-old grandson brought the child to a doctor, whom she informed of her suspicion that the boy had been beaten by his father. The physician was of the opinion that this could indeed have been the reason for the injuries and subsequently reported the instance to the child welfare authorities. After the child's father maintained that he had not injured his son, criminal proceedings were initiated against the grandmother because she had expressed a wrong (or at least unproven) suspicion, and she was found guilty of the offence of 'defamation without better knowledge'.

81 *Vajnai v Hungary* App no 33629/06 (2010) 50 EHRR 44.
82 Ibid, paras 52–53.
83 Ibid, para 55.
84 Ibid, para 54.
85 Ibid, para 46.
86 *Juppala v Finland* App no 18620/03 (2010) 51 EHRR 4.

The judgment shows clear parallels to the jurisprudence of the German Constitutional Court: the ECtHR elaborated at length on the necessity of balancing the countervailing interests (freedom of expression v protection from unfounded defamation)[87] and highlighted that the incriminated behaviour was meant to protect a child from abuse. Owing to 'every adult's moral duty to defend a child's interests', private persons acting in good faith to this end 'should not be influenced by fear of being prosecuted'.[88] Once again, the Court also made reference to the 'chilling effect' that the respective criminal laws might have on the exercise of the freedom of expression.[89] In the end, the ECtHR held that the grandmother's conviction violated her rights under Article 10(1) ECHR.

C. Conclusion

This list of judgments is not meant to create the impression that the Constitutional Court or the ECtHR is overly critical as regards the review of criminal law provisions. There are many decisions indicating the opposite.[90] But the case-law analysed above at least allows for a few tentative conclusions as to the 'constitutional maximum' of criminal law.

First, criminal sanctions are, in part due to their blaming effect, to be regarded as particularly serious interferences with human rights. But if a personal reproach is inherent in every criminal punishment, this must be taken into account when the level of the penalty is fixed in a particular case. Otherwise the criminal court would risk imposing a sanction which is disproportionate and constitutionally unacceptable. As regards the spectrum of constitutionally acceptable criminal sanctions, the following conclusion can be drawn: whereas the death penalty is per se explicitly prohibited, other forms of punishment may also be impermissible. In particular, this has been held to be the case for life imprisonment if it does not leave the convicted person any hope of ever being released again. Likewise, any penalty that results in a particular humiliation may not be imposed. In this regard, both Courts even apply a quite similar standard by demanding that the individual must not become a mere object in the hands of the authorities ('object formula', interpreting the protection of human dignity).

[87] Ibid, paras 41–45.

[88] Ibid, para 42.

[89] Ibid, para 43.

[90] BVerfGE 90, 145–226 (1994) (punishability of the import of minimal amounts of cannabis products for personal use does not violate the Constitution as long as substantive and procedural law provide regulations that allow the refraining from punishment); BVerfGE 90, 241–54 (1994) (denial of holocaust is not protected by the right to free speech); BVerfGE 120, 224–73 (2008) (making incest between brother and sister a criminal offence does not infringe upon the principle of proportionality); ECtHR, *Sürek v Turkey* App no 26682/95 Reports 1999-IV, 7 BHRC 339 (publication of letters with harsh criticism of Turkish military actions against the Kurdish minority is not protected by Art 10 ECHR as it amounts to hate speech); *Lindon, Otchakovsky-Laurens and July v France* App nos 21279/02 and 36448/02 (2008) 46 EHRR 35 (conviction of 'public defamation' for the publication of a novel which sharply attacks the leader of an extremist party does not constitute a violation of Art 10 ECHR).

Secondly, the prohibition inherent in every criminal offence cannot be justified by any legitimate aim, but – as the ECtHR puts it – only by a 'pressing social need'. In particular, it is insufficient that the danger caused by the criminalised conduct is merely hypothetical.

And finally, even if there is a legitimate aim that justifies the prohibition of a certain conduct, it is still necessary to balance the need for criminal laws with conflicting human rights. In this regard, the case-law discussed above at least shows a certain tendency: whenever an activity is of particular relevance for the democratic functioning of society, the threshold for the constitutionality of its penalisation is especially high.

IV. Preconditions for the Use of Criminal Law

The preceding considerations can be summarised as follows: criminal law allows states to impose sanctions that curtail the individual's rights most seriously. Therefore, it is on the one hand a particularly attractive means of law enforcement. It is expected to promote the public sense of justice by affirming elementary rules of conduct and to serve the effective deterrence of dangerous behaviour. On the other hand, its powerful impact and potential 'chilling effect' creates the need to restrict the scope of criminal offences. To use a common German expression, criminal law is the state's 'sharpest sword'. From the point of view of human rights, however, it is also a double-edged sword which should be handled with care. Maybe this conclusion does not appear to be very innovative, but what is interesting is that both Courts follow a very similar line in this respect. This allows us to deduce some parameters for the use of criminal law[91] which do not just fit within a single legal order, but which can be generalised. Of course this in no way excludes the possibility that legal orders require additional rules (such as *nulla poena sine culpa*) to be respected.[92]

A. Strict Proportionality Test

In order to comply with the universal obligation to respect human rights, both the 'constitutional minimum' and the 'constitutional maximum' of criminal law must be respected. To this aim, both Courts basically apply a strict proportionality test. In doing so, they stress the protected interest ('pressing social aim') and weigh it against conflicting human rights affected by the respective prohibition. As regards other aspects of proportionality, especially the question of whether there is a less

[91] In detail see Appel (n 4) 569–93; Lagodny (n 4) 511–32.

[92] Appel (n 4) 585–89, develops a requirement of coherent criminal laws (based on the principle of equality). However, this can hardly be deduced from the jurisprudence of the ECtHR and the German Constitutional Court.

severe instrument than criminal sanctions to achieve the legal goal, the courts concede a broad margin of appreciation to the legislature.[93] In this regard, the German Constitutional Court appears to follow an even more generous approach than the ECtHR.[94] If, from time to time, it refers to the concept of criminal law as *ultima ratio*[95] – the state's instrument of last resort – this is, therefore, not meant as a strict measure of judicial control but rather paraphrases the whole proportionality test, which takes account of the particularities of criminal law.[96]

These parallels in the jurisprudence of both courts should be of particular importance for German scholars since they reveal that criminal law concepts that are often regarded as typically German (such as that of *Rechtsgüter*[97]) are not totally unfamiliar to other legal orders. Consequently there is not just a need, but also a possibility to discuss them at a European level.

B. The Principle of Legality

Apart from the proportionality requirement, one further fundamental principle serves to establish a 'constitutional minimum' and a 'constitutional maximum' of criminal law: the principle of legality, according to which it must be possible to foresee whether an act will entail punishment. Compared to the principle of proportionality, which is a general measure for the constitutionality of state activities, it is probably linked even more closely to the tasks and risks of criminal law: effective deterrence can hardly be achieved if the law does not make clear which activities are forbidden.[98] Likewise, the precise definition of an offence creates the confidence that acts not covered by the respective provision will not be punished. Thus, the principle of legality helps to avoid the already mentioned 'chilling effect' of criminal law provisions on the exercise of basic rights. This function becomes clearly visible in a judgment of the German Constitutional Court with regard to a criminal conviction for the blockade of military barracks during an anti-war demonstration (which had been regarded as coercion, § 240 StGB).[99] The Court held that the protestors could not reasonably have foreseen that a sit-in would be interpreted as 'violence' and therefore make them criminally liable.[100]

Of course it needs to be taken into account that the principle of legality cannot be applied to all legal systems in the same way, and may require modification for

93 BVerfGE 110, 226, 262 (para 129).

94 The exclusion of hypothetical risks as a sufficient justification for criminal laws in *Vajnai v Hungary* (n 81) para 46 appears as an aspect of necessity rather than as one of legitimate aim.

95 See, for instance, BVerfGE 39, 1, 47 (para 162); 88, 203, 258 (para 176).

96 In this sense also Roxin (n 21) § 2 para 101.

97 For the debate on this issue see the volume edited by R Hefendehl, A von Hirsch and W Wohlers, *Die Rechtsgütertheorie* (Baden-Baden, Nomos, 2003).

98 Indeed, the principle of *nulla poena sine lege* can also be derived from the purposes of criminal punishment, see Roxin (n 21) § 5 paras 22–23.

99 BVerfGE 92, 1–25 (1995). In an earlier decision (BVerfGE 73, 206–61 (1986)), there had been no majority among the judges in order to declare the respective conviction unconstitutional.

100 Ibid, 18 (paras 61–62).

systems based on common law. However, the ECtHR's jurisprudence on Article 7(1) of the Convention demonstrates that the foreseeability criterion can also be applied in this context, although with a slightly more generous approach.[101]

V. Concluding Remarks

At the end of this chapter, it is time to return to the initial thesis: the relationship between the protection of human rights and criminal law is indeed ambivalent. In a limited number of cases, the state is obliged to protect human rights by means of criminal law. But the reverse constellation – the liberalising effect of the doctrine of human rights in the field of criminal law – is even more important. The development of a criminal law system that respects the 'constitutional minimum' as well as the 'constitutional maximum' of criminal law can be considered as one of the major steps towards a full implementation of the rule of law, a process which is not at all completed yet.

This conclusion is of particular importance if one considers new tendencies which can be summarised as the international dimension of criminal law. In a time when the approximation of national criminal-law systems is at the top of the agenda, national legislatures are often not entirely free in their decision whether to make an act a criminal offence: parliaments are bound by international obligations, particularly by those formulated by the European Union. Looking at recent EU directives and framework decisions, for example in the field of combating terrorism,[102] it is quickly noticeable that these legal instruments mostly focus on the protective role of criminal law. On the basis of Article 83(2) of the Treaty on the Functioning of the European Union (TFEU), EU Member States might even be compelled to criminalise a certain behaviour in order to guarantee the effectiveness of Union law – without the additional requirement of any 'pressing social need'.[103] Such an interpretation would neglect the risks that arise from an excessive criminalisation and be inconsistent with a proportionate use of criminal law as argued above.[104] For all these reasons it appears highly desirable that the 'constitutionalisation' of criminal law continues, albeit now also at the European level.

[101] For instance, it is sufficient that the development of judicial interpretation is 'consistent with the *essence of the offence* and could be *reasonably* foreseen': *SW v The United Kingdom* App no 20166/92 Series A no 335-B(1995), (1996) 21 EHRR 363, para 36 (emphasis added). For the criterion of foreseeability in general, see *Kokkinakis v Greece* App no 14307/88 Series A no 260-A (1993), (1994) 17 EHRR 397, para 52.

[102] Framework Decision 2008/919/JHA [2008] OJ L330/21, amending Framework Decision 2002/475/JHA on combating terrorism [2002] OJ L164/3.

[103] Two decisions of the European Court of Justice hint in the same direction, see case C-176/03 *Commission v Council* [2005] ECR I-7879, para 48 and case C-440/05 *Commission v Council* [2007] ECR I-9097, para 66.

[104] See European Criminal Policy Initiative, 'A Manifesto on European Criminal Policy' (2009) *Zeitschrift für Internationale Strafrechtsdogmatik* 707 (available in English online at www.zis-online.com).

3

Eroding the Structure of the European Convention?

The Public Interest in Prosecutions for Serious Crime

ANDREW ASHWORTH

In this chapter I will argue that the European Court of Human Rights in Strasbourg has begun to move away from some basic doctrines of European human rights law, and that some of its recent pronouncements in criminal cases raise questions about the fundamental structure of the European Convention on Human Rights (ECHR), notably in relation to Article 6. Two particular aspects of Article 6 are questioned: first, to what extent should 'public interest' factors be relevant in determining whether the right to a fair trial under Article 6 has been violated? Secondly, under what circumstances should the use of evidence obtained through violation of another Convention right render a trial unfair under Article 6? The movements to which I draw attention are not apparent in all judgments on criminal matters, but there is sufficient evidence of differences in the Court's approaches to justify an examination of the lines of argument.

I will begin in section I by setting out the structure of the Convention; section II considers the general approach to Article 6 in the late 1990s; section III examines the way in which, in recent cases, the Court has begun to cite the public interest in prosecutions for serious crime as a reason for taking a different approach; in section IV the Court's approach to Article 3 is set out, and in section V the Court's approach to the interaction between Articles 3 and 6 is examined; finally, section VI returns to the question of the interaction between Articles 8 and 6, and discusses the extent to which it is compatible with the Court's other judgments and with the structure of the Convention itself.

I. The Structure of the Convention

The structure of Convention rights may be elucidated by looking first at Article 15, which singles out certain rights for special treatment:

> Article 15
>
> (1) In time of war or other public emergency threatening the life of the nation any High Contracting Party may take measures derogating from its obligations under this Convention to the extent strictly required by the exigencies of the situation, provided that such measures are not inconsistent with its other obligations under international law.
>
> (2) No derogation from Article 2, except in relation to deaths resulting from lawful acts of war, or from Article 3, 4 (paragraph 1) and 7 shall be made under this provision . . .

The thrust of Article 15 is that it is permissible for states to derogate from various Convention rights if the conditions for doing so are satisfied, but that no derogation at all is allowed from four rights. This immediately establishes an order of priority, placing these four rights in a specially protected category. The non-derogable rights are:

- the right to life (Article 2),
- the right not to be subjected to torture or inhuman or degrading treatment (Article 3),
- the right not to be subjected to forced labour (Article 4(1)), and
- the right not to be subjected to retrospective criminal laws or penalties (Article 7).

The fact that these rights are non-derogable indicates that they are the most basic of the fundamental rights in the Convention. Of course, their meaning and reach are subject to interpretation, and in that sense they are not *absolute* rights – or, at least, not until the scope of their application has been finally determined. But it is plain that they are not intended to give way to 'public interest' considerations: the metaphor of 'balancing' should not be applied when considering the scope of these rights.

Another category of Convention rights might be termed qualified or prima facie rights – the right is declared, but it is also declared that it may be interfered with on certain grounds, so long as the restriction is as minimal as possible. Examples of this type of right are the right to respect for private life (Article 8), the right to freedom of thought and religion (Article 9), the right to freedom of expression (Article 10), and the right to freedom of assembly and association (Article 11). All these qualified rights appear in the Convention with a second paragraph, which states that each right may be subject to interference, if it can be established that such interference is 'necessary in a democratic society' on one of the grounds listed in the right's second paragraph. The jurisprudence of the

Strasbourg Court interprets the second paragraphs of these Articles in such a way as to impose meaningful limitations on state interference with the rights, chiefly through the doctrine of proportionality.

Situated between non-derogable rights and qualified rights is an intermediate category, which is less easy to label and less easy to assess. In the European Convention this category includes the right to liberty and security of the person (Article 5) and the right to a fair trial (Article 6). One might refer to the rights in this intermediate category as 'strong rights', to demonstrate that they have a strength which is not qualified to the extent that the rights in Articles 8–11 are qualified. Indeed, the rights in Articles 5 and 6 are not at all qualified on the face of the Convention. In the internal logic of the Convention, this is a significant distinction – it suggests that, although strong rights are less fundamental than the non-derogable rights, any arguments for curtailing a strong right must at least be more powerful than the kind of 'necessary in a democratic society' argument that is needed to establish the acceptability of interference with one of the qualified rights.

If this analysis is accepted, then it raises doubts about some of the more extravagant statements of the Strasbourg Court, which have been cited in some subsequent judgments. Consider, for example, the much-cited statement of the Court in its judgment in *Sporrong and Lönnroth v Sweden*:[1]

> [T]he Court must determine whether a fair balance was struck between the demands of the general interest of the community and the requirements of the protection of the individual's fundamental rights. The search for this balance is inherent in the whole of the Convention and is also reflected in the structure of Article 1.[2]

The first part of the final sentence is surely extravagant: it cannot seriously be suggested that when determining whether there has been a breach of Article 2 or Article 3 it is relevant to weigh the public interest against the individual's right. That has never formed part of Article 2 decisions, and we will see that in Article 3 it would be most unusual. Thus the first part of the final sentence was not intended as an authoritative pronouncement on the proper approach to all questions under the Convention, despite its unguarded terms. More accurate is the second part of the final sentence, which brings the issue specifically to the interpretation of Article 1 of Protocol 1 (the right to peaceful enjoyment of possessions), which was the subject-matter of the case. Indeed, it could be argued that the two sentences are taken out of context, in the way that they are commonly cited, since the words immediately preceding the quoted passage are 'for the purposes of the latter provision', which is a direct reference to Article 1 of Protocol 1. It is therefore submitted that this statement from *Sporrong and Lönnroth v Sweden* should not be taken out of context and used as a basis for the argument that, in any case arising under the Convention, a court must balance the individual's right against the general interests of the community.

[1] *Sporrong and Lönnroth v Sweden* App no 7151/75 Series A no 52 (1982), (1983) 5 EHRR 35.
[2] Ibid, para 69.

II. Establishing the General Approach to Article 6

The argument above was about the structure of the Convention and its logical implications for the broad 'public interest' arguments on which governments often rely. We must now look at some details of how the Strasbourg Court has reacted to 'public interest' arguments when they have been advanced as possible limitations on rights that form part of the general right to a fair trial in criminal cases, a right safeguarded by Article 6. Three examples of the approach of the Court in the late 1990s may be given.

First, in *Saunders v United Kingdom*[3] the question was whether the privilege against self-incrimination was an implied right, falling within the general right to a fair trial under Article 6; if so, whether it applied in this case; and, if so, whether it should be upheld as against the pressing social importance of combating serious fraud. Having answered the first two questions in the affirmative, the Court considered the third question and stated:

> [The Court] does not accept the Government's argument that the complexity of corporate fraud and the vital public interest in the investigation of such fraud and the punishment of those responsible could justify such a marked departure as that which occurred in the present case from one of the basic principles of a fair procedure . . . The general requirements of fairness contained in Article 6, including the right not to incriminate oneself, apply to criminal proceedings in respect of all types of criminal offences without distinction, from the most simple to the most complex. The public interest cannot be invoked to justify the use of answers compulsorily obtained in a non-judicial investigation to incriminate the accused during criminal proceedings.[4]

This is a broad statement of principle. It is not entirely unambiguous, since the Court did not offer a concluded opinion on 'whether the right not to incriminate oneself is absolute or whether infringements of it may be justified in particular circumstances'.[5] But the terms of its dismissal of the government's 'public interest' argument are powerful.

Two years later the Court had to deal with its first case of entrapment in the context of attempts to bring drug traffickers to justice. In *Teixeira de Castro v Portugal* (1998)[6] the Court found that the applicant had been entrapped by police officers into committing the offence of supplying drugs. One of the government's arguments was that proactive methods of law enforcement were vital in order to combat drug trafficking. The Court's reply was as follows:

> The use of undercover agents must be restricted and safeguards put in place even in cases concerning the fight against drug-trafficking. While the rise in organized crime undoubtedly requires that appropriate measures be taken, the right to a fair administra-

[3] *Saunders v United Kingdom* App no 19187/91 Reports 1996-VI, (1997) 23 EHRR 313.
[4] Ibid, para 74.
[5] Ibid.
[6] *Teixeira de Castro v Portugal* App no 25829/94 (1999) 28 EHRR 101.

> tion of justice nevertheless holds such a prominent place that it cannot be sacrificed for the sake of expedience. The general requirements of fairness embodied in Article 6 apply to proceedings concerning all types of criminal offence from the most straightforward to the most complex. The public interest cannot justify the use of evidence obtained as a result of police incitement.[7]

This is a clear and unqualified statement of the relationship between Article 6 and 'public interest' arguments.

Perhaps the high water mark of this approach was reached in *Heaney and McGuinness v Ireland* (2000),[8] where the Court held that the convictions of the two applicants for the offence of failing to give an account of their movements at a particular time violated their privilege against self-incrimination. The offences formed part of Irish anti-terrorist law, and the government relied on this strong 'public interest' argument to claim that any curtailment of the privilege against self-incrimination was justified in order to combat terrorism. The Court's response was uncompromising:

> The Court . . . finds that the security and public order concerns of the Government cannot justify a provision which extinguishes the very essence of the applicants' right to silence and their right not to incriminate themselves guaranteed by Article 6(1) of the Convention.[9]

Once again, the Court reasserts the priority of the guarantees of a fair trial in Article 6 over arguments based on the alleged[10] public interest.

III. The Resurgence of 'Public Interest' Arguments?

In the last few years the Court has had to deal with a range of different situations in which governments have pressed arguments based on the 'public interest'. Sometimes these arguments are phrased in terms of proportionality, a term with several uses in Convention jurisprudence. The doctrine of proportionality is most relevant when determining the justification for interferences with qualified rights such as those in Articles 8–11; very few judgments on Articles 5 or 6 regard it as relevant. When the notion of proportionality is introduced into discussions of the limits of Article 6 rights, the purpose is to draw into the debate various 'public interest' arguments. These are the very arguments that were excluded in the three

[7] Ibid, para 36.

[8] *Heaney and McGuinness v Ireland* App no 34720/97 (2001) 33 EHRR 12.

[9] Ibid, para 58.

[10] The word 'alleged' is interposed here to make the point that any argument advanced under the title 'public interest' must be examined carefully, rather than simply accepted. For example, should a court require evidence that the existence of a particular law does advance the 'fight against terrorism', rather than simply accepting the government's assertion that it is necessary? Does the importance of preventing arbitrary uses of power by officials against citizens form part of the 'public interest' too?

judgments cited in section II above, but we will see that they are now being regarded by the Court as relevant in certain circumstances.

In *O'Halloran and Francis v United Kingdom* (2007)[11] the question was whether a particular offence in English law – that committed by the owner of a motor vehicle who fails to comply with a request from the police to state who was driving the vehicle at a particular time – is compatible with the privilege against self-incrimination. The Grand Chamber held that it is, concluding:

> Having regard to all the circumstances of the case, including the special nature of the regulatory regime at issue and the limited nature of the information sought by a notice under section 172 of the Road Traffic Act 1988, the Court considers that the essence of the applicants' right to remain silent and their privilege against self-incrimination has not been destroyed.[12]

This conclusion marked an unusual step in the Court's decision-making. In every previous case in which an element of compulsion had been found, the Court held that the privilege against self-incrimination was violated. On this occasion, the Court felt able to conclude that there were other factors in the case which, in conjunction with the relatively low level of compulsion, were not sufficient to 'destroy the very essence' of the privilege against self-incrimination. Thus the Court held that account should be taken of (i) the fact that the compulsion is part of a regulatory scheme that fairly imposes obligations on vehicle owners and drivers in order to promote safety on the roads; (ii) the fact that the information required is the simple, specific and restricted fact of who was driving, rather than a general account of movements or answers to wide-ranging questions; and (iii) that the particular statutory offence contains a safeguard, in the form of a defence of due diligence, which allows a conscientious owner to avoid criminal liability. These factors suggest a kind of proportionality judgment, and indeed the Court quoted extensively from the leading United Kingdom decision on the point, which emphasises the importance of achieving a balance and seeking proportionality when dealing with this issue.[13] The Court itself did not state that the question of compatibility with Article 6 is to be determined by reference to a proportionality assessment, but its conclusion that the particular features of this offence did not destroy the essence of the applicants' rights seems to imply some such assessment.

More explicit is another recent judgment of the Grand Chamber, that in *Jalloh v Germany* (2006).[14] This was a case in which the police had been observing a drug dealer operating on the street, and when they arrested him he swallowed the 'bubble' of drugs he had in his mouth. The police asked him to take an emetic so that they could recover the bubble, but he refused. At the police station four police officers held him down while a doctor administered an emetic, after which he

[11] *O'Halloran and Francis v United Kingdom* App nos 15809/02 and 25624/02 (2008) 46 EHRR 21.

[12] Ibid, para 62.

[13] That decision is *Brown v Stott* [2003] 1 AC 681, and the leading judgment of Lord Bingham is quoted extensively by the Court in *O'Halloran*.

[14] *Jalloh v Germany* App no 54810/00 (2007) 44 EHRR 32.

regurgitated one bubble of cocaine. The Grand Chamber considered the case under Article 3 and Article 6. For present purposes, the Court's assessment of whether the conduct of the police amounted to a violation of the privilege against self-incrimination is relevant:

> In order to determine whether the applicant's right not to incriminate himself has been violated, the Court will have regard, in turn, to the following factors: the nature and degree of compulsion used to obtain the evidence; the weight of the public interest in the investigation and punishment of the offence at issue; and the use to which any material so obtained is put . . . As regards the weight of the public interest in using the evidence to secure the applicant's conviction, the Court observes that . . . the impugned measure targeted a street dealer who was offering drugs for sale on a comparably small scale and was finally given a six months' suspended prison sentence and probation. In the circumstances of the instant case, the public interest in securing the applicant's conviction could not justify recourse to such a grave interference with his physical and mental integrity.[15]

This passage of the judgment is noteworthy because the Grand Chamber clearly stated that the weight of the public interest in prosecuting this offence is a relevant consideration, and did so without any reference to *Saunders v United Kingdom* and to the other judgments cited in section II above, which indicate that the seriousness of the crime has no bearing on whether or not there has been a violation of the privilege against self-incrimination. The implication of this passage from *Jalloh* is clearly that, in cases where the offence is very serious (unlike small-time drug dealing), this might lead to the conclusion that the use of compulsion might be permissible and a violation of the privilege against self-incrimination might not be found.

IV. The Interpretation of Article 3

In respect of Article 3, the Grand Chamber in *Jalloh v Germany* held that the actions of the police subjected the applicant to inhuman and degrading treatment. While the Court accepted that there might be cases of medical urgency that required a forcible medical intervention, the activities of a small-time street dealer in drugs could not justify this:

> Any recourse to a forcible medical intervention in order to obtain evidence of a crime must be convincingly justified on the facts of a particular case. This is especially true where the procedure in intended to retrieve from inside the individual's body real evidence of the very crime of which he is suspected. The particularly intrusive nature of such an act requires a strict scrutiny of all the surrounding circumstances. In this connection, due regard must be had to the seriousness of the offence at issue . . . The Court notes that drug trafficking is a serious offence. It is acutely aware of the problem

[15] Ibid, paras 117 and 119.

> confronting contracting states in their efforts to combat the harm caused to their societies through the supply of drugs. However, in the present case it was clear before the impugned measure was ordered that the street dealer on whom it was imposed had been storing drugs in his mouth and could not, therefore, have been offering drugs for sale on a large scale . . .[16]

In this passage the Court recognises, as it did in *Teixeira de Castro v Portugal*,[17] that it is difficult for states to combat drug trafficking. Whereas in *Teixeira* the Court followed this with an affirmation of the need to uphold Convention rights, in this case the Court seemed to accept that in a serious drug-trafficking case (unlike the present facts) it might be justifiable to use methods that would normally be regarded as inhuman or degrading treatment.

Subsequent judgments of the Court have moved away from the *Jalloh* approach, although without referring to it. Thus in *Saadi v Italy* (2008)[18] the Grand Chamber rejected the argument that, in considering whether a person should be returned to a country where he or she faced a real possibility of being subjected to a violation of Article 3, weight should be given to the interests of the community in which he was currently residing and the risks presented. The Court recognised the 'immense difficulties' faced by states in protecting their communities from terrorist violence, but held that this could not 'call into question the absolute nature of Article 3'. The Court went on:

> Since protection against the treatment prohibited by Article 3 is absolute, that provision imposes an obligation not to extradite or expel any person who, in the receiving country, would run the real risk of being subjected to such treatment. As the Court has repeatedly held, there can be no derogation from that rule . . . It is not possible to weigh the risk of ill-treatment against the reasons for the expulsion in order to determine whether the responsibility of a state is engaged under Article 3, even where such treatment is inflicted by another state. In that connection, the conduct of the person concerned, however undesirable or dangerous, cannot be taken into account . . .'[19]

That last sentence points in precisely the opposite direction to the passage from *Jalloh* cited above, and is consistent with the great preponderance of authorities on Article 3.

Further evidence that *Jalloh* was out of line on this point comes from another decision of the Grand Chamber, *Gäfgen v Germany* (2008).[20] The relevant point here appears from the following passage:

> The Court, having regard to all the circumstances of the applicant's interrogation by E, observes that he was subjected to sufficiently real and immediate threats of deliberate

[16] Ibid, paras 71 and 77. However, in para 99 the Court's summary of the effect of Art 3 states that 'the Convention prohibits in absolute terms torture and inhuman or degrading treatment or punishment, irrespective of the victim's conduct', a formulation that seems inconsistent with its earlier acceptance that the 'public interest' is relevant.

[17] *Castro* (n 6).

[18] *Saadi v Italy* App no 37201/06 (2009) 49 EHRR 30.

[19] Ibid, para 138.

[20] *Gäfgen v Germany* App no 22978/05 (2009) 48 EHRR 13.

> ill-treatment . . . made for the purpose of extracting a statement from him, which must be regarded as an aggravating element. The Court would like to underline in this connection that in view of the absolute prohibition of treatment contrary to Article 3 irrespective of the conduct of the person concerned and even in the event of a public emergency threatening the life of the nation – or, a fortiori, of an individual – the prohibition on ill-treatment of a person in order to extract information from him applies irrespective of the reasons for which the authorities wish to extract a statement, be it to save a person's life or to further criminal investigations.[21]

The final sentence of that passage is surely sufficient to show how far out of line the *Jalloh* judgment was in suggesting that the seriousness of the offence under investigation should be relevant in determining whether or not there had been a violation of Article 3. As the vast majority of judgments on Article 3 affirm, the prohibitions on torture and on inhuman and degrading treatment apply irrespective of how dangerous the applicant is thought to be or how serious or detestable the applicant's conduct has been.

V. The Relationship between Article 3 and Article 6

If the prosecution relies upon evidence obtained through a violation of Article 3 in a subsequent trial, is that relevant to whether or not the trial is fair (Article 6)? Only in recent years has this question been confronted by the Court, and the answer remains somewhat unclear. The Grand Chamber in *Jalloh v Germany* adopted a strong, though not unwavering, stance on the proper approach. Its general pronouncement was limited to cases of torture:

> Incriminating evidence – whether in the form of a confession or real evidence – obtained as a result of acts of violence or brutality or other forms of treatment which can be characterised as torture – should never be relied on as proof of the victim's guilt, irrespective of its probative value. Any other conclusion would only serve to legitimate indirectly the sort of morally reprehensible conduct which the authors of Article 3 of the Convention sought to proscribe or, as it was so well put in the US Supreme Court's judgment in the *Rochin* case, to 'afford brutality the cloak of law'.[22]

However, that statement was carefully differentiated from the Court's subsequent assessment of the proper approach where the misconduct amounts only to inhuman and degrading treatment. Thus:

> Although the treatment to which the applicant was subjected did not attract the special stigma reserved to acts of torture, it did attain in the circumstances the minimum level of severity covered by the ambit of the Article 3 prohibition. It cannot be excluded that on the facts of a particular case the use of evidence obtained by intentional acts of

[21] Ibid, para 69.
[22] *Jalloh* (n 14) para 105; the reference is to *Rochin v California* 342 US 165 (1952).

> ill-treatment not amounting to torture will render the trial against the victim unfair irrespective of the seriousness of the offence allegedly committed, the weight attached to the evidence and the opportunities which the victim had to challenge its admission and use at his trial.[23]

The Court followed the 'it cannot be excluded that' formulation with a clear statement that the relationship between Articles 3 and 6 is left open when the mistreatment does not attain the level of torture. Clearly the Court took the view that the reasoning that it applied to torture – that to allow a court to act on the evidence would be indirectly to give legitimacy to behaviour that is morally reprehensible – does not apply to mere inhuman and degrading treatment, despite the fact that all those forms of mistreatment are encompassed in an Article that is often referred to as fundamental and as enshrining 'one of the most fundamental values of democratic societies'.[24] Not only that, but the Court envisaged that the question whether a trial is fair when the prosecution relies on evidence obtained through a violation of Article 3 depends to some extent on the seriousness of the offence charged. In this case the Court found that the applicant's fair trial right was violated because he had been subjected to inhuman and degrading treatment, and there was insufficient public interest in doing so when he was merely a street dealer. Again, this implies (contrary to the authorities cited in section IV above) that if the applicant had been charged with a serious offence the Court might have held that 'the public interest' justified it in overlooking the fact that the evidence was obtained through a breach of Article 3.

In *Gäfgen v Germany* the Court simply followed the *Jalloh* formulation, without engaging with the distinctions drawn in that case.[25] There are two aspects to the *Jalloh* formulation: one is that it accords with the special treatment of torture that is evident in Article 15 of the United Nations Convention against Torture and Other Cruel, Inhuman or Degrading Treatment or Punishment;[26] the other is that it does so without giving a clear reason that applies to torture and not to inhuman and degrading treatment. Yet the conclusion drawn by the Court is that, in relation to the effect on the fairness of a trial, reliance on evidence obtained by inhuman and degrading treatment (as opposed to torture) is regarded as on a par with reliance on evidence obtained by a breach of Article 8.

[23] *Jalloh* (n 14) para 106.

[24] *Jalloh* (n 14) para 99.

[25] *Gäfgen* (n 20) para 99.

[26] See, to the same effect, the judgment of Lord Bingham in *A (FC) v Secretary of State for the Home Department* [2005] UKHL 71, para 53.

VI. The Relationship between Article 8 and Article 6

The Strasbourg Court often repeats the assertion that the admissibility of evidence 'is primarily a matter for regulation under national law'.[27] The Court's invariable position has been that reliance by the prosecution on evidence obtained through a breach of Article 8 does not automatically render a trial unfair under Article 6. Thus in *Khan v United Kingdom*[28] the Court held that there was a violation of Article 8, because the use of listening devices was not sufficiently governed by a legal framework at that time, but went on to hold that the use of evidence obtained by this listening device, as the main part of the prosecution case, did not render the trial unfair under Article 6. So long as the defendant has the possibility of challenging the authenticity of the evidence, and so long as the trial court has a discretion to exclude the evidence, there may be no violation of Article 6. In his dissenting opinion, Judge Loucaides argued that such reasoning defies the structure of the Convention:

> This is the first case which comes before the Court where the only evidence against an accused in a criminal case which also led to his conviction, was evidence secured in a manner contrary to the provisions of Article 8 of the Convention . . . I cannot accept that a trial can be fair, as required by Article 6, if a person's guilt for any offence is established through evidence obtained in breach of the human rights guaranteed by the Convention.

However, the Court has continued to adopt the same approach. It did so in *PG and JH v United Kingdom*,[29] but in her dissenting opinion Judge Tulkens again drew attention to wider questions of the structure of the Convention:

> I do not think that a trial can be described as 'fair' where evidence obtained in breach of a fundamental right guaranteed by the Convention has been admitted during that trial. As the Court has already had occasion to stress, the Convention must be interpreted as a coherent whole (see *Klass v. Germany* 1978, paras. 68–69) . . . In concluding that there has not been a violation of Article 6, the Court renders Article 8 completely ineffective. The rights enshrined in the Convention cannot remain purely theoretical or virtual . . .

Both dissenting judges point to the obligation of member states (under Article 1) to ensure that all articles of the Convention are safeguarded, and argue that the Convention's structure is undermined if a trial is conducted on the basis of evidence obtained through violation of one of the Convention's articles.

[27] *Gäfgen* (n 20) para 96, citing the leading decision in *Schenk v Switzerland* App no 10862/84 Series A no 140 (1988), (1991) 13 EHRR 242, and the recent decision in *Heglas v Czech Republic* App no 5935/02 (2009) 48 EHRR 44. Interestingly, the Court also cites a judgment that rejected the application of this general assertion, *Castro* (n 6).

[28] *Khan v United Kingdom* App no 35394/97 (2000), (2001) 31 EHRR 45.

[29] *PG and JH v United Kingdom* App no 44787/98 (2008) 46 EHRR 51.

However, the Court's general or majority position seems to be that there is a separation between a violation of Article 8 and a violation of Article 6. In other words, the Court's view seems to be that the way to deal with a violation of Article 8 is to provide a remedy to the person who suffered from the breach, a remedy that might be found in an award of damages or perhaps a reduction in sentence. But the criminal trial is something separate, with its own fairness criteria, and the origins of the prosecution evidence do not affect this.

The problem with this separation thesis is that the Court is inconsistent about it. Plainly the Court does not support the separation thesis in cases of torture; it regards any evidence obtained by torture as rendering the trial unfair. We have seen that it does not apply that reasoning to inhuman and degrading treatment, and we now see that it does not apply that reasoning to evidence obtained by a breach of Article 8. In these cases, the separation thesis is regarded as appropriate; breach of Article 8 (or of Article 3, in respect of inhuman or degrading treatment) is regarded as a separate matter, calling for a separate remedy, and does not affect the fairness of the criminal trial based upon it.

In *Heglas v Czech Republic*[30] the Court brought together the two lines of argument that have been the focus of this chapter. The Court found a breach of Article 8 in the unlawful recording of a conversation between the applicant and another person, and then had to decide whether the prosecution's reliance on evidence obtained by that violation rendered unfair the trial for robbery with violence. The Court developed the previous case law:

> The general requirements of fairness provided in Article 6 apply to all criminal proceedings, whatever the type of offence involved. It remains that, in order to determine whether the proceedings as a whole have been fair, the weight of the public interest in the prosecution of a particular offence and the sanction of its author may be taken into consideration and put in the balance with the interest of the individual that the incriminating evidence be gathered lawfully. However, the considerations of public interest cannot justify measures emptying the applicant's rights of defence of their very substance, including that of not contributing to its own incrimination guaranteed by Article 6 of the Convention.[31]

The Court went on to hold that the evidence obtained by a violation of Article 8 was not crucial to the case, and then added, tellingly for our purposes, the following paragraph:

> As regards the weight of the public interest in the use of that evidence to find the applicant guilty, the Court observes that the measure was aimed at the author of a serious offence which caused injuries to a third party, and who was finally imposed a nine-year sentence.[32]

This exposes the Court's position with clarity: this is the corollary of the finding in *Jalloh*, and so we now know that the requirements of a fair trial are held to vary

[30] *Heglas v Czech Republic* App no 5935/02 (2009) 48 EHRR 44.
[31] Ibid, para 87, with a reference to *Heaney* (n 8).
[32] Ibid, para 91.

according to the seriousness of the offence with which the defendant is charged. This passage was recently repeated by the Grand Chamber in *Bikov v Russia*:[33] the issue in *Bikov* was different and so the Court was not called upon to interpret or apply *Heglas*, but the Grand Chamber cited it without disagreement.[34]

VII. Conclusions and Questions

The purpose of this chapter has been to identify some significant changes in the interpretation of certain articles of the Convention relevant to criminal cases. It is not claimed that these changes are confirmed or complete, but sufficient evidence has been adduced from Strasbourg judgments in the first decade of the new century to cast doubt on the structure of the Convention and on some of its hitherto established doctrines. Article 3 has been revered as enshrining 'one of the most fundamental values of democratic societies',[35] but how fundamental is it if (a) courts are beginning to divide it into two parts of different strength (ie the torture prohibition, and the prohibition on inhuman or degrading treatment), or if (b) there are circumstances in which the application of Article 3 depends on the seriousness of the offence allegedly committed by the defendant, or if (c) the Court treats as fair a criminal trial in which the prosecution uses evidence obtained through violation of Article 3? The last point also carries over to the relationship between Article 8 and Article 6: if the prosecution uses evidence obtained through a breach of Article 8, does this have any implications for the fairness of the trial? Can the two issues fairly be treated as separate, or should the Convention be read as a unified whole? In relation to Article 6 itself, is the privilege against self-incrimination an implied right that applies to all criminal cases, from the lowest to the highest, as the judgments of the 1990s maintained; or is it a right that may give way to 'the public interest', ie to the seriousness of the offence being investigated? The answers to these questions have immense implications for the future of human rights guarantees in criminal cases, and yet the manner in which the Court and the Grand Chamber have introduced these changes, or at least inconsistencies, into their judgments means that there has been no principled debate about the issues. Points made in the dissenting judgments have rarely been addressed in the majority judgments, creating doubts about the structure of the Convention and leading to unfortunate weaknesses in the developing doctrines.

[33] *Bikov v Russia* App no 4378/02 (2009); [2010] Crim LR 413.
[34] Ibid, para 100.
[35] *Jalloh* (n 14) para 99.

4

The 'Constitutionalisation' of Labour Law: Possibilities and Problems

ACL DAVIES

For many years now, there has been considerable interest among labour lawyers in the human rights perspective on their subject. Statutory developments such as the Sex Discrimination Act 1975 and the Race Relations Act 1976 can be seen as early examples of the movement to protect rights at work, albeit without much explicit use of rights language. In the 1980s and early 1990s, as the trade union movement came under attack, some theorists drew on international human rights instruments as a benchmark against which to critique domestic developments. The interest in human rights has increased in recent years with the enactment of the Human Rights Act 1998 (HRA) and with developments in EU law, both of which make it possible to present rights arguments directly to the courts in labour law cases. This has prompted some commentators to suggest that the subject is undergoing a process of 'constitutionalisation'.

However, the attitude of labour lawyers towards human rights has long been somewhat ambivalent. Whilst rights can be used to advance the interests of workers, there is a concern that too great a focus on workers' rights might undermine the collective dimensions of labour law. This concern stems both from early common law cases on the 'right to work', in which the courts questioned closed shop arrangements, and from statutory developments in the 1980s which enhanced the rights of individual trade union members as against their unions. Thus, constitutionalisation may bring problems as well as benefits in the particular context of labour law.

This chapter will argue that fears about the constitutionalisation of labour law are exaggerated and that more explicit use of human rights arguments in the legislature and the courts is a positive development. However, the impact of these arguments has been limited: the rights of workers and their unions have been treated as one factor among many to be taken into account rather than as having particular weight in the reasoning process. The government and the legislature have continued to place considerable emphasis on other policy concerns alongside the need to protect workers' rights, and (with some exceptions) the domestic courts have continued to show considerable 'deference' to employers' economic arguments.

I. Constitutionalisation

The term 'constitutionalisation' has no clearly accepted meaning. For the purposes of this chapter, it will be taken to refer to the developing possibility of making explicit use of human rights arguments both in the courts and in the legislative process, in a context in which those arguments may have some degree of binding force in domestic law. This definition seeks to capture the reasons why the constitutionalisation of labour law might be seen as a relatively novel development.[1]

The UK government has been bound in international law to uphold workers' human rights for many years. Historically, the United Kingdom played a key role in the creation and development of the International Labour Organization (ILO). The United Kingdom was a founding signatory of the European Convention on Human Rights (ECHR) and has permitted individuals to petition the Court in Strasbourg since 1966. The United Kingdom is also a signatory to the European Social Charter 1961 (ESC), another Council of Europe instrument, which relates specifically to protection of socio-economic rights, though the United Kingdom has yet to ratify the protocol on collective complaints or the Revised Social Charter of 1996. Traditionally, the UK government has argued that these international commitments should be implemented through the normal legislative process rather than through human rights guarantees enforceable in the domestic courts. Thus, the obligation under Article 11 ECHR to uphold freedom of association might be fulfilled through a detailed body of legislation on trade unions rather than by incorporating Article 11 directly into domestic law. This fits with the United Kingdom's tradition of having no written constitution and no formal bill of rights.

Growing dissatisfaction with this general approach led to the enactment of the HRA 1998, which came into force in 2000. This statute allows litigants to invoke most of the rights contained in the ECHR in the domestic courts. The enactment of the HRA reflects a desire to allow the domestic courts – not just the ECtHR – to adjudicate on human rights questions. The HRA represents a compromise between the desire to afford greater judicial protection to human rights and an attempt to preserve the sovereignty of Parliament, a fundamental principle of the British constitution. The HRA does not empower the courts to strike down Acts of Parliament if they infringe Convention rights. Instead, it requires them to follow a two-stage process. First, they must attempt to interpret the statute in question consistently with those rights.[2] Second, if this is impossible, the courts may issue a 'declaration of incompatibility'.[3] This is merely an expression of opinion and does not oblige

[1] In labour law, constitutionalisation is particularly associated with the work of Hugh Collins. See H Collins, 'Utility and Rights in Common Law Reasoning: Rebalancing Private Law through Constitutionalization', *LSE Legal Studies Working Paper* No 6/2007, and 'Beyond the Third Way in Labour Law', available at www.fljs.org/section.aspx?id=2481 (last visited 14 April 2011).

[2] HRA 1998, s 3.

[3] Ibid, s 4.

Parliament to take steps to amend the offending legislation. The Act's framers assumed that political pressure would be sufficient to ensure that amendments would be passed in most cases. The courts are to 'take into account' Convention jurisprudence when deciding cases.[4] The Act brings about two further significant changes. One is that public bodies are now obliged to act in accordance with human rights when exercising their powers.[5] The courts can enforce this obligation through judicial review. The other is that the courts themselves may take the Convention rights into account when developing the common law, though the exact scope of their obligation to do so remains a matter of debate.[6]

A number of Convention rights have relevance to employment law. The most obvious is freedom of association (Article 11), but there are others, including freedom of expression (Article 10), the right to respect for private life (Article 8), and the (limited) right not to be subjected to discrimination (Article 14). Since the Convention is only directly binding upon public bodies, it is not possible for an employee outside the public sector simply to go to court and argue that his or her employer breached Convention rights. However, it is possible to argue that the courts should develop the common law in line with the Convention, to ask for a statute to be interpreted compatibly with the Convention, or to challenge a statute's compatibility with the Convention, even in a case against a private employer. Moreover, although the legislature is not bound to legislate compatibly with Convention rights, the possibility that a court might issue a declaration of incompatibility has raised the profile of human rights considerations during the legislative process.

The HRA and the Convention are not the only factors to consider. EU law is becoming more focused on human rights, and this inevitably has an impact on English law. The United Kingdom has been a member of the European Union (then European Communities) since 1973. As is well known, successive treaty amendments have expanded the European Union's competence in employment law and it now has power to legislate on many significant topics such as discrimination, health and safety, working conditions, termination of employment, and information and consultation.[7] Pay, freedom of association, and the right to strike are, however, specifically excluded.[8] Most EU legislation takes the form of directives. These identify the end to be achieved but allow each Member State a discretion as to the method of achieving that end.[9] The United Kingdom has a relatively good record of implementing directives although it is notorious for its hostility towards new proposals in the employment field. The European Court of Justice (ECJ) (now the Court of Justice of the European Union, CJ) has played a significant role in developing anti-discrimination law in particular.[10]

[4] Ibid, s 2.
[5] Ibid, s 6.
[6] This follows from the courts' own status as public bodies within HRA 1998, s 6.
[7] Art 153 TFEU.
[8] Art 153(5) TFEU.
[9] Art 288 TFEU.
[10] Under Art 157 TFEU in particular.

The European Union has become increasingly focused on human rights in recent years as part of an attempt to appeal more to its sometimes rather sceptical citizens. The ECJ has developed some important jurisprudence on fundamental rights,[11] and in 2000, the Member States proclaimed the EU Charter of Fundamental Rights. The Charter is a comprehensive statement of human rights. It contains civil and political rights (drawing heavily on the ECHR), but also includes a wide range of economic and social rights.[12] This makes it potentially very significant in the employment sphere: much more so than the ECHR. Now that the Lisbon Treaty has entered into force, the Charter has become legally binding, and the CJ has begun to cite its provisions.[13] However, the Charter is designed only to constrain the Union institutions (and the Member States when they are implementing Union law) rather than to create new competences.[14] And, as we shall see below, the effect of the Court's jurisprudence in labour law has been mixed. Importantly, the principle of supremacy means that EU law has a much greater impact on domestic law than does the Convention, even after the HRA. The national courts must follow the precedents set by the CJ, and if national legislation is incompatible with EU law, the courts can set it aside.[15]

This brief overview has demonstrated that whilst human rights arguments are by no means new in labour law, their status has changed in recent years. The enactment of the HRA has made it possible to invoke Convention rights in the domestic courts and has raised their profile in the legislative process. EU law is growing in importance as a source of human rights norms in domestic law. These developments give rise to the suggestion that – at least in a formal sense – a process of constitutionalisation is taking place.

This chapter will begin by considering a possible objection to the greater use of rights arguments in labour law: that their focus on the individual might undermine the subject's traditional emphasis on the achievement of worker protection through the collective strength of workers in trade unions (section II). It will then consider some recent examples of the legislature's reaction to human rights concerns, by exploring the statutory changes enacted in the light of the ECtHR's decisions in *Wilson v United Kingdom*[16] and *ASLEF v United Kingdom* (section III).[17] It will then examine the use of human rights arguments in the courts, looking in particular at *Pay v Lancashire Probation Service*[18] (on the application of Convention rights in the context of employers' dismissal decisions) and recent cases on the compatibility of industrial action legislation with Article 11 ECHR (notably

[11] See, generally, P Craig and G de Búrca, *EU Law*, 5th edn (Oxford, OUP, 2011) ch 11.

[12] For a helpful critique, see D Ashiagbor, 'Economic and Social Rights in the European Charter of Fundamental Rights' (2004) 1 *European Human Rights Law Review* 62.

[13] Case C-341/05 *Laval v Svenska Byggnadsarbetareförbundet* [2007] ECR I-11767, [2008] 2 CMLR 9, para 90.

[14] Art 51 of the Charter of Fundamental Rights of the European Union [2000] OJ C364/1.

[15] See, generally, Craig and de Búrca (n 11) ch 9.

[16] *Wilson v United Kingdom* App nos 30668/96, 30671/96 and 30678/96 [2002] ECHR 552, (2002) 35 EHRR 20.

[17] *ASLEF v United Kingdom* App no 11002/05 [2007] ECHR 184, (2007) 45 EHRR 34.

[18] *Pay v Lancashire Probation Service* [2004] ICR 187 (EAT).

Metrobus v Unite the Union[19] and *London Midland v ASLEF*[20]) in the domestic courts, and at the well-known *Viking*[21] and *Laval*[22] decisions of the ECJ on the right to strike in EU law (section IV).

II. Individualism and Collectivism

As a statement of civil and political rights, the ECHR is focused on the individual. English labour law, by contrast, has traditionally focused on protecting the ability of workers to act collectively through trade unions. In the light of 1980s policies, in which individual rights were used to undermine the trade union movement, it is not surprising that many English labour lawyers regarded the HRA with suspicion. They feared that it would entrench the individualistic approach in English law and make collectivist reforms unattainable. This section will first analyse the collectivist critique in more detail. It will be argued that some versions of the collectivist critique are overstated. The section will then explore the outlook of the ECtHR. The discussion will demonstrate that the ECtHR is, in fact, attuned to the need to interpret rights with regard to the collective context.

The collectivist critique of individual rights can take at least two forms. A broad version of the critique is to the effect that any legal protection for individual rights might undermine trade unions. Kahn-Freund, the great advocate of collective laissez-faire, took the view that legal rights for individual workers would remove their incentive to join a trade union.[23] Although such rights might protect workers' immediate interests, their long-term wellbeing would best be served through strong collective bargaining. However, this argument is difficult to sustain. First, trade unions are unlikely ever to achieve universal coverage of the workforce, because some groups of workers are difficult to organise. Unless the law intervenes, these workers would be left without basic protections against discrimination, unfair dismissal and so on. Second, trade unions are democratic organisations and as such must focus on protecting the interests of the majority of their members. Members who are in the minority on a particular issue may find that their rights are ignored. Third, the presence of legal rights does not necessarily take away the value of being a union member. The union may be able to negotiate for protection above and beyond that granted by the law. It may also be able to help individuals with the daunting task of enforcing their legal rights. Thus, few, if any, modern labour lawyers would regard individual rights as inherently inappropriate.

[19] *Metrobus v Unite the Union* [2009] EWCA Civ 829, [2010] ICR 173.

[20] *London Midland v ASLEF* [2011] EWCA Civ 226, [2011] ICR 848.

[21] Case C-438/05 *International Transport Workers' Federation v Viking Line ABP* [2007] ECR I-10779, [2008] 1 CMLR 51.

[22] *Laval* (n 13).

[23] O Kahn-Freund, 'Legal Framework' in A Flanders and H Clegg (eds), *The System of Industrial Relations in Great Britain* (Oxford, Blackwell, 1954) 66.

There is, however, a less radical version of the collectivist critique of individual rights that does have some force in relation to English labour law as it stands at present. It is that the use of individual rights *in trade union law in particular* may undermine unions' ability to function effectively. On this view, the problem with individual rights is that they prioritise individuals' choices over the views of the majority. Rights are incompatible with successful trade unionism because this requires (with some exceptions) that individuals accept majority decisions and act in ways which express solidarity with their colleagues.[24] For example, English law restricts unions' ability to discipline individuals who refuse to take part in a strike, even if the strike is supported by a majority of the workforce and is otherwise lawful.[25] Although this preserves the individual's freedom to make a difficult decision which may have serious financial consequences, it does inhibit unions' ability to organise a well-supported and effective strike. The ILO, which places considerable emphasis on the autonomy of trade unions,[26] has condemned the United Kingdom's trade union legislation on a number of occasions.[27]

The HRA gives effect to Article 11 ECHR in English law. This protects the right to form and join associations, including trade unions. Because this forms part of a civil and political rights instrument, there has been a worry that it would reinforce the problem of individualism just identified: that it would prioritise individual rights at the expense of collective activities. However, the force of this argument depends on the ECtHR's approach to Article 11. As this section will demonstrate, the fear of individualism is unfounded, for two reasons. First, when faced with direct clashes between individual rights and collective interests, the Court has shown a sound grasp of the issues at stake and has given appropriate weight to collective interests. Second, in recent case-law the Court has broadened its interpretation of Article 11 so that it protects collective bargaining and the right to strike. Thus, the overall tenor of the right has become much more collective in nature.

It is true that the ECtHR has been relatively individualistic in its approach to the 'closed shop', in which individuals are required to join a trade union in order to work in a particular workplace.[28] In *Sørensen and Rasmussen v Denmark*, [29] although the Court said that 'compulsion to join a particular trade union may not always be contrary to the Convention', it also noted that closed shops were 'not an indispensable tool for the effective enjoyment of trade union freedoms'.[30] This

[24] JM Barbalet, *Citizenship: Rights, Struggle and Class Inequality* (Milton Keynes, Open University Press, 1988) 26.

[25] Trade Union and Labour Relations (Consolidation) Act 1992 (hereafter TULRCA), ss 64–65.

[26] ILO, Freedom of Association and Protection of the Right to Organise Convention (Convention No 87, 1948), Arts 2, 3 and 8. See also Committee on Freedom of Association, *Digest of Decisions* (1996), paras 331–32.

[27] See, for example, ILO Committee on Freedom of Association, case nos 1618 and 1730.

[28] The closed shop is effectively unlawful in English law as a result of TULRCA 1992, ss 137 and 152–53.

[29] *Sørensen and Rasmussen v Denmark* App nos 52562/99 and 52620/99) Reports 2006-I, (2008) 46 EHRR 29, para 54.

[30] Ibid, para 75.

suggests that the Court would uphold a closed shop only in exceptional circumstances. However, this approach is not out of line with the international jurisprudence.

Although the ILO allows states to decide whether or not to permit unions and employers to agree to closed shops,[31] the European Committee on Social Rights has interpreted the ESC as prohibiting the closed shop altogether,[32] and it is also expressly prohibited in the Universal Declaration of Human Rights.[33] Thus, it is not appropriate to conclude from the closed shop cases alone that the ECtHR is excessively individualistic in its outlook.

The validity of the collectivist critique of the ECHR must therefore turn on its treatment of issues of trade union membership other than the closed shop. Does it follow the ILO in respecting unions' autonomy, or is it likely to reinforce English law's approach of prioritising the rights of individuals? The *ASLEF* case indicates that the ECtHR is in fact fully aware of the need to strike a balance between the rights of the individual and the rights of the trade union.[34]

ASLEF, a trade union, discovered that one of its members was also an active member of the far-right British National Party. The union's rules provided that members of organisations with aims and objectives opposed to those of the union could be excluded or expelled. The union sought to expel the member under this provision. In doing so, it fell foul of English legislation which prohibited unions from using membership of a political party as a ground of exclusion or expulsion.[35] The Employment Appeal Tribunal (EAT) mitigated the force of the legislation somewhat by holding that the union would not be liable where its decision was attributable solely to the individual's *activities* as a member of the political party.[36] However, it was found on the facts that ASLEF had expelled the individual because of his membership, not his activities, so the union was forced to readmit him as a member and was potentially liable to pay him compensation.[37] In response to these proceedings, the government amended the legislation to confirm the distinction drawn by the EAT between membership and activities.[38] Nevertheless, it remained unlawful for a union to exclude or expel an individual solely for *membership* of a political party. ASLEF challenged this legislation in the ECtHR.

The Court began by pointing out that 'the right to form trade unions involves, for example, the right of trade unions to draw up their own rules and to administer

[31] International Labour Conference, 43rd Session, 1959, Report of the Committee of Experts, Report III (Part IV), para 36.

[32] ESC Secretariat, Digest of the Case Law of the ECSR (2005) 30.

[33] Art 20(2).

[34] *ASLEF* (n 17). For an excellent discussion of the issues written prior to the ECtHR's decision, see J Hendy and KD Ewing, 'Trade Unions, Human Rights and the BNP' (2005) 34 *Industrial Law Journal* 197.

[35] Then TULRCA 1992, s 174(4)(a)(iii).

[36] *ASLEF v Lee*, UKEAT/0625/03/RN (2004), paras 28–30.

[37] *Lee v ASLEF*, 7 October 2004 (unreported).

[38] TULRCA 1992, s 174, as amended, Employment Relations Act 2004, s 33.

their own affairs'.[39] It cited various sources for this proposition, including ILO Convention Number 87.[40] It went on to note that since individuals can choose whether or not to join a union, unions should have the equivalent right to decide who to admit to membership: 'Article 11 cannot be interpreted as imposing an obligation on associations or organisations to admit whosoever wishes to join.'[41] This meant that the UK legislation was in breach of Article 11, so it fell to the government to justify its interference with the union's rights. The Court accepted that the government was seeking to protect the individual's political freedoms. However, it concluded that the government had failed to strike the correct balance between those freedoms and the rights of the trade union. The Court stated that trade unions 'are not bodies solely devoted to politically neutral aspects of the well-being of their members, but are often ideological, with strongly held views on social and political issues'.[42] On this view, it was legitimate for the union to set membership rules with some political content. There was no evidence to suggest that the union had erred in its application of these rules to the individual's case. From the individual's perspective, there was no real hardship involved in the loss of his union membership. It did not inhibit his political activities or his freedom of expression. Since there was no closed shop, he did not stand to lose his job as a result of the union's decision. Moreover, he would continue to benefit from collective bargaining because the results of ASLEF's bargaining efforts would be afforded to all workers, not just to its own members. Overall, the Court concluded that the union's right to choose its members was the most important consideration and that the union had suffered a violation of its Article 11 rights.

The collectivist approach adopted by the Court in *ASLEF* in the context of a clash between the interests of a union and an individual member has been strongly reinforced by its recent interpretation of the *content* of Article 11. Historically, the Court held that, whilst Article 11 required that trade unions should be able to take steps to protect their members' interests,[43] signatory states enjoyed a wide margin of appreciation in deciding exactly what possibilities should be made available to unions for this purpose.[44] Thus, there was no obligation on states to protect a right to engage in collective bargaining or to strike,[45] though where a State chose to offer a right to strike the Court would engage in (limited) review of the proportionality of any restrictions on the right.[46] However, in *Demir v Turkey*, the Court took three bold steps.[47] First, it departed from its earlier, limited case-law on the scope of Article 11. Second, it referred to the jurisprudence of the ILO and the

[39] *ASLEF* (n 17), para 38.
[40] ILO (n 26).
[41] *ASLEF* (n 17), para 39.
[42] Ibid, para 50.
[43] *National Union of Belgian Police v Belgium* (1979–80) 1 EHRR 578, 591.
[44] *Schmidt and Dahlströhm v Sweden* (1979–80) 1 EHRR 578.
[45] For example, *Swedish Engine Drivers' Union v Sweden* (1979–80) 1 EHRR 617; *Schmidt* (n 44).
[46] *UNISON v UK* [2002] IRLR 497.
[47] *Demir v Turkey* (2009) 48 EHRR 54. For discussion, see KD Ewing and J Hendy, 'The Dramatic Implications of *Demir and Baykara*' (2010) 39 *Industrial Law Journal* 2.

ESC in interpreting the right. And third, it held that the right to engage in collective bargaining was protected by Article 11. Turkish law's annulment of a collective agreement between a civil service trade union and a municipal government therefore constituted a violation of this right. In *Enerji Yapi-Yol Sen v Turkey*, the Court went a step further, holding that the right to strike was an 'important aspect' of unions' ability to protect their members' interests.[48] It found that a ban by the Turkish government on a one-day strike by civil servants was disproportionate and thus a violation of Article 11.

The responses of the UK government and courts to these decisions will be discussed below.[49] For present purposes, the important point is that the Court has adopted a collectivist approach to Article 11, both in the context of a clash between a union and a member (in *ASLEF*) and in interpreting the right more generally (as in *Demir* and *Enerji*). It is important to approach these developments with some caution: the facts of *Demir* and *Enerji* involved quite clear-cut violations of the relevant rights, so the Court might be less willing to intervene in more marginal cases. Nevertheless, now that the Court has accepted the relevance of the ILO and ESC jurisprudence, it will be hard for it to turn back from the collectivist route.

III. The Constitutionalisation of Labour Legislation

It was noted above that the constitutionalisation of labour law, through EU law and through the ECHR, might be expected to have some impact on the legislature. EU law is binding in domestic law, so although it is possible to enact a statute that is incompatible with EU law, a court could disapply it. Under the HRA, the courts are obliged to uphold statutes that are incompatible with Convention rights, but they do have power to issue a declaration of incompatibility. This prospect has led to a greater degree of interest within the executive and the legislature as to whether or not proposed legislation is compatible with the Convention,[50] reinforced by an obligation on the minister proposing a bill to indicate whether or not it is thought to infringe Convention rights.[51]

In this section, we will consider two examples of legislation intended to change English law to bring it into line with ECtHR decisions. Both examples have met with a mixed reception from labour law commentators. They illustrate the complexities of interpreting the ECtHR's decisions and reconciling them with domestic concerns.

[48] *Enerji Yapi-Yol Sen v Turkey* (68959/01), judgment 21 April 2009, quoted in Ewing and Hendy (n 47) 14.

[49] Sections III.B and IV.B.

[50] The United Kingdom has a parliamentary executive and it is generally the case that a government with a reasonable parliamentary majority can control the legislature.

[51] HRA 1998, s 19.

A. *Wilson v United Kingdom*

In *Wilson*, the employer was seeking to terminate its relationship with the union and offered a pay rise to those workers who were willing to accept a so-called 'personal contract' instead of a collectively bargained contract.[52] Mr Wilson, who was unwilling to give up collective bargaining and was thus denied the pay rise, claimed that he had been discriminated against on grounds of trade union membership. His claim failed in the House of Lords.[53] One of the main reasons for this was that the House of Lords adopted a narrow definition of membership which did not include obtaining the benefits of collective bargaining. The ECtHR held that the government had not complied with its positive obligation to secure Mr Wilson's enjoyment of his Article 11 rights. It said:

> It is of the essence of the right to join a trade union for the protection of their interests that employees should be free to instruct or permit the union to make representations to their employer or to take action in support of their interests on their behalf. If workers are prevented from so doing, their freedom to belong to a trade union, for the protection of their interests, becomes illusory. It is the role of the State to ensure that trade union members are not prevented or restrained from using their union to represent them in attempts to regulate their relations with their employers.[54]

One of the key points emerging from this decision is that the Article 11 right protects more than just union membership per se. It also affords protection to the use of union services: in this case, asking the union to make representations to the employer.[55]

Under s 146 TULRCA 1992, a worker has a right not to be subjected to any detriment (whether by action or deliberate omission) to prevent or deter trade union membership, prevent or deter participation in union activities, or prevent or deter the use of union services. The last of these three elements, the protection for the use of union services, was added in 2004 in response to the *Wilson* decision.[56] At first glance, it appears to reflect the ECtHR's views. However, the definition of union services for this purpose explicitly excludes collective bargaining.[57] The employer can therefore lawfully subject individuals to detriment or dismissal if they are seeking to make use of their union to negotiate on their behalf in the collective bargaining process. This is clearly incompatible with the ECtHR's ruling in *Wilson*, which

[52] *Wilson* (n 16). In the UK, trade union recognition is often voluntary: the union simply persuades the employer to engage in bargaining, perhaps by threatening industrial action. This means that the employer is legally free to withdraw recognition of the union at any time provided that it can persuade the workforce to accept the change. The position is more complicated where the union achieves statutory recognition under Schedule A1 of the Trade Union and Labour Relations (Consolidation) Act 1992, but this will not be considered in detail here because it was not relevant in *Wilson*.

[53] *Associated Newspapers v Wilson* [1995] 2 All ER 100.

[54] *Wilson* (n 16) para 46.

[55] KD Ewing, 'The Implications of *Wilson* and *Palmer*' (2003) 32 *Industrial Law Journal* 1, 7–9.

[56] Employment Relations Act 2004, ss 30–31.

[57] TULRCA 1992, s 145B(4). See AL Bogg, 'Employment Relations Act 2004 – Another False Dawn For Collectivism?' (2005) 34 *Industrial Law Journal* 72, 74–75.

required states to protect individuals not just in respect of their union membership but also in respect of asking their union to represent them in negotiations with the employer.

Also in response to *Wilson*, the government brought in two new provisions to address the specific fact situation in which the employer offers inducements to the workforce. New s 145A TULRCA 1992 gives a worker a right not to have an offer made to him or her to induce him or her to give up union membership, or to refrain from using union services or participating in union activities. New s 145B gives a worker the right not to have an offer made to him or her which, in conjunction with offers made to other workers, would have the effect of stopping collective bargaining. Because of the exclusion of collective bargaining from the definition of union services in the other provisions already examined, this is in fact the only right English law gives workers in respect of collective bargaining. Commentators have, however, identified weaknesses in these provisions. As a result, they may not be a particularly effective practical tool for the protection of workers' Article 11 rights. First, the employer's attack on trade unionism must be its 'sole or main' purpose. This allows employers to argue that their purpose was something else – business reorganisation, for example – with the anti-union purpose as a minor side effect.[58] Second, the main remedy under ss 145A and 145B is an award of £3,500 in compensation.[59] This relatively small sum may not deter employers from offering inducements. Some employees may be happy to give up union membership or collective bargaining in return for the inducements. Those who are unwilling to give up their rights may not find it worthwhile to take the employer to a tribunal for minimal compensation.

A final problem is that the government did not accept the need to enact any rights for unions themselves as part of this programme of reform.[60] In *Wilson*, the ECtHR clearly stated that the unions' rights had been violated:

> [The Court] considers that, by permitting employers to use financial incentives to induce employees to surrender important union rights, the respondent State has failed in its positive obligation to secure the enjoyment of the rights under Article 11 of the Convention. This failure amounted to a violation of Article 11, as regards both the applicant trade unions and the individual applicants.[61]

Both Bogg and Ewing have argued that this required fundamental changes to English law to give unions as well as individuals a remedy against employer strategies designed to bring about derecognition.[62] This point is of particular significance in practice. Although individual rights not to be discriminated against on trade union grounds are clearly necessary to the existence of trade unions, they may not be sufficient. This is because individuals may be reluctant to enforce their

[58] Bogg (n 57) 74.

[59] TULRCA 1992, s 145E.

[60] Department of Trade and Industry (DTI), *Review of the Employment Relations Act 1999* (2003), paras 3.16–3.17.

[61] *Wilson* (n 16) para 48.

[62] Bogg (n 57) 73; Ewing (n 55) 11–13.

rights, either because of the costs of litigation or because they fear the employer's reaction. A remedy of some kind for the union would considerably enhance the effectiveness of the statutory regime.

Thus, although English law does contain protections for workers against discrimination by their employers on trade union grounds, some aspects of the law are clearly in breach of Article 11 and others are, arguably, weak in the protection they offer. The government has failed to comply fully with the spirit – and sometimes even the letter – of the *Wilson* decision. The main reason for this seems to be that the *Wilson* decision did not fit with the then Labour government's pro-business agenda. The government (despite the Labour Party's close links with the trade union movement) had an ambivalent view of unions, regarding them as beneficial but only when they worked in 'partnership' with employers.[63] One of the practical manifestations of the government's attitude was a desire to prevent the unions from regaining significant power by maintaining as much 1980s legislation as possible. This included allowing employers the freedom to derecognise a union and – most importantly – to have the freedom to use certain 'tactics' (such as detrimental treatment and inducements) to bring about that result.[64] It is possible that the courts may be able to remedy English law's current failures using their interpretative powers under s 3 HRA,[65] but for reasons to be discussed below, this seems unlikely in practice. It may therefore be necessary for unions to take more cases to the ECtHR in order to clarify the precise requirements of Article 11 in this context.

B. *ASLEF v United Kingdom*

The case of *ASLEF v United Kingdom* was discussed above.[66] It will be recalled that the union challenged English law's rules barring unions from excluding or expelling individuals on the basis of their membership of a political party. The ECtHR held that the union should have been allowed to expel the member in question because the member would not have suffered particular hardship beyond the loss of membership itself, and because union autonomy was an important value to be upheld. As with *Wilson*, there is evidence of an unenthusiastic response from the UK government, though important changes were also introduced as amendments in the legislature.

The government's initial proposal was to remove all references to political party membership from s 174 TULRCA, leaving unions free to adopt and enforce their own rules on this topic.[67] However, when the proposal was put before Parliament, concern was expressed by the Joint Committee on Human Rights

[63] DTI, *Fairness at Work* (Cm 3968, 1998) ch 4.
[64] Ibid, paras 3.12–3.13.
[65] For scepticism on this point see Bogg (n 57) 75.
[66] Above (n 17).
[67] Department for Business, Enterprise and Regulatory Reform, *ECHR Judgment in the ASLEF v UK Case – Implications for Trade Union Law, Government Response to Public Consultation* (2007).

that this approach would not afford sufficient safeguards to union members.[68] As a result, s 174 as amended allows unions to exclude or expel an individual for membership of a political party, but only where a detailed set of conditions is met.[69] The conditions are that: membership of the political party is contrary to a rule of the trade union, or membership of the political party is contrary to an objective of the trade union where it is reasonably practicable to ascertain that objective; the decision to exclude or expel is taken in accordance with the union's rules; the individual is given notice of the proposal to exclude or expel him or her and the reasons for this, he or she is given a fair opportunity to make representations and those representations are considered fairly by the union; and it must not be the case that the exclusion or expulsion would cause the individual to lose his or her livelihood or suffer exceptional hardship.[70]

These various conditions reflect statements in the ECtHR's judgment in *ASLEF*, so on one level it can be argued that they ensure a high degree of compliance with the detailed requirements of the decision. Indeed, the safeguards could be seen as a means of reconciling the strong protection of the union's Article 11 rights in the *ASLEF* decision with concern for the Article 10 and 11 rights of the affected individual. However, commentators have argued that the effect of the conditions may be to make the law unnecessarily restrictive.[71] For example, the ECtHR noted that the affected individual would not lose his job as a result of being expelled from the union because the closed shop is unlawful. This is reflected in the amended s 174 in the requirement that the exclusion or expulsion should not lead to loss of livelihood or undue hardship. However, the stipulation relating to loss of livelihood seems superfluous because of the ban on the closed shop. The stipulation relating to undue hardship is, as Ewing has argued, difficult to interpret.[72] It leaves discretion to the courts to find hardship in a particular case which may deter unions from invoking the power to exclude or expel on political grounds.

Perhaps more importantly, the government (as it had done after *Wilson*) focused solely on the immediate issue raised by the *ASLEF* case: the interaction between union membership and membership of a political party.[73] It is arguable that the principle of autonomy enunciated in that case (and which underlies other relevant instruments, such as ILO Convention No 87 and the ESC) has broader implications for English law on trade union membership. The starting presumption of English law is that unions are *only* permitted to set membership rules within certain statutory constraints. This presumption ought to be reversed to comply with the principle of autonomy: unions should be free to set their own membership rules unless there is a good reason for restricting that freedom within

[68] See Joint Committee on Human Rights, Seventeenth Report of Session 2007–8 (HL 95/HC 501, 2008).

[69] Employment Act 2008, s 19, amending TULRCA 1992, s 174.

[70] TULRCA 1992, s 174(4A)–(4H).

[71] KD Ewing, 'Implementing the *ASLEF* decision – a victory for the BNP?' (2009) 38 *Industrial Law Journal* 50.

[72] Ibid, 55.

[73] DTI (n 67) 12.

Article 11(2). Such restrictions might include requirements to comply with anti-discrimination law and to apply union rules in a fair and objective manner. Again, however, the government's ambivalent attitude towards the trade union movement might have helped to explain its reluctance to engage in a wholesale review of the legal regime.

C. Conclusion

Both examples considered in this section show a welcome degree of engagement on the part of the government and the legislature with human rights issues in labour law. However, we have also seen some of the difficulties associated with turning an ECtHR decision on a specific case, albeit expressed in fairly broad terms, into a detailed legislative response. For labour lawyers, the process has been a disappointing one in which apparently radical ECtHR decisions have been translated into modest domestic changes. This reflects the role of domestic values and policy concerns – in *Wilson*, a concern with employer flexibility, and in *ASLEF*, a concern with the political rights of the individual – in the legislative process. There is no simple cause and effect relationship between an ECtHR decision and a legislative change.

IV. Constitutionalisation and the Courts

Let us now turn our attention to the approach of the courts in human rights cases in labour law. Although our main focus in this chapter is on the domestic courts, their approach must be considered in the context of decisions of the ECtHR and ECJ. It is, of course, difficult to generalise across these different courts and across different types of case. However, a common theme of considerable respect for the needs of employers does emerge from all the case-law in this area. Borrowing a term from the administrative law literature, this might be summed up as judicial 'deference' towards employers. The reasons for this deferential attitude vary from case to case, and we will explore these reasons in this section.

It should be noted that judicial deference to employers is a familiar theme in labour law.[74] There is a common perception among labour lawyers that the courts do not favour employee interests in litigation. In domestic law, the deferential application of the reasonableness test in unfair dismissal cases is often cited as an example of this phenomenon. In EU law, there are examples of deference in the way in which both domestic courts and the ECJ have allowed employers to justify unequal pay using the market forces defence. In these respects, deference in

[74] For detailed discussion, see ACL Davies, 'Judicial Self-Restraint in Labour Law' (2009) 38 *Industrial Law Journal* 278.

human rights cases is not a new phenomenon. However, it might have been expected that the ability to invoke human rights arguments directly might strengthen employees' claims. On the evidence so far, such arguments have only had limited success.

A. *Pay v Lancashire Probation Service; Pay v United Kingdom*

For many years, commentators have expressed concern that English law allows employers too much scope to monitor employees' activities both within and outside the workplace.[75] The HRA might have the potential to improve employees' protection in this area, but so far, the signs are not encouraging. Unfortunately, the ECtHR has reinforced the domestic courts' cautious approach.

The ECHR protects the right to respect for private and family life (Article 8) and freedom of expression (Article 10). Employers may be tempted to infringe these rights in various ways, for example, through surveillance in the workplace, or through attempts to prevent employees from engaging in certain activities outside work, such as political campaigning. Sometimes, these infringements might be justified. Alcohol testing might be appropriate where workers' jobs involve operating dangerous machinery; controls on political activities might be appropriate for certain public sector workers. The value of framing these issues in terms of Convention rights is that the employer must satisfy the proportionality test. In other words, the employer must show that it is pursuing a legitimate aim and that it has struck a balance between its needs and the employee's rights. The burden of justification under the HRA should be a heavy one.

The case of *Pay v Lancashire Probation Service* illustrates both the potential of the HRA in this area and the problems with the courts' current approach.[76] Mr Pay was a probation officer. His employers discovered that he performed in fetish clubs in his spare time, and ran a company selling products relating to bondage, domination and sadomasochism on the internet. Although there was no criticism of his work, he was dismissed on the grounds that these activities might harm the reputation of the Probation Service. Mr Pay brought a claim for unfair dismissal. English unfair dismissal law employs a two-stage approach.[77] First, the employer must demonstrate the reason for the dismissal. Second, the tribunal must apply a reasonableness test. This involves deciding whether or not the employer acted within a 'band of reasonable responses' in dismissing the employee for the stated reason.[78]

Under s 3 HRA, the courts are under a duty to interpret statutes so as to make them compatible with the Convention rights. In *Pay*, the EAT accepted that the

[75] H Collins, *Justice in Dismissal* (Oxford, Clarendon Press, 1992) ch 6.

[76] *Pay* (n 18). For a useful discussion of the case, see L Vickers, 'Unfair Dismissal and Human Rights' (2004) 33 *Industrial Law Journal* 52.

[77] Employment Rights Act 1996, s 98.

[78] *Iceland Frozen Foods v Jones* [1983] ICR 17; *Foley v Post Office* [2000] ICR 1283.

reasonableness test should be construed in accordance with Convention rights. Thus, the dismissal would be found to be unreasonable and unfair if the employer had violated the employee's Convention rights.[79] Although the *Pay* case involved a public authority, the Probation Service, which was obliged to act in conformity with human rights under s 6 HRA, the s 3 obligation is applicable in all cases regardless of the public or private status of the defendant. Thus, private employers will also be expected to show respect for employees' Convention rights if they are to demonstrate that their dismissal decisions are fair. There is, as yet, no clear authority on this point, but it has been suggested in *Pay* and elsewhere and is clearly correct in principle.[80]

However, the outcome of the *Pay* case on the facts is disappointing and illustrates the courts' reluctance to apply the proportionality test at an appropriate level of intensity.[81] The tribunal found, and the EAT accepted, that the claimant's Article 8 rights were not engaged because his activities took place in public.[82] The Probation Service accepted that his Article 10 rights had been infringed but argued that it was acting to maintain the reputation of the service (particularly with victims of sex offenders) and that dismissal was a proportionate sanction. Whilst it must be the case that an employer has a legitimate concern to maintain its reputation, the EAT failed to explore in any detail the various stages in the argument. In particular, the EAT did not question the employer's assertions that victims of crime would find out about Mr Pay's activities outside work, or that they would connect them with his work, or that the reputation of the Probation Service would be damaged if either of these things occurred. Thus, the application of the proportionality test on the facts of the case was highly deferential to the employer's perception of the situation.[83]

The ECtHR then considered the *Pay* case and ruled that it was inadmissible.[84] Although it was prepared to assume that Article 8 might be engaged as well as Article 10, it found that the proportionality test was satisfied. The Court adopted a similarly deferential attitude:

> Given the sensitive nature of the applicant's work with sex offenders, the Court does not consider that the national authorities exceeded the margin of appreciation available to them in adopting a cautious approach as regards the extent to which public knowledge of the applicant's sexual activities could impair his ability effectively to carry out his duties.[85]

Thus, although the Court recognised that dismissal was a severe sanction, it found that it was not disproportionate on the facts.

[79] *Pay* (n 18) para 35.

[80] Ibid, paras 31–35; see also *X v Y* [2003] ICR 1138; *Copsey v WWB Devon Clays Ltd* [2005] EWCA Civ 932; [2005] ICR 1789.

[81] For a different view, see Vickers (n 76).

[82] *Pay* (n 18) paras 36–38.

[83] Ibid, paras 39–46.

[84] *Pay v United Kingdom* App no 32792/05 (2009) 48 EHRR SE2.

[85] Ibid, 26.

These are disappointing results. In principle, the proportionality test requires the courts to consider the legitimacy of the employer's aim and to balance this against the individual's rights. There is no evidence of this in the EAT's decision in *Pay*, and indeed it would be no exaggeration to say that the invocation of the HRA did not advance the claimant's case beyond ordinary unfair dismissal.[86] Although the ECtHR did consider the proportionality test a little more fully – recognising that protecting the employer's reputation was a legitimate aim and then considering the relationship between the aim and the sanction – it did not subject the employer's arguments to detailed critical scrutiny. In both courts, it appears that deference to the employer's expertise in the management of its own reputation was the deciding factor.

B. Industrial Action and Article 11 ECHR

The regulation of industrial action in English law is a complex matter and this is not the place for a detailed account. In simple terms, English law's approach is to provide trade unions and strike organisers with an immunity from the liability they would otherwise incur in tort (such as for inducing breach of contract by the striking workers) provided that certain conditions are met. There are two broad sets of conditions. First, the strike must take place 'in contemplation or furtherance of a trade dispute' as defined in the statute (though the court in ruling on the lawfulness of the strike is not required to consider the merits of the dispute).[87] Second, the union organising the strike must follow a series of highly complex procedures in which it must ballot the relevant workers and must provide the employer with a series of notices relating to the ballot and the strike.[88] From this, it can be seen that English law does not formally provide a 'right' to strike. This would not necessarily be objectionable if the immunity achieved the same practical effect. However, this is not the case. Employers often succeed in obtaining interim injunctions to prevent strikes from taking place by arguing that the union has failed to comply with one or more of the detailed balloting or notice requirements. As a result, the UK has been condemned by the ILO and others for failing to provide an appropriate level of protection for the right to strike. The UK government has ignored the ILO's criticisms.

In recent years, attention has turned to the possibility that the ECHR might protect the right to strike. Coupled with the HRA, this would provide unions with an opportunity to challenge the UK's restrictive strike laws in the domestic courts on a case-by-case basis. As we saw above, Article 11 ECHR does not expressly include protection of the right to strike, and the Court was initially reluctant to recognise a right to strike other than as one of the many options states might provide to trade

[86] See also V Mantouvalou and H Collins, 'Private Life and Dismissal' (2009) 38 *Industrial Law Journal* 133.

[87] TULRCA 1992, s 219.

[88] Ibid, ss 226–35.

unions for the protection of their interests.[89] Eventually, in *Enerji Yapi-Yol Sen v Turkey*,[90] the Court accepted that the right to strike was an essential right within Article 11. We will now examine two cases with contrasting outcomes in which the Court of Appeal was called upon to consider the relevance of this new ECtHR ruling to English law on industrial action.[91]

In the case of *Metrobus v Unite the Union*, the Court of Appeal was invited to use s 3 HRA to construe the statutory rules on ballot notification to make them compatible with Article 11 ECHR.[92] The law requires unions to give three notices to the employer: a notice that a ballot is to take place,[93] a notice of the result of the ballot,[94] and a notice of industrial action.[95] The employer argued that the union had failed to provide the second of these notices 'as soon as reasonably practicable', and that the union had failed to supply the required information about the employees involved in the proposed action in all three notices. The Court of Appeal upheld these claims, though (unlike the trial judge) it was prepared to disregard an insignificant typing error in two of the union's notices relating to the number of employees affected.

Giving the leading judgment, Lloyd LJ considered the impact of Article 11 on the statutory provisions. He held that the test to be applied was whether the restrictions were proportionate, given the need to balance the interests of workers and unions against those of employers. Without detailed discussion, he found that the notice requirements were a legitimate type of restriction on industrial action.[96] This meant that the question of balance was at the heart of the case: 'The question is whether [the restrictions] go too far because of their complexity, detail and rigidity, so as to attenuate excessively the exercise of this aspect of the Article 11 rights.'[97] He noted the union's submission that both the ILO and the ESC Committee had condemned the procedural provisions of English industrial action law on this ground.[98] However, in relation to the specific provisions at issue in the case – the requirement to provide the ballot result 'as soon as reasonably practicable' and the requirement to explain the union's calculation of the numbers of affected employees – he held that they did not amount to disproportionate restrictions on the union's Article 11 rights.

Again, this decision can be regarded as deferential in tone. The court is concerned to protect the interests of employers. This is particularly evident from its

[89] See, for example, *Schmidt and Dahlströhm v Sweden* (1979–80) 1 EHRR 637, 644.

[90] *Enerji* (n 48). For discussion with reference to *Metrobus*, see Ewing and Hendy (n 47).

[91] It is worth noting that the government has shown no interest in reviewing the law in the light of the *Enerji* decision. It seems unlikely that it will do so unless a union obtains a ruling directly against the UK.

[92] *Metrobus* (n 19). For discussion see R Dukes, 'The Right to Strike under UK Law: Not Much More than a Slogan?' (2010) 39 *Industrial Law Journal* 82.

[93] TULRCA 1992, s 226A.

[94] Ibid, s 231A.

[95] Ibid, s 234A.

[96] *Metrobus* (n 19) para 104.

[97] Ibid.

[98] Ibid, para 49.

rejection of the argument made on behalf of the union that democratic requirements in industrial action should be regarded as a benefit to the members rather than as a matter for the employer.[99] Moreover, there is a further dimension of deference to the government and the legislature. Because the case concerned the interpretation of legislation, the court clearly regarded it as inappropriate to disrupt the balance struck in the statute unless there were very strong grounds for doing so. This is evident from references to the legislative history and to the government's consultation exercises on the topic.[100] However, this is problematic both in principle and in the particular context of Article 11. In principle, whilst the government is under an obligation in international law to comply with Convention rights, the court is under an obligation to make its own decision on the matter: it cannot simply assume that the government has understood the requirements correctly. In the context of Article 11, the ECtHR's jurisprudence has undergone significant development in recent years, so it cannot be assumed that legislation that was considered to be Convention-compatible at the time of its enactment has necessarily remained so in the light of these developments.

However, some hope is offered by the more recent case of *London Midland v ASLEF.*[101] Again, the case concerned breaches of the union's procedural obligations. At first instance, an injunction had been granted to stop the strike on various grounds which were subsequently rejected by the Court of Appeal. Two of the most important grounds were that ballot papers had been sent to two workers who were not in fact entitled to vote, and that the union had failed to provide the employer with accurate information when giving notice of the ballot. The Court of Appeal adopted a much more pro-union construction of the relevant statutory provisions. In relation to the balloting mistake, it was held that this was protected by the exception for 'small accidental failures' in s 232B because the union believed that it was balloting the right constituency but because of 'human errors and failings' it had gone wrong.[102] In relation to the notification mistake, it was held that the statute did not require the union to collect information specifically for the purpose of notifying the employer, but simply to make use of information it already had (unless it knew that the information was inaccurate).[103] Perhaps most interestingly, Elias LJ suggested (obiter) that the de minimis principle might also apply to notification errors even though there is no equivalent of s 232B in this area, because there was 'no justification for reading section 232B as being intended to cut back on such defences as the law would have allowed before it was implemented'.[104]

So what brought about this alteration in approach? Since the decision in *Metrobus* is a decision of the Court of Appeal, it was not possible for the union to

[99] Ibid, para 40.
[100] Ibid, para 103.
[101] *London Midland* (n 20).
[102] Ibid, para 56.
[103] Ibid, para 71.
[104] Ibid, para 86.

revisit the argument made in that case that the complexity of the balloting and notification provisions constituted a breach of Article 11 in itself. However, Article 11 did play some role in the decision. The Court of Appeal used Article 11 to reject the argument – often accepted in the past – that the immunities should be construed strictly against the trade unions:

> The common law's focus on the protection of property and contractual rights is necessarily antithetical to any form of industrial action since the purpose of the action is to interfere with the employer's rights. The statutory immunities are simply the form which the law in this country takes to carve out the ability for unions to take lawful strike action. It is for Parliament to determine how the conflicting interests of employers and unions should be reconciled in the field of industrial relations. But if one starts from the premise that the legislation should be strictly construed against those seeking the benefit of the immunities, the effect is the same as it would be if there were a presumption that Parliament intends that the interests of the employers should hold sway unless the legislation clearly dictates otherwise. I do not think this is now a legitimate approach, if it ever was. In my judgment the legislation should simply be construed in the normal way, without presumptions one way or the other.[105]

This is potentially a very significant shift in judicial attitudes towards the immunities, recognising that they are in truth a means of providing a right to strike and should be interpreted accordingly.

Nevertheless, it remains to be seen how the case-law will develop. It is possible that a differently composed Court of Appeal might not support the *London Midland* approach. That there are significant divisions in the court is evidenced by the strong differences of opinion expressed in another recent case, *British Airways v Unite*.[106] More fundamentally, a 'full' Article 11 challenge to the balloting and notification requirements can now only be brought if a case reaches the Supreme Court. Even then, there may be difficulties. The most important objection to the balloting and notification provisions is their extreme complexity taken as a whole. But in most cases, the union will only have infringed perhaps two or three particular requirements. These may not seem unduly burdensome by themselves and it may be difficult for an English court, proceeding on a case-by-case basis, to see – or evaluate – the regime as a whole. And even in *London Midland*, Elias LJ noted the importance of deferring to Parliament's overall assessment of how the balance should be struck between unions and employers.[107] At the time of writing, the RMT union is challenging the balloting and notification provisions before the ECtHR.[108] The outcome of this case will be of critical importance in determining the future approach of the UK courts to the law on industrial action.

[105] Ibid, para 9.

[106] *British Airways Plc v Unite the Union* [2010] EWCA Civ 669, [2010] ICR 1316.

[107] *London Midland* (n 20), para 9.

[108] RMT Press Release, 24 May 2010. See: www.rmt.org.uk/Templates/Internal.asp?NodeId=136488 (last accessed 29 April 2011).

C. *Viking* and *Laval*

Our third example is drawn from EU law and involves some important decisions of the ECJ. These decisions have been well documented elsewhere and our discussion of them will be brief.[109] However, they illustrate particularly well the potential for conflict between workers' rights and employers' economic rights. In these cases, the ECJ recognised for the first time that the right to strike was a fundamental right in EU law. However, because EU law prioritises economic rights, the significance of this recognition of the right to strike was limited in practice. Again, employers' rights prevailed.

In *Viking*, the employer wished to reflag a ferry from Finland to Estonia.[110] This constitutes an exercise of freedom of establishment under Article 43 of the EC Treaty (now Article 49 TFEU). The Finnish trade union representing the crew, in conjunction with the International Transport Workers' Federation (ITF), organised a blockade of the employer's ships in protest at the decision. This blockade was highly effective. The employer sought an injunction to stop the industrial action, arguing that Article 43 was horizontally applicable to the trade unions and that their action infringed the Article. The ECJ, on a reference from the High Court in London, held that Article 43 was engaged and that it was for the national court to determine whether or not the unions' action was proportionate in the light of the guidance it provided.

In *Laval*, a Latvian firm won a contract to repair school buildings in Sweden.[111] It wanted to use its own workers to perform the contract. Under Swedish law, it was expected to agree their terms and conditions with a local trade union. No agreement could be reached and the firm was unable to perform the contract because of a blockade of its sites by the union. The firm argued that its Article 49 EC (now Article 56 TFEU) freedom to provide services had been infringed by the requirement to negotiate the workers' terms and conditions with the union. This case was somewhat more complicated than *Viking* because the treatment of

[109] See, for example, C Barnard, 'Internal Market v Labour Market: A Brief History' in M de Vos (ed), *European Union Internal Market and Labour Law: Friends or Foes?* (Antwerp and Oxford, Intersentia, 2009); C Barnard, 'A Proportionate Response to Proportionality in the Field of Collective Action' (2012) 37 *European Law Review* 117; ACL Davies, 'One Step Forward, Two Steps Back? The Viking and Laval cases in the ECJ' (2008) 37 *Industrial Law Journal* 126; C Joerges and F Rödl, 'Informal Politics, Formalised Law and the "Social Deficit" of European Integration: Reflections after the Judgments of the ECJ in Viking and Laval' (2009) 15 *European Law Journal* 1; C Kilpatrick, 'Laval's Regulatory Conundrum: Collective Standard-Setting and the Court's New Approach to Posted Workers' (2009) 34 *European Law Review* 844; J Malmberg and T Sigeman, 'Industrial Actions and EU Economic Freedoms: the Autonomous Collective Bargaining Model Curtailed by the European Court of Justice' (2008) 45 *Common Market Law Review* 1115; P Syrpis and T Novitz, 'Economic and Social Rights in Conflict: Political and Judicial Approaches to their Reconciliation' (2008) 33 *European Law Review* 411. On UK disputes raising these issues, see C Kilpatrick, 'British Jobs for British Workers? UK Industrial Action and Free Movement of Services in EU Law', *LSE Legal Studies Working Paper* No 16/2009; C Barnard, '"British Jobs for British Workers": the Lindsey Oil Refinery Dispute and the Future of Local Labour Clauses in an Integrated EU Market' (2009) 38 *Industrial Law Journal* 245.

[110] *Viking* (n 21).

[111] *Laval* (n 13).

posted workers is governed by Directive 96/71/EC, the Posted Workers Directive. It is clear from the judgment that the Court wished to comment on Sweden's reliance on collective bargaining for the implementation of the directive even though the terms of the directive itself could not be enforced against the trade union in that case. Again, the Court held that the firm's Article 49 rights had been infringed and that a proportionality test should be used to assess the union's conduct.

In both decisions, the ECJ recognised that the right to strike was a fundamental right in EU law. It cited various international sources and, for the first time, relied upon the EU Charter of Fundamental Rights.[112] This is a positive aspect of the decision because, as noted above, the EU Charter is one of the few ways in which economic and social rights – of greater relevance to labour law than civil and political rights, in most cases – might be given effect in English law. However, the right to strike was treated as a defence to employers' economic rights under the Treaty. This meant that the right could only be exercised where it could be defended as a proportionate restriction on the employer's economic freedoms. As I have argued elsewhere, the ECJ's guidance on the proportionality test is quite limiting from the perspective of the trade union movement.[113]

It is important to emphasise that the ECJ could not easily have decided these cases differently.[114] The Member States chose to include free movement rights in the Treaty, and from the Court's perspective it is difficult to argue that these rights – which are fundamental in EU law – could be trumped by a right to strike which, pre-Lisbon, had an uncertain legal status in the EU context. Reform will probably need to come from outside the Court: either via the so-called Monti II Regulation recently proposed by the Commission,[115] or through the EU's accession to the ECHR (where, as we have seen, the right to strike is now protected under Article 11).[116] But from a non-EU perspective, the priority given to the employer's economic rights in *Viking* and *Laval* is surprising. The right to strike is an internationally recognised human right and, at the very least, the case should be regarded as raising a conflict of rights. This would not preclude a decision that there are limits on the extent of legitimate trade union action – the right to strike is inevitably subject to conditions and limitations because of the harm strikes can cause – but such limits would need to be explained and justified. We normally think in terms of proportionate *restrictions* on the right to strike, rather than proportionate *exercise* of the right to strike.

[112] *Viking* (n 21) para 77; *Laval* (n 13) para 90.

[113] Davies (n 109).

[114] Though for an interesting discussion of some of the options, see C Barnard, 'A Proportionate Response' (n 109) 117.

[115] Commission, Proposal for a Council Regulation on the Exercise of the Right to Take Collective Action within the Context of the Freedom of Establishment and the Freedom to Provide Services (COM (2012) 130 final).

[116] See *Enerji* (n 48) and Ewing and Hendy (n 47).

D. Conclusion

The *Viking* and *Laval* decisions do, of course, arise in quite a different context to *Pay* and *Metrobus*, discussed above. The underlying legal regime and the reasoning both differ accordingly. However, all these decisions reinforce the view that the constitutionalisation of labour law, in the sense of more explicit use of human rights arguments, is not a straightforwardly beneficial development from the perspective of workers and unions. The interests of employers are a powerful force, and the characterisation of workers' interests using the language of fundamental rights does not appear to tip the scales as strongly in their direction as one might have expected. The decision in *London Midland* may offer some hope, but it is too early to claim that it has transformed the courts' approach.

V. Concluding Remarks

In recent years, the enactment of the HRA and, to a lesser extent, the increasing emphasis on rights jurisprudence in EU law, have shifted the debate about workers' rights from an abstract plane to a more practical one. Rights arguments can now be used in the domestic courts in many labour law cases. In turn, this has given greater immediacy to the role of rights arguments in the legislative process even though, under the HRA at least, Parliament is free to legislate contrary to Convention rights if it so chooses. In this formal sense, it can be said that labour law is undergoing a process of constitutionalisation.

Although labour lawyers have drawn on rights reasoning when evaluating the law, there has long been a concern, particularly in the trade union context, that too great an emphasis on the rights of individual workers might undermine collective activity. It was argued above that, in the ECHR context at least, this concern has not so far arisen in practice. The ECtHR's decision in *ASLEF* shows an awareness of the importance of collective autonomy and demonstrates that a court concerned with individual rights may sometimes decide that they are outweighed by the rights of the group as a whole. It is true that the ECtHR is hostile to the closed shop but many labour lawyers would now accept that this extreme form of collectivism is difficult to defend. The Court has also started to recognise the broader role of Article 11 in protecting collective activities through decisions such as *Demir* and *Enerji*.

Thus, the constitutionalisation of labour law has not had any significant negative effects, but has it had any positive ones? From the evidence so far, I would argue that the positive effects are limited. The government has legislated in response to ECtHR decisions against the UK and, although this is not a new phenomenon in itself, it is arguable that the process has been taken somewhat more seriously because of the prospect of the domestic courts being called upon to examine the legislation in the light of the ECtHR jurisprudence. However, other considerations have intervened, such as the concern to preserve employers' flexibility or to ensure that unions do not have too much power, and the resulting legislation reflects a combination of these forces, not just the ECtHR's decisions. In the courts, there has been a greater acceptance of the relevance of human rights arguments, both domestically and in the ECJ. However, the traditional concerns of upholding employers' discretion and protecting them against disruptive industrial action (domestically) and upholding their economic freedoms (in the ECJ) have largely outweighed the rights arguments. Again, rights are treated as one factor to take into account, rather than as a factor with inherent weight or importance.

It is possible that this is just the first stage of constitutionalisation. Perhaps there will be a second stage, in which giving effect to rights will come to be regarded as an overwhelmingly important goal of legislation, and in which the courts will scrutinise any apparent infringement of rights with considerable rigour. The most likely source of such a development is ongoing pressure from Strasbourg on the UK government, the domestic courts and the CJ, and perhaps the *London Midland* decision is the start of a new trend. Constitutionalisation in this form would have transformative potential in labour law. It would change the reasoning process, so that rights would be regarded as having particular weight, and in some (though by no means all) instances, it would change the outcome for workers and their unions. It remains to be seen whether or when we will see this deep form of constitutionalisation of labour law in the United Kingdom.

5

The Human Rights Act 1998, Horizontality and the Constitutionalisation of Private Law

ALISON L YOUNG

The Human Rights Act 1998 is heralded as initiating a sea change to the way in which the United Kingdom constitution protects human rights, and its impact upon public law is well known. Prior to its enactment, human rights were only protected in an indirect as opposed to a direct manner. If an administrative body were to act contrary to a human right, this was not, in and of itself, sufficient to overturn the action or decision of the administration as an unlawful act. Rather, an individual would need to demonstrate that contravening a human right amounted to an act or decision that was unreasonable. Section 3 of the Act makes it unlawful for a public authority to act contrary to a right guaranteed by the European Convention on Human Rights (Convention or ECHR). Not only does this provide the individual with a better cause of action, but it also provides courts with the means to evaluate the actions of the administration directly to determine their compatibility with human rights, focusing predominantly on the substance of the decision, as opposed to the process through which the decision was made.[1] In addition, courts apply a more stringent test of review to determine the legality of discretionary decisions of the administration. The traditional *Wednesbury*[2] unreasonableness standard has been replaced by a test of proportionality.[3] Finally, courts have a greater power to review legislation. The Human Rights Act does not empower the judiciary to overturn legislation that is contrary to Convention rights. However, section 3(1) of the Act requires the judiciary to read and give effect to legislation in a manner compatible with Convention rights, so far as it is possible to do so. This contrasts with the previous powers of the court, based upon principles of interpretation, which presumed that Parliament would not wish to legislate contrary to its international obligations. This only enabled the court to choose a Convention-compatible interpretation of legislation in order to

[1] For an illustration, contrast the decision of the Court of Appeal in *R v Ministry of Defence ex parte Smith and Grady* [1996] QB 517 with the decision of the European Court of Human Rights in *Smith & Grady v United Kingdom* App nos 33985/96 and 33986/96 Reports 1999-VI (1999) 29 EHRR 493, [1999] IRLR 74.

[2] *Associated Provincial Picture Houses v Wednesbury Corporation* [1948] 1 KB 223.

[3] *R v Home Secretary ex parte Daly* [2001] UKHL 26, [2001] 2 AC 532.

resolve ambiguity.[4] When such an interpretation is not possible, courts of the level of the High Court or above have the power to make a declaration of incompatibility,[5] which places considerable political pressure upon Parliament to modify legislation so as to ensure its compatibility with Convention rights.

This sea change in the protection of human rights can be regarded as part of the process of the constitutionalisation of public law.[6] What is less frequently analysed is the extent to which the Act has 'constitutionalised' private law. The aim of this chapter is to investigate this phenomenon. It will do so in three stages. First, it will analyse what is meant by the phrase 'constitutionalisation', recognising the different meanings that can be given to this term in the English legal system, with its preference for a political as opposed to a legal constitution, and its adherence to the principle of parliamentary sovereignty, which prevents constitutional legislation from overturning non-constitutional legislation (section I below). Having explained possible forms of constitutionalisation, the chapter will then examine the extent to which horizontality could lead to the constitutionalisation of the content of private law (section II below). It will be argued that it is difficult to assess the impact of the Act upon constitutionalisation. This is for three reasons: the ambiguity surrounding the definition of constitutionalisation; the difficulty in determining the precise form of horizontality adopted in English law; and the extent to which constitutionalisation was taking place before the enactment of the Human Rights Act 1998. It will argue, however, that this indeterminacy is a strength as opposed to a weakness. It enables the adoption of a flexible approach, allowing English law to adopt different means of paying regard to human rights in different areas, ensuring that the means adopted is best suited to balancing the competing rights claims that arise in horizontal protections of human rights. This, in turn, facilitates a deeper form of constitutionalisation than the mere incorporation of Convention rights into English law (section III below).

I. The Meaning of Constitutionalisation

The term 'constitutionalisation' is widely used. Recent claims have been made regarding the constitutionalisation of the European Union;[7] international trade

[4] *R v Secretary of State for the Home Department ex parte Brind* [1991] 1 AC 691.

[5] Human Rights Act 1998, s 4.

[6] See J Jowell, 'Beyond the Rule of Law: Towards Constitutional Judicial Review' [2000] *Public Law* 671 for an account of this process of constitutionalisation, examining how this was occurring prior to as well as after the enactment of the Human Rights Act 1998.

[7] See eg K Lenaerts, 'Constitutionalism and the Many Faces of Federalism' (1990) 38 *American Journal of Comparative Law* 205; JHH Weiler, *The Constitution of Europe: 'Do the New clothes have an Emperor?' and Other Essays on European Integration* (Cambridge, CUP, 1999); JHH Weiler and Marlene Wind (eds), *European Constitutionalism Beyond the State* (Cambridge, CUP, 2003); and Koen Lenaerts and Damien Gerard, 'The Structure of the Union According to the Constitution for Europe: The Emperor is Getting Dressed' (2004) 29 *European Law Review* 289. See also Koen Lenaerts and Marlies Desomer, 'Bricks for a Constitutional Treaty of the European Union: Values, Objectives and Means'

law;[8] intellectual property law;[9] the right to freedom of expression in English law;[10] and judicial review, both general[11] and specific.[12] Despite its wide use – and some would argue misuse – there is little precise agreement as to the meaning of the term, or as to its application to private law. Added to this is the complexity inherent in the definition of 'constitutional' in the United Kingdom, given its predominantly political as opposed to legal constitution. This section will first dispel two myths regarding the meaning of constitutionalisation, before establishing a framework from which the constitutionalisation of private law, and the impact of the Human Rights Act 1998, can be assessed.

First, it would be wrong, and too simplistic, to reject the application of constitutionalisation to English law given that English law does not have, nor arguably could it ever have, a constitution, in the sense of a set of principles contained in a document that are entrenched and which override legislation. This defeatist analysis is too narrow and fails to recognise the different layers of meaning that we apply to the term 'constitutional'. Principles can be 'constitutional' without forming part of a legally binding and entrenched 'constitution'. Second, it would also be wrong to dismiss the impact of the Human Rights Act to the process of constitutionalisation by seeing 'constitutionalisation' as the formation of values and principles that underpin the law and, potentially, the relationship between the citizens and the state. This definition is too broad: not all principles and values are 'constitutional'. If we define 'constitutionalisation' in this manner, it is arguable that the common law, resting on principles that have developed over time, has been 'constitutionalised' since its inception.

These myths are illustrative of two sets of general meanings of the term. First, constitutionalisation refers to the ideal of the formation of a set of principles, normally based upon liberalism, that are prior to and confine government. Second, constitutionalisation can refer more loosely to the development of principles, perhaps through a dialogue between the governors and the governed, which constitute

(2002) 27 *European Law Review* 377; D Halberstam, 'The Bride of Messina: Constitutionalisation and Democracy in Europe' (2005) 30 *European Law Review* 775; P Eleftheriadis, 'The Idea of a European Constitution' (2007) 27 *Oxford Journal of Legal Studies* 1; Schepel, 'Reconstructing Constitutionalisation: Law and Politics in the European Court of Justice' (2000) 20 *Oxford Journal of Legal Studies* 457; A Dyevre, 'The Constitutionalisation of the European Union: Discourse, Present, Future and Facts' (2005) 30 *European Law Review* 165; and P Craig, 'The Constitutionalisation of Community Administration' (2003) 28 *European Law Review* 840.

[8] D Cass, 'The Constitutionalisation of International Trade Law: Judicial Norm-generation as the Engine of Constitutional Development in International Trade' (2001) 12 *European Journal of International Law* 39.

[9] C Geiger, '"Constitutionalising" Intellectual Property Law: The Influence of Fundamental Rights on Intellectual Property Rights in the European Union' (2006) *International Review of Intellectual Property and Competition Law* 371.

[10] I Loveland, *Political Libels: A Comparative Study* (Hart, Oxford, 2000); I Loveland, 'The Constitutionalisation of Political Libels in English Common Law' [1998] *Public Law* 633; I Loveland, 'Freedom of Political Expression: Who Needs the Human Rights Act?' [2001] *Public Law* 233.

[11] J Jowell, 'Beyond the Rule of Law: Towards Constitutional Judicial Review' [2000] *Public Law* 671.

[12] S Singh Juss, 'Constitutionalising Rights without a Constitution: The British Experience Under Article 6 of the Human Rights Act 1998' (2006) 27 *Statute Law Review* 29.

that particular society.[13] Both of these general senses of constitutionalisation can be applied to English law. The Human Rights Act 1998 provides for a means of incorporation of the ECHR in English law. It provides a list of civil liberties that are regarded as constraining government, even though in English law this is achieved not through the ability to strike down legislation, but to read and give effect to provisions of legislation, so far as possible, in a manner compatible with Convention rights,[14] and, where this is not possible, to make a declaration of incompatibility,[15] prompting Parliament to amend the legislation in question either through the enactment of primary or secondary legislation.[16] The Act also adds to the development of rights and values underpinning English law, adding a new set of values that frame the development of private law. Although the rights are derived from the Convention, decisions of the courts have re-interpreted these rights. The manner in which Convention rights are incorporated into English law can be seen as part of an ongoing dialogue between the courts and the legislature, refining these rights, which become values that form part of the UK constitution. Regardless of whether we regard constitutionalisation as resting on liberal or other values, we can determine the extent to which the Human Rights Act has altered these values, both as confines on governmental power and as to the refinement of the values that constitute the UK constitution.

Having established a general account of the meaning of constitutionalisation, attention also needs to be paid to the manner in which private law can become constitutionalised. Most assessments focus on the content of private law. If it can be shown that the content of private law has been modified, particularly through the incorporation of liberal rights deriving from the Human Rights Act, then we can determine the extent to which the Act has added to the process of constitutionalisation of English law.[17] However, there are also three further dimensions from which constitutionalisation can be measured. First, there can be a constitutionalisation of procedure, which can occur in at least three ways. Article 6 ECHR may lead to the development of procedural rights which in turn facilitate constitutionalisation through developing mechanisms that enable the institutions of government to be held to account for their actions.[18] In addition, a need to protect Convention rights may be read into the rules of civil procedure.[19] Moreover, courts may modify the process of the trial, particularly through enabling representations from third parties who may be more generally affected by the issue before the court.

[13] This distinction is drawn by M Loughlin, 'Constitutionalisation: A Twenty-fifth Anniversary Essay' (2005) 25 *Oxford Journal of Legal Studies* 183, 183–84.

[14] Human Rights Act 1998, s 3(1).

[15] Ibid, s 4.

[16] Ibid, s 10.

[17] See, for example, Cass (n 8); Schepel (n 7); and Geiger (n 9).

[18] Singh-Juss (n 12).

[19] See, for example, the impact of the Human Rights Act 1998, s 12(4), requiring the courts to give particular regard to the Convention right of freedom of expression found in Art 10 ECHR, which the courts have used not only as means of incorporating the right to freedom of expression, but also of the right to privacy, through Art 10(2) ECHR in *Douglas v Hello! (1)* [2001] 1 QB 967.

Second, constitutionalisation may occur through the development of a set of institutions, or a network of institutional frameworks that facilitate the development and application of constitutional values.[20] Third, constitutionalisation may occur through a modification of the process of adjudication itself. Whilst common law adjudication predominantly applies principles of inductive reasoning, constitutional adjudication is more deductive. Consequently, the process of adjudication in the private law could be said to be constitutionalised through the way in which the judiciary refer to general principles, or frame their conclusions as deriving from the application of general rights.[21]

To assess how far the Human Rights Act 1998 has facilitated a process of constitutionalisation, therefore, we need to analyse private law to determine how far its content, procedural rights, civil procedures, and judicial reasoning have modified, either through the incorporation of the rights found in the Act itself, or through the facilitation of a dialogue concerning the adoption of these rights as part of the values that underpin and constitute English law. Space precludes an analysis of the whole of private law.[22] Instead, an account will be given of the process through which the Human Rights Act has achieved horizontal effect, focusing in particular upon the Article 10 ECHR right to freedom of expression and the Article 8 ECHR right to privacy to illustrate the manner in which the Human Rights Act has constitutionalised English private law. [23]

II. Horizontality and the Human Rights Act 1998

Horizontality occurs when human rights obligations are placed upon private individuals. As such, determining the extent to which the Human Rights Act has facilitated horizontality can provide one benchmark by which to measure how far the Act has influenced the process of constitutionalisation of the private law. It is clear that the Human Rights Act enjoys a form of horizontal effect. This provides one of the main ways in which the Act has constitutionalised private law. By requiring individuals to uphold Convention rights, the content of private law has been modified to reflect the set of liberal rights found in the ECHR. This section will argue, however, that it is wrong to equate horizontality with constitutionalisation. To do so is both over- and under-inclusive. Moreover, it cautions against merely examining one form of horizontality, recognising that horizontality, and constitutionalisation, can occur in ways other than the operation of sections 6(1) and 6(3)(a) of the Act. Finally, it will argue that difficulties surrounding the

[20] See Cass (n 8).

[21] See M Rosenfeld, 'Constitutional Adjudication in Europe and the United States: Paradoxes and Contrasts' (2004) 2 *International Journal of Constitutional Law* 633.

[22] For a more detailed discussion of the impact of the Human Rights Act on private law, see D Hoffman, *The Impact of the UK Human Rights Act on Private Law* (Cambridge, CUP, 2011).

[23] This area has been chosen as it provides the strongest examples of possible constitutionalisation.

description of the form of horizontality taken by the Act and a potential divergence between the form and substance of horizontality make it difficult to determine the precise extent to which the horizontal effect of Convention rights created by the Human Rights Act has constitutionalised English private law.

A. The Relationship between Horizontality and Private Law

Horizontality and the constitutionalisation of private law are not coterminous. To merely evaluate the way in which horizontality has occurred following the implementation of the Act would provide an account of constitutionalisation that was both too narrow and too broad. It would be too broad as obligations to uphold Convention rights may be placed upon private individuals through the operation of public law as well as private law. This occurs through the operation of section 6 of the Human Rights Act 1998. Section 6 provides that it is unlawful for a public authority to act contrary to Convention rights. Section 6(3)(b) includes 'any person certain of whose functions are functions of a public nature' as public authorities, albeit limiting their obligation to uphold Convention rights to decisions and actions taken when performing this public function.[24] As such, it is possible that individuals who are private – in the sense of not being part of the structure of the state, or funded predominantly by the state – are nevertheless required to uphold Convention rights.[25] However, section 6(3)(b) is regarded as creating an obligation in public as opposed to private law, this obligation normally being upheld through an action for judicial review, or where the illegality of the conduct of the body in question is raised as a defence in private law proceedings.

An illustration of how section 6(3)(b) can impose obligations upon a private individual is found in *Poplar Housing v Donoghue*.[26] Poplar Housing was a housing association, to which housing stock had been transferred by Tower Hamlets, a local authority. As a housing association, it was a private-sector body. Yet the court determined that it was providing a public function. As such, it would have to comply with Articles 8 and 6 ECHR when taking decisions to terminate tenancies. This obligation, albeit placed upon a private sector body, was of a public law nature. Consequently, the imposition of the obligation to comply with Convention rights did not require any modification of the content of private law. The nature of the tenancy agreement between Poplar Housing and Donoghue was not modi-

[24] Despite the functional focus of s 6(3)(b) itself, concerns as to the composition of a body performing a public function, and of its enmeshment with the state, have also been deemed relevant to the determination of whether a body is a 'public authority' for the purposes of the Human Rights Act 1998. See *Poplar Housing and Regeneration Community Association Limited v Donoghue* [2002] QB 48; *R (Heather) v Leonard Cheshire Foundation* [2002] EWCA Civ 366, [2002] 2 All ER 936; *YL v Birmingham City Council* [2007] UKHL 27 and *R (Weaver) v London and Quadrant Housing Trust* [2009] EWCA Civ 58, [2009] 4 All ER 865.

[25] Ian Leigh refers to this as 'public authority' horizontality. See I Leigh, 'Horizontal Rights, the Human Rights Act and Privacy: Lessons from the Commonwealth?' (1999) 48 *International and Comparative Law Quarterly* 57, 74–85.

[26] *Poplar Housing and Regeneration Community Association Limited v Donoghue* [2002] QB 48.

fied. However, if Poplar Housing had exercised its rights under the tenancy agreement in such a manner that breached Articles 8 or 6 ECHR, then this unlawful act could be raised by Donoghue as a defence to the repossession proceedings brought by Poplar Housing.

Equating horizontality with the process of constitutionalisation of private law is also under-inclusive, omitting ways in which the Human Rights Act may facilitate constitutionalisation through an incorporation of Convention rights. The main way in which horizontality occurs in English law is through the combined operation of sections 6(1) and 6(3)(a) of the Act. As discussed above, section 6(1) prohibits public authorities from acting in a manner incompatible with Convention rights. Section 6(3)(a) expressly includes courts and tribunals in the definition of a public authority. Consequently, it is unlawful for a court or tribunal to act in a manner incompatible with Convention rights. This provides the main means through which constitutionalisation of private law occurs, as courts modify provisions of private law to comply with Convention rights, thereby imposing obligations to uphold Convention rights upon private individuals. However, when modifying private law in this manner, courts may also modify the way in which private law imposes obligations upon public bodies. This provides an example of constitutionalisation of the private law, in that the content of private law may be modified in order to incorporate Convention rights.

In addition, section 8 of the Human Rights Act empowers the courts to award damages as a remedy for those whose Convention rights have been breached by a public authority. The existence of this section may give rise to constitutionalisation of the private law in two ways. First, the existence of the remedy is a possible example of constitutionalisation in and of itself, providing a framework through which those whose rights have been harmed may recover damages. Second, the existence of section 8 may be used as a justification for developing the common law to ensure that it mirrors Convention rights. An illustration of these forms of constitutionalisation is found in *Chief Constable of the Hertfordshire Police v Van Colle*.[27] The case concerned the question whether, when an individual has alerted the police to evidence that another has threatened to kill or inflict violence against that person, that individual, or his relatives, should be able to recover damages, should the negligent actions of the police lead to the death of or harm to the individual in question. As well as the possible claim in tort law, there could, in certain circumstances, also be a claim under the Human Rights Act that the police had failed to uphold the positive duty of the state with regard to the right to life found in Article 2 ECHR. Lord Bingham recognised that the existence of liability under the Human Rights Act could not be used to ground the development of a new tort mirroring the Convention right, but that in some instances the common law 'had evolved in a direction signalled by the Convention'.[28] Lord Brown reached the opposite conclusion, arguing that the existence of liability under the Human

[27] *Chief Constable of the Hertfordshire Police v Van Colle* [2008] UKHL 50, [2009] 1 AC 225.

[28] Ibid, [58]. Lord Bingham referred in particular to the Court of Appeal decision in *D v East Berkshire Community Trust* [2003] EWCA Civ 1151, [2004] QB 558, [55]–[88].

Rights Act rendered a development of the common law redundant; that common law liability and liability under the Human Rights Act served different purposes and, therefore, should be kept separate.[29] This divergence of opinion illustrates the tension between these two possible forms of constitutionalisation.

B. The Relationship between Horizontality and Sections 6(1) and 6(3)(a)

Sections 6(1) and 6(3)(a) of the Human Rights Act provide the main means through which an obligation to uphold Convention rights may be imposed upon private individuals. However, as indicated above, it is not the only means through which horizontality can occur in English law. As such, to rely solely upon an analysis of these provisions would give too narrow an account of the constitutionalisation of private law.

First, constitutionalisation of the private law can occur through section 3(1) of the Act. A Convention-compatible interpretation of statutory provisions can be used to impose obligations upon private individuals through the modification of provisions of private law. This can be illustrated by the case of *Ghaidan v Godin-Mendoza*,[30] where a Convention-compatible reading of paragraph 2 of Schedule 1 to the Rent Act 1977 created an obligation on a private landlord to treat the surviving homosexual partner of a statutory tenant as a 'spouse' and, therefore, a statutory tenant. As such, Mr Ghaidan was unable to obtain an order for possession of the flat, as to do so would restrict the right to family life of Mr Godin-Mendoza. Constitutionalisation occurred as Convention rights were read in to the content of private law, restricting the way in which Mr Ghaidan could exercise his private law rights.

Second, section 12 of the Human Rights Act 1998 creates a specific form of remedial horizontality, requiring the court to pay specific attention to the Article 10 right of freedom of expression when determining whether to grant injunctions restraining publication.[31]

Third, the mere existence of the Act itself may give rise to horizontal effect. The existence of the Act may trigger a shift in the common law, giving rise to the creation of new obligations, facilitating the process of constitutionalisation by modifying the content of private law in order to ensure its content is compatible with Convention rights.

In addition, focusing merely upon the operation of sections 6(1) and 6(3)(a) is too broad. These sections can apply to functions of the court other than that of deciding private law cases, including when adjudicating disputes between a private individual and institutions of the state. In *R (A) v Secretary of State for the*

[29] Ibid, [136]–[139].

[30] *Ghaidan v Godin-Mendoza* [2004] UKHL 30, [2004] 2 AC 557.

[31] See eg *Douglas v Hello! Ltd (1)* (n 19).

Home Department[32] Keene LJ argued that section 6(1) required that courts, when reviewing a detention order, decide for themselves whether the detention order was compatible with Article 5 ECHR. Only then could the court be assured that it was acting lawfully by ensuring that its decision did not contravene Convention rights.[33] The court's duty under section 6(1), therefore, may require the court to adopt more stringent forms of judicial review, requiring a modification of the standards of public as opposed to private law.[34] Section 6(1) also applies to criminal law adjudication. In *R v Mushtaq*,[35] 'public authority' in section 6(3)(a) was interpreted to include the judge and the jury. As such, it was unlawful for the judge, when directing the jury, to invite them to act in a manner that would contravene the Article 6 ECHR right against self-incrimination of the defendant.[36] This is an example of the possible constitutionalisation of criminal as opposed to private law.

C. Clarifying the Scope of Horizontality

As will already be apparent from the above discussion, there are four main sources of horizontal effect found in the Human Rights Act 1998: section 3(1); section 12; a combination of sections 6(1) and 6(3)(a); and a combination of sections 6(1) and 6(3)(b). In addition, the Act itself can be said to give rise to a form of horizontal effect. To add to the confusion, academic commentary has created a plethora of terminology, both to differentiate between the types of horizontal effect created by the different sources of horizontality, as well as to more precisely delineate between the forms of horizontal effect that may have, or have, been created by the combination of sections 6(1) and 6(3)(a).[37] The focus in this subsection

[32] *R (A) v Secretary of State for the Home Department* [2007] EWCA Civ 804, [2007] All ER (D) 461.

[33] Ibid, [73]–[75]. Keene LJ also argued that s 6(1) motivated the conclusion of the House of Lords in *Huang v Secretary of State for the Home Department* [2007] UKHL 11, [2007] 2 WLR 581, which concluded that, when carrying out a statutory appeal, the special immigration authorities were to decide for themselves as to whether a particular immigration decision was compatible with Convention rights, as opposed to carrying out a function of secondary review.

[34] Although public liability horizontality may arise here.

[35] *R v Mushtaq* [2005] UKHL 25, [2005] 1 WLR 1513.

[36] Ibid, [52]–[54], Lord Roger and [70]–[75], Lord Carswell.

[37] See, for example, K Ewing, 'The Human Rights Act and Parliamentary Democracy' (1999) 62 *Modern Law Review* 79; M Hunt, 'The Horizontal Effect of the Human Rights Act' [1998] *Public Law* 423; I Leigh, 'Horizontal Rights, the Human Rights Act and Privacy: Lessons from the Commonwealth?' (1999) 48 *International and Comparative Law Quarterly* 57; B Markesenis, 'Privacy, Freedom of Expression and the Horizontal Effect of the Human Rights Bill: Lessons from Germany' (1999) 115 *Law Quarterly Review* 47; G Phillipson, 'The Human Rights Act, "Horizontal Effect" and the Common Law: a Bang or a Whimper?' (1999) 62 *Modern Law Review* 824; T Raphael, 'The Problem of Horizontal Effect' (2000) *European Human Rights Law Review* 493; R Singh, 'Privacy and the Media after the Human Rights Act' (1998) *European Human Rights Law Review* 722; Sir William Wade, 'The United Kingdom's Bill of Rights' in I Hare and C Forsyth (eds), *Constitutional Reform in the United Kingdom: Practice and Principles* (Oxford, Hart, 1998) 62; AL Young, 'Horizontality and the Human Rights Act 1998' in K Ziegler (ed), *Human Rights and Private Law: Privacy as Autonomy* (Oxford, Hart, 2007) 35 and 'Mapping Horizontal Effect' in D Hoffman (ed), *The Impact of the UK Human Rights Act on Private Law* (Cambridge, CUP, 2011) 16.

will be to analyse the horizontal effect created by sections 6(1) and 6(3)(a). A discussion of the impact of other forms of horizontality has already been given in the previous subsections, delineating how an awareness of these forms of horizontality is required to give a more complete account of the extent to which the Human Rights Act has had an impact on the constitutionalisation of private law. The description of the horizontal effect created by sections 6(1) and 6(3)(a) has not yet been discussed and has given rise to the most academic and judicial controversy in English law.

To understand the extent to which these sections have created a form of horizontal effect, and thereby determine the extent to which they have contributed to the constitutionalisation of private law, we need first to delineate between different forms of horizontal effect. The first distinction we need to draw is that between direct and indirect horizontal effect. Direct horizontal effect occurs when an individual pleads a breach of a Convention right in and of itself before the court, obtaining redress against another individual. Indirect horizontal effect occurs when the applicant pleads other legal provisions, which are in turn interpreted so as to contain or reflect the human right in question. It is the alternative legal provision itself that imposes the obligation, which reflects or mirrors the obligation found in a Convention right.[38]

One settled matter in English law is that Convention rights can only create indirect as opposed to direct horizontal effect.[39] This choice helps to determine the extent to which the Act has facilitated the constitutionalisation of private law. This can be understood when we analyse an alternative method of drawing the distinction between direct and indirect horizontal effect, which focuses on the perspective of the individual who is made subject to an obligation to uphold Convention rights as opposed to the perspective of the claimant seeking to protect their Convention rights. When examined from this perspective, direct horizontal effect occurs when *an individual* is made subject to constitutional or human rights obligations, being required to act in a manner that respects the constitutional human rights of others. Indirect horizontal effect occurs when *the law* is made subject to constitutional or human rights. Individuals may then face an obligation to uphold human rights through a modification of the law which has itself been modified to ensure that it complies with constitutional or human rights.[40]

[38] Phillipson (n 37) and Hunt (n 37) at 428–34.

[39] *Campbell v MGN* [2004] UKHL 22, [2004] 2 AC 457. See also the judgment of Lord Phillip of Worth Matravers MR in *Douglas v Hello! (3)* [2005] EWCA Civ 595, [2006] QB 125, [50]. However, there is also academic commentary prior to this case which argued to the contrary and which advocates the adoption of direct horizontal effect. See Wade (n 37) 61, 63–64; HRW Wade, 'Horizons of Horizontality' (2000) 116 *Law Quarterly Review* 217; J Morgan 'Privacy, Confidence and Horizontal Effect: 'Hello' Trouble' (2003) 62 *Cambridge Law Journal* 444, 467–68; J Morgan, 'Privacy in the House of Lords, Again' (2004) 120 *Law Quarterly Review* 563, 566; and D Beyleveld and S Pattinson, 'Horizontal Applicability and Horizontal Effect' (2002) 118 *Law Quarterly Review* 623, 634–45.

[40] S Gardbaum, 'Where the (State) Action is' (2006) 4 *International Journal of Constitutional Law* 760; and G Taylor, 'The Horizontal Effect of Human Rights Provisions: the German Model and its Applicability to Common-Law Jurisdictions' (2002) 13 *King's College Law Journal* 187, 190–95.

This helps to explain how the Human Rights Act may provide for a more wide-ranging, albeit weaker, form of constitutionalisation in English law. Indirect horizontal effect requires the modification of English private law, as opposed to creating freestanding rights that are added to English law. This may give rise to a more wide-ranging form of constitutionalisation, as it provides an opportunity for all existing doctrines of private law to be examined, in order to determine how far they comply with Convention rights. This creates further opportunities to examine existing provisions, perhaps catching ways in which the law may be modified to incorporate values underpinning Convention rights which would not have triggered a freestanding right under direct horizontal effect. Moreover, it allows for Convention rights to be merged into existing provisions of private law, stimulating developments of the law, as opposed to merely replacing provisions that contradicted Convention rights.

Constitutionalisation of private law occurring through indirect horizontal effect has, possibly, greater longevity than that occurring through direct horizontal effect – it may remain even if the Human Rights Act is overturned. If Convention rights were to have direct horizontal effect, then the horizontal effect in question would derive from the Act itself. As such, if the Act were to be overturned, the horizontal effect of Convention rights would also lapse.[41] The same is not true of indirect horizontal effect, which works through the modification of provisions of private law. Although overturning the Human Rights Act would remove any possible obligation of the court to ensure that private law mirrored or reflected Convention rights, the private law that had been altered so as to impose an obligation to uphold Convention rights could remain.[42]

However, although possibly broader in effect, the constitutionalisation that occurs through indirect horizontal effect is weaker in strength than that created by direct horizontal effect. If Convention rights were to have direct horizontal effect, they would be clearly recognised as distinct, constitutional rights. In legal systems that delineate more clearly between constitutional and other rights, particularly those that allow constitutional rights to override legislation, this provides a stronger protection of rights and a stronger form of constitutionalisation, because the rights given horizontal effect derive from the Constitution and cannot be overridden by legislation. The same is not true of indirect horizontal effect, where the rights are incorporated into ordinary legal provisions and, in a sense, lose part of their constitutional status in that this law could be overturned by legislative provisions. This weaker effect, however, is not due to the form of horizontal effect chosen by the court, but due to the nature of the United Kingdom's constitution and the Human Rights Act itself.

[41] Of course, it is possible that further developments of the common law would occur, so as to maintain an obligation for private individuals to uphold Convention obligations. However, this would not be a form of direct horizontal effect.

[42] Although it would be possible for these precedents which expanded the common law to be distinguished and no longer followed, given the overturning of the Human Rights Act 1998.

What has given rise to more difficulty, however, has been the classification of the form of indirect effect created by the Act. Not only is this dispute prevalent in the literature, but there is also no clear, legally authoritative resolution of this issue. This makes it difficult to determine the precise extent to which horizontality has constitutionalised private law. Moreover, this lack of clarity is exacerbated by a distinction between the form and the substance of horizontal effect found in some of the more recent case law.

There are two main parameters that determine the form of indirect horizontal effect. First, different models of indirect horizontal effect place varying degrees of obligation upon the court to modify private law. The court may be required to modify private law, or merely empowered to do so. In addition, different restrictions may be placed upon the court's ability to develop new causes of action. Courts may be required or permitted to create new causes of action, forbidden from using the law to develop new causes of action, or only allowed to create new causes of action when this would be no more than a merely incremental development of the law. Courts may also be required to recognise Convention rights or values as fundamental principles of the common law, or just as principles of the common law. Clearly, the stronger the obligation placed upon the court, the greater the potential constitutionalisation of private law.

Second, courts may be required or enabled to modify the common law in order to ensure its compatibility with Convention rights, or in order to ensure its compatibility with the values underpinning Convention rights. The choice between Convention rights and values does not affect the scope or strength of constitutionalisation of the private law, but rather its form. If private law is modified so as to reflect Convention rights, then this will produce a form of constitutionalisation closer to the incorporation of liberal rights within English law. If private law is to be modified so as to reflect the values underpinning Convention rights, then the Act will facilitate constitutionalisation that may be closer to an establishment of values that constitute the values of the United Kingdom, influenced by, but not necessarily completely reflecting, the statement of liberal constitutional values found in the ECHR.

Clarity surrounding the form of indirect effect adopted in English law, therefore, would provide a clearer account of the possible extent of the constitutionalisation of private law. However, there is little certainty as to the precise model adopted by the courts. In addition, the judiciary appear to be reluctant to discuss the precise form of indirect horizontal effect that should be applied in English law. If anything, judicial pronouncements dictate in favour of flexibility, where the weight to be given to Convention values depends upon the specific context. In *Campbell v MGN*,[43] Lord Hoffmann appeared to require the courts to incorporate the values underpinning Convention rights as fundamental values in the common law, as can be illustrated by the following:

[43] *Campbell v MGN* [2004] UKHL 22, [2004] 2 AC 457.

> This House decided in *Wainwright v Home Office* [2003] UKHL 53, [2003] 4 All ER 969, [2003] 3 WLR 1137 that there is no general tort of invasion of privacy. But the right to privacy is in a general sense one of the values, and sometimes the most important value, which underlies a number of more specific causes of action, both at common law and under various statutes. One of these is the equitable action for breach of confidence, which has long been recognised as capable of being used to protect privacy.

Privacy is recognised as 'sometimes the most important value' which would appear to suggest that the value of privacy, as opposed to the right of privacy found in Article 8 ECHR may, on occasion, be regarded as a fundamental principle. It may also mean that the value of privacy is merely recognised as an ordinary principle that may be the most important principle given the circumstances, even when this is merely allocated ordinary weight.

In the same case, Baroness Hale placed a stronger obligation upon the court, requiring the court to develop the common law not only to reflect the values underpinning Convention rights, but the Convention rights themselves:

> The 1998 Act does not create any new cause of action between private persons. But if there is a relevant cause of action applicable, the court as a public authority must act compatibly with both parties' convention rights. In a case such as this, the relevant vehicle will usually be the action for breach of confidence.[44]

Neither Lord Hoffmann nor Baroness Hale gave a more detailed justification for why they adopted a particular model, Lord Hoffmann seeing this as unnecessary because the law had already developed to ensure that Articles 8 and 10 ECHR would be sufficiently protected in English law.[45] Nor was there a detailed discussion of the divergence between these two models.[46]

Further confusion is caused by the way in which the courts have developed the tort of breach of confidential information following *Campbell v MGN*. Although it is clear that English law only adopts a model of indirect horizontal effect, the extent to which the tort of breach of confidential information has been modified in order to incorporate Convention rights produces an effect that is much closer to that of direct horizontal effect. This can be illustrated by the recent Court of Appeal decision of *McKennitt v Ash (McKennitt)*. Loreena McKennitt was a well-known Canadian folk singer who had striven to ensure that her private life was guarded from public scrutiny. Ash was a close friend of McKennitt who, following the breakdown of their friendship, wrote a book detailing aspects of McKennitt's private life that McKennitt wished to keep private. McKennitt sought an injunction to prevent further publication of the book, in reliance on a breach of privacy and breach of confidence. Buxton LJ, giving the leading judgment and the only judgment that provided a detailed analysis of the manner in which English law

[44] Ibid, [132].

[45] Ibid, [53].

[46] For a discussion of the judicial reluctance to determine the precise model of indirect horizontal effect, see G Phillipson, 'Clarity Postponed: Horizontal Effect after *Campbell*' in H Fenwick, R Masterman and G Phillipson (eds), *Judicial Reasoning under the UK Human Rights Act* (Cambridge, CUP, 2007) 143.

protects privacy, did not expressly state that Convention rights had direct substantive horizontal effect.[47] He was also careful to explain that there was no domestic tort of invasion of privacy. Instead protections of Article 8 and article 10 are 'shoehorned' into the tort of breach of confidence.[48] However, the content of the tort of breach of confidence was entirely dictated by the content of Articles 8 and 10,[49] an approach confirmed in both the Court of Appeal and the Supreme Court, applying not only to 'privacy'-based injunctions and super-injunctions, but also anonymity orders.[50] When interpreted in this manner, the impact of indirect horizontal effect upon the constitutionalisation of private law is closer to that of direct effect. It is still the case that principles of the common law are being modified, giving rise to a possibly broader and more permanent form of constitutionalisation than that found under direct effect. However, by using the content of Convention rights to determine the very content of the tort, constitutionalisation is much closer to the adoption of liberal principles, which override the previous confines of the common law, than a system of values that becomes enmeshed with pre-existing legal principles.

III. Lessons from Freedom of Expression and Privacy

Both the right to freedom of expression and the right to privacy have become constitutionalised in English law. However, the extent and the cause of this constitutionalisation differ. An analysis of these two areas, therefore, not only provides a series of practical examples from which to examine the process of constitutionalisation following the Human Rights Act, but also provides the opportunity to examine its strengths and weaknesses. It will be shown that the Human Rights Act is part of a larger process of constitutionalisation. In addition, this process of constitutionalisation has been influenced not only by the ECHR, but also by decisions from other common law jurisdictions – most notably those of the United States, Australia and New Zealand. Nevertheless, the Act has added greater legitimacy to these developments. In particular, the Act appears to be influencing the judicial reasoning process, although it is not yet the case that the courts have developed deeper theoretical justifications either of the form or process of the constitutionalisation of private law, or of the rights that have become constitutionalised.

[47] Ibid, 374.

[48] *McKennitt v Ash* [2006] EWCA Civ 1714, [2007] 3 WLR 194, [8].

[49] N Moreham, 'Privacy and Horizontality: Relegating the Common Law' (2007) 123 *Law Quarterly Review* 373, 375–76.

[50] *Murray v Express Newspapers Plc* [2008] EWCA Civ 446, [2008] 3 WLR 1360; *Donald v Nutili* [2010] EWCA Civ 1276; *Application by Guardian and News Media Limited in Ahmed v HM Treasury Limited* [2010] UKSC 1; *Hutcheson (formerly known as KGM) v News Group Newspapers* [2011] ECWA Civ 808.

The Article 8 ECHR right to privacy has triggered a constitutionalisation of the tort of breach of confidence that has radically altered the content of the law. As discussed above, English law had no general tort of privacy prior to the enactment of the Human Rights Act 1998, and this still remains the case.[51] However, the right to privacy is now protected in all but name, following amendments to the tort of breach of confidential information. First, the tort of breach of confidential information rested upon the establishment of a duty of confidence, that duty being breached by the individual who disclosed the confidential information to the detriment of the owner of that information. As confirmed in *Campbell v MGN*, the tort can now occur even when there is no duty of confidence, resting upon the classification of the published information as confidential, so much so that Lord Nicholls re-christened the tort as the 'misuse of private information'.[52] More importantly, as discussed above, the tort has effectively become the means through which Articles 8 and 10 ECHR are incorporated into English law. When determining whether the tort has been established, the court first examines whether there was a reasonable expectation of privacy with regards to the information in question and, if established, determines whether the right to freedom of expression outweighs the right to privacy.[53]

However, although the Human Rights Act, particularly the combination of sections 6(1) and 6(3)(a) may have acted as the catalysts for the constitutionalisation of this area of the law, it can also be regarded as part of its incremental development. Judicial statements supporting the extension of the tort of breach of confidence to include disclosures of private information, regardless of whether that information was disclosed in breach of confidence or otherwise, can be found in case law pre-dating the enactment of the Human Rights Act.[54] The Act provided further impetus for this change, as well as modifying the justification of the tort of breach of confidence, moving away from the protection of an equitable interest towards a rights-based focus of the need to balance the right to privacy and the right to freedom of expression.[55] The Act not only prompts further constitutionalisation, building on previous developments, but also marks a shift in judicial reasoning, with Convention rights operating in the foreground, delineating the content of the tort, as opposed to operating in the background.

There is less evidence of a drastic change to the content of the private law in order to protect the right to freedom of expression.[56] The area in which the right to freedom of expression has had the greatest impact upon the constitutionalisation of private law is the tort of defamation, particularly concerning political

[51] *Wainwright v Home Office* [2003] UKHL 53, [2004] 2 AC 406.

[52] *Campbell v MGN* [2005] UKHL 61, [2005] 1 WLR 3394, [15].

[53] See, for example, the reasoning of the judiciary in *McKennitt v Ash* (n 48) and *Murray v Express Newspapers plc* (n 50).

[54] See, most notably, *AG v Guardian (2)* [1990] 1 AC 109, 281 and Laws LJ in *Hellewell v CC of Derbyshire* [1995] 1 WLR 804, 807.

[55] See, in particular, *Campbell v MGN* (n 52) [16] and [19] (Lord Nicholls), [45] and [51] (Lord Hoffmann), [86] and [114]–[125] (Lord Hope) and [135] (Baroness Hale).

[56] See K Oliphant, 'Defamation' in Hoffman (ed) (n 37) 195.

libels. The recognition of the need to protect freedom of expression has led the courts to modify the content of the private law – by prohibiting local authorities from bringing defamation actions to protect their reputation[57] as well as adapting the defence of qualified privilege to include circumstances in which the media communicates information to the public at large, provided that, in doing so, it complies with the standards of responsible journalism (the *Reynolds* privilege)[58] – a development which has led some of their Lordships to question how far the *Reynolds* privilege is an extension of qualified privilege, seeing it instead in terms of a new defence.[59] This suggests that the constitutionalisation of this area of the law is greater than was at first perceived. These developments, however, took place, for the most part, before the enactment of the Human Rights Act and were influenced by developments in other common law jurisdictions, particularly decisions of the US Supreme Court.[60] The court was convinced that no further alteration would be required, as English private law mirrored the requirements of Article 10 ECHR.[61] Once more, the Act appears to function more as a justification for further developing nascent constitutionalisation in the common law. It provides a catalyst not necessarily for radically altering the content of the common law, but for bolstering the recognition of the right to freedom of expression as a fundamental or constitutional right.[62]

It would be wrong, however, to use this as evidence of the lack of influence of the Act in the process of constitutionalisation. First, although the Act itself has not prompted a similar alteration in the content of private law as found with regard to the right to privacy, this is not because of a lack of importance of the Act, or due to the lack of importance of the right to freedom of expression, but rather because private law had already begun a process of constitutionalisation, which was merely crystallised and legitimised by the Act.[63] Second, the Act has had a greater impact upon two other aspects of private law – the judicial reasoning process and upon procedural aspects of the common law. In addition, there is a nascent recognition of an institutional constitutionalisation of the media.

[57] *Derbyshire County Council v Times* [1993] AC 534.

[58] *Reynolds v Times* [2001] 2 AC 127.

[59] *Jameel v Wall Street Journal Europe SPRL* [2006] UKHL 44, [2007] 1 AC 359, [46], [50] and [57] (Lord Hoffmann) and [146] (Baroness Hale). See also *Flood v Times Newspapers Limited* [2012] UKSC 11.

[60] *Derbyshire County Council v Times* (n 57), drew in particular upon the decision of the Supreme Court of Illinois in *City of Chicago v Tribune* [1923] 139 NE 86 and of the US Supreme Court in *New York Times v Sullivan* (1964) 376 US 254. Ian Loveland argues that these decisions have influenced the common law precisely because they drew upon old common law authorities, as opposed to being more specifically derived from the requirements of the First Amendment to the US Constitution, which protects the right to freedom of expression, Loveland, 'Freedom of Political Expression' (n 10) 243–44.

[61] *Derbyshire County Council v Times* (n 57) at 551 (Lord Keith) and *Reynolds v Times* (n 58) at 203 (Lord Nicholls).

[62] *Reynolds v Times*, ibid (n 58) (Lord Steyn).

[63] See Loveland, *Political Libels* (n 10); Loveland, 'The Constitutionalisation of Political Libels (n 10) 633; I Loveland, '*Reynolds v Times Newspapers* in the House of Lords' [2000] *Public Law* 351; Loveland, 'Freedom of Political Expression (n 10); E Barendt, 'Freedom of Expression in the United Kingdom under the Human Rights Act' (2009) 84 *Indiana Law Journal* 851.

A clear example of the modification of the judicial reasoning process can be seen by contrasting the judgment of Bingham CJ, as he then was, in the Court of Appeal decision of *Reynolds v Times* (*Reynolds*),[64] decided before the Human Rights Act, with his judgment as Lord Bingham in the House of Lords in *McCartan Turkington Breen v Times Newspapers Limited* (*McCartan*).[65] In *Reynolds* Lord Bingham began his analysis of whether English law should develop the law of qualified privilege, as advocated by Lord Lester QC, by distilling the requirements of the defence by analysing the case law.[66] Lord Lester had argued that *Derbyshire County Council v Times* (*Derbyshire*) supported the broadening of the defence of qualified privilege, as, in that case, their Lordships had accepted the existence of the chilling effect, which harmed freedom of expression by deterring the media from publishing information. A constitutionalised approach to judicial reasoning, with its focus on broad principles from which specific applications can be derived, would have been more sympathetic to Lord Lester's argument. Lord Bingham, however, rejected his argument in stating that 'in our judgment, on a proper reading, the *Derbyshire* case leaves this question completely open, and we think it dangerous to speculate how their Lordships would have decided the present question had it fallen for decision'.[67] Lord Bingham's reasoning is more inductive than deductive. He does not regard the chilling effect as being conclusively established as a general principle, to be applied by analogy in other more specific cases. Rather, he regards *Derbyshire* as establishing one instance in which the court accepted the chilling effect, but was reluctant to see this as general authority to extend the acceptance of the chilling effect principle beyond the specific facts and circumstances of *Derbyshire*. This is illustrative of a more inductive, common-law reasoning process as opposed to a more deductive reasoning process found in the application of more general constitutional principles.

In a similar manner, Lord Bingham treats the decisions of the European Court of Human Rights (ECtHR) cited in that judgment in a narrow manner, arguing that the case law cited did not specifically require the creation of the defence of qualified privilege advocated by Lord Lester, as opposed to analysing more broadly whether the cases were illustrative of a general principle that could be furthered by the modification of the defence of qualified privilege.[68] He does consider the context of the right to freedom of expression at the end of his judgment, when forming his conclusions, arguing in particular that to extend the defence of qualified privilege would be to fail to balance the right to freedom of expression and the protection of an individual's reputation in the correct manner, as well as being contrary to English authority.[69]

[64] *Reynolds v Times* (n 58).
[65] *McCartan Turkington Breen v Times Newspapers Limited* [2001] 2 AC 277.
[66] *Reynolds v Times* (n 58) 160–70.
[67] Ibid, 171.
[68] Ibid, 172–73.
[69] Ibid, 176–78.

In *McCartan* their Lordships were asked to determine whether a meeting in a private home, to which journalists and some members of the public had been invited, was a 'public meeting', such that a report of the meeting would benefit from the defence of qualified privilege under section 7 of the Defamation Act (Northern Ireland) 1955. Here, Lord Bingham begins his analysis by focusing upon the right to freedom of expression, in particular the need for a free press in a modern democracy.[70] This is then used to shape his interpretation of the statute.[71] He applies constitutional reasoning to the case, furthering constitutionalisation of the judicial reasoning process as well as to the content of private law.

Second, the Human Rights Act has furthered the constitutionalisation of procedural aspects of private law. This has occurred not only through the interpretation of section 12 of the Human Rights Act 1998,[72] but also through the manner in which the court exercises its inherent jurisdiction to grant a court order requiring the disclosure of the identity of sources of information where it can be demonstrated that the individual in question has participated in, or was involved in, the commission of a civil or criminal wrong,[73] as well as the role of section 10 of the Contempt of Court Act 1981. In *Ashworth Hospital Authority v MGN Ltd*[74] it was made clear that the court was required to scrutinise all such court orders strictly, in order to ensure that they did not interfere with the right to freedom of expression.[75] In particular, the court was required to pay attention to the potential 'chilling effect' created by court orders requiring the disclosure of a journalist's source of information, where journalists may prefer not to publish information for fear of having to reveal, and therefore potentially lose, a confidential informant.[76] This development has given rise to a perceived greater reluctance to grant court orders than was evident prior to the enactment of the Human Rights Act,[77] as well as providing further evidence of a shift in judicial reasoning, with the courts laying greater emphasis upon the content of Article 10, as interpreted by decisions of the ECtHR. Again, this development is part of a process of constitutionalisation, triggered in part by the enactment of section 10 of the Contempt of Court Act 1981, with the Act providing further legitimacy and clarity to the constitutionalisation process.[78] In addition, the process of the hearing itself is becoming constitution-

[70] *McCartan Turkington Breen v Times Newspapers Limited* (n 65) [1].

[71] See I Loveland, 'Freedom of Political Expression: who needs the Human Rights Act?' [2001] *Public Law* 233, 237.

[72] For an analysis of the extent to which this section has modified the content of procedural requirements of the private law, see A McColgan, 'Privacy, Freedom of Expression and the Grant of Interim Injunctions' (2008) 27 *Civil Justice Quarterly* 23.

[73] *Norwich Pharmacal Co v Customs and Excise Commissioners* [1974] AC 133, [1973] 2 All ER 943.

[74] *Ashworth Hospital Authority v MGN Ltd* [2002] UKHL 29, [2002] 4 All ER 193.

[75] Ibid, [50] (Lord Woolf).

[76] Ibid, [61] (Lord Woolf).

[77] See, for example, H Fenwick and G Phillipson, *Media Freedom under the Human Rights Act* (Oxford, OUP, 2006).

[78] It is unclear how far the courts regarded s 10 of the Contempt of Court Act 1981 as motivated by the need to ensure compatibility with Art 10 ECHR and there was disparity between decisions of the English court and the ECtHR as to the application of s 10. See the contrasting views of Schiemann LJ in *Camelot Group plc v Centaur Communications Ltd* [1999] QB 124, 128 and Sedley LJ in *Financial*

alised. For example, in *McKennitt* a variety of media organisations had applied to intervene in the case, hoping to present arguments in favour of the right to freedom of expression. Although the Court of Appeal did not grant these institutions the permission to intervene it did, with the consent of the parties, both ask the parties to take note of their detailed submissions in their application to intervene and state that the court itself would take note of these submissions.[79] This is evidence of a more constitutionalised judicial process, with the court being willing to take account of deeper arguments, recognising more general issues that may arise from the development of the private law than the implications for the two parties before the court.

A more subtle shift is evidenced by the way in which the media is starting to be recognised not only as a beneficiary of the right to freedom of expression, but also for its constitutional role, as the 'fourth estate'. The role of the press in promoting democratic speech played a role in the background to the development of the law in *Derbyshire.* Lord Nicholls remarked in more detail on the role of the media in *Reynolds*, recognising the

> importance of the role discharged by the media in the expression and communication of information and comment on political matters. It is through the mass media that most people today obtain their information on political matters. Without freedom of expression by the media, freedom of expression would be a hollow concept. The interest of a democratic society in ensuring a free press weighs heavily in the balance in deciding whether any curtailment of this freedom bears a reasonable relationship to the purpose of the curtailment.[80]

Although not expressly referred to as a constitutional role, the court is protecting the right to a free press because of the importance of the media in both reporting and commenting upon political information, thus facilitating democracy. This role is also recognised in *McCartan*, focusing on the role of the media as a conduit of information, as well as its role in investigatory journalism. This recognition formed part of the justification for the development of the emerging reportage defence – allowing media institutions the ability to benefit from providing a fair and accurate report of libellous accusations without having to take steps to determine the truth of these allegations.[81] The recognition of the role of the media is influenced by decisions of the ECtHR, in particular *Lingens v Austria.* [82] However, this influence is not conclusive. English law has developed the defence of reportage

Times Ltd v Interbrew SA [2002] EWCA Civ 274; *X Ltd v Morgan-Grampian (Publishers) Ltd* [1991] 1 AC 1; and *Goodwin v United Kingdom* (1996) 22 EHRR 123. This disparity is recognised by Lord Woolf in *Ashworth Hospital Authority v MGN Ltd* (n 74) [38].

[79] *McKennitt v Ash* (n 48) 196.

[80] *Reynolds v Sunday Times* (n 58) 200.

[81] See *Al Faigh v HH Saudi Research and Marketing UK Ltd* [2001] All ER (D) 48 (Nov); *Charman v Orion Publishing Group Ltd* [2007] EWCA Civ 972, [2008] 1 All ER 750; *Roberts v Gable* [2007] EWCA Civ 721, [2008] QB 502; G Busuttil, 'Reportage: A Not Entirely Neutral Report' (2009) *Entertainment Law Review* 44. 'Reportage' has now been confirmed by the Supreme Court as a species of the *Reynolds* privilege, see *Flood v Times Newspapers Limited* (n 59).

[82] *Lingens v Austria* App no 9815/82 (1986) 8 EHRR 407.

through its interpretation of common law principles recognising the freedom of the press. Yet this defence was not required by – and may even contradict – requirements of the ECHR.[83] Moreover, the defence of reportage is difficult to reconcile with principles of defamation law, particularly the repetition rule.[84] The nascent recognition of the potential constitutional role of the media provides further evidence of a constitutionalisation of the judicial reasoning process. This occurs as the judiciary is reasoning from general principles, recognising the need to apply these principles in the context of the UK constitution. This process operates differently from the 'bottom-up' reasoning of the common law, where a series of specific examples work together to produce general legal principles.

IV. Conclusion

The examples of the right to freedom of expression and the right to privacy demonstrate how the Human Rights Act adds legitimacy to the growing process of constitutionalisation of English private law, a process influenced by developments in other common law jurisdictions as well as the more frequent reference to the ECHR. The impact of the Act depends upon the extent to which this constitutionalisation process was taking place before the advent of the Act, as well as the way in which the requirements of the ECHR have been read to fit in with existing principles of private law. The largest shift is not necessarily in the content of the law, but in the way in which the judiciary has become more willing to focus directly as opposed to indirectly upon these rights, recognising their constitutional status through recognising their fundamental nature and using them more explicitly to shape the content of private law. This illustrates a more fluid and flexible process of constitutionalisation, one that enables these constitutional rights to become more firmly embedded in English private law, without requiring a drastic overhauling of the principles of private law.

The variety of means through which horizontal effect may occur in English law adds to this flexibility. This is not a weakness, but a strength of English law. It produces a deeper sense of constitutionalisation, focusing not merely upon the incorporation of a particular subset of liberal rights, but a firmer and more lasting development of constitutional principles, stimulating a deeper recognition of the need to develop principles that facilitate legitimate government. This in turn facilitates a deeper process of constitutionalisation more apt for a predominantly political as opposed to a legal constitution.

[83] Busuttil (n 81) 49–50.
[84] Ibid, 48.

6

Constitutionalisation of Freedom of Contract in European Union Law

CARSTEN HERRESTHAL

I. Introduction

One of the most interesting challenges accompanying the process of harmonising Member States' private law within the Common Market are issues that go beyond the scope of those areas of the law that are traditionally separately addressed in public and private German law. As is generally known, neither primary nor secondary EU law makes a distinction between private law and public law. This is partly due to the fact that only specific competences are conferred on the EU legislature and the fact that EU regulation is subject-matter oriented. As a result, freedom of contract under EU law is located in EU law as well as German private and public law.

The following chapter will first address some basic, uncontroversial assumptions with regard to EU law as well as to the relationship between EU law and Member States' law. Second, a definition of the term 'constitutionalisation' will follow which will reveal its two-fold meaning. Third, the fundamental principle of freedom of contract and its functions will be analysed. Fourth, structural deficits in the European Union that endanger freedom of contract will be pointed out. Finally, some instruments that could overcome these shortcomings will be identified.

The aim of this contribution is to strengthen the principle of freedom of contract in EU law and in the Member States' private law which results from the harmonisation within the European Union. Thus, the following chapter will point to several structural deficits that may predetermine the level of protection of freedom of contract in EU law as well as the level of regulation[1] within the European Union. The overriding concern of this contribution is not to argue for a specific level of protection of freedom of contract, but to express concern that structural shortcomings and institutional deficits in the EU legal system may determine the level of protection of freedom of contract in the private law within the European

[1] In the following 'regulation' is taken to mean any limitation of the freedom of contract by the state or authorised by the state.

Union. Without doubt, there should be an intensive discussion about the adequate level of protection of the individual in private law. This protection, along with others, is the subject matter of European consumer protection law and European anti-discrimination law. But this very valuable discussion could be without significance if the level of protection is predetermined by structural shortcomings in the EU legal system. Thus, the latter must be addressed. Moreover, those structural shortcomings often result in a level of overprotection of other interests from the perspective of freedom of contract.[2]

II. Basic Assumptions with Regard to the EU Legal System

A. Ordoliberalism as One of the Foundations of the EU

The first basic assumption concerns the economic theory of ordoliberalism. It is quite uncontested that the theory of ordoliberalism is one of the main foundations of the economic constitution of the European Union.[3] Moreover, the fundamental aim of the European Union is still to extend market competition and freedom of contract across the borders of the Member States within the internal market.[4] The principle of freedom of contract is one of the most important structural issues in a liberal market order. Nevertheless, private law in the Member States is characterised by a paradox today:[5] those rules in the national private law

[2] See below section VI.

[3] See CF Ophüls, 'Grundzüge europäischer Wirtschaftsverfassung' (1962) 124 *Zeitschrift für Handelsrecht* 136 ff; for further details with regard to the impact of the German concept of *Wirtschaftsverfassung* on the foundations of EU law, see H-J Mestmäcker, 'Offene Märkte im System unverfälschten Wettbewerbs in der europäischen Wirtschaftsgemeinschaft' in *Festschrift für Böhm* (Karlsruhe, CF Müller, 1965) 345 ff; T Oppermann, CD Classen and M Nettesheim, *Europarecht*, 5th edn (Munich, CH Beck, 2011) § 18, paras 1–6; W Möschel, 'Wettbewerbspolitik aus ordoliberaler Sicht' in O von Gamm (ed), *Strafrecht, Unternehmensrecht, Anwaltsrecht, Festschrift für Gerd Pfeiffer* (Cologne, Carl Heymanns, 1988) 707 ff; S Grundmann, W Kerber and S Weatherill, 'Party Autonomy and the Role of Information in the Internal Market – an Overview' in S Grundmann, W Kerber and S Weatherill (eds), *Party Autonomy and the Role of Information in the Internal Market* (Berlin, de Gruyter, 2001) 20; P Müller-Graff, 'Basic Freedoms – Extending Party Autonomy across Borders' in ibid, 136; J Basedow, 'Freedom of Contract in the European Union' (2008) 6 *European Review of Private Law* 901, 921; recently H Collins, 'The European Economic Constitution and the Constitutional Dimension of Private Law' (2009) 5 *European Review of Contract Law* 71, 75 ff (provisions of the treaties posses many characteristics of an economic constitution); for a broader discussion of the economic foundations of the European Union see W Zippel (ed), *Ökonomische Grundlagen der Europäischen Integration* (Munich, Franz Vahlen, 1993); W Molle, *The Economics of European Integration*, 5th edn (Aldershot, Ashgate, 2006) 9 ff; for the opposite opinion cf J Rutgers, 'The European Economic Constitution, Freedom of Contract and the DCFR' (2009) 5 *European Review of Contract Law* 95.

[4] See Müller-Graff (n 3) 137 ff.

[5] See also F Bydlinski, 'Kriterien und Sinn der Unterscheidung von Privatrecht und öffentlichem Recht' (1994) 194 *Archiv für die civilistische Praxis* 319, 328 f; F Bydlinski, '"Privatrechtsgesellschaft" und Rechtssystem' in K Schmidt and E Schwark (eds), *Unternehmen, Recht und Wirtschaftsordnung.*

that are heavily criticised by referring to the principles of a liberal market order and the principle of freedom of contract often have their origin in European law.[6] The main reason is the large set of rules included in EU law which interferes heavily with freedom of contract and the corresponding principle of personal autonomy. Thus, today the EU legal system departs from the economic foundations of the process of European integration and a legal system ensuring competition in the internal market.[7] As mentioned above, it is debatable whether the level of protection provided by the EU law is adequate; nevertheless, there should be no doubt that according to the legal and economic foundations of the European Union, the principle of freedom of contract is a necessary and fundamental element within the EU legal system.

B. Freedom of Contract as a Principle in the EU Member States' Legal Orders

Freedom of contract[8] is described as the possibility of individuals to determine legal relations according to their respective wills.[9] This principle embraces two major elements: the principle of self-determination and the principle of responsibility of the individual. It goes without saying that the principle of freedom of contract as determined by those two elements is an important privilege; moreover, this principle plays a significant role in the Member States' constitutions and in their private laws.[10] Freedom of contract is one of the most important topics for private law in general and for contract law in particular.[11] As mentioned above, the principle is closely related to the ordoliberal approach regarding the economic constitutions in some of the Member States.[12] Some authors trace the principle

Festschrift für P Raisch (Cologne, Heymanns, 1995) 9 f; F Bydlinski, 'Formale Freiheitsethik und andere Ethiken im Privatrecht' in S Kessal-Wulf, M Martinek and P Rawert (eds), *Formale Freiheitsethik oder materiale Verantwortungsethik* (Berlin, de Gruyter, 2006) 99, 104 (with regard to Austria).

[6] Cf H Micklitz, 'A Comment on Party Autonomy and Consumer Regulation in the European Community – A Plea for Consistency' in Grundmann et al (n 3) 197, 198 (majority of the EU regulation restricts freedom of private parties).

[7] With regard to the European foundations cf also D Gerber, 'Constitutionalizing the Economy: German Neo-liberalism, Competition Law and the "New" Europe' (1994) 42 *American Journal of Comparative Law* 25, 27 ff; W Sauter, 'The Economic Constitution of the European Union' (1998) 4 *Columbia Journal of European Law* 27, 29 f.

[8] In the following the term 'freedom of contract' is used in a very broad sense which equates to the German concept of *Privatautonomie* [individual autonomy].

[9] See BVerfGE 72, 155, 170; W Flume, *Allgemeiner Teil des BGB, II*, 4th edn (Berlin, Springer, 1992) § 1/1; likewise D Coester-Waltjen, 'Constitutional Aspects of Party Autonomy and Its Limits – The Perspective of Law' in Grundmann et al (eds) (n 3) 41.

[10] See J Beatson, *Anson's Law of Contract*, 29th edn (Oxford, Oxford University Press, 2010) 4 (freedom of contract is 'a reasonable social ideal' that plays a significant role in every national economy); Micklitz (n 6) 197 (national legal orders deeply grounded in the concept of autonomy and individual responsibility); Basedow (n 3) 902 (foundational tenet).

[11] See Grundmann et al (eds) (n 3) 3, 4.

[12] Basedow (n 3) 905.

back to the French Revolution.[13] The principle has been eroded throughout the twentieth century; this is especially true at the level of the Member States. This erosion was caused, among other things, by reactions of the private law to changes in the structure of the Member States' economies. Additionally, private law of the Member States was hit substantially by the political trend in the 1970s and 1980s.

With regard to *English* law, the protection of freedom of contract by Article 8 of the European Convention on Human Rights (ECHR) may directly influence English private law through the Human Rights Act 1998. Freedom of contract is recognised as the most basic principle of the English law of contract.[14] One might even argue that in English law, too, freedom of contract is of higher rank than simple Acts of Parliament, if one accepts that English law has established a hierarchy of norms by the adoption of the Human Rights Act.

In German law[15] freedom of contract is a fundamental right protected by the German Constitution. The principle is part of the individual freedom which is covered by Article 2(1) of the German Constitution.[16] Due to its character as a constitutional right, the principle is of a higher rank than rules in the Civil Code [*Bürgerliches Gesetzbuch*, BGB]. Moreover, freedom of contract is the most basic principle of German contract law. Of course there are constraints to this principle by the constitutional order because restrictions of freedom of contract by statutory or judge-made law are legitimate. Nevertheless, those restrictions have to comply with the due process of law and the principle of reasonableness.

In the following sections, the erosion of freedom of contract due to structural deficits of the structure of private law in the European Union, that is, within the legal order that covers EU law and Member States' law, will be analysed.

C. Private Law Influenced by Fundamental Rights in the National and European Legal Order

A basic assumption of the following analysis is that private law in general is not separate from fundamental rights protected by the Member States' constitutions,

[13] See J Ghestin, G Goubeaux and M Fabre-Magnan, *Traité de Droit Civil – Introduction Générale*, 4th edn (Paris, LGDJ, 1994) paras 134 ff.

[14] See P Atiyah, *The Rise and Fall of Freedom of Contract* (Oxford, Oxford University Press, 1979) 35; with regard to US law cf G Alexander, 'The Limits of Freedom of Contract in the Age of Laissez-Faire Constitutionalism' in FH Buckley (ed), *The Fall and Rise of Freedom of Contract* (Durham, Duke University Press, 1999) 25.

[15] For a discussion of the foundations of this principle see W Fikentscher, 'Vertrag und wirtschaftliche Macht' in *Festschrift für Hefermehl* (Munich, CH Beck, 1971) 41; W Flume, 'Rechtsgeschäft und Privatautonomie' in E v Caemmerer and E Friesenhahn (eds), *Festschrift zum 100jährigen Bestehen des Deutschen Juristentags* (Karlsruhe, CF Mueller, 1960) 135; F Rittner, 'Über das Verhältnis von Vertrag und Wettbewerb' (1988) 188 *Archiv für die civilistische Praxis* 101; F Bydlinski, *Privatautonomie und objektive Grundlagen des verpflichtenden Rechtsgeschäfts* (Vienna, Springer, 1967); L Fastrich, *Richterliche Inhaltskontrolle im Privatrecht* (Munich, CH Beck, 1992); S Lorenz, *Der Schutz vor dem unerwünschten Vertrag* (Munich, CH Beck, 1997); M Wolf, *Rechtsgeschäftliche Entscheidungsfreiheit und vertraglicher Interessenausgleich* (Tübingen, Mohr Siebeck, 1970).

[16] See BVerfGE 8, 274; BVerfGE 74, 109.

but that it is substantially influenced by them.[17] The principle of freedom of contract and its limits can be based on constitutional law in a narrow sense in many Member States.[18] With regard to German law there is intense discussion and manifold solutions concerning the influence of (constitutionally protected) fundamental rights on (statutory) private law rules. For the following analysis it is sufficient to highlight the prevailing opinion under German law.[19] According to this opinion, rules of private law must be interpreted in accordance with the fundamental rights of the Constitution. Thus, general clauses in statutory law are the main gateway for the fundamental rights in the Constitution to influence private law. By way of representative example, one can point to cases of surety bonds of family members which are entered into due to an emotional commitment of the family member and which may result in ruinous liability of the family member. The Federal Constitutional Court held that in those situations the infringement of the self-determination of the family member granting the surety may render a contract contrary to public policy and thus void under § 138(1) BGB.[20] In those cases a general clause in private law (§ 138(1) BGB) provides the way for the application of the fundamental rights.

Moreover, those cases reveal a second aspect of the influence of constitutional law on statutory law. The fundamental rights as protected by the Constitution may also include the duty of the state to protect this right of the citizen against other citizens. Thus, the interpretation of statutory private law in accordance with constitutional rights has to consider this duty of the state, too. As a result, under German law the statutory private law rules have to be interpreted in accordance with the freedom of contract of the citizens; this freedom must not be infringed by the state or by other citizens.

Moreover, the Member States' private law is also heavily influenced by EU treaty law.[21] These fundamental freedoms prohibit all constraints of the protected freedom from Member State regulation, including private law rules.[22] As a result, there is a duty to interpret national private law in accordance with EU primary law, which includes the interpretation in accordance with the fundamental freedoms of EU law.[23]

[17] With regard to European private law cf D Friedmann and D Barak-Erez (eds), *Human Rights in Private Law* (Oxford, Hart Publishing, 2001); G Vettori, *Diritto Dei Contratti e 'Costituzione' Europea* (Milan, Giuffrè, 2005); O Cherednychenko, 'EU Fundamental Rights, EC Fundamental Freedoms and Private Law' (2006) 4 *European Review of Private Law* 23 ff; O Cherednychenko, 'Fundamental Rights and Contract Law' (2006) 2 *European Review of Contract Law* 489 ff; for a comparison of the functioning of fundamental rights in private law of certain Member States cf G Brüggemeier, A Colombi Ciacchi and G Comandé (eds), *Fundamental Rights and Private Law in the European Union, I. A Comparative Analysis*, 2nd edn (Cambridge, Cambridge University Press, 2010).

[18] Coester-Waltjen (n 9) 42.

[19] For discussion see C-W Canaris, *Grundrechte und Privatrecht* (Berlin, de Gruyter, 1999).

[20] See BVerfGE 89, 214.

[21] Likewise Grundmann et al (eds) (n 3) 9.

[22] For a discussion of the influence of EU fundamental freedoms on private law see T Körber, *Grundfreiheiten und Privatrecht* (Tübingen, Mohr Siebeck, 2004).

[23] See C Herresthal, *Rechtsfortbildung im Europarechtlichen Bezugsrahmen* (Munich, CH Beck, 2006) 250 ff.

D. EU Law Prevailing Over Member States' Law

The last basic assumption for the following analysis is concerned with the relationship between Member States' law and EU law. In general, primary and secondary EU law prevails over Member States' law, which is also true for the Member States' constitutional law. Nevertheless, according to the German Federal Constitutional Court this general rule does not apply if the essence of fundamental rights protected by the German Constitution would be affected by EU law. Thus, EU law does not prevail over an entrenched, unchangeable core of those rights protected by Article 79(3) of the German Constitution. Since this provision is interpreted in a very narrow sense, secondary EU law has considerable power to restrict substantially the constitutional guarantee of freedom of contract. Thus, the German Constitution is no longer an effective means to prevent EU law from limiting freedom of contract. As a result, EU law is decisive for limits of freedom of contract within the area of the EU and the internal market.[24] In addition, the bulk of current regulation in the Member States' private law has its origins in EU law.[25] Taking this into consideration, there is a strong argument that the protection of freedom of contract at the level of EU law is of paramount importance today. It has replaced the protection of this principle by the Member States' constitutions in terms of relevance. This is especially true with regard to those limits that derive from the economic constitution.

III. The Two Elements of Constitutionalisation of Fundamental Rights

With regard to the title of this chapter, the term 'constitutionalisation' needs some clarification in the international context. In German law as well as in European private law this term is used with various meanings. In this chapter, the term is used to indicate the normative effect of the (unwritten) principle of freedom of contract on primary EU law. The constitutionalisation of this principle contains two aspects:[26] a downward perspective and an upward perspective.[27]

First, the downward perspective is concerned with the extension of constitutional rules, especially fundamental rights, into private law or – more generally –

[24] See Grundmann et al (n 3) 3.

[25] Likewise ibid, 5.

[26] For further discussion of this term see T Barkhuysen and S Lindbergh (eds), *Constitutionalisation of Private Law* (Leiden, Martinus Nijhoff Publishers, 2006).

[27] Besides, there is a discussion about the status and formation of a European constitution as such; for example, whether the treaties and the primary law outside the treaties already qualify as a European constitution in the traditional sense, since the Treaty provides legitimacy to and the control of the exertion of Union powers and thus constitutes somehow a constitution, cf C Calliess (ed), *Verfassungswandel im Europäischen Staaten- und Verfassungsverbund* (Tübingen, Mohr Siebeck, 2007).

into non-constitutional legislation (simple Acts of Parliament). The most important means to reach this result is the interpretation of Acts of Parliament in light of and consistent with the constitutional rule. Thereby constitutional rules and the fundamental principles enshrined in the constitution are enforced in private law. This holds especially true for the constitutionalisation of private law in Germany. The interpretation in light of and consistent with constitutional principles is the most powerful instrument for enforcing the values these principles embrace in private law.[28] The reform of English company law was partly based on this assumption too.[29] In general, this meaning of constitutionalisation of fundamental principles is also accepted with regard to European private law.[30]

Second, there is an upward perspective. According to this viewpoint, the specific content of the most significant values and principles in a legal system, especially constitutional values and principles, derives in part from rules outside the realm of constitutional law.[31] The reason is that fundamental values and principles are generalised in very abstract rules on the constitutional level. The inferior rules of non-constitutional private law provide for the differentiation of those values and principles. Thus, the process of substantiation of constitutional fundamental principles and values by non-constitutional law has an effect on the content of the constitutional rules. This dynamic process resembles the paradigm of the process of substantiation of general clauses: the more precise rule is influenced by the abstract principle laid down in the general clause and the substantiation of the general clause by the more precise rule relates back to the content of the general rule and the principle covered therein. This may be called a 'feedback mechanism'. One example of this process of substantiation is the constitutionalisation of freedom of contract in the legal orders of the Member States.

These two elements of the term 'constitutionalisation' apply also with regard to the principle of freedom of contract in European primary law. The first element is concerned with the requirement of protection of the still-unwritten principle of freedom of contract in primary EU law. The guarantee of freedom of contract on the level of primary EU law sets the material standard for secondary EU law. As mentioned above, regarding the level of European integration and the broad impact of EU law on the Member States' private law, there is a strong need for an

[28] See G Schuppert and C Bumke, *Die Konstitutionalisierung der Rechtsordnung* (Baden-Baden, Nomos, 2000) 9 ff.

[29] See 'Modern Company Law – For a Competitive Economy – Developing a Framework – A Consultation Document from the Company Law Review Steering Group' (DTI Pub URN 00/656 March 2000) 8, 151 ff.

[30] See B Hess, 'Anmerkung' (2006) 61 *Juristenzeitung* 540 f (constitutionalisation in the sense of *Überformung* of European private law by European fundamental rights); cf with regard to the development of EU law C Möllers, 'Verfassungsgebende Gewalt – Verfassung – Konstitutionalisierung.Begriffe der Verfassung in Europa' in A von Bogdandy (ed), *Europäisches Verfassungsrecht: Theoretische und dogmatische Grundzüge*, 2nd edn (Berlin, Springer, 2009) 59 ff; A Colombi Ciacchi, 'The Constitutionalization of European Contract Law: Judicial Convergence and Social Justice' (2006) 2 *European Review of Contract Law* 167 ff.

[31] In this sense E-J Mestmäcker, 'Einleitung' in U Immenga, E-J Mestmäcker and J Basedow (eds), *EG-Wettbewerbsrecht*, 1st edn (Munich, CH Beck, 1997–98) paras 1–9 (constitutionalisation of personal liberties in EU law).

independent supranational regime embracing the principle of freedom of contract. Mere reliance on the private law of the Member States' legal system and the freedom of contract anchored therein is no longer sufficient.[32] The principle of freedom of contract needs to be established at the level of primary EU law as the lodestar for the EU legislature when enacting secondary EU law, and for the European courts when interpreting secondary EU law.

Conversely, detailed rules of secondary EU law substantiate the (unwritten) principles of primary EU law. This is also true for the principle of freedom of contract. It relates back to the general principle, substantiates its content and should provide for the fundamental value as 'law in action'. Nevertheless, its limits are still determined by primary EU law, even though its content needs to be concretised by secondary EU law.

IV. Freedom of Contract

A. The Scope of Freedom of Contract

The core content of freedom of contract is mostly uncontroversial.[33] The principle embraces the freedom to enter into a contract, the freedom to select the contractual partner and the freedom of classification and content.

B. The Significance of Freedom of Contract in the Legal System

i. The Fundamental Means of Self-Determination of One's Legal Affairs

The main function of freedom of contract is to enable the parties to shape their legal affairs independently.[34] Moreover, the result of this self-determined organisation of legal affairs – contracts and their agreed-upon content – is respected and enforced by the state. Thus, the parties to a contract have the opportunity and right to pursue their personal preferences and aims when entering into the contract and shaping its contents. In principle, there should be no state interference with private preferences; there should be no constraint by the state to pursue officially determined preferences. In addition, the state has to provide for the means to enable the parties to pursue their preferences; the parties to the contract need more than merely a formal grant of the right, they also need the material chance to pursue their interests.

[32] Likewise F Rittner, 'Die wirtschaftliche Ordnung der EG und das Privatrecht' (1990) 45 *Juristenzeitung* 838, 841; U Immenga, 'Editorial' (1993) 4 *Europäische Zeitschrift für Wirtschaftsrecht* 169.

[33] See Basedow (n 3) 905 f.

[34] See A Bruns, 'Die Vertragsfreiheit und ihre Grenzen in Europa und den USA' (2007) 62 *Juristenzeitung* 385, 390.

ii. Prerequisite for the Functioning of a Market Economy

As is generally known, the competence to pursue one's own preferences is the fundamental prerequisite for the functioning of a liberal market economy. The market provides for the opportunity to exchange information and to pursue personal preferences without coordination by the state. Thus, freedom of contract and the establishment of a market economy are closely related.[35] Markets and trade on markets are nothing other than elementary emanations of a civil society and of freedom of contract. Mandatory regulation is a severe interference with the free market and with freedom of contract because individual preferences are no longer exclusively decisive for the content of a legal relationship.

iii. The Evolutionary Potential of the Law

Finally, the evolutionary potential of the law depends strongly on the principle of freedom of contract. With freedom of contract in private law, the parties may react to changes in the economic, social and political order by adapting their legal relationships. They may amend their legal relationships, reacting to a change of the (legal) order or of their preferences; likewise they may enter into new legal relationships. Freedom of contract provides for the necessary flexibility with regard to the content and the adaptation of legal relationships. This is the main advantage of dispositive rules in private law compared to mandatory rules. A mandatory rule may not be as well adapted to the changed structure of the area it seeks to regulate; the balancing of interests and legal preferences underlying the mandatory rule may quickly become obsolete owing to a change of circumstances. Regulation by the national or European legislature requires time, if the EU legislature reacts at all. This may not be the case because the envisaged changes may affect only a few Member States. Contractual parties usually react more precisely and quickly than the legislature.

C. The Protection of Freedom of Contract in EU Law

Even though there is a broad consensus that freedom of contract should be the guiding principle in European private law,[36] and that freedom of contract is part

[35] See C-W Canaris, 'Wandlungen des Schuldvertragsrechts – Tendenzen zu seiner Materialisierung' (2000) 200 *Archiv für die civilistische Praxis* 273, 292 ff; E-J Mestmäcker, 'Über die normative Kraft privatrechtlicher Verträge' (1964) 19 *Juristenzeitung* 441, 443; W Zöllner, 'Die politische Rolle des Privatrechts' (1988) 28 *Juristische Schulung* 329, 330; E Hoppmann, 'Moral und Marktsystem' (1990) 41 *Jahrbuch für die Ordnung von Wirtschaft und Gesellschaft (Ordo)* 3, 5; D Reuter, 'Freiheitsethik und Privatrecht' in F Bydlinski and T Mayer-Maly (eds), *Die ethischen Grundlagen des Privatrechts* (Vienna, Springer, 1994) 111.

[36] See KJ Hopt, 'Disclosure Rules as a Primary Tool for Fostering Party Autonomy' in Grundmann et al (eds) (n 3) 251 f; Advocate General Trstnjak in Case C-331/05 *Internationaler Hilfsfonds v Kommission* [2007] ECR I-5475, para 93 (Union legal order and the legal orders of the Member States are based on the ides of freedom and individual responsibility); Advocate General Ruiz-Jarabo Colomer in Case C-106/03 *Vedial v Harmonisierungsamt für den Binnenmarkt* [2004] ECR I-9573 para 28.

of the general principles of the European Union,[37] it is not explicitly mentioned in the Treaties. Before the enactment of the Lisbon Treaty, there were two different approaches to justify freedom of contract being part of primary EU law. First, freedom of contract may be derived from the protection of free movement within the European Union. Free movement requires free choice of individuals and of enterprises on both the consumer and the supply sides of the market. Therefore, free movement calls for freedom of contract.[38] As a result, EU law must protect the freedom to enter into contracts as well as the freedom to shape their contents from discrimination and other restrictions imposed by Member States' law. According to this opinion, the economic rationale of European integration is to be extended to comprise freedom of contract across the Member States' borders within the internal market.

According to the second approach, freedom of contract is included in the notion of a free market economy as well as in the general freedom of action as part of the general principles of European primary law. In general, freedom of contract is part of primary EU law, and its content is derived from the constitutional traditions of the Member States.[39]

The European Court of Justice (since the entry into force of the Lisbon Treaty in 2009 known as the Court of Justice and hereafter referred to as the CJ) first mentioned the principle of freedom of contract in the 1970s.[40] After this and until the 1990s, the CJ followed a merely descriptive approach: the CJ made descriptive references to the principle but did not develop a coherent approach to freedom of contract in EU law. In and of itself the principle of freedom of contract has never been addressed or defined in the decisions of the Court.[41] Nevertheless, the main elements of freedom of contract – freedom to enter into a contract, the freedom

[37] Likewise Micklitz (n 6) 198; Basedow (n 3) 921; Müller-Graff (n 3) 136; cf N Jansen and R Zimmermann, 'Restating the Acquis communautaire? A Critical Examination of the Principles of the Existing EC Contract Law' (2008) 71 *Modern Law Review* 505, 518 (freedom of contract is taken for granted).

[38] See Müller-Graff (n 3) 134 f; P Müller-Graff, 'Privatrecht und Europäisches Gemeinschaftsrecht' in P Müller-Graff and M Zuleeg (eds), *Staat und Wirtschaft in der EG* (Baden-Baden, Nomos, 1987) 27 f; Micklitz (n 6) 199; for critics see Basedow (n 3) 907 f; S Grundmann, 'Information, Party Autonomy and Economic Agents in European Contract Law' (2002) 39 *Common Market Law Review* 269, 277 ff; S Grundmann, 'The Concept of the Private Law Society: After 50 Years of European and European Business Law' (2008) 4 *European Review of Private Law* 553, 560 f; O Remien, *Zwingendes Vertragsrecht und Grundfreiheiten des EG-Vertrages* (Tübingen, Mohr Siebeck, 2003) 178 f.

[39] Likewise Coester-Waltjen (n 9) 42, 48; H-W Rengeling, *Grundrechtsschutz in der Europäischen Gemeinschaft* (Munich, CH Beck, 1993) 135; P von Wilmowsky, 'Der internationale Verbrauchervertrag im EG-Binnenmarkt' (1995) 4 *Zeitschrift für Europäisches Privatrecht* 735; Remien (n 38) 178.

[40] See Case C-151/78 *Sukkerfabriken Nykøbing Limiteret v Ministry of Agriculture* [1979] ECR 1, paras 19–20; for further discussions see D Laumann, *Der privatrechtliche Vertragsschluss in der Rechtsprechung des Europäischen Gerichtshofes* (Frankfurt, Peter Lang, 2005) 68; Basedow (n 3) 911 f.

[41] Likewise Basedow (n 3) 911. Nevertheless, there are some irritating references of the CJ to the *Member States' guarantee* of this principle, cf Case C-421/05 *City Motors Groep v Citroën Belux* [2007] ECR I-653, para 24; Case C-125/05 *VW-Audi Forhandlerforeningen obo Vulcan Silkeborg v Skandinavisk Motor Co* [2006] ECR I-7637, para 47 ('the contractual freedom of the parties, as exercised under the applicable national law').

to choose the parties to a transaction, the freedom to amend the contract, freedom of form, and the freedom to design the content of the contract – are acknowledged by the CJ.[42] Recently there have been some references to tangible interpretative principles derived from a normative understanding of contractual freedom, often with regard to what were then Articles 81 and 82 EC (Articles 101 and 102 TFEU).[43]

Thus, irrespective of the source of the principle of freedom of contract in EU law, the principle gives the parties the right to shape the content of their contract in an international setting.[44] As mentioned above, those privately arranged relationships require recognition by a legal system. To sum up, there was no comprehensive safeguard of freedom of contract in primary EU law.[45]

The same is true after the enactment of the Treaty of Lisbon. There are, of course, some safeguards in the Treaty because the Charter of Fundamental Rights of the European Union[46] has become binding EU law[47] and of equal rank as the Treaties. Nevertheless, the fundamental principle of freedom of contract is still not explicitly mentioned in the Charter despite its fundamental significance for a market economy in the legal order of all Member States and its guarantee by EU primary law. In Article 6 of the Charter the general right to liberty pertains to the principle of personal liberty (that is, physical movement).[48] Only certain aspects of freedom of contract are protected in the provisions of the Charter: Article 12 provides for the right to assembly, Article 15 for the right to engage in work, Article 16 guarantees the freedom to conduct a business in accordance with EU law and national laws and practices,[49] and Article 17 guarantees the right to property.

[42] See Case C-499/04 *Werhof v Freeway Traffic Systems* [2006] ECR I-2397, para 23 (a contract is characterised by the principle of freedom of the parties to arrange their own affairs, according to which, in particular, parties are free to enter into obligations with each other); Case C-240/97 *Spain v Commission* [1999] ECR I-6571, paras 99 ff (right of parties to amend contracts concluded by them is based on the principle of contractual freedom and cannot, therefore, be limited in the absence of EU rules imposing specific restrictions in that regard); Joined Cases C-90/90 & C-91/90 *Jean Neu v Sécrétaire d'Etat à l'Agriculture* [1991] ECR I-3617, para 13 (right to freely choose the transaction partner).

[43] See Case T-24/90 *Automec v Commission* [1992] ECR II-2223, paras 50–52 ('freedom of contract must remain the rule').

[44] See Grundmann et al (eds) (n 3) 5.

[45] For a different opinion see Basedow (n 3) 909, who, nevertheless, admits that there are 'extensive limitations' on the freedom of contract in primary EU law.

[46] Charter of Fundamental Rights of the European Union [2000] OJ C364/01.

[47] See Art 6(1) Treaty of Lisbon amending the Treaty on the European Union and the Treaty establishing the European Community [2007] OJ C306/1, 13.

[48] See N Bernsdorff, 'Artikel 6 Recht auf Freiheit und Sicherheit' in J Meyer (ed), *Kommentar zur Charta der Grundrechte der Europäischen Union*, 3rd edn (Baden-Baden, Nomos, 2011) Art 6, para 11.

[49] For the relevance of this right see O Remien, 'Europäisches Privatrecht als Verfassungsfrage' (2005) 6 *Europarecht* 699, 716; Bernsdorff (n 48) Art 16, para 12.

V. Structural Deficits in EU Law Endangering Freedom of Contract

European integration comes along with an extensive transfer of regulation from the Member State level to the EU level. In the light of this, restrictions on freedom of contract principally result from a structural deficit. Regulation remaining at Member State level is controlled by the fundamental freedoms of EU law, and regulation on the level of the European Union – secondary EU law in directives and regulations. Both levels of regulation generate a new problem: how is freedom of contract to be protected in the light of EU regulation and the influence of EU law on Member States' regulation?

Some check on secondary legislation which may restrain freedom of contract results from primary EU law. The 'principle of an open market economy with free competition' (Article 119 TFEU, ex-Article 4(1) EC) tends to prohibit any restriction of cross-border activities by the European Union without due justification. Limitations on freedom of contract by EU regulation in general are addressed by Article 345 TFEU (ex-Article 295 EC), which relates to Member States' competence to regulate property ownership. Nevertheless, there is no general answer to the question of which criteria are applicable and which remedies are available if the European Union intervenes in the market economy using regulatory means.

Taking into consideration the above-mentioned functions of freedom of contract,[50] the scope of this principle is crucial for striking the balance between an open market economy and regulation on the level of EU law. While the principle is acknowledged as a fundamental right in EU law and as a principle of primary EU law, it is still given insufficient effect. According to the two elements of the constitutionalisation of a fundamental principle,[51] freedom of contract needs to have a substantial impact on secondary EU law on the one hand; on the other hand, secondary EU law needs to contribute to the content of the principle in primary EU law.

With regard to this process of fleshing out freedom of contract in EU law and its current deficits, the key questions are how far the insufficient protection of freedom of contract on the level of EU law is predetermined by structural deficiencies of the EU legal system and to what extent the constraints of freedom of contract in EU law are due to EU regulation. In other words, to what extent is the process of substantiation of freedom of contract in EU law determined by the structure of the EU legal system, and does the EU legal system provide for more or less protection of freedom of contract compared to Member States' legal systems?

In the following sections, several structural deficiencies of the EU legal system will be identified. These deficiencies result in a weak position of freedom of

[50] See above section IV.B.
[51] See above section III.

contract in EU law and insufficient limits for its restriction by the EU legislature and judiciary.[52] While the academic literature has addressed individual threats to freedom of contract,[53] deficiencies resulting from the underlying structure of EU legislation and judicial interpretation have not been analysed so far. Nevertheless, such deficiencies may result in substantial and arbitrary restrictions of freedom of contract in EU law because they do not follow from any consideration or balancing of the interests at hand. Instead, the outcome is pre-determined by the structure of EU legislation and adjudication.

A. The Insufficient Substantiation of Freedom of Contract

i. Freedom of Contract as a Fundamental Right in EU Law

The status of freedom of contract in EU law is a constitutional question.[54] Thus, the first apparent structural deficit is the insufficient substantiation and concretisation of freedom of contract as a fundamental right in primary EU law. In general, fundamental rights at the level of EU law have not gained the same importance as an effective means to limit the EU legislature, the European judiciary, and the national legislature[55] when compared to the role of fundamental rights in Member States' law.[56] The situation with regard to freedom of contract – up to now and even after the enactment of the Treaty of Lisbon – is exacerbated because it has virtually no textual basis in the Treaties.[57]

a. Insufficient Protection by the Court of Justice and in Secondary EU Law

The principle of freedom of contract still lacks a precise scope in EU law, whereas the growing amount of EU legislation results in an increasing number of limitations on freedom of contract.[58] Nevertheless, the content of freedom of contract

[52] Whilst the structure and the characteristics of primary EU law are certainly the focus of the analysis, nevertheless the experience and the findings of the discussion of this issue in the Member States' law provide for valuable insights. There is no reason to ignore these findings of the Member States' legal systems; nevertheless, for the latter opinion see Grundmann et al (eds) (n 3) 10.

[53] Cf eg W Canaris, 'Verfassungs- und europarechtliche Aspekte der Vertragsfreiheit in der Privatrechtsgesellschaft' in P Badura and R Scholz (eds), *Festschrift für Peter Lerche* (Munich, CH Beck, 1993) 873 (regarding Directive 99/44/EC of the European Parliament and of the Council of 25 May 1999 on certain aspects of the sale of consumer goods and associated guarantees [1999] OJ L171/12.

[54] Likewise Grundmann et al (eds) (n 3) 3.

[55] The Member States are bound by the fundamental rights of primary EU law 'when they implement Community rules'. See Case C-292/97 *Karlsson* [2000] ECR I-2737, para 37; Case C-2/92 *R v Ministry of Agriculture ex p Bostock* [1994] ECR I-955, para 16; Case C-260/89 *Elliniki Radiophonia Tiléorassi v Pliroforissis* [1991] ECR I-2925, paras 42–45; Herresthal (n 23) 68 ff.

[56] Likewise U Di Fabio, 'Wettbewerbsprinzip und Verfassung' (2007) 3 *Zeitschrift für Wettbewerbsrecht* 264, 274 f.

[57] See above section IV.C and Grundmann et al (eds) (n 3) 10.

[58] See C Kirchner, 'Wandlungen oder Erosion der Privatautonomie: Rechtsvergleichende, rechtsmethodische und rechtspolitische Anmerkungen' in K Riesenhuber and Y Nishitani (eds), *Wandlungen oder Erosion der Privatautonomie?* (Berlin, de Gruyter, 2007) 313 (process of erosion with regard to freedom of contract on the level of EU law).

in EU law still requires a more precise shape, especially in terms of precise definitions.[59]

As mentioned above, the fundamental right to pursue a business present in primary EU law incorporates the principle of freedom of contract.[60] Nevertheless, the latter right has not been sufficiently and materially substantiated by the CJ, even though one may identify the most important elements in its decisions.[61] Thus, there are no precise definitions of the content of the principle. For example, there is a random distinction between the freedom to enter a contract and the freedom to shape its content. Therefore, the outstanding significance of the latter is not sufficiently emphasised by the CJ. Moreover, the qualification of freedom of contract as a negative or personal liberty (defensive right) and its function of protecting the *status negativus* (the right to be protected from the state) is not yet sufficiently stressed. The duty of the European Union to protect freedom of contract of EU citizens with regard to possible intrusion by other parties has not been wholly accepted either.

Because of this lack of substantiation freedom of contract carries only marginal weight in cases of conflict with other fundamental principles and when being balanced against these interests. Moreover, the particular weight of freedom of contract as the fundamental principle in a market economy in the case of a balancing of interests has not been stressed by the CJ yet. Likewise there is so far no clarity as to the requirements of justification the EU legislator has to meet when restricting freedom of contract.

Furthermore, there are no precise mechanisms that protect freedom of contract from restrictions by the legislature, as there is no sufficient analytical separation between the scope of the right and its legitimate restrictions. While freedom of contract as a constitutional right is well protected in the Member States' law against abrogation by particular protection mechanisms, similar mechanisms are still missing in EU law. Thus, according to the CJ, restrictions may be justified even by reference to social functions.[62]

As a result, there is as yet neither a coherent concept of freedom of contract nor a strong mechanism against its undue restriction in EU law.[63] Freedom of contract

[59] For general criticism of the CJ adjudication on fundamental rights see T Kingreen, 'Artikel 52 Grundrechte-Charta' in C Calliess and M Ruffert (eds), *EUV/AEUV*, 4th edn (Munich, CH Beck, 2011) paras 48, 56, 71; M Nettesheim, 'Zur grundrechtlichen Prüfdichte des EuGH' (1995) 3 *Europäische Zeitschrift für Wirtschaftsrecht* 106 ff; M Ruffert, 'Grundrecht der Berufsfreiheit' in D Ehlers (ed), *Europäische Grundrechte und Grundfreiheiten*, 3rd edn (Berlin, de Gruyter, 2009) § 16.3, para 39; for a different but unconvincing approach, see B Heiderhoff, 'Vertrauen versus Vertragsfreiheit im europäischen Verbrauchervertragsrecht' (2003) 4 *Zeitschrift für Europäisches Privatrecht* 769, 778 (EU law solely intends the protection of cross-border party autonomy).

[60] See above section IV.C.

[61] See above section IV.C. For a different opinion see Basedow (n 3) 913 (comprehensive recognition in the jurisprudence of the CJ).

[62] With regard to the right of freedom to pursue trade or professional activities see Case 44/79 *Hauer v Rheinland-Pfalz* [1979] ECR 3727, para 7; Case 234/85 *Freiburg v Keller* [1986] ECR 2897, para 8.

[63] See Kirchner (n 58) 310 (lack of a constitutional system of values that is also binding for private law); for the opposite opinion see Grundmann et al (eds) (n 3) 7 (without further explanations).

is still protected by the fundamental market freedoms extending across the Member States.[64] But the scope of protection by the fundamental freedoms is very limited, because restrictions may be justified by the public interests, a very broad and unpredictable concept of possible justification. Besides, the wide range of EU policies in the Treaties which an EU legislator has to consider increases the scope of EU action and discretion up to the border of arbitrariness. Thus, there is an obvious need for the CJ to confirm the existence of freedom of contract as a fundamental right in the European legal order by a precise substantiation of its content and of its legitimate restrictions. Those deficits on the EU level are key for the protection of freedom of contract in the internal market; the Member States' protection of the principle is no longer sufficient due to the amount and intensity of EU regulation. Furthermore, areas of law in which the protection of freedom of contract by the Member States is still ensured[65] are continuously reduced by EU legislation.

The same is true with regard to the European legislature – the picture is unclear at best. There are some references in EU legislation affirming individual responsibility and acknowledging freedom of contract, especially in recitals of directives.[66] Also, multiple references to the dangers of an abuse of freedom of contract can be found. In those directives and regulations, the recital makes reference to freedom of contract and points out that the rule under consideration is a necessary exception or intended to prohibit the abuse of freedom of contract. Nevertheless, EU private law regulation contains almost exclusively mandatory provisions and, thus, substantial restrictions of freedom of contract.[67] The substantial weight of conflicting interests, such as consumer protection and non-discrimination, contributes substantially to this.

b. The Lack of Judicial Review as a Main Reason for the Insufficient Protection

The main reason for the insufficient substantiation of freedom of contract in primary EU law lies in the lack of primary judicial review of secondary EU law with regard to the violation of fundamental rights.[68] Whereas national constitutional law has developed subtle case-by-case rules for legitimate restrictions of freedom of contract, those rules are still lacking in EU law. As a result, case-law from the European courts on freedom of contract is very rare.[69]

[64] See Müller-Graff (n 3) 131; P Müller-Graff, 'Europäisches Gemeinschaftsrecht und Privatrecht – das Privatrecht der europäischen Integration' (1993) 46 *Neue Juristische Wochenschrift* 13, 14.

[65] Eg the Member States' legislation outside the scope of application of primary and secondary EU law.

[66] See Recital no 8 of Directive 1999/44/EC of the European Parliament and of the Council of 25 May 1999 on certain aspects of the sale of consumer goods and associated guarantees [1999] OJ L171/12.

[67] See Basedow (n 3) 903.

[68] Those instruments in German law include the constitutional complaint and the constitutional review of statutes by the constitutional court. For an overview of these instruments see M Sachs, *Verfassungsprozessrecht*, 3rd edn (Stuttgart, Mohr Siebeck, 2010).

[69] See Micklitz (n 6) 199.

The TFEU provides only the reference for a preliminary ruling (Article 267), infringement procedure (Article 258) and proceedings for annulment (Article 263). The reference for a preliminary ruling results in the interpretation of EU law in an isolated case. Up to now, the CJ has refrained from making fundamental rights more effective through preliminary rulings. The procedure requires national courts to refer a question for a preliminary ruling. Moreover, the decisions of the CJ are usually very short and without substantial discussion of the issues.[70] This contributes to the vague content of freedom of contract as a legal concept in EU law.[71] The procedures under Articles 263 and 258 TFEU are limited too. Only few parties are entitled to bring an action. Individuals and legal entities may rely only on Article 263 TFEU; actions by EU institutions and Member States will largely depend on political considerations.

ii. Market Intervention: Regulated Markets

Another structural deficit is related to heavily regulated markets.[72] Regulated markets contradict an 'open market economy with free competition' (Articles 119(1), 120 TFEU). Those markets are characterised by intensive EU regulation and an approval of Member States' regulations by the European Union, and their number was extended by the recent amendments of the Treaties. Those 'discontinuities' are to the detriment of the protection of an area of personal freedom and free competition by freedom of contract. Since interferences with free competition are the rule in those markets, freedom of contract is heavily restricted. It should be mentioned that, until now, the CJ did not render any regulation in the area of the Common Agricultural Policy (Articles 38 TFEU ff) void.[73] On the contrary, the CJ has granted the EU legislature broad discretion. Thus, areas outside legitimate regulation have not yet been identified.[74]

Freedom of contract is not just limited in the exceptional case of regulated markets; there is an eminent risk that the separation of both areas is not strictly respected. Needless to say, it is possible to impose stricter limits on freedom of contract in certain areas of law for constitutional reasons. But the intrusion into freedom of contract in those heavily regulated areas may spill over to other areas

[70] For further references see KJ Hopt, 'Reform der europäischen Gerichtsbarkeit – Überlegungen zur aktuellen Reformdiskussion' (2002) 66 *Rabels Zeitschrift für ausländisches und internationales Privatrecht* 589, 598 n 31; R Streinz, 'Der "effet utile" in der Rechtsprechung des Gerichtshofes der Europäischen Gemeinschaften' in O Due, M Lutter and J Schwarze (eds), *Festschrift für Ulrich Everling* (Baden-Baden, Nomos, 1995) 1491, 1508; N Röttgen, *Die Argumentation des Europäischen Gerichtshofes: Typik, Methodik, Kritik* (diss. Bonn, 2001); with a positive connotation G Hirsch, 'Das Rechtsgespräch im EuGH' (2002) 31 *Zeitschrift für Unternehmens- und Gesellschaftsrecht* 15.

[71] For a different opinion see Micklitz (n 6) 199 (little opportunity to give the courts' opinion on the concept).

[72] See also Kirchner (n 58) 308 (process of erosion of freedom of contract caused by EU law).

[73] For criticism see also R Streinz, 'Artikel 15 Grundrechte-Charta' in R Streinz (ed), *EUV/AEUV* 2nd (Munich, CH Beck, 2012) para 5; Ruffert (n 59) § 16.3, para 3.

[74] See Case C-306/93 *SMW Winzersekt v Rheinland-Pfalz* [1994] ECR I-5555, para 22; Case C-44/94 *R v Minister of Agriculture ex p National Federation of Fishermen's Organisations* [1995] ECR I-3115, para 57.

of the law. Instead of narrowly drawn exceptions, those areas may result in broadening the scope for restrictions of freedom of contract in EU law in general. For example, the proportionality test with regard to restrictions on freedom of contract that applies in the context of regulated markets is less strict, and therefore needs to be distinguished from the general proportionality test applied in the context of unregulated markets. However, this distinction has not been made by the CJ yet.

iii. Harmonisation Measures

Another structural deficit is the missing link between the concept of internal market and the principle of freedom of contract. Market-building through harmonisation of the Member States' laws implies only the need for common rules in the internal market and makes no assumption about the quality of the common rules. There is no link between harmonisation and protection of autonomy of parties to a contract thus far.[75] Thus, harmonisation factually reduces freedom of contract and results in potential welfare losses due to inflexible regulation based on the knowledge available. The quality of a uniform rule is, therefore, not directly addressed by the CJ or the Commission either.

One major policy goal of the European Union is to extend freedom of contract across the internal market. Nevertheless, the European Union relies heavily on regulatory action as a means to reach this aim.[76] The reason is the rule of exemption,[77] created by the CJ. Whereas generally a national restriction is justified if it serves a legitimate requirement, such justification of Member State regulation is excluded if the EU legislature has harmonised the area of law, creating a binding common standard across the EU. Therefore, the subject matter is regulated at the level of EU law (harmonising directives) to overcome obstacles to freedom of contract across the European Union created by Member State regulation. The result is a transfer of regulatory requirements from national level to the EU level.[78]

This process is accompanied by an obvious risk that has materialised. Extending freedom of contract across the borders by EU regulation may result in substantial restrictions. For example, mandatory regulation in the area of consumer protection is limiting freedom of contract in the internal market. However, the cross-border liberalisation is flanked by restricting regulation; thus, the harmonisation of the Member States' law in fact reduces freedom of contract. Moreover, there is a strong argument for potential welfare losses due to inflexible regulation based on the (limited) knowledge available. The quality of the uniform rule has been – up to now – not directly addressed by the CJ or the Commission.

[75] Likewise S Weatherill, 'Justifying Limits to Party Autonomy in the Internal Market' in Grundmann et al (eds) (n 3) 175.

[76] See Müller-Graff (n 3) 146 ff.

[77] See Case 261/81 *Rau Lebensmittelwerke v De Smedt* [1982] ECR 396, para 12, with further references.

[78] See Müller-Graff (n 3) 147.

iv. Insufficient Substantiation and the Rule of Law

Furthermore, the formal[79] and material requirements that may justify a restriction of the fundamental freedoms as well as of the fundamental rights are not sufficiently substantiated under EU law. The CJ has not established coherent principles in its case-law with regard to the balancing of the general interest against 'the limitations justified on grounds of public policy, public security or public health'.[80] The same is true for the 'public interest' of the European Union[81] or the Member States, which may justify restrictions of fundamental rights in primary EU law.

The same applies to the proportionality test. The proportionality principle is embedded in several Treaty provisions (Articles 5(4) TEU, 36, 45 III, 52(1), 102 lit (a), 106(2) TFEU), but there is no adequate outline of this test in EU (case) law.[82] Usually, the CJ balances the interests of the policy pursued by the EU legislature on the one hand against freedom of contract on the other hand. In doing so it prioritises one of the interests and then considers whether the restriction of the other interest is justified or whether the EU legislature made an obvious error in their balancing.[83] This vague test merely eliminates absolutely inappropriate limitations of freedom of contract.[84] Moreover, the absolute protection of the core of fundamental rights like freedom of contract has not been elaborated yet, but is blurred by the proportionality test.[85] Without doubt, this is one of the main reasons for the small number of cases in which the CJ held a constraint of a fundamental right to be unlawful. Of course the Commission may enforce the proportionality test by

[79] For the vague requirements regarding the provision of legality see D Ehlers, 'Allgemeine Lehren' in D Ehlers (ed), *Europäische Grundrechte und Grundfreiheiten*, 3rd edn (Berlin, de Gruyter, 2009) § 14, para 67 (fundamental rights), § 7, para 92 (fundamental freedoms).

[80] See Case C-109/04 *Kranemann v Nordrhein-Westfalen* [2005] ECR I-2421, para 33; Case C-55/94 *Gebhard v Consiglio dell'Ordine* [1995] ECR I-4156, para 37; Case C-208/00 *Überseering v Nordic Construction Co* [2002] ECR I-9919, para 92 (overriding requirements relating to the general interest 'may, in certain circumstances and subject to certain conditions, justify restrictions on freedom of establishment'). For overriding requirements relating to the general interest, see C Herresthal, 'Vertragsrecht' in K Langenbucher (ed), *Europarechtliche Bezüge des Privatrechts* (Baden-Baden, Nomos, 2005) § 2, para 58 (besides others protection of the interests of creditors, minority shareholders, employees and even the taxation authorities); Müller-Graff, Artikel 15 EGV, in R Streinz (n 73), para 107 f.

[81] Case 5/88 *Wachauf v Bundesamt für Ernährung* [1989] ECR 2609, para 18; Case C-292/97 *Karlsson* [2000] ECR I-2737, para 45.

[82] Likewise Ehlers (n 79) § 7, para 109 f 96, § 14 para 71; Bernsdorff (n 48), Art 15, para 18; T von Danwitz, 'Der Grundsatz der Verhältnismäßigkeit im Gemeinschaftsrecht' (2003) 9 *Europäisches Wirtschafts- und Steuerrecht (EWS)* 393, 395 ff; in detail O Koch, *Der Grundsatz der Verhältnismäßigkeit in der Rechtsprechung des Gerichtshofs der Europäischen Gemeinschaften* (Berlin, Duncker & Humblot, 2003). For an example regarding the adjudication of the European courts see Case C-22/94 *Irish Farmers Association v Minister for Agriculture* [1997] ECR I-1809, para 27.

[83] See I Pernice, 'Gemeinschaftsverfassung und Grundrechtsschutz – Grundlagen, Bestand und Perspektiven' (1990) 43 *Neue Juristische Wochenschrift* 2409, 2415 f; Ruffert (n 59) § 16.3, paras 37 ff.

[84] For a justification of this broad limitation referring to the complexity of the legislative process see Case C-233/94 *Germany v European Parliament* [1997] ECR I-2405, paras 54 ff.

[85] See ECJ, 13.12.1979, Case 44/79 (Hauer), 1979, ECR 3727 para 5; see also I Pernice and F Meyer, 'Nach Art 6 EUV' in E Grabitz and M Hilf (eds), *Das Recht der Europäischen Union*, 40th edn (Munich, CH Beck, 2009) para 305.

recourse to the action for annulment (Article 263 TFEU).[86] Despite this, the level of protection of freedom of contract under EU law is a far cry from that provided by the Member States.[87]

Furthermore, EU law lacks a concept analogous to the so-called concept of 'practical congruency' [*praktische Konkordanz*] found in German law[88] – the fair balance of fundamental freedoms and fundamental rights involved in a case.[89] Even though the CJ states that the exercise of fundamental rights can and must be reconciled with the exercise of the fundamental freedoms of the Treaty,[90] the content of this obligation to solve the conflict of fundamental rights[91] is rather unclear.

As a result, there is no effective judicial review of the EU legislation, and there is no effective balancing of interests where freedom of contract is restricted.[92]

B. The Structural Weakness of Fundamental Freedoms and Freedom of Contract

i. Individual Freedom v Social Regulation

Another deficit relates to the structural weakness of fundamental freedoms and freedom of contract compared to social standards. This weakness originates from the differences between the European economic constitution and the welfare state aspects of EU law.

First, the 'open market economy with free competition' requires and fosters cross-border transactions, cross-border competition and freedom of contract within the internal market. Thus, the market approach is closely linked with cross-border transactions. Social standards provide for substantive rules that apply *without* the requirement of a cross-border transaction in the Member States.

Furthermore, there is a functional difference. The content of the European economic constitution, at least where it does not concern the competence to

[86] Case C-68/95 *T Port v Bundesanstalt für Landwirtschaft* [1996] ECR I-6065, para 49.

[87] For a different opinion see BVerfGE 102, 147, 165 f. The Court referred to this claim as a residual measure for the protection of fundamental rights. Thus, the essentially equal protection of fundamental values under EU law, as compared with the German Constitution, was affirmed by the Federal Constitutional Court.

[88] The same term is used by Streinz (n 73), Art 26 AEUV, para 36; and Ruffert (n 59), Art 2 EGV, para 10.

[89] For the resulting legal uncertainty see Ehlers (n 79) § 7, para 86; cf also § 14, para 47.

[90] C-112/00 *Schmidberger v Austria* [2003] ECR I-5659; C-265/95 *Commission v France* [1997] ECR I-6959.

[91] See Case 5/73 *Balkan-Import-Export v Hauptzollamt Berlin-Packhof* [1973] ECR 1091, para 24; Case 29/77 *SA Roquette Frères v French State* [1977] ECR 1835, paras 29–31; Case 139/79 *Maizena v Council* [1980] ECR 3393, para 23; Case C-280/93 *Germany v Council* [1994] ECR I-4973, para 47; Case C-44/94 *R v Minister of Agriculture ex p National Organisation of Fishermen's Organisations* [1995] ECR I-3115, para 37; recently Case C-557/07 *LSG-Gesellschaft zur Wahrnehmung von Leistungsschutzrechten v Tele2 Telecommunication* [2009] ECR I-1227 para 29.

[92] See also Streinz (n 73), Art 16 GR-Charta, para 4; Ruffert (n 59) § 16.3, para 37 f.

harmonise, is negative, in the sense that its rules prohibit state intervention of the European Union and of the Member States. In contrast, social standards are introduced by substantive rules into the European and national legal orders. Hence, the principles of a market economy, such as freedom of contract, may lack sufficient weight in a conflict with welfare state rules. In the balancing of interests the formal and seemingly empty principle of freedom of contract may be outweighed by substantive content of welfare state principles.[93] Thus, due to their content, market principles that safeguard the freedom of the parties, such as freedom of contract, seem to be weaker if compared to welfare state principles.[94]

To be clear at this point, this chapter does not argue against appropriate social standards within the European Union but rather against the predetermination of the outcome of the balancing of interests and of an appreciation of values by the structure of the rules. With regard to market principles and social welfare standards, there is the risk that the latter will prevail due to their structure. Thus, the necessary general appreciation of the European welfare state values and principles of the market economy, including freedom of contract, is still missing. There is an inherent danger of expanding social standards because an effective proportionality test that includes a thorough balancing of interests is still lacking.[95] Conflicts between the principles of a free market economy and new social policies may therefore be expected.

ii. Insufficient Respect for the Structure of Member State Legal Systems

In general, EU law does not stipulate whether the Member States have to transform EU directives into national public or private law. Moreover, EU law ignores the specific structure of private law within the different Member States. This initially appears to allow Member States to implement EU law in a way that fits best with the structure of the Member States' legal systems. Nevertheless, EU rules often need to be implemented in national *private* law rules. This is especially true for rules on consumer protection. There is obviously no possibility to implement the rules of directives on consumer sales, consumer credit and travel contracts into public law rules, because these rules concern the content of those contracts. Thus, although EU law in directives, especially directives on consumer protection, does not stipulate the specific structure of the Member States' private law, it does require specific rules of private law. Moreover, EU law requires with those provisions that certain conflicting interests are included in the balancing exercise, as

[93] Regarding the German constitutional order, the situation is completely different. There is a textual anchor in the Constitution for the principle of freedom of contract (Art 2(1)), and there is a longstanding tradition concerning the adjudication of the freedom of the individual, which includes the notion of freedom of contract. Moreover, the decisions of the German Federal Constitutional Court resulted in a differentiated scheme of the right to individual freedom. Finally, those decisions led to substantial 'weight' of this right, which has to be outweighed by possible welfare principles.

[94] Likewise F Rittner, 'Über den Vorrang des Privatrechts' in A Dieckmann (ed), *Festschrift für Wolfram Müller-Freienfels* (Baden-Baden, Nomos, 1986) 509, 522.

[95] For further criticism see Streinz (n 73) Art 16 GR-Charta, para 4; Ruffert (n 59) § 16.3, paras 38 f.

well as the level of protection of freedom of contract in Member States' *private* law as far as those rules apply.

Moreover, EU law ignores problems of implementation of those private law rules which result from the specific structure of private law and of private law institutions in the Member States. The Member States have to implement *private* law rules with far-reaching restrictions on freedom of contract in national law.

In the case of minimum harmonisation, EU provisions may require Member States to increase consumer protection; in the case of maximum harmonisation, the level of protection in the directive binds Member States. In neither case would they strengthen freedom of contract. Thus, the Member States have to implement those rules in national law. If the coherence of the national law is endangered by the implementation, a Member State may expand the application of those provisions to other situations. Restrictions of freedom of contract may, therefore, extend to further areas of the law.

C. Promotion of Justice instead of the Principle of Freedom of Contract

Like Member State law, EU law is characterised by the fundamental antagonism of private initiative and state policy. The fundamental freedoms of the Treaty are intended to restrict national regulation; they have deregulatory and liberalising effects on Member State law. However, re-regulation has recently been enhanced at European level. This is done quite often by mandatory rules under the label of harmonisation. Those rules do not leave room for party disposition and thus foster the freedom of the individuals only with regard to *entering* into cross-border transactions, if at all, but not with regard to the *content* of those transactions.

Moreover, concerning the process of harmonisation of European private law using mandatory rules, the EU legislature has not recognised the fundamental distinction between promoting social justice and freedom of contract yet. German law distinguishes between contractual justice [*Vertragsgerechtigkeit*] and freedom of contract [*Vertragsfreiheit*]. Regarding contractual justice there is a more liberal approach, which accentuates the formal equivalence of the parties and the due process of law; the opposite opinion, the welfare state approach, accentuates the material equivalence of the parties. With regard to freedom of contract, one may distinguish between freedom of contract by law and freedom of contract in fact. The recent process in German private law is concerned with the substantiation of freedom of contract and the guarantee of freedom of contract in fact.

In EU law this distinction has not yet been recognised. Moreover, there is a tendency to emphasise justice over freedom of contract at the EU level, with significant effects on personal freedom and the free market economy. The substantiation of freedom of contract results in the protection of effective freedom of choice. This aim may be reached by the protection of freedom of choice in specific situations regarding the formation of a contract, such as the duty to inform and the right of withdrawal in distance contracts, doorstep sales and e-commerce. This substantiation may strengthen the personal responsibility of the parties by isolated measures.[96]

In contrast, the substantiation of justice is concerned with the substantial equivalence of the parties' interests in the contract. The principal measures to protect the weaker party to the contract are mandatory provisions.[97] This approach provides for a far-reaching limitation of self-determination due to material requirements affecting the content of a contract,[98] for example by prohibiting specific clauses in a contract clause or by prescribing mandatory rules and the right of withdrawal for certain types of contract.

The EU legislature has up to now disregarded the fundamental difference of both approaches.[99] This is even worse since the European Union subscribes to an 'open market economy with free competition'. Therefore, the substantiation of justice requires a thorough justification. The reasons are quite obvious: this approach is accompanied by a substantial impact on freedom of contract and a tendency towards paternalism. The 'just content' of a contract is highly disputed and exposed to influences by political compromises as well as the impact of lobby groups. There are public choice arguments like lobbying, self-interest of legislation, and active judicial intervention[100] that argue against this second approach. Thus, the corrective standard of fairness should only be applied in very exceptional circumstances.[101] Nevertheless, EU law reflects a clear tendency towards the second approach. First, regulations concerned with the protection of consumers do not have a reference point or substantial counterpart at the level of EU principles. Thus, the recitals of directives on consumer protection do not recall the fundamental relationship between freedom of contract and social regulation before they embark on the justification of a particular measure of social regulation. Furthermore, the majority of mandatory legal instruments in secondary EU law do not make reference to freedom of contract. Second, mandatory provisions have assumed an ever-increasing significance in EU legislation, resulting in a far-reaching intrusion into freedom of contract.[102]

[96] R Zimmermann, 'European Contract Law: General Report' (2007) 15 *Europäische Zeitschrift für Wirtschaftsrecht* 455, 462 (contract as a means of promoting the self-determination of those who wish to conclude a contract); R Zimmermann, *The New German Law of Obligations* (Oxford, Oxford University Press, 2005) 205 ff.

[97] See M Meli, 'Social Justice, Constitutional Principles and Protection of the Weaker Contractual Party' (2006) 2 *European Review of Contract Law* 159 ff.

[98] Thus, the question at hand is not limited to the determination of the adequate balancing of freedom of contract and mandatory private law. See G Wagner, 'Die soziale Frage und der Gemeinsame Referenzrahmen' (2007) 1 *Zeitschrift für Europäisches Privatrecht* 180, 193 f.

[99] Likewise Zimmermann, 'European Contract Law: General Report' (n 96) 462 (*preserve* rather than *restrict* private autonomy); G Wagner, 'Die soziale Frage und der Gemeinsame Referenzrahmen' (2007) 1 *Zeitschrift für Europäisches Privatrecht* 180, 196 f.

[100] See Hopt (n 36) 250 f.

[101] See Coester-Waltjen (n 9) 45.

[102] For a different opinion see Basedow (n 3) 918. According to Basedow the limitations barely exceed what has been commonplace in national law for decades; this statement is not convincing especially with regard to the level of EU consumer protection and moreover with regard to anti-discrimination regulation on the basis of Art 19 TFEU; see also ibid, 921, whereupon the interference with the freedom to select a contractual partner has already reached a problematic level due to EU anti-discrimination regulation.

To be sure here, the broad variety of business forms in the dynamic internal market puts the limits of freedom of contract in the centre of interest. But the regulatory needs in a post-industrial society demand common principles and a common approach to the limits and restrictions of party autonomy. There is a need for general principles of private law from which the principles of contract law and the law of obligations must dependably arise.[103]

D. Insufficient Judicial Review of Secondary EU Law

Another structural deficit relates to the insufficient judicial review of secondary EU law by the CJ. Secondary law has to comply with primary EU law,[104] even though the Treaty refers only to formal – and not to substantive – requirements (Article 13(2) TEU, Article 288 TFEU).[105] The same is true of the hierarchy between (also unwritten) primary law and secondary law.[106] The intensity of the court's review is decisive for the compliance with these principles.[107] There is a plethora of examples of judicial review by the CJ of the *formal* requirements of the Treaty with regard to secondary law. The paradigm cases are those concerned with tobacco advertising. In the first *Tobacco Advertising* case,[108] the CJ required an actual obstacle to cross-border trade within the internal market that resulted from the divergence of rules in different Member States. In the second *Tobacco Advertising* decision,[109] the mere possibility of interference with cross-border trade sufficed to uphold the directive on the basis of Article 114 TFEU.[110] The wording of this decision, as well as the generous test for whether these requirements are met by the European legislature, has been reinforced by more recent decisions of the CJ.[111] There is a strong argument that such a broad interpretation of Article 114 TFEU is in conflict with the principle of conferred powers (which limits the power of the European Union to competences conferred by the Member States). It has to be kept in mind that, according to the Federal Constitutional Court, this principle is decisive for the legitimacy of European acts.[112]

The same criticisms apply to the judicial review of *substantive* requirements by the CJ. Regarding secondary law there is rarely a judicial review of substantive

[103] According to Basedow (n 3) 916, there is a broad degree of variation and no overall coherence of EU interference with parties' freedom of contract.

[104] See Case 44/79 *Hauer v Rheinland-Pfalz* [1979] ECR 3727, para 14.

[105] See Schroeder in R Streinz (n 73) Art 288 AEUV, para 17.

[106] See Nettesheim in E Grabitz and M Hilf (n 85) Art 288 AEUV, para 224.

[107] See also Weatherill (n 75) 191; W Van Gerven, 'Remedies for Infringement of Fundamental Rights' (2000) 10 *European Public Law* 262.

[108] Case C-376/98 *Germany v European Parliament* [2000] ECR I-8498, paras 76 ff.

[109] Case C-380/03 *Germany v European Parliament* [2006] ECR I-11573, paras 36 ff.

[110] For criticism see C Maierhöfer, 'Anmerkung' (2007) 62 *Juristenzeitung* 463 ff; C Hillgruber, 'Die Verwirklichung des Binnenmarktes durch Rechtsangleichung' in R Krause, W Veelken and K Vieweg (eds), *Recht der Wirtschaft und der Arbeit in Europa. Gedächtnisschrift für Wolfgang Blomeyer* (Berlin, Duncker & Humblot, 2004) 602.

[111] Case C-301/06 *Ireland v European Parliament and Council* [2009] ECR I-628 paras 60–72.

[112] See BVerfGE 89, 155, 187 f.

requirements of primary law.[113] There is presently no case in which the CJ has declared a rule in a directive void because of a violation of fundamental rights under primary EU law.[114] Also, there is only one decision which declares a rule of a regulation void due to the violation of property rights as part of EU fundamental rights.[115] Moreover, to date the CJ has found a violation of fundamental rights of (unwritten) primary law, with one exception,[116] only with regard to decisions of the EU institutions.[117] Thus, substantive judicial review has only been developed in a rudimentary fashion.[118] It has to be mentioned that this is not caused by a lack of cases but by the lack of review. The CJ grants the European Union and the Member States a wide range of discretion in choosing measures of intervention. Moreover, there are serious doubts whether the court system of the EU is capable of producing the range of precedents that is needed by civil justice.[119]

In sum, there is an urgent need for substantive judicial review, including review for compliance with fundamental rights under EU law.[120] This would support the development of fundamental rights in primary EU law, including freedom of contract, because the CJ would have to define the content, limits and indispensible core of these rights. This is also required by the German Federal Constitutional Court. As mentioned above the Court demands an essentially equal protection of the fundamental rights under EU law. Taking the judicial review of the CJ into consideration, the protection of fundamental rights under EU law has not been effective. Fundamental rights amount to mere law in the books and to a hypothetical limit on legislative acts. It is highly questionable whether there is a protection of freedom of contract in primary EU law which is essentially equivalent to that in national law. This would require a more systematic enforcement of the fundamental right and annulment of secondary EU law which infringes freedom of contract. This deficit has to be addressed, rather than embellished by vague references to the structure of the legal system.[121]

According to the opposite opinion, the few and very broad requirements for the content and the validity of secondary law are predetermined by the structure of the lawmaking process within the European Union. Otherwise the Member States could refuse to implement secondary law in their legal orders, claiming its

[113] Cf also M Jestaedt, 'Diskriminierungsschutz und Privatautonomie' (2005) 64 *Veröffentlichungen der Vereinigung Deutscher Staatsrechtslehrer* 298, 322.

[114] Likewise ibid, 324.

[115] Joined Cases C-402/05 & C-415/05 *Kadi v Council* [2008] ECR I-6351, paras 355 ff. For a thorough analysis of the main issue of these cases, the relationship between international law and European law, see K Ziegler, 'Strengthening the Rule of Law, but Fragmenting International Law: The Kadi Decision of the ECJ from the Perspective of Human Rights' (2009) 9 *Human Rights Law Review* 288 ff.

[116] Above *Kadi v Council* (n 115).

[117] See Case C-404/92 *X v Commission* [1994] ECR I-4737, paras 17–24.

[118] Likewise Müller-Graff (n 3) 148 f.

[119] Likewise Basedow (n 3) 916.

[120] See also Canaris (n 35) 363 f (lack of ambition of the European courts). With regard to secondary law and the fundamental freedoms see C Schönberger, 'Hierarchisierungen im Gemeinschaftsrecht' (2003) 38 *Europarecht* 600.

[121] See Jestaedt (n 113) 322 f, fnn 97, 99 (primary law provides for secondary law only weak limitations).

invalidity.[122] This opinion is objectionable for two reasons. First, according to the CJ, there is a presumption of the validity of EU law which may be rebutted only by the CJ.[123] Second, the structure of the lawmaking process does not justify the dilution of freedom of contract. On the contrary, the need for the CJ to substantiate those fundamental rights needs to be emphasised. In the light of this, the argument that a diluted version of freedom of contract, with marginal requirements derived from primary law as a standard of validity of secondary law, is in the interest of the Member States cannot be accepted. It is supported by the claim that secondary law often is an expression of the coordination of the Member States' positions and an agreement of the Member States in the Council of Ministers.[124] The opposite is true: freedom of contract is an individual liberty which is protected against interference by the state. The cooperation of the Member States and decision-making of the governments of the Member States in the Council of Ministers are state regulation, and thus they may interfere with the essence of freedom of contract.

For example, Article 19 TFEU is a competence clause that confers the substantiation of certain fundamental rights (of non-discrimination) within EU law upon the EU legislature. Accordingly, secondary EU law on this issue is legitimate, but there is no hint about the balancing of interests with regard to anti-discrimination law and freedom of contract. The limits of constraints of freedom of contract have not been defined yet. Therefore, there is an inherent risk of a so-called anchor effect: while the principle of non-discrimination is explicitly mentioned in the Treaty, freedom of contract is not.

E. The Area-specific Harmonisation of Private Law: Specific Welfare State Intervention v General Party Autonomy

The EU legislature addresses specific problems of limited scope in an isolated fashion, resulting in selective mandatory provision. There is no general, thought-through policy of the EU legislature. Moreover, punctiform harmonisation measures are adopted without regard to the structure of Member State legal systems. The European Union is concerned with the specific issue at hand (for example, roaming prices[125]) and specific issues of unfairness or injustice. Thus, there is a structural danger to freedom of contract because social regulation will often prevail over freedom of contract in a balancing of values. The reason is that the structure of the balancing of interests in those specific situations tends to contrast the specific case of injustice or unfairness with the general principle of freedom of contract. The result is that often greater weight will be accorded to the more

[122] Cf Schönberger (n 120) 603; Jestaedt (n 113) 323 fn 99.

[123] Case C-44/98 *BASF v Präsident des Deutschen Patentamts* [1999] ECR I-6269, paras 48 ff.

[124] Jestaedt (n 113) 323 fn 99; Schönberger (n 120) 603.

[125] Cf Regulation 717/2007/EC of the European Parliament and the Council of 27 June 2007 on roaming on public mobile telephone networks within the Union and amending Directive 2002/21/EC, [2007] OJ L171/32.

precise, detailed social standards over the general principle of freedom of contract. For example, the protection from discrimination on the basis of race or sex in case of a tenancy contract will prevail over the broad principle of freedom of contract. Thus, there is a strong need to reflect on the general balance of interests with the principle of freedom of contract.

Moreover, specific social regulations of the European Union may result in severe infringements of the autonomy of the contracting parties at Member State level. The Member State may be forced on grounds of coherence of its legal system or political opportunity to extend the regulation to other areas of the law. This is also a means to avoid so called reverse discrimination against the Member States' citizens.

F. Dilution of Political Responsibility

Furthermore, political responsibility tends to be diluted in the political process. It is difficult for the EU citizen to hold one legislature to account for a Member State's rule restricting freedom of contract which implements EU law. The EU legislature will point to the national legislature because an EU directive will primarily lay down a particular aim, whereas the measures used to reach this aim are left to the Member State. Moreover, the executive power of the Member State is involved in the process of law-making on a European level, and the Member State's legislature may extend the EU law rule to other areas of the law. At the same time, the Member State's legislature will point to the EU legislature because EU law provides for a mandatory aim that restricts freedom of contract; the Member State merely chooses the implementing measures. Moreover, the extension of the EU directive to other areas not covered by it shall reduce the possibility of incoherence the implementation of the EU measure might cause in the national legal system and from the perspective of equal treatment under the law.

With regard to consumer protection there is an additional structural deficit: the Member States agreed upon the desirability of political action in this field without any particular sensitivity for the constitutional limits.[126] This is true even though there was the requirement of unanimity in the Council. On the contrary, the problem of unanimity is consent. It is hard to reach but it may pre-empt any discussion about constitutional limits of the intended rule. Unanimity paved the way for the extension of the scope of EU action, since there was no concern for the Member States that consumer protection was the real aim of the measures, for which the European Union lacked competence. Likewise, the shift of responsibility from the Member States to the European Union (Commission) has remained in the dark.[127]

In general, today there is leeway for Member States' politicians and chances to negotiate behind closed doors in Brussels over EU initiatives and to mislead the

[126] Likewise Weatherill (n 75) 183.
[127] See Micklitz (n 6) 202.

Member States' citizens with regard to the true motives of the government. If a Member State's government is pushed at home to pass certain regulatory measures, it may, on the one hand, refer to the nature of the issue as affecting the whole European Union or even to an ongoing initiative on the EU level to show that regulation by an individual Member State is not feasible. On the other hand, the Member State may make the citizens believe that it fought for progress on the issue, but that due to the strong resistance of other Member States it was not possible to reach the intended goal. On this basis it is no surprise that the harmonisation within the internal market did not stop regulatory activism, but rather led to more regulation. The leeway was used by the European Union and by the Member States in opposite ways. Regulation wanted by the legislature was pushed and supported on the EU level but justified to the citizens by the pressure of other Member States towards regulation.

G. Tendency to Increase the Level of Protection

Finally, the structure of the balance of interests will usually result in an excess of consumer protection, anti-discrimination and other EU regulation. EU consumer protection law is shaped as minimum protection of consumers in all Member States, no matter which level of consumer protection the Member State provides. Thus, EU law does not take other measures in the Member States' laws into account. Harmonisation leads to an increased level of protection in the Member States because the protection by EU law is added to the measures already enacted in the Member States' laws. Even though there is the possibility of reducing the level of consumer protection in the national legal system because of the protection by EU law, this is – due to political realities – only a theoretical possibility.

Moreover, EU law is extended by the national legislatures where the limits of the regulation are unclear in order to ensure correct implementation into Member States' law. Furthermore, the structure of the Member States' legal systems – for example, the German system – may provide for further extension of the rules that originate from EU law. The German legal system, for example, is characterised by the distinction between 'general' and 'specific' parts of codified areas of law. Thus, the Member State has to decide whether to interpret the more general clauses in accordance with EU law as well (in addition to the specific rules) or whether to resort to a divided, context-dependent interpretation of the Member State's rule.

VI. Conclusion: Measures to Foster Autonomy of Parties to a Contract in EU Law

One may conclude that in Member State legal orders freedom of contract is seldom trumped by other constitutionally protected principles, whereas in primary

EU law freedom of contract is protected only in exceptional circumstances. There is primarily an inherent need for a constitutionalisation of freedom of contract in EU law. Furthermore, such a constitutional right then should be reflected in secondary law which has to define the content of freedom of contract more precisely.

Possible measures to foster freedom of contract in EU law directly result from the above-mentioned structural deficits, but freedom of contract in primary EU law must be protected more explicitly. Freedom of contract should be added to the text of the EU Charter of Fundamental Rights.

The CJ ought to consider freedom of contract more extensively and more explicitly. The CJ has to make an effort to provide for a substantiation of freedom of contract. Since the EU Charter on Fundamental Rights provides the European Union with its own catalogue of rights, reference to decisions of the European Court of Human Rights might become less prominent in the future.

The test of conformity of secondary EU law with the formal and substantive requirements of primary EU law needs to be a mandatory part of judicial review. Thus, directives have to be annulled if they violate primary EU law in proceedings under Article 263 TFEU and to be disapplied in preliminary ruling proceedings under Article 267 TFEU. The European Union is, quite literally, a union based on the rule of law, a *Rechtsgemeinschaft*. Thus, EU institutions are not beyond control, whether their acts are in accordance with primary and secondary EU law.[128] The principle of subsidiarity – the political weapon of the Member States to strike down EU regulatory action[129] – needs to get activated in the political discourse. Political responsibility for specific regulations needs to be attributed to the legislature, and the legislative process in turn needs to be shaped in a way that enables such accountability.

[128] See Case 294/83 *Parti écologiste 'Les Verts' v European Parliament* [1986] ECR 1339, paras 44 ff; Opinion 1/91 [1991] ECR I-6102, para 21.

[129] See Micklitz (n 6) 201.

7

Anti-discrimination Legislation

A Paradigm Shift in the Protection of Human Rights?

PETER M HUBER

When dealing with anti-discrimination issues, the German legal order is confronted with quite a few problems. These problems are exemplified by the constitutional development since 1949, and also by the reluctance with which the non-discrimination directives of the European Union have been implemented into the national legal order. At the core of these difficulties, however, lie axiomatic differences between the common- and civil-law spheres, between basic ideas on the role of the state, different perspectives on the relationship between individual and state and quite different approaches to the scrutiny of state actions.

I. The Constitutional Prohibition of Discrimination

The *Grundgesetz* [Basic Law, GG], the German Constitution of 1949, contains several prohibitions of discrimination, most of them laid down in Art 3. They range from gender-oriented guarantees (Art 3(2)) to those aimed at equal protection by law without regard to race, origin, religion or other criteria (Art 3(1)).

A. Prohibition of Discrimination between Men and Women

When the *Parlamentarische Rat*, the Parliamentarian Council of 65 elected representatives of the West German states that was called upon to draft the *Grundgesetz* convened in 1948/49, its initial plan was to maintain the level of equal protection the Constitution of 1919 [*Weimarer Reichsverfassung*, WRV] had guaranteed. This would have meant that women would have only enjoyed equal protection as citizens, that is, as far as political rights were concerned. Article 109(2) WRV was understood as to provide merely a basis for universal suffrage. The right to vote had been extended to women after the end of World War I and the end of the monarchy. It neither entailed equality rights in private law, such as the right of women to start a business of their own, nor did it attempt to create factual equality of men and women. This is evidence that four years after World War II, the fathers and mothers of the Constitution were not concerned much about discrimination on grounds of sex.

Elisabeth Selbert, one of four female members of the *Parlamentarische Rat* and a highly esteemed expert on constitutional matters within the Social Democratic Party of Germany (SPD), did not accept this state of affairs. Not only did she intervene against the idea of merely maintaining the standards of the beginning of the century, but she also organised a media campaign in which hundreds of women from all over the country demanded that the new constitution had to look forward. In the end the wording of Art 3(2) GG was changed to read: 'Men and women enjoy equal protection by the law.' This was intended not only as a political programme, but, like all fundamental rights guaranteed by the constitution, as a binding norm for the legislative, executive and judicial branches of government (Art 1(3) GG).

Because the equality clause was meant to be constitutionally binding, its application was suspended until 31 March 1953 (Art 117(1) GG) in order to give the legislature enough time to adjust the legal order to the demands of the new constitution. Nevertheless, it would take another two decades until the legislature would turn Art 3(2) GG from mere 'law in the books' into 'law in action'. Even today, 60 years after the Basic Law came into force, (hidden) discrimination on the basis of sex cannot be regarded as overcome. It has been only a few years since the *Bundesverfassungsgericht* [Federal Constitutional Court] made it clear that the laws regulating marriages and family names have to respect the guarantees against discrimination.[1]

B. Guarantees against Discrimination in other Areas

Beyond the equal protection clause in Art 3(2) GG, the Basic Law contains several other guarantees against discrimination. Article 3(3) GG states that nobody shall be privileged or discriminated against on the grounds of descent, race, language, origin, belief or religious or political convictions. Moreover, in 1994 the article was amended in order to protect disabled persons; its second sentence now reads: 'Nobody shall be discriminated against on grounds of disability.'

Guarantees against discrimination laid down in the constitution are primarily directed at the public administration and public service. Article 33(3) GG, for example, strengthens the general civil rights with respect to freedom of religion by proclaiming that access to jobs in the public administration or entitlements earned within it must not depend on religious affiliation. Moreover, this section

[1] *Entscheidungen des Bundesverfassungsgerichts* (BVerfGE) 84, 9 ff – *Family Names* (according to § 1355(2) of the German Civil Code [*Bürgerliches Gesetzbuch*, BGB], previous version).

affirms that nobody shall be disadvantaged because he or she adheres to a particular religious denomination or philosophical conviction [*Weltanschauung*].

II. The Paradigm Shift in Fundamental Rights Dogmatics in the Equal Protection Clause

Since the 1970s a paradigm shift in the theory of fundamental rights has affected equal protection clauses and guarantees against discrimination. Although the original understanding of fundamental rights considered them to be guarantees for the individual against the state and other public authorities, legal theory became more interested in whether and to what extent fundamental rights also have an effect within society. This was particularly the case in regard to a horizontal dimension of fundamental rights in legal relationships between individuals. Keeping in mind that fundamental rights not only secure individual interests against the state, but also are general principles which affect every corner of the legal order,[2] the Bundesverfassungsgericht developed the concept of *Schutzpflicht* [duty to protect]. In its first decision on abortion[3] in 1975, the Bundesverfassungsgericht held that based on Art 2(2) GG (right to life) in conjunction with Art 1(1) GG (human dignity), the legislature has a constitutional duty to protect unborn children by criminal law.[4] Since then the idea has been extended to all other spheres of life, ranging from the risks of nuclear energy, noise and chemical weapons to the protection of employees against their employers, debtors against banks, and to a myriad other relationships.

Along with this development, guarantees against discrimination can also be understood as duties for the state in general, and the legislature in particular, to protect citizens against discrimination from third parties. But it has been a long way to reach this understanding of non-discrimination and there is still a long way to go towards its full implementation.

A. *Extramarital Children*

Discrimination against children born out of wedlock was obvious when the Basic Law came into force in 1949. Article 6(5) GG states that legislation must ensure that those children would enjoy the same conditions for their physical and spiritual welfare and the same position in society as children born within marriage. However, it took the legislature almost 20 years to fulfil this requirement, and it did so only after the Bundesverfassungsgericht had issued an ultimatum demanding it. In its decision of 29 January 1969, the court ruled that if the legislature did

[2] The leading case is BVerfGE 7, 198, 205 – *Lüth*.

[3] BVerfGE 39, 1 ff – *Abortion I*.

[4] The concept has been maintained, but after reunification it was altered to grant broader discretion to the legislature, BVerfGE 88, 203 ff – *Abortion II*.

not fulfil its duty under Art 6(5) GG by a reform of the statutes concerning the legal position of children born out of wedlock by the end of the fifth election period of the Bundestag,[5] Art 6(5) GG would be applied directly, and all contrary provisions of the German Civil Code [*Bürgerliches Gesetzbuch*, BGB] would become null and void.[6]

B. Constitutional Amendment of Prohibition of Sex Discrimination

At the end of the 1980s the Bundesverfassungsgericht began to redefine the guarantee against discrimination concerning men and women (Art 3(2) GG), changing the original prohibition against discrimination on the basis of sex into a general obligation of the state to foster and promote rights for women.[7] This jurisprudence was codified in an amendment of Art 3(2) in 1994, when the second sentence was added. It reads: 'The state promotes equal opportunities of women and men and will minimize existing disadvantages.'

III. Europeanisation of the Guarantees against Discrimination

Twenty years ago Europeanisation of fundamental rights and freedoms started to become a serious challenge to the Member States' legal orders. The influence of European law on all aspects of equal protection and guarantees of non-discrimination cannot be overstated. This is in contrast to the scant protection of individuals against EU authorities which can still be considered to be somewhat underdeveloped: the *Kadi*[8] and the *Schecke*[9] decisions were the first examples in 50 years of jurisprudence of the European Court of Justice (ECJ) in which acts of EU organs have been annulled because they violated fundamental rights. In respect to the prohibition of discrimination, European law and the ECJ have always been ahead of the level guaranteed by the German constitution.[10] The ECJ realised earlier than German courts that there is a link between equal protection clauses and the principle of proportionality. It therefore pays greater attention to the peculiarities of the single case as can be observed in regard to the question of

[5] That is, the autumn of 1969.

[6] BVerfGE 25, 167, 173.

[7] BVerfGE 85, 191ff – *Prohibition of Work at Night*; 89, 276 ff – *§ 611a BGB*.

[8] Joined Cases C-402/05 P and C-415/05 P *Yassin Abdullah Kadi and Al Barakaat International Foundation v Council and Commission* [2008] ECR I-6351; Joined Cases C-453/03, C-11/04, C-12/04 and C-194/04 *ABNA Ltd and others v Secretary of State for Health and others* [2005] ECR I-10423, paras 85 ff.

[9] Joined Cases C-92/09 and C-93/09 *Volker and Markus Schecke GbR and Hartmut Eifert v Land Hessen* [2010] ECR I-11063.

[10] As interpreted by the BVerfG.

whether quotas are permissible (section A).[11] Furthermore, the European Union has realised several legislative measures to promote non-discrimination (section B). Some of them have caused serious problems for Member States, for example, the prohibition of age discrimination by EU law (section C).

A. Quotas

The more modern approach of the ECJ is especially notable in the area of sex discrimination.[12] Until the end of the 1990s, the debate in Germany focused more or less on the question whether fixed percentages for female employees (rigid quotas) in public administration violated the constitution. This debate could not be settled satisfactorily within the national legal framework, but it became more or less irrelevant in the light of Europeanisation of the question. EU law not only provides equal protection of men and women under Arts 8, 157 TFEU (ex-Arts 3(2), 141 EC) and Art 2(4) of Directive 76/207/EC, but also states the obligation of EU organs to secure equal opportunities in everyday life. The Directive empowers the EU institutions to take measures that reduce existing differences between the sexes and allows Member States to introduce similar instruments.

The ECJ has shaped this programme during the last two decades significantly. It has shifted the burden of proof that promotion decisions were non-discriminatory to the public administration in the situation where part-time civil servants or employees were promoted less quickly than their colleagues working full time.[13] However, it has consistently and rightly denied the introduction of rigid quotas. In its *Kalanke* decision[14] the ECJ insisted that, even if such rules exist in the national legal order, a male applicant must have the possibility to raise (extraordinary) arguments in an individual case to allow or force the public administration to give him precedence over equally qualified, competing women. However, in its *Hellmuth Marschall* decision,[15] the ECJ approved flexible quotas, which means that if women are considered to be equally suited for a job from the perspective of qualifications, professional capability and other suitability criteria, they may be given priority as long as they are under-represented in certain careers. But this privilege must not be applied automatically, absolutely and unconditionally:

> Unlike the rules at issue in *Kalanke*, a national rule which, as in the case in point . . . contains a saving clause does not exceed those limits if, in each individual case, it provides for

[11] See M Brenner and PM Huber, 'Europarecht und Europäisierung im Jahr 1997' (1999) 114 *Deutsches Verwaltungsblatt* 764, 776; PM Huber, 'Das Kooperationsverhältnis zwischen BVerfG und EuGH in Grundrechtsfragen – Die Bananenmarktordnung und das Grundgesetz' (1997) 8 *Europäische Zeitschrift für Wirtschaftsrecht* 517, 520; U Kischel, 'Zur Dogmatik des Gleichheitssatzes in der Europäischen Union' (1997) 24 *Europäische Grundrechte-Zeitschrift* 1 ff; in contrast see the view of the Administrative Court Frankfurt/Main (1997) 8 *Europäische Zeitschrift für Wirtschaftsrecht* 182, 190.

[12] PM Huber, *Recht der Europäischen Integration*, 2nd edn (Munich, Vahlen, 2002) § 8, paras 48 ff.

[13] Case C-1/95 *Hellen Gerster v Freistaat Bayern* [1997] ECR I-5253 ff.

[14] Case C-450/93 *Eckhard Kalanke v Freie Hansestadt Bremen* [1995] ECR I-3051, 3078, para 24.

[15] Case C-409/95 *Hellmuth Marschall v Land Nordrhein-Westfalen* [1997] ECR I-6363.

> male candidates who are equally as qualified as the female candidates a guarantee that the candidatures will be the subject of an objective assessment which will take account of all criteria specific to the individual candidates and will override the priority accorded to female candidates where one or more of those criteria tilts the balance in favour of the male candidate. In this respect, however, it should be remembered that those criteria must not be such as to discriminate against female candidates.[16]

This means that 'soft quotas', which provide that in individual cases male applicants do at least have an opportunity to override the priority of female competitors, can be regarded simply as an instrument of promotion and do not entail discrimination on the grounds of sex.

The ECJ has maintained this line of thinking, although the TEC was amended in 1999 when the Treaty of Amsterdam introduced what is now Art 157(4) TFEU (ex-Art 141(4) TEC). Until today the relation between this provision and the older jurisprudence of the ECJ has not been completely clarified, although Art 157 TFEU is primary EU law, whereas Art 2 of Directive 76/207/EC, the basis of the ECJ's jurisprudence, is only secondary EU law. It is still an open question whether Art 157(4) TFEU allows 'rigid quotas'. In its *Badeck* decision the ECJ ruled that to rely on Art 157(4) TFEU would only be necessary if a national law was in conflict with Art 2(4) of Directive 76/207/EC,[17] which can be interpreted as allowing 'rigid quotas'.[18] Half a year later, however, in its *Katarina Abrahamsson* decision, the ECJ held that what is now Art 157(4) TFEU cannot be interpreted in such a way that 'it allows a selection method of the kind at issue in the main proceedings which appears, on any view, to be disproportionate to the aim pursued'.[19]

It seems that under the ECJ's perspective Art 157(4) TFEU has not brought substantial change but has only codified what had already been the law. Women may therefore only be given preference over male competitors if they are under-represented in a certain area; if the difference between the respective merits is not so great as to give rise to a breach of the requirement of objectivity in making appointments [*qualifikatorisches Patt*]; if the precedence is not granted automatically and unconditionally; and if all applications are treated in a way that allows for an objective assessment and a consideration of individual aspects.[20] In contrast, 'positive discrimination' that goes beyond these criteria must be considered a breach of Arts 2(1) and 4 of Directive 76/207/EC and Art 157(4) TFEU.[21]

This approach seems to be much better suited to the nuances of the specific situations than the general and abstract approach developed under Art 3(2) GG, which until today has not been able to solve the problems with rigid quotas in a satisfactory way.

[16] Ibid, para 33.

[17] Case C-158/97 *Georg Badeck v Hessischer Ministerpräsident* [2000] ECR I-1875.

[18] In this sense see also C Starck, 'Anmerkung' (2000) 55 *Juristenzeitung* 670, 671 f.

[19] Case C-407/98 *Katarina Abrahamsson and Leif Anderson v Elisabet Fogelqvist* [2000] ECR I-5539, para 55.

[20] *Badeck* (n 17) para 38.

[21] M Brenner and PM Huber, 'Europarecht und Europäisierung in den Jahren 2000/2001' (2001) 116 *Deutsches Verwaltungsblatt* 1013 ff.

B. EU Non-discrimination Legislation in General

Until the turn of the millennium the focus of non-discrimination legislation was on the relationships between citizens and Member States. Things changed in 1999 when the Treaty of Amsterdam introduced what is now Art 19 TFEU (ex Art 13 TEC), a rule that was generally considered as the result of attempts to fight racism and xenophobia.[22] In addition to criteria that are traditionally considered to be 'suspicious', such as race, ethnic origin, religion or philosophical conviction, and which can be found both in Art 14 ECHR and in national constitutions, Art 19 TFEU lists 'new' criteria such as age, disability and sexual orientation.

The European Union has embraced this provision wholeheartedly. In 2000, only a year after the Treaty of Amsterdam came into force, the Council of the European Union passed a Community Action Programme to combat discrimination (2001–06),[23] which paved the way for extensive legislation to come. In the same year the European Union adopted Directive 2000/43/EC implementing the principle of equal treatment between persons irrespective of racial or ethnic origin[24] and Directive 2000/78/EC establishing a general framework for equal treatment in employment and occupation.[25] This legislative push has continued. In 2008, for example, the European Commission made a proposal for a directive on implementing the principle of equal treatment between persons, irrespective of religion or belief, disability, age or sexual orientation.[26]

The idea that eliminating racism, xenophobia and other forms of discrimination could entail a duty of the European Union and the Member States to protect citizens and foreigners from becoming victims of discrimination caused a fundamental shift of paradigm in the understanding of non-discrimination guarantees. Although legal doctrine in this area has only caught up with what had already been accepted in regard to liberty rights,[27] it can be taken for granted that when ratifying the Treaty of Amsterdam neither Parliament nor anybody else was aware of the fact that, once empowered, the European Union would immediately start to fulfil the duty to protect through extensive legislation. This may explain why opposition in Parliament, professional associations and almost the entire academic community of lawyers have fought the above-mentioned non-discrimination directives so fiercely. However, the protests were too late; the directives had already entered into force, and the Member States were under an obligation to implement them into their respective legal systems.[28]

[22] R Streinz, 'Artikel 13 EGV' in R Streinz (ed), *EGV/EUV* (Munich, CH Beck, 2003) para 1.

[23] [2000] OJ L303/23.

[24] [2000] OJ L180/22.

[25] [2000] OJ L303/16.

[26] COM (2008) 426 final, 2 July 2008.

[27] See above section II.

[28] P Badura, 'Gleiche Freiheit im Verhältnis zwischen Privaten – Die verfassungsrechtliche Problematik der Umsetzung der EG-Diskriminierungsrichtlinien in Deutschland' (2008) 68 *Zeitschrift für ausländisches öffentliches Recht und Völkerrecht* 347 ff; G Britz, 'Diskriminierungsschutz und

C. Age Discrimination

In Germany, special problems arose with the development of the 'suspicious' criterion of age and with the *Mangold* decision of the ECJ, the leading case in this area.[29] In the years after the crash of the so-called 'new economy', unemployment in Germany had risen to the frightening number of almost five million people, among them many elderly people over 50 years of age. One of the reasons for this development seemed to be that employers avoided hiring older employees because they feared it would be impossible to dismiss them under German employment law. Parliament therefore passed a law – the Part-time Work and Fixed-term Contract Act 2003 [TzBfG],[30] which suspended the respective rules on dismissal for employees above the age of 52 in order to promote employment of such employees. But the ECJ held that this measure, which was meant to improve the situation of older employees, was discrimination on the grounds of age and went against the relevant general principle of EU law. Although it was doubtful whether a general principle of non-discrimination on the basis of age actually existed in EU law and whether the *Mangold* decision had to be considered as an ultra vires act,[31] there are also some arguments in favour of the ECJ's judgment. The strongest is that Art 21(1) of the EU Charter on Fundamental Rights (EUCFR) mentions the criterion of age. With some reluctance, Germany accepted the ruling of the ECJ in the end.

IV. Public Authorities and Institutions

A last aspect of anti-discrimination policy has to be mentioned: the establishment of public authorities and institutions which are supposed to strengthen the effectiveness of fundamental rights, among them equal protection clauses and non-discrimination guarantees. Leaving the Venice Commission and the 'Commission against racism and intolerance of the Council of Europe' aside, it is the European Fundamental Rights Agency (FRA) which deserves attention.

On 1 March 2007 the FRA was established in Vienna, after the Council of the European Union had passed Regulation 168/2007/EC on 15 February. Its most

Privatautonomie' (2005) 64 *Veröffentlichungen der Vereinigung der Deutschen Staatsrechtslehrer* 355 ff; M Jestaedt, 'Diskriminierungsschutz und Privatautonomie' (2005) 64 *Veröffentlichungen der Vereinigung der Deutschen Staatsrechtslehrer* 298 ff; for a more favourable view cf R Uerpmann-Wittzack, 'Gleiche Freiheit im Verhältnis zwischen Privaten: Art. 3 Abs. 3 GG als unterschätzte Verfassungsnorm' (2008) 68 *Zeitschrift für ausländisches öffentliches Recht und Völkerrecht* 359 ff.

[29] Case C-144/04 *Werner Mangold v Rüdiger Helm* [2005] ECR I-9981.

[30] § 14(3) of the *Gesetz über Teilzeitarbeit und befristete Arbeitsverträge* of 23 December 2002 (2002) *Bundesgesetzblatt I* 4607.

[31] BVerfG (2010) 63 *Neue Juristische Wochenschrift* 3422 ff and the dissenting opinion of Judge Landau.

important task is to advise EU organs and Member States in fundamental rights matters and to assist with the implementation of EU rules into the legal system of the Member States. The FRA therefore collects data, information and analysis on the state of fundamental rights in the European Union; works on methods and standards to improve the quality of these data, information and analysis and their comparability; and does research on fundamental rights problems. Moreover, it encourages the cooperation of the so-called civil society and tries to make the public aware of fundamental rights issues. The FRA is entrusted with organising cooperation and a permanent dialogue between all institutions, organisations and people working in the field of fundamental rights. Additionally, the FRA organises 'round tables', which take place not only in Vienna, but in other European capitals too. Against this background the FRA is described as an 'operational instrument for human rights policies in the EU',[32] which will not only improve the mutual understanding between the Member States but also ensure that the requirements of Arts 6 and 7 TEU are fulfilled.

V. Non-discrimination Guarantees as Education Guidelines?

This development, which leads to the widespread application of fundamental rights in private relationships, is not without problems. Fundamental rights, originally intended to safeguard private rights and interests against interference from the state and later from the European Union, have not only changed into legally binding duties to protect one citizen against the other, thus diminishing the scope of political decisions. By creating special authorities and institutions to promote fundamental rights, to organise campaigns for individual behaviour according to the values the fundamental rights entail, they have also become public duties which justify and even demand interference of the European Union or the Member States in private rights and interests. It is not without irony that the perfection of fundamental rights ends up in a sort of decay. Once strongholds of individual freedom and equal protection, whose violation provided standing before courts, fundamental rights in general[33] and non-discrimination guarantees in particular are in danger of mutating into mere guidelines for the political agenda of second-rank authorities. From this perspective an unbound leviathan – be it the European Union or the Member States – threatens to endanger our liberty and self-determination.

[32] *European Parliament resolution of 15 March 2007 on compliance with the Charter of Fundamental Rights in the Commission's legislative proposals: methodology for* systematic *and rigorous monitoring (2005/2169(INI))*, [2007] OJ L301E/229 and *Bundesrats-Drucksache* 567/05.

[33] For tendencies in that direction see BVerfGE 105, 252 ff – *Glykol*; 105, 279 ff – *Osho.*

8

The Human Rights Act 1998 and the Development of Administrative Law in the United Kingdom

ANTHONY BRADLEY

I. Introduction

If there is one fact about the constitution of the United Kingdom which is known to all students of comparative public law, it is that it is in essence an unwritten constitution. There is no a priori reason why the United Kingdom could not join most other states in the world by equipping itself with a single constitutional text to serve as the foundation for its system of public law. Nothing in the juridical orthodoxy associated with AV Dicey's *Law of the Constitution* makes such a development impossible.[1] But socio-political circumstances in the United Kingdom during the last three centuries have never required a step of this kind to be taken, and lawyers trained in the common law tradition often see no need for a single constitutional document. Undoubtedly, *if* circumstances did call for such a step, the resulting text would include a chapter devoted to the protection of fundamental rights. But, as will be shown below with regard to the Human Rights Act 1998 (HRA), the historical background in the United Kingdom has often caused movements for reform to take the form of piecemeal accommodation against that background, avoiding the need for a complete 'transformation scene' (as in a theatre when the revolving stage transports the actors in a trice from, say, the dining hall of a noble palace to a forest clearing). In a process of incremental change, reformers may find their task easier if they can downplay the extent of a change and present a development as having fewer implications than may turn out to be the case.

When some 30 years ago, it became necessary in the United Kingdom to take seriously the early jurisprudence of the European Court of Human Rights (hereafter

[1] See AW Bradley, 'The Sovereignty of Parliament – Form or Substance?' in J Jowell and D Oliver (eds), *The Changing Constitution*, 7th edn (Oxford, OUP, 2011) ch 2; and M Gordon, 'The Conceptual Foundations of Parliamentary Sovereignty: Reconsidering Jennings and Wade' [2009] *Public Law* 519.

the Strasbourg Court),[2] I found it relevant to look at the Canadian experience, including both the Bill of Rights of 1960 and the Canadian Charter of Rights and Freedoms, in an attempt to assess the constitutional significance of giving greater protection to human rights in the United Kingdom. In 1982 Professor Walter Tarnopolsky wrote:

> [F]or most of the time the important issue concerning a Bill of Rights is not whether it will provide authority for judicial review of legislative action, but rather whether it will induce the judiciary to review and restrain administrative action.[3]

At that time, this emphasis seemed to me to be worth developing with regard to the European Convention on Human Rights (ECHR), and in 1983 I wrote:

> [T]o a surprising extent there are points of comparison and resemblance between administrative law and the Convention system . . . One practical objective of the Convention system is to enable attention to be drawn to shortcomings in the national system of legal protection for the individual . . . Developments at Strasbourg may stimulate administrative lawyers [in the United Kingdom] to look again at such problems as executive discretion, bureaucratic secrecy and the provision of compensation for those who suffer a failure of justice . . . [Incorporation of the ECHR in United Kingdom law] would be of value even without attempting to curb the legislative supremacy of Parliament. It would be unfortunate if the perceived constitutional difficulty [the legislative supremacy of Westminster] were to be a total bar to all movement towards better protection of the individual in UK law.[4]

The aim of the present chapter is to consider whether this conclusion was well founded or whether it must now be seen as hopelessly tentative and faint hearted. A rather different picture of the evolving landscape of public law today appears in Thomas Poole's illuminating article, 'The Reformation of English Administrative Law'. His opening passage is challenging:

> We are witnessing a reconfiguration in the law of judicial review, intimations of which can be found on the surface of both the cases and the commentary. The language of *Wednesbury* unreasonableness and *ultra vires* increasingly gives way to talk about rights, proportionality and deference. This semantic recasting of judicial review reflects deeper mutations that go to the very heart of the discipline . . . Rights and substantive review, like Cinderella, have escaped subservient positions to take centre stage.[5]

In the discussion which now follows, it may be helpful from an analytical viewpoint to note that the arrival of protection for human rights in the United Kingdom in the form of the HRA includes both aspects that are '*internal*' to administrative law

[2] See AW Bradley, 'The United Kingdom before the Strasbourg Court 1975–1990' in W Finnie, C Himsworth and N Walker (eds), *Edinburgh Essays in Public Law* (Edinburgh, Edinburgh University Press, 1991).

[3] W Tarnopolsky, 'Enacting a Bill of Rights: The Legal Problems' (1982) 2 *Oxford Journal of Legal Studies* 122, 125, quoted by AW Bradley, 'The ECHR and Administrative Law – First Impressions' (1983) 21 *Osgoode Hall Law Journal* 609, 613.

[4] Bradley (n 3) 633, 635.

[5] T Poole, 'The Reformation of English Administrative Law' (2009) 68 *Cambridge Law Journal* 142, 142, 244.

(those that concern the reasoning and processes adopted in administrative litigation), and '*external*' aspects (those that delimit the jurisdiction of the administrative judge with reference to other constitutional actors, such as the institution and processes of Parliament). It is easier to declare this formal distinction than it is to apply it to every aspect of the subject, but the effects of the distinction may be seen in our study of a recent decision by the UK courts.

As for the structure of those courts, it will be known that the appellate jurisdiction that had long been exercised by the Law Lords (the Lords of Appeal in Ordinary) sitting as members of the House of Lords in the palace of Westminster is now exercised by the Supreme Court for the United Kingdom.[6] Although in name a new court – and the change is potentially significant for public understanding of the role of the judiciary – the 12 Law Lords have become Justices of the Court, and their jurisdiction is essentially the same as the appellate jurisdiction of the former House of Lords.[7]

II. A Case Study: *R (Wright) v Secretary of State for Health*[8]

This case arose from the Care Standards Act 2000, an Act which followed earlier legislation that sought to protect children from abuse by adults[9] by seeking to give similar protection to vulnerable adults (for example, elderly residents in retirement homes) against the risk of abuse by unsuitable care workers. The statutory procedure began with a duty on the employer of staff in residential or care homes to report to the Department of Health every instance in which one of their employees was dismissed (or resigned) when a complaint of misconduct harming or placing a vulnerable person at risk of harm had been made. It was the duty of the department to make a *provisional* listing of the individual in a list, the 'protection of vulnerable adults list' (the POVA list), if the department was of the opinion that *the employer* 'reasonably considered' the employee to have been guilty of relevant misconduct and that the individual was unsuitable to work with vulnerable adults. It might take six or nine months for the department to decide whether the provisional listing should be confirmed or set aside.

[6] Part 3 of the Constitutional Reform Act 2005 came into effect in October 2009, when the Supreme Court began to sit in a building at Westminster but outside the precincts of Parliament.

[7] In addition to the appellate jurisdiction of the House of Lords, the jurisdiction to decide 'devolution issues' arising from the devolution of legislative and executive powers to authorities in Scotland, Wales and Northern Ireland has been transferred from the Judicial Committee of the Privy Council to the Supreme Court. Constitutional Reform Act 2005, s 40 and schedule 9.

[8] *R (Wright) v Secretary of State for Health* [2009] UKHL 3, [2009] 2 All ER 129. Earlier decisions in *Wright* are at [2006] EWHC 2886 (Admin), [2007] 1 All ER 825; and [2007] EWCA Civ 999, [2008] 1 All ER 886.

[9] Protection of Children Act 1999.

The effect of including a name on the list, whether a provisional or a confirmed entry, was to prevent the individual from being employed in any employment subject to the listing procedure; the effect of listing was also extended automatically to a ban on working with children. Once a listing was confirmed by the department, the individual had a right to appeal to the Care Standards Tribunal (a judicial body) for a decision to be made on the available evidence. The statute also provided that *after nine months* on the provisional list, and only after that time, the individual had a right to apply to the tribunal for a decision as to whether the listing should be *confirmed* or *discontinued*. The four claimants in the case were all registered nurses. Mrs Wright had worked for eight years in care homes before being placed provisionally on the POVA list; it took two years from her dismissal for her provisional listing to be confirmed by the department. Thereafter she appealed successfully to the tribunal. Three other claimants in the case were provisionally included on the POVA list for eight months or more before the department decided to end the listings. It will be evident that for the claimants to lose their employment on the basis of complaints or assertions of facts that were not eventually upheld would indeed be serious; and the procedure was inherently likely to cause injustice.

The two main issues raised by the case were: (1) did the Care Standards Act 2000 breach the rights of the care workers that arose under Articles 6(1) (right to a fair hearing) and 8 (right to respect for private and family life) of the ECHR, and if so, (2) what remedy (if any) could the court give the claimants under the HRA? Before we consider the response of the judges to these questions, some further observations on the background to the issues are necessary.

III. Some Observations

The facts of the case may seem very mundane, compared with (for instance) cases under the HRA arising from the British government's decision to invade Iraq[10] or from the war against terrorism,[11] but at stake is a basic principle of administrative law: the right of the individual to be heard before a decision is made against him or her involving allegations of misconduct. The principle has long been protected by the rules of natural justice at common law, as broadened in the last 40 years into a general duty to act fairly.[12] Although occasional suggestions were made that fairness had a substantive content in the case of an excessively harsh decision,[13] in the 1980s fairness was perceived to be essentially a procedural matter:

[10] *R (Gentle) v Prime Minister* [2008] UKHL 20, [2008] AC 1356; *R (Al-Skeini) v Defence Secretary* [2007] UKHL 685, [2008] AC 153 (application of HRA in Iraq).

[11] See notes 32 and 52 below and Birkinshaw, chapter 14 in this volume.

[12] See *Ridge v Baldwin* [1964] AC 40. The innumerable later cases include *R v Home Secretary, ex p Doody* [1994] 1 AC 531.

[13] *R v Barnsley Corporation, ex p Hook* [1976] 3 All ER 452.

> The function of the court is to see that lawful authority is not abused by unfair treatment and not to attempt itself the task entrusted to that authority by the law.[14]
>
> Judicial review is concerned not with the decision, but with the decision-making process . . . Judicial review is not an appeal from a decision, but a review of the manner in which the decision was made.[15]

However, the second citation overstates the position. Judicial review includes challenges to a decision claiming that the subject-matter or motivation for a decision is ultra vires or, exceptionally, that a decision can be held to be *Wednesbury* unreasonable ('so unreasonable that no reasonable public authority could have made it').[16] Moreover, the courts in the 1990s expressly applied a more searching scrutiny by way of judicial review where the decision impinged on fundamental human rights.[17] Judicial review for unfairness at common law was formerly justified by reference to the presumed intention of the legislature,[18] and thus it was vulnerable to being limited or excluded altogether by express legislation.

Although the subject-matter involved the right to be heard, which has long been protected by principles of judicial review at common law, it is notable that the arguments and judgments in *Wright* were based entirely on ECHR issues. But for the HRA, the application for judicial review could not have been made with any prospect of success. The relevant provisions of the HRA are the following:[19]

- Section 2 requires the UK courts to take account of all relevant decisions made by the European Court of Human Rights at Strasbourg.
- By section 3, all legislation whenever enacted 'must be read and given effect' in a way that is compatible with ECHR rights 'so far as it is possible to do so' (this was a new duty imposed on the court which, as we shall see below, goes far beyond the normal principles of statutory interpretation).
- By section 4, when it is 'not possible' by the process of interpretation under section 3 to remove a clash between the ECHR and primary legislation, a superior court may make a 'declaration of incompatibility'. The effect of such a pronouncement is that the statutory provision remains in operation, notwithstanding the declaration of incompatibility, but the declaration opens the way under section 10 for the incompatibility to be removed by the making of secondary legislation, subject to a special parliamentary procedure.
- By section 6, all public authorities (including the courts) are obliged to act consistently with the ECHR, and are acting unlawfully if they do not do so, except where they are prevented from doing so by primary legislation.

[14] *R v Chief Constable of North Wales, ex p Evans* [1982] 3 All ER 141, 143 (Lord Hailsham).

[15] Ibid, 154 (Lord Brightman).

[16] See *CCSU v Minister for the Civil Service* [1985] AC 374 (especially Lord Diplock's analysis of the grounds for judicial review).

[17] See n 38.

[18] See C Forsyth (ed), *Judicial Review and the Constitution* (Oxford, Hart Publishing, 2000); M Elliott, *Constitutional Foundations of Judicial Review* (Oxford, Hart Publishing, 2001).

[19] Full accounts of the Human Rights Act 1998 and of the extensive case law may be found in A Lester and D Pannick (eds), *Human Rights Law and Practice*, 3rd edn (London, LexisNexis, 2009), and in R Clayton and H Tomlinson (eds), *The Law of Human Rights*, 2nd edn (Oxford, OUP, 2009).

- By section 7, a person who claims that a public authority is acting unlawfully within the meaning of section 6 may rely on the Convention rights in question whenever they are relevant to any court or tribunal proceedings; however, judicial review is the default procedure for enforcing Convention rights.
- By section 8, a court or tribunal which finds that there has been a breach of Convention rights may grant such remedies as are within its power – including (in the civil courts) the payment of compensation on the same basis of 'just satisfaction' as when this remedy is awarded under Art 41 ECHR.
- By section 19, every government bill introduced into Parliament must be accompanied by a statement from a minister to the effect that the bill is compatible with Convention rights (or that the bill is not so compatible but the government wishes the bill to proceed). Such statements are subject to scrutiny in Parliament by the Joint Committee on Human Rights.

When a prima facie breach of Convention rights arises from the application of primary legislation, one key issue that often arises for the court is to decide whether a solution by means of interpretation under section 3 HRA is *possible*. If this is held not to be possible, the court must then decide whether to make a declaration of incompatibility under section 4 HRA.

There is extensive case-law that illustrates the different approaches that the superior courts may adopt under section 3 in deciding what is 'possible' by means of interpretation. To decide whether a particular interpretation is 'possible' requires the court to exercise a broad and potentially controversial power that would not have been available to it apart from the HRA, but the scheme of the Act makes it clear that there are limits to this power, and that this is not a solution available to the court whenever there is a clash between primary legislation and a Convention right.

One leading authority is *Ghaidan v Godin-Mendoza*, in which the House of Lords held by a majority of 4 to 1 that the definition of 'married couple' contained within the Rent Acts (which expressly included relationships short of marriage in which a man and woman were living together) could be read as including same-sex partnerships, so that the survivor of such a partnership was entitled to take over the protected tenancy on the death of the partner.[20] Dealing with the power of interpretation under section 3 HRA, Lord Nicholls said:

> Parliament cannot have intended that in the discharge of this extended interpretative function the courts should adopt a meaning inconsistent with a fundamental feature of legislation . . . Parliament has retained the right to enact legislation in terms which are not Convention-compliant.[21]

Drawing on the analogy of judicial application of legislation to give an effect consistent with European Union law, Lord Rodger said that the courts

[20] *Ghaidan v Godin-Mendoza* [2004] UKHL 30, [2004] 2 AC 557.
[21] Ibid, para 33.

> could supply by implication words that are appropriate to ensure that legislation is read in a way which is compatible with Convention rights . . . [By] its very nature, an implication will go with the grain of the legislation. By contrast, using a Convention right to read in words that are inconsistent with the scheme of the legislation or with its essential principles as disclosed by its provisions . . . falls on the wrong side of the boundary between interpretation and amendment of the statute.[22]

Having made a detailed analysis of earlier cases in which the courts had granted declarations of incompatibility under section 4 HRA, Lord Steyn said:

> [w]hat is necessary . . . is to emphasise that interpretation under section 3(1) is the prime remedial remedy and that resort to section 4 [to make a declaration of incompatibility] must always be an exceptional course. In practical effect there is a strong rebuttable presumption in favour of an interpretation consistent with Convention rights.[23]

The dissenting judge, Lord Millett, held that to rewrite the Rent Acts so that they applied to same-sex couples involved 'questions of social policy which should be left to Parliament'.[24] However, the majority judges in *Ghaidan* were plainly influenced by the consideration that if Parliament were today to legislate to define the extent of protection for controlled tenancies, it would be very likely to include an express provision permitting same-sex couples to take the benefit of the legislation; discrimination on grounds of sexual orientation was 'by common accord . . . not acceptable, without more, as a basis for different legal treatment'.[25]

It will be evident from this illustration that the judges are required by the HRA to embark on considerations that would otherwise have been outside the traditional sphere of statutory interpretation.

IV. The Response of the Judges to the Claims in *Wright*

Against this background, we may now examine the response of the three courts that dealt with the claim of the nurses. They all did so by studying the Strasbourg jurisprudence, since the claim of the nurses raised issues as to the application of articles 6(1) and 8 ECHR that required decision. However, it is not necessary to examine the details of that case-law here.

In the Administrative Court, Stanley Burnton J held that the effect of provisional listing in barring Mrs Wright's employment in caring for adults or children was a determination of her civil rights and obligations within the meaning of Article 6(1) ECHR, and that the procedure followed by the Department of Health was in breach of Article 6(1) in that it did not provide for a right to hearing before an impartial and independent tribunal (the Care Standards Tribunal) until months after the

[22] Ibid, para 121.
[23] Ibid, para 50.
[24] Ibid, para 101.
[25] Ibid, para 9 (Lord Nicholls).

listing had taken effect. The judge also held that the listing was calculated to interfere with Mrs Wright's personal relationships with colleagues and the vulnerable persons with whom she had worked, and with others. The listing thus breached her rights under Article 8, since although it was for a legitimate purpose, it was unfair and disproportionate. The judge made a declaration of incompatibility under section 4 HRA.

In the Court of Appeal, the majority (Dyson and Jacob LJJ) agreed with Stanley Burnton J that provisional listing of a care worker on the POVA list engaged Article 6(1) ECHR and that her right to a 'fair and public hearing' before this took effect was not respected by the statutory procedure. The denial of the right to make representations was 'a denial of one of the fundamental elements of the right to a fair determination of a person's civil rights, namely the right to be heard'.[26] However, to counter the risk of unfairness, section 3 HRA required the Care Standards Act to be read as giving the individual the right to make representations to the Department of Health before she was placed provisionally on the list, except only if the department considered on reasonable grounds that the delay that this would cause would place vulnerable adults at risk of harm. In effect, the majority judgment read an additional procedural step into the Care Standards Act.

Different reasoning was adopted by May LJ: he agreed that provisional listing engaged Article 6(1), but held that overall the legislation was both fair and in the public interest, without the need for reading in additional procedure; in particular, the care worker who wished to challenge her provisional listing could do so by applying for judicial review if she had 'a knock-out reason for saying that the provisional listing should not have been made'.[27] The Court of Appeal thus unanimously (albeit for differing reasons) set aside the declaration of incompatibility made by the Administrative Court.

In the House of Lords, the single judgment was given by Lady Hale. She noted that the additional procedural step read into the act by the Court of Appeal had been accepted by the Department of Health, but she did not consider that this met the essential fault in the legislation, which denied the care worker her fundamental right to be heard 'before imposing on her possibly irreparable damage to her employment or prospects of employment'.[28] In her view, the additional procedural step read into the act by the Court of Appeal still allowed irreparable damage to be done, and did not enable the true urgency of a case to be assessed. Lady Hale held therefore that the Care Standards Act 2000 was inconsistent with both Articles 6(1) and 8 ECHR and that the defect could not be cured satisfactorily by reading in extra words. The Administrative Court's declaration of incompatibility was accordingly restored.

We may now assess the constitutional significance of this decision, by which the judges held to be seriously unfair legislation that had been passed by Parliament

[26] [2008] 1 All ER 886, para 106.
[27] Ibid, para 69.
[28] [2009] 2 All ER 129, para 28.

a few years previously to protect vulnerable adults against the risk of harm or abuse. This outcome was the direct effect of the HRA, as the express terms of the Care Standards Act 2000 made it virtually impossible for the claimants to rely on the common law grounds of judicial review. Thus Parliament in the HRA had brought about a change in the relationship between the legislature and the courts that involved a significant extension of the power of the courts. We do not know when the Department of Health must have realised that the scheme under the Care Standards Act 2000 was vulnerable to a human rights challenge: it may be relevant that it was enacted just two months before the HRA came into effect, so that passage of the bill was not preceded by a minister's statement that the bill's provisions were compatible with the ECHR.

Nevertheless, was the outcome in *Wright* a significant challenge to the authority of Parliament and Whitehall in political or institutional terms? The judges all stressed that the POVA list served the public interest: the dispute was not about the existence of the list, but about the procedure that should be observed in maintaining the list.[29] Moreover, even before the Court of Appeal had heard the case, new legislation replaced the Care Standards Act with a wholly different scheme that came into operation in October 2008.[30] Accordingly, the House of Lords' decision provides an uncontroversial example of the HRA operating to protect the rights of individuals against unfair treatment at the hands of Parliament and government. Since Parliament had already provided a new legislative scheme, the decision gave rise to no constitutional 'dialogue'.[31]

The decision in *Wright* thus provides a sharp contrast with the impact of the House of Lords' decision in the 'Belmarsh prison' case, *A v Secretary of State for the Home Department*.[32] In that case, the Law Lords issued a declaration of incompatibility in respect of the indefinite detention authorised by Parliament in 2001 for foreigners suspected of involvement in terrorism who could neither be placed on trial for criminal offences nor be deported. This decision was made despite argument by the Attorney General for the government that the courts were in danger of exceeding their legitimate role in a democracy. The judges rejected this argument, taking the understandable view that in reviewing the scheme for indefinite detention, they were fulfilling the mandate that Parliament had expressly vested in them by the HRA. In fact, it was inevitable that the decision in the Belmarsh prison case would lead to further legislation; this provided for control orders – a form of house arrest rather than detention – which in turn was

[29] See eg [2008] 1 All ER 886, para 44.

[30] The Safeguarding Vulnerable Groups Act 2006 brought together three different schemes for barring unsuitable persons from working with children and vulnerable adults. The need for a more integrated scheme had been identified by the Report on the Bichard Inquiry (HC 653, 2003–04).

[31] TR Hickman, 'Constitutional Dialogue, Constitutional Theories and the HRA' [2005] *Public Law* 306.

[32] *A v Secretary of State for the Home Department* [2004] UKHL 56, [2005] 2 AC 68 (indefinite detention of foreigners suspected of terrorist conduct declared incompatible with ECHR Art 5); A Tomkins, 'Readings of *A v Secretary of State for the Home Department*' [2005] *Public Law* 259.

challenged on Convention grounds.[33] In this sensitive area, it might be said that the 'dialogue' contemplated by the framers of the HRA is continuing.

V. The Significance of the HRA within Administrative Law

As the *Wright* case has shown, the HRA enables a new array of legal claims to be made when official decisions are challenged by judicial review.[34] All statutory schemes of regulation and control are subject to scrutiny on Convention grounds, and this has been particularly evident in respect of immigration law, the branch of executive power that gives rise to more cases of judicial review than any other. The HRA has profoundly altered the task of the immigration judge, so that (as the House of Lords has held) the primary task of that tribunal is to decide on the facts whether the removal of a non-citizen from the United Kingdom is or is not consistent with the individual's rights under Article 8 ECHR; it is not a secondary, reviewing function limited to the traditional grounds of judicial review.[35] Numerous immigration decisions have been made that are dependent on Convention arguments.[36] When taken with decisions raising human rights issues in other areas of public law, as in *Wright*, the HRA had a significant impact on the judicial workload of the House of Lords.[37] This impact is now felt by the Supreme Court of the United Kingdom which, as we have seen, took over the appellate functions of the House of Lords with effect from October 2009.

One frequent criticism of the grounds for judicial review in administrative law in English law has been based on the straitjacket of '*Wednesbury* unreasonableness', which has appeared to limit judicial review on substantive grounds to the rare cases in which officials had 'taken leave of their senses'. Already before the advent of the HRA, this ground of review had been reworked to take account of

[33] See Prevention of Terrorism Act 2005; and *Secretary of State for the Home Department v JJ* [2007] UKHL 46, [2008] AC 440.

[34] See also AW Bradley, 'The Human Rights Act and Judicial Review' in M Supperstone, J Goudie and P Walker (eds), *Judicial Review*, 3rd edn (London, Butterworths, 2005) ch 4.

[35] *Huang v Secretary of State for the Home Department* [2007] UKHL 11, [2007] 4 All ER 15.

[36] They include *EB (Kosovo)* [2008] UKHL 41, [2008] 4 All ER 28 (effects of official delay on Article 8 factors); *AL (Serbia)* [2008] UKHL 42, [2008] 4 All ER 1127 (whether amnesty for immigrant families in breach of ECHR Art 14 by omitting single persons); *Beoku-Betts* [2008] UKHL 39, [2008] 4 All ER 1148 (decision must take account of effect of removal on all members of B-B's family unit, not merely its effect on B-B); *Chikwamba* [2008] UKHL 40, [2009] 1 All ER 363 (general policy requiring C to leave United Kingdom for Zimbabwe even when she would be entitled to return to the United Kingdom – breach of Art 8); *EM (Lebanon)* [2008] UKHL 64, [2009] 1 All ER 559 (removal of Moslem boy of 7 to Lebanon – breach of Art 8 – 'utterly compelling humanitarian grounds against removal').

[37] See S Shah and T Poole, 'The Impact of the HRA on the House of Lords' [2009] *Public Law* 347.

the human rights context of certain judicial review cases.[38] Even so, this gave too limited scope for review to enable many Convention rights to be protected. To meet the requirements of the ECHR, judicial review decisions raising Convention issues frequently now turn on the substantive test of proportionality.[39]

Notwithstanding these changes in the grounds of judicial review as a matter of administrative law, protection of Convention rights under the HRA has not meant the wholesale reform of the common law rules that restrict payment of compensation for loss caused by unlawful administrative decisions. The procedural rules for judicial review now include provision for claiming damages when, on the facts that support a claim for judicial review, a claim may also be made in the law of tort. But merely because an administrative decision has been quashed by judicial review, there is no liability in English law to compensate for loss that the decision has caused.[40]

A vivid instance of this defect in the law is provided by the decision of the House of Lords in *Jain v Trent Health Authority*.[41] Mr and Mrs Jain were owners of a nursing home which, without any warning or prior notice, was closed down under a magistrate's order obtained by the health authority. The patients were immediately dispersed. Over four months later, the owners emerged victorious from the Registered Homes Tribunal, which held that there had never been any sufficient grounds to justify the immediate closing of the home. But it was a pyrrhic victory since their business had already collapsed. The owners sued the health authority in tort for the economic loss that they had suffered, but without success. The House of Lords held that the authority owed no duty of care to the owners on which a claim for negligence could be based.

The facts in *Jain* occurred before the HRA came into effect. However, in delivering the leading judgment, explaining why the claim in negligence failed, Lord Scott notably went off the judicial *piste* by examining what would have been the position if the HRA had already been in operation. He concluded that Mr and Mrs Jain could have shown that their rights to a fair hearing (Article 6(1) ECHR) and to peaceful enjoyment of their possessions (Article 1, First Protocol, ECHR) had been breached, and 'that they would have been entitled to compensation under domestic law'[42] (since claims to 'just satisfaction' under Article 41 ECHR have effect in the UK law by reason of section 8 HRA). Lord Scott endorsed an earlier observation by Lord Brown dealing with the effect of the HRA in providing a financial remedy for breaches of Convention rights: 'it is quite simply unnecessary now to develop the

[38] See especially *R v Ministry of Defence (ex p Smith)* [1996] QB 517 (policy of excluding homosexuals from armed forces) and the Strasbourg sequel of *Smith v United Kingdom*, App nos 33985/96 (2000) 29 EHRR 493.

[39] See Poole (n 5) 146–47 for some leading citations.

[40] See eg *Dunlop v Woolahra Council* [1988] AC 473. Also Justice/All Souls report, *Administrative Justice – Some Necessary Reforms* (1988) ch 11.

[41] *Jain v Trent Health Authority* [2009] UKHL 4, [2009] 1 All ER 957.

[42] Ibid, para 18. This *obiter* view was supported by Lady Hale and Lord Neuberger.

common law to provide a parallel cause of action'.[43] This provides a revealing insight into the factors that may influence the exercise by senior judges of their power to steer the development of the common law.

If we return once more to the *Wright* case, we see at once that the declaration of incompatibility granted by the court did not provide a remedy for the months during which, in breach of their Convention rights, the claimants were unable to gain employment as care workers. Fortunately, the existence of section 8 HRA is known to the Royal College of Nursing, who had represented the claimants and, following the *Wright* decision, some 80 to 90 claims to compensation from similarly placed nurses were pending.[44] This does not mean that these claims would necessarily succeed. In *R (Greenfield) v Secretary of State for the Home Department*,[45] the House of Lords strongly discouraged litigation that sought compensation for every infringement of Convention rights and emphasised that national courts must follow the lead of the Strasbourg Court in holding that the focus of the Convention is the protection of human rights, not the award of compensation; it was observed that the HRA had not created a new tort in English law. In *Greenfield*, a convicted prisoner complained that he did not have a fair hearing when he was required under prison disciplinary rules to serve additional days of imprisonment for a drug offence. It does not follow that an equally restrictive attitude to compensation should be taken in all Convention cases, and indeed the House in *Greenfield* warned of the 'risk of error if Strasbourg decisions given in relation to one article of the Convention are read across as applicable to another'.[46] Since it is now unlikely that the common law of negligence will be developed to provide a remedy for economic loss caused by unlawful administrative action, much as some tort lawyers may regret this, there is a strong argument to be made that the Administrative Court should be granted power on judicial review to award compensation in cases where such an award is necessary in the interests of justice.[47]

Space does not permit discussion of other aspects of administrative law that have been affected by the HRA. These include (a) the meaning of a 'public authority' for human rights purposes,[48] (b) the extent to which article 6(1) ECHR has affected formal structures for official decision-making,[49] and (c) whether the

[43] In *Van Colle v Chief Constable of Hertfordshire* [2008] UKHL 50, [2008] 3 All ER 977, para 136. Lord Brown's view is not universally supported. And cf L Blom-Cooper, 'When the Private Lawyer Should Go Public' [2009] *Public Law* 195.

[44] Information supplied by the Royal College of Nursing legal department.

[45] *R (Greenfield) v Secretary of State for the Home Department* [2005] UKHL 14, [2005] 2 All ER 240. See also *Ali v Head Teacher of Lord Grey School* [2006] UKHL 14, [2006] 2 All ER 457.

[46] *Greenfield* [2005] UKHL 14, para 7. Cf R Clayton, 'Damage Limitation: The Courts and HRA Damages' [2005] *Public Law* 429.

[47] See M Fordham, 'Monetary Awards in Judicial Review' [2009] *Public Law* 1. Also T Cornford, 'Administrative Redress: The Law Commission's Consultation Paper' [2009] *Public Law* 70.

[48] See *YL v Birmingham City Council* [2007] UKHL 27, [2008] AC 95 (a decision that was soon reversed by the Health and Social Care Act 2008, s 145).

[49] *R (Alconbury Developments) v Environment Secretary* [2001] UKHL 23, [2001] 2 AC 295; *Runa Begum v Tower Hamlets LBC* [2003] UKHL 5, [2003] 2 AC 430; *Ali v Birmingham City Council* [2010] UKSC 8, [2010] 2 All ER 175. And see Bradley (n 34).

decision maker must expressly articulate a rights-based approach in the making of decisions[50] and, if the decision maker has done so, the weight that should be attributed to this.[51]

VI. Constitutional Significance of Developing Administrative Law

In the 1990s, the campaign for incorporation of the ECHR in UK law was largely driven by a demand for more effective judicial review, including the protection of substantive rights, and the wish of some senior judges to be in a position to adjudicate on human rights claims in national courts, rather than forcing individuals who wished to enforce their Convention rights to go to Strasbourg. Support for incorporation of the ECHR also came from those who were dissatisfied with the country's unwritten constitution and wished to bring about a new 'constitutional settlement'. In the event, enactment of the HRA has enabled UK courts to apply the extensive jurisprudence of the Strasbourg Court directly, without having to contend at the same time with intermediate complexities resulting from the manner in which the Convention has been given effect in national law.

One result of the HRA has been to increase the significance of the ECHR for the making of public policies, and the judiciary have (whether willingly or not) become more involved in the scrutiny of policy making. This has been particularly evident in the many cases concerned with aspects of the 'war against terror' following 9/11.[52] But other examples include the impact of article 2 ECHR (the right to life) on administrative procedures for inquiring into near-suicide attempts by prisoners,[53] and whether the scheme of social assistance for disabled persons breaches article 14 ECHR (prohibition of discrimination) by distinguishing between homeless and other claimants.[54] Such examples necessarily give rise to discussion, sometimes involving an acute level of political controversy, of whether the HRA requires the judiciary to go too far beyond the traditional role of the courts by causing them to review the merits of decisions taken by government or in Parliament.

As for the effect of human rights protection on the process of judicial review and on judicial reasoning, the extensive citation of European and comparative case-law by advocates and judges is now commonplace. The extended sphere for judicial decision-making is not always welcomed by government, especially as

[50] *R (SB) v Denbigh High School* [2006] UKHL 15, [2007] 1 AC 100; and *Belfast City Council v Miss Behavin' Ltd* [2007] UKHL 19, [2007] 3 All ER 1007.

[51] These issues are fully examined in Poole's article (n 5).

[52] See note 32 above and *Secretary of State for the Home Department v AF (No 3)* [2009] UKHL 28, [2009] 3 All ER 643.

[53] *R (JL) v Secretary of State for Justice* [2008] UKHL 68, [2009] 2 All ER 521.

[54] *R (RJM) v Secretary of State for Work & Pensions* [2008] UKHL 63, [2009] 2 All ER 556.

regards the effect of the ECHR in restricting the deportation of foreigners whose presence in the United Kingdom is considered to be undesirable.[55] Some sections of public opinion and the media deplore the HRA as another instance of the evil influence of Europeanisation.[56] It is possible that the existence of the Supreme Court may be a lightning conductor for such attacks. The Conservative party's manifesto for the general election in May 2010 declared that 'to protect our freedoms from state encroachment and encourage greater social responsibility, we will replace the Human Rights Act with a UK Bill of Rights'. The coalition government that took office in 2010 tried to bridge the abyss on this issue that exists between Conservative and Liberal Democrat attitudes by creating a commission to examine proposals for a Bill of Rights for the United Kingdom, but in 2012 the commission's report on the fundamental issues in dispute was still awaited.[57] Whether or not the commission reports in favour of such a Bill of Rights, it is clear that, so long as the United Kingdom remains a party to the ECHR, commitment to the rights protected by the Convention would necessarily be at the heart of a UK Bill of Rights.

Repeal of the HRA remains a legal possibility, although this would be seen as a profoundly backward step by the liberal community. The manner in which the HRA gave legal effect in the United Kingdom to the Convention rights has generally been considered to be an ingenious and well-drafted compromise, respecting on the one hand the parliamentary basis for government and on the other the need to enable the courts to protect rights and freedoms against excessive claims by the state. The political backlash to the HRA reflected in the Conservative party's manifesto in 2010 might well have been greater if the HRA scheme had not expressly allowed for the continuing legislative power of Parliament. Certainly the HRA is a statute of constitutional significance, as it has made possible judicial review of Acts of Parliament, giving powers to the superior courts that stop short only at the power to quash legislation that is inconsistent with the ECHR. This does not mean that the HRA is part of a written constitution but, given the tradition of parliamentary sovereignty, the HRA is immensely significant as a major step towards the constitutionalisation of public law in the United Kingdom.[58]

[55] The lengthening line of cases includes *Chahal v United Kingdom* App no. 22414/93 (1997) 23 EHRR 413, *A v United Kingdom* App no 3455/05 (2009) 26 BHRC 1, and *Othman (Abu Qatada) v United Kingdom* App no 8139/09 (2012) 32 BHRC 62.

[56] One decision by the Supreme Court that gave rise to excessive criticism of the HRA was *R(F) v Home Secretary* [2010] UKSC 17, [2010] 2 All ER 707 (lifelong inclusion of sex offenders in police register imposing restrictions on private life: statute incompatible with Art 8 ECHR because no scope for review).

[57] In July 2011, the commission gave interim advice to the Government on reforms to the Strasbourg Court that it considered to be urgently needed.

[58] For a theoretical analysis of the HRA from an unduly narrow Diceyan perspective, see A Young, *Parliamentary Sovereignty and the HRA* (Oxford, Hart Publishing, 2009). For a very different discussion, see the issues raised by HRA sceptics in articles such as KD Ewing, 'The Futility of the HRA' [2004] *Public Law* 829 and KD Ewing and J-C Tham, 'The Continuing Futility of the HRA' [2008] *Public Law* 668. For a cogent reply, see A Kavenagh, 'Judging the Judges under the HRA – Deference, Disillusionment and the "war on terror"' [2009] *Public Law* 287. And for a stimulating survey, see T Hickman, *Public Law after the Human Rights Act* (Oxford, Hart Publishing, 2010).

Part Two

Balancing Human Rights

9

Human Rights Protection in Multipolar Legal Relationships

SOPHIE-CHARLOTTE LENSKI

I. Introduction

Human rights protection in Germany is of a quite different nature in private law than in administrative and criminal law.[1] Criminal law and administrative law are determined by the principle of direct vertical application of fundamental rights. In these areas of law the state on the one hand and the individual on the other hand face each other in a relationship of super- and subordination. The fundamental rights situation here is clear: the individual is protected by the fundamental rights, while according to Article 1(3) Basic Law the state is bound by them, whether it acts as legislature, executive or judiciary.[2]

More complex to answer, however, is the question how fundamental rights affect private law, for in private law a relationship of super- and subordination does not exist. Instead, private law is determined by individuals acting on a level of co-equality. Both of the individuals in this relationship can rely on their fundamental rights. So in this relationship it is a debatable point against whom the fundamental rights have an effect or who is restricted by them.

According to prevailing legal doctrine and established jurisprudence, fundamental rights do not restrict the individual, as it is the individual who is protected

[1] This binary division regarding the effect of fundamental rights, however, does not change the fact that in general, fundamental rights bind the three branches of law, see H Jarass, 'Grundrechte als Wertentscheidungen bzw. objektivrechtliche Prinzipien in der Rechtsprechung des Bundesverfassungsgerichts' 110 *Archiv des öffentlichen Rechts* 363, 378, who distinguishes this general effect from the indirect horizontal effect. K Schlaich and S Korioth, *Das Bundesverfassungsgericht*, 7th edn (Munich, CH Beck, 2007) para 322, seem to be right when assuming that the effect of fundamental rights is even stronger in public law than in private law.

[2] Nevertheless in criminal law there may be cases in which, apart from the relationship of super- and subordination from the state to the delinquent, fundamental rights positions of an individual (especially the victim) may be of importance, see Zimmermann, ch 2 of this volume. These effects, however, only influence the duty to protect of the state but do not change the basic vertical direct effect of fundamental rights.

by them. Therefore a direct horizontal effect of fundamental rights in private law does not exist.[3]

However, private law is not an area of law where individuals face each other without any link to the state. When relations between individuals become subject to private law, the state engages in this relationship, either through legislation which regulates the legal relationships on an abstract level, or civil courts which adjudicate specific disputes. When legislating or adjudicating in this way, the state is bound by fundamental rights. Therefore the fundamental rights have an indirect horizontal effect on private law.[4]

In the so-called *Görgülü* decision, however, the Federal Constitutional Court contrasted the concept of multipolar fundamental rights situations with the conventional idea of indirect horizontal effect. To a certain extent it thereby changed the perspective on that concept.

In the following sections the concept of multipolarity will be contrasted with the idea of indirect horizontal effect in order to determine whether the term 'multipolarity' describes a sustainable concept to deal with the effect of fundamental rights on private law according to German constitutional law.

II. Indirect Horizontal Effect of Fundamental Rights

Currently, the doctrine of indirect horizontal effect of fundamental rights is, despite the numerous modifications of explanation in detail,[5] the prevailing model to describe how fundamental rights affect private law. Individuals are not bound by fundamental rights, but the state is restricted by them when legislating in the area of private law or applying private law through the courts.

[3] See W Rüfner, 'Grundrechtsadressaten' in J Isensee and P Kirchhof (eds), *Handbuch des Staatsrechts der Bundesrepublik Deutschland*, vol 5 (Heidelberg, CF Müller, 1992) § 117 para 59; K Hesse, *Grundzüge des Verfassungsrechts der Bundesrepublik Deutschland*, 20th edn (Heidelberg, CF Müller, 1995) para 355; H Dreier, 'Vorbemerkung' in H Dreier (ed), *Grundgesetz*, vol 1, 2nd edn (Tübingen, Mohr Siebeck, 2004) para 98; this opinion is not shared by the Federal Labour Court [*Bundesarbeitsgericht*, BAG], BAGE 1, 185, 193 f, which, however, later dissociated itself from this point of view, see BAGE 48, 122, 138 f; 52, 88, 97 f.

[4] See K Stern, *Das Staatsrecht der Bundesrepublik Deutschland* vol III/1 (Munich, CH Beck, 1988) 1531; H-J Papier, 'Drittwirkung der Grundrechte' in D Merten and J-J Papier (eds), *Handbuch der Grundrechte in Deutschland und Europa*, vol 2 (Heidelberg, CF Müller, 2006) § 55, para 27. For a critical review of what was then a new development of fundamental rights' direct and indirect horizontal effect, see E Forsthoff, 'Die Umbildung des Verfassungsgesetzes' in H Barian, E Forsthoff and W Weber (eds), *Festschrift für Carl Schmitt* (Berlin, Duncker & Humblot, 1959) 35, 45 f.

[5] See for the different models, which, however, mostly lead to identical results, Dreier (n 3) para 99.

A. Fundamental Rights Protection when Legislating and Adjudicating Private Law

When legislating in the area of private law, the state is bound by fundamental rights in the same way it always is when acting as legislator. The laws it enacts have to be in accordance with fundamental rights, and the laws may impair the fundamental rights only to the extent to which the impairment can be justified under the Basic Law. They particularly have to be in accordance with the principle of proportionality.

With regard to legislation one has to distinguish between specific rules with relevance for the fundamental rights on the one hand and so-called 'general clauses' on the other.[6] On the one hand, when enacting specific rules, the legislature defines the factual requirements and the legal consequence of one specific legal issue. One example for this kind of legislation can be found in family law. According to Article 1626a of the German Civil Code, only the mother has the right of parental custody for a child if the parents are not married and do not agree to joint custody. In this case the legislature balances the unmarried mother's parental right, the unmarried father's parental right and the best interest of the child on an abstract level by law. Factual conditions and legal consequence are clearly defined.[7]

So-called general clauses, on the other hand, are not characterised by such clearly defined factual prerequisites and legal consequences. General clauses are rules which are highly in need of interpretation, for example when the law attaches legal consequences to terms like 'illegitimacy', 'unlawfulness' or 'legitimate legal interest'.

The protection of privacy in German private law provides examples of such general clauses. If an individual wants to intervene against publications interfering with his privacy, he can only refer to an analogous application of section 1004 of the German Civil Code. The provision contains a claim for a prohibitory injunction for the owner of movable things or immovable property but is also applied by analogy to infringements of other rights than property, for example the right of privacy. If property or another right is interfered with, the right holder may require the disturber to remove the interference. If further interferences are to be feared, the right holder may seek a prohibitory injunction. The legislature does not define the term 'interference'. Moreover, the term has to be interpreted by the courts for every single case. But in any case, when interpreting and applying the term, the courts are bound by fundamental rights.

These different instances of fundamental rights affecting legislation and adjudication are reflected in constitutional review by the Federal Constitutional Court.

[6] See Jarass (n 1) 377.

[7] For the constitutionality of this balancing see Decisions of the Federal Constitutional Court [*Bundesverfassungsgericht*, BVerfG], BVerfGE 107, 150.

Regarding specific rules the Federal Constitutional Court normally reviews whether the rule itself is in accordance with fundamental rights. Regarding general clauses, in contrast, the Federal Constitutional Court reviews whether the rule has been interpreted and applied in accordance with the Basic Law.[8]

B. Fundamental Rights as an Objective System of Values

Despite the fact that the legislature and the courts are bound by fundamental rights, the legal relations in private law remain legal relations between two individuals, and individuals are not the addressees of fundamental rights. Therefore, the question arises in which way the legislature and the courts have to consider the fundamental rights.

The Federal Constitutional Court derived the obligation to consider fundamental rights from the principle that fundamental rights do not have direct effect in private law, but that they shape it because fundamental rights establish an objective system of values. The Federal Constitutional Court held that

> far from being a value-free system the Constitution establishes an objective system of values in its section on fundamental rights, and thus expresses and reinforces the value of the fundamental rights. This system of values, centring on the freedom of the human being to develop in society, must apply as a constitutional axiom throughout the whole legal system: it must direct and inform legislation, administration, and judicial decisions. It naturally influences private law as well; no rule of private law may conflict with it, and all such rules must be construed in accordance with its spirit.[9]

Therefore, the Federal Constitutional Court traces the fundamental rights' indirect horizontal effect back to the objective dimension of fundamental rights. As fundamental rights establish an objective system of values, the legislator and the judge also have to obey them in the area of private law. With this idea the Federal Constitutional Court, on the one hand, avoids the problem that fundamental rights are not binding between individuals. At the same time the Court does not alienate the fundamental rights in private law from their subjective roots. If a court does not interpret a general clause in the manner required by fundamental rights, it does not only objectively violate the law. The civil court – in the words of the Federal Constitutional Court – 'contravenes not only objective constitutional law by misconceiving the content of the objective norm underlying the basic law, but also, by its judgment, in its capacity as a public authority, contravenes the Constitution itself, which the citizen is constitutionally entitled to have respected by the judiciary'.[10]

[8] According to a consistent line of jurisprudence, the Federal Constitutional Court examines whether there has been a 'Verletzung spezifischen Verfasssungsrechts', a violation of specific constitutional law, not whether laws other than constitutional ones have been violated, see BVerfGE 18, 85, 92; S Korioth, 'Bundesverfassungsgericht und Rechtsprechung ("Fachgerichte")' in P Badura and H Dreier (eds), *Festschrift 50 Jahre BVerfG*, vol 1 (Tübingen, Mohr Siebeck, 2001) 55, 81; E Benda and E Klein, *Verfassungsprozessrecht*, 2nd edn (Heidelberg, CF Müller, 2001) para 654.

[9] BVerfGE 7, 198, 205 (translation by the author).

[10] BVerfGE 7, 198, 206 f; BVerfGE 89, 214, 229 f.

To a certain extent these considerations of the Federal Constitutional Court appear contradictory. Fundamental rights as subjective rights appear as an objective system of values, because they cannot have a direct effect on private law. At the same time the Court establishes a new subjective right to have the fundamental rights recognised as an objective system of values. Both parties in a private law legal relationship can refer to this right.

This possibility of both parties laying an equal claim to fundamental rights, however, is not fully realised in the Federal Constitutional Court's jurisprudence. The affected party can invoke the Federal Constitutional Court by means of a constitutional complaint if the civil court infringed the party's fundamental rights, and the Constitutional Court can review the judgment. However, only the party which was unsuccessful in the civil proceeding can lodge a constitutional complaint. Therefore, only the infringement of the claimant's rights is examined from a subjective point of view. The other party's fundamental rights are only taken into account as far as they are part of the objective system of values established by the fundamental rights. The perspective from which the Federal Constitutional Court reviews a case therefore depends on the question of which party prevailed in the civil litigation.

Trying to resolve these random effects, the Federal Constitutional Court in such cases modifies its way of examining the fundamental rights infringement compared to constellations of direct vertical fundamental rights effect. When applying fundamental rights on the basis of indirect horizontal effect, the Federal Constitutional Court first invokes the traditional doctrinal system of fundamental rights as defensive rights against the state. It examines whether a measure is within the scope of protection of a fundamental right, whether there is an interference and, as part of the justification, which restrictions on the specific fundamental right are permissible. When applying the proportionality test, however, it does not apply the criteria of proportionality in the narrow sense as it does in vertical fundamental rights situations. It does not examine whether one individual's use of fundamental rights can justify the interference with another individual's fundamental rights, but balances the conflicting fundamental rights, a process which in German is called 'practical concordance'. The court brings the conflicting fundamental rights into proportionate balance on an equal level so that none of the conflicting fundamental rights can claim more importance than the other.[11] However, in the end this concept cannot explain exactly how the subjective and the objective dimension of fundamental rights protection intertwine.

[11] Hesse (n 3) para 317 f; H Maurer, *Staatsrecht I*, 6th edn (Munich, CH Beck, 2010) para 60.

III. Multipolar Fundamental Rights Situations

A few years ago, the Federal Constitutional Court introduced a new legal term to this settled legal doctrine of indirect horizontal effect: the multipolar fundamental rights situation. Originally it developed this legal term in its so-called *Görgülü* decision in the context of human rights protection in multi-level systems. However, it has carefully begun to use it in other contexts.

A. The *Görgülü* Decision

The *Görgülü* decision is based on the following facts: the complainant, Mr Görgülü, was the father of a child born outside of marriage. The mother gave the child up for adoption one day after the birth and declared her prior consent to adoption by the foster parents, with whom the child had been living since its birth. For five years Mr Görgülü brought a number of judicial proceedings, including a constitutional complaint, which ultimately were unsuccessful, to obtain custody and to be granted a right of access. In response to his individual application, the European Court of Human Rights (ECtHR) held unanimously that the decision on custody and the exclusion of the right of access by the German courts violated Article 8 of the European Convention for the Protection of Human Rights and Fundamental Freedoms (ECHR). It held that in cases in which the family connections to a child demonstrably existed, the state had a duty to work towards uniting a natural parent and his or her child. It stated that, at the very least, the complainant must be given access to his child.[12]

Implementing this ruling, the local German court granted custody to Mr Görgülü and granted him a right of access by way of a temporary injunction of the court's own motion. The Higher Regional Court overturned the temporary injunction on the complainant's right of access. In his constitutional complaint against this decision, the complainant alleged the violation of his fundamental rights because the Higher Regional Court disregarded international law and failed to recognise the binding effect of the decision of the ECtHR.

This chapter will not explain all aspects of the controversial ruling of the Federal Constitutional Court concerning the binding effect of judgments of the ECtHR; most of them are without relevance in this context. Instead only the Court's considerations concerning the concept of multipolar fundamental rights situations will be examined. The Federal Constitutional Court held:

> If, in concrete application proceedings in which the Federal Republic of Germany is involved, the ECtHR establishes that there has been a violation of the Convention, and if this is a continuing violation, the decision of the ECtHR must be taken into account

[12] *Görgülü v Germany* App no 74969/01 [2004] ECHR 89; also reported in (2004) 57 *Neue Juristische Wochenschrift* 3397, 3399.

in the domestic sphere, that is, the responsible authorities or courts must discernibly consider the decision and, if necessary, justify understandably why they nevertheless do not follow the international-law interpretation of the law. Precisely in cases in which national courts, as in private law, have to structure multipolar fundamental rights situations, it is always important that various subjective legal positions are sensitively weighed against each other, and if there is a change in the persons involved in the dispute or a change in the actual or legal circumstances, this weighing up may lead to a different result. There may therefore be constitutional problems if one of the subjects of fundamental rights in conflict with another obtains an ECtHR judgment in his or her favour against the Federal Republic of Germany and German courts schematically apply this decision to the private-law relationship, with the result that the holder of fundamental rights who has 'lost' in this case and was possibly not involved in the proceedings at the ECHR would no longer be able to take an effective part in the proceedings as a party.[13]

B. The Case of *Caroline von Hannover*

At first glance the problem of multipolarity according to the Federal Constitutional Court seems to be a speciality of human rights protection in multi-level systems.[14] The Federal Constitutional Court held that as the ECtHR is not integrated into the national legal system, it can only declare a violation or non-violation of the ECHR. If the Court finds that there has been a violation of the Convention it can provide a remedy to the injured party; however, it is not entitled to refer the case to a national court. Therefore, so argues the Federal Constitutional Court, the ECtHR's decision could in a given case be one sided, not considering the conflicting human rights in a multipolar legal relationship in a balanced way.

These considerations, however, are only relevant for the question of how far the judgments of the ECtHR are binding for national courts. They are irrelevant in deciding how convincing the concept of multipolar fundamental rights situations is. With good reason, the Federal Constitutional Court therefore used the term in other decisions in totally different contexts.[15] However, it did not clarify which dogmatic relevance it attributes to the concept and in which relation it stands to the idea of indirect horizontal effect.

[13] (2003) 56 *Neue Juristische Wochenschrift* 3407, 3410.

[14] In the scholarly literature as well the term is adopted mainly in this context, see AD Luch, *Das Medienpersönlichkeitsrecht – Schranke der 'vierten Gewalt' Der Grundrechtsschutz in der Europäischen Union* (Munich, Herbert Utz, 2008) 260 f; G Ziegenhorn, *Der Einfluss der EMRK im Recht der EU-Grundrechtecharta* (Berlin, Duncker & Humblot, 2009) 233 f; C Grabenwarter, 'Das mehrpolige Grundrechtsverhältnis im Spannungsfeld zwischen europäischem Menschenrechtsschutz und Verfassungsgerichtsbarkeit' (eds) *Völkerrecht als Wertordnung. Festschrift für Christian Tomuschat* (Kehl, Engel, 2006) 193 f; W Hoffmann-Riem, 'Kontrolldichte und Kontrollfolgen beim nationalen und europäischen Schutz von Freiheitsrechten in mehrpoligen Rechtsverhältnissen' (2006) 33 *Europäische Grundrechte Zeitschrift* ; M Pelonpää, 'Kontrolldichte des Grund-und Menschenrechtsschutzes in mehrenpoligen Rechtsverhältnissen' (2006) 33 *Europäische Grundrechte Zeitschrift* 483 f.

[15] BVerfG (2009) 28 *Neue Zeitschrift für Verwaltungsrecht* 240, 241; BVerfG, 1 BvR 2532/07 of 12 December 2007 (not reported, available at www.bundesverfassungsgericht.de); BVerfGE 115, 205, 232; BVerfGE 114, 1, 61.

In fact, the ECtHR's intervention into the German system of fundamental rights protection did have an impact in the field of private law; it caused a change of perspective towards a multipolar point of view. This can be demonstrated with another example, which originally put on the agenda the question of how far decisions of the ECtHR are binding for German courts: the case of *Caroline von Hannover*, a case concerning the conflict between the right of privacy and freedom of expression.[16] In this case, the ECtHR rendered a judgment which declared that a prior decision of the Federal Constitutional Court violated Caroline von Hannover's right to protection of her private life laid down in Article 8 ECHR. Since then the Federal Constitutional Court's jurisprudence has changed. A recent decision seized on the concept of multipolar fundamental rights situations.

i. The ECtHR's Judgment

Since the beginning of the 1990s, Princess Caroline von Hannover has been campaigning in various European countries to prevent photographs about her private life from being published in the tabloid press. She has on several occasions unsuccessfully applied to the German courts for an injunction preventing any further publication of a series of photographs which had appeared in the 1990s in German magazines, claiming that they infringed her right to protection of her private life and her right to control the use of her image.

In a landmark decision of 1999,[17] the Federal Constitutional Court granted the applicant's request for an injunction regarding the photographs in which she appeared with her children on the ground that their need for protection of their privacy was greater than that of adults.[18] However, the Court considered that the applicant had to tolerate the publication of photographs of her taken in public places, even if they showed her in scenes from her daily life rather than engaged in her official duties. In its decision the Court referred to the freedom of the press and to the public's legitimate interest in knowing how such a person generally behaved in public.[19]

The ECtHR declared that the Federal Constitutional Court's decision violated Article 8 ECHR. The ECtHR considered the decisive factor in balancing the protection of private life against freedom of expression was that the published photographs and articles contributed to a debate of general interest. While the general public might have a right to information, including, in special circumstances, information about the private life of public figures, they did not have such a right in this instance. The ECtHR concluded that the general public did not have a legitimate interest in knowing Caroline von Hannover's whereabouts or how she behaved generally in her private life, even if she appeared in places that could not

[16] See KS Ziegler, 'The Princess and the Press: Privacy after Caroline von Hannover v. Germany' in KS Ziegler (ed), *Human Rights and Private Law: Privacy as Autonomy* (Oxford, Hart Publishing, 2007) 189 f.

[17] BVerfGE 101, 361.

[18] BVerfGE 101, 361, 385 f.

[19] BVerfGE 101, 361, 391 f.

always be described as secluded and were easily accessible to the public. Even if such a public interest existed, just as there was a commercial interest for the magazines to publish the photographs and articles, those interests had to yield to the applicant's right to the effective protection of her private life.[20]

This decision has been very controversial in Germany.[21] The interesting point about this is that the decisive factors for balancing the conflicting fundamental rights laid down by the ECtHR on an abstract level in fact hardly differ from those factors laid down by the Federal Constitutional Court.[22] For example, the Federal Constitutional Court also stated that in balancing the freedom of expression against conflicting personality rights, it has to be determined whether there is a serious and relevant discussion of questions which substantially concern the public or whether there is merely a dissemination of private matters which only satisfy curiosity.[23]

The difference between the ECtHR and the Federal Constitutional Court therefore lies on a specific, not on an abstract level, because the Federal Constitutional Court always avoided taking into consideration whether a publication made a contribution to a debate of general interest or not.[24]

ii. The Federal Constitutional Court's New Caroline *Decision*

After the ECtHR's judgment, the German civil courts did not implement the new guidelines set by the Strasbourg judges in a uniform way.[25] In 2007 the Federal Court of Justice rendered a landmark decision concerning the conflict between the freedom of the press and the right of privacy.[26] This decision again arose from a dispute between Caroline von Hannover and the tabloid press. Again the princess wanted to prevent any further publication of a series of photographs.

On this occasion the Federal Court of Justice modified its jurisprudence and adjusted it to that of the ECtHR. It therefore interdicted the further publication of most, but not all, of the photographs that were the subject of the dispute. Consequently the publisher as well as the princess lodged a constitutional complaint. On the occasion of these complaints the Federal Constitutional Court

[20] (2004) 57 *Neue Juristische Wochenschrift* 2647, 2649 f.

[21] See F Gersdorf, 'Caroline-Urteil des EGMR—Bedrohung der nationalen Medienordnung'(2005) 50 *Archiv für Presserecht* 221 f; C Grabenwarter, 'Caroline-Urteil des EGMR—Bedrohung der nationalen Medienordnung' (2004) 49 *Archiv für Presserecht* 309 f; A Halfmeier, 'Privatleben und Pressefreiheit – Rechtsvereinheitlichung par ordre de Strasbourg' (2004) 49 *Archiv für Presserecht* 417 f; R Vetter and N Warneke, 'Zur Abgrenzung von Pressefreiheit und Schutz der Privatsphäre' 2004) 119 *Deutsches Verwaltungsblatt* 1226 f.

[22] See A Heldrich, 'Persönlichkeitsschutz und Pressefreiheit nach der Europäischen Menschenrechtskonvention' (2004) 57 *Neue Juristische Wochenschrift* 2634, 2636; S-C Lenski, 'Der Persönlichkeitsschutz Prominenter unter EMRK und Grundgesetz'(2005) 24 *Neue Zeitschrift für Verwaltungsrecht* 50, 51.

[23] BVerfGE 34, 269, 283; 101, 361, 391.

[24] See Lenski (n 22) 51.

[25] See K-N Peifer, 'Zur Reichweite des Persönlichkeitsschutzes Prominenter in Bezug auf die Veröffentlichung von Fotos aus dem Privat- und Alltagsleben' (2008) 111 *Gewerblicher Rechtsschutz und Urheberrecht* 547, 548.

[26] BGHZ 171, 275.

could now set new constitutional measures, taking into account the ECtHR's case law. In doing so the Federal Constitutional Court again used the term of multipolar fundamental rights situations,[27] although in comparison to the *Görgülü* decision this aspect was not a central point. On the whole, however, one can find distinct differences concerning the argumentation after the ECtHR's decision.

The first difference concerns the decisive factors in balancing the conflicting fundamental rights. In this new *Caroline* decision, the Federal Constitutional Court for the first time answers the question how far a publication makes a contribution to a serious and relevant discussion of questions which substantially concern the public.[28] For the first time the Court, in balancing the freedom of the press and the right of privacy, not only decides the question of how seriously the individual's privacy is interfered with, but also considers the interest the public has in information when weighing the freedom of the press.

The question how to balance the conflicting rights raises a more conceptual question, which appears at another point of the judgment. In the new *Caroline* decision, the Federal Constitutional Court does not only examine the scope of protection of, the interference with, and the constitutional justification for, each fundamental right separately. Rather, it combines the examination of the fundamental rights of the publisher on the one hand and the fundamental rights of the princess on the other. By doing so, the Court connects the examination of the freedom of the press and the right of privacy when balancing the conflicting fundamental rights. Therefore, the conflict between the fundamental rights is not just discussed within the proportionality test in a narrow sense. The Court instead examines the scope of protection, and the interference with and restrictions of the fundamental right in a parallel way for both fundamental rights. Only within the proportionality test does the Court again combine the examination of the two fundamental rights by balancing them on an equal level. In doing so the Federal Constitutional Court applies the idea of multipolar legal relationships – it not only examines one fundamental right in an isolated way, but combines the examination of both fundamental rights without having to refer to the objective dimension of fundamental rights.

IV. Conclusions

Against the background of this decision one has to ask how far the concept of multipolar fundamental rights situations is able to replace the idea of indirect horizontal effect. The decision of the Federal Constitutional Court in the case *Caroline von Hannover* seems to imply this development. But how generalisable are the Court's findings in this case?

[27] BVerfGE 120, 180, 212.
[28] BVerfGE 120, 180, 215 f.

If one wanted to hold on to the objective reasoning of the horizontal effect of fundamental rights, the generalisability would be denied and the specific procedural constellation emphasised. The specific constellation of the case lies in the fact that both parties to the civil litigation – the publisher and Caroline von Hannover – lodged constitutional complaints against the judgment of the Federal Court of Justice. The Federal Constitutional Court joined the two constitutional complaints procedures. Due to the fact that the two cases were joined, the parallel examination of the two fundamental rights appears the logical consequence.

However, the fact that the cases were joined is not the cause but rather the consequence of the new perspective on fundamental rights in private law as multipolar fundamental rights situations. The Federal Constitutional Court is free to decide which complaints to join. Neither the Basic Law nor the Federal Constitutional Court Act imposes an obligation to join constitutional complaints under certain circumstances. It is the Federal Constitutional Court's decision whether to do so or not. Additionally, in the new *Caroline* decision there was no logical need to join the cases. In each of the original complaints, different publications and different photographs were subject to the constitutional complaints. Moreover, by consolidating the complaints the Federal Constitutional Court carried out its change of perspective towards the multipolar fundamental rights situation.

The new perspective of multipolar fundamental rights situations facilitates a view that locates the conflicting fundamental rights at the same level without having to refer to the objective dimension of fundamental rights. This enables courts to balance the conflicting fundamental rights on an equal basis. This new approach is applied in the *Caroline* decision, where the Federal Constitutional Court not only weighs the importance of the right of privacy on a concrete level but also considers the importance of the freedom of the press by examining how far a publication contributes to a debate of general interest. We will see if the Federal Constitutional Court will follow up this idea in its future jurisprudence.

10

Empirical Research in Rights-based Judicial Review of Legislation

PAUL YOWELL

I. Introduction

The standard method courts use to determine whether government action violates human rights is proportionality. In many cases this is a fact-sensitive inquiry. Because proportionality concerns the efficacy of means and the nature and acceptability of side effects, questions about empirical causality are built into it, in various respects. In judicial review of legislation, proportionality is typically formulated as an inquiry involving all or some combination of the following steps:

1. *Legitimacy*: Does the legislative measure pursue a legitimate aim?
2. *Suitability* (or rationality): Are the means chosen by the legislature suitable for the intended purpose?
3. *Necessity* (or minimal impairment): Are other, less restrictive means capable of producing the same result?
4. *Balancing* (or proportionality *stricto sensu*): Does the measure strike an appropriate balance between the 'state interest' and the burden on the individual right (or interest protected by the right)?[1]

According to the Canadian Supreme Court, the proportionality inquiry required by section 1 of the Canadian Charter of Rights and Freedoms 'is by its very nature a fact-specific inquiry':

> In determining proportionality, [a court] must determine the actual connection between the objective and what the law will in fact achieve; the actual degree to which it impairs the right; and whether the *actual* benefit which the law is calculated to achieve outweighs the *actual* seriousness of the limitation of the right. In short, s. 1 is an exercise

[1] Eg T Tridimas, *The General Principles of EU Law* (Oxford, OUP, 1999) 92; *R v Oakes* [1986] 1 SCR 103, paras 69–71.

> based on the facts of the law at issue and the proof offered of its justification, not on abstractions.[2]

Here 'actual' signifies a concern with facts, actualities. The European Court of Human Rights (ECtHR) holds that in order to demonstrate conformity with the principle of proportionality, national authorities must show 'that they based their decisions on an acceptable assessment of the relevant facts'.[3] The US Supreme Court has stated that 'underlying questions of fact may condition the constitutionality of legislation'.[4] (While US courts do not use the term 'proportionality', they often use tests of rationality, minimal impairment, and balancing that resemble the steps listed above.[5]) In cases involving a rights-based challenge to the constitutionality of legislation, courts regularly assess the results of research in economics, psychology, sociology, medicine, and other fields, especially when assessing the strength of the state's interest in legislation, but also for other aspects of the proportionality inquiry. Such evidence may be presented by the government in defence of a law, or by a claimant seeking to demonstrate the unconstitutionality of a law.

This chapter will discuss the origins of this method of judicial review of legislation and consider whether courts have institutional capacities that are fit for the purpose. Most judges do not have scientific training, and courts, unlike legislatures, generally lack dedicated staff and other internal resources for acquiring and evaluating factual information. Empirical sources may be submitted by parties or found by judges through their own investigation; on occasion courts appoint expert witnesses to provide testimony on factual issues. An analysis of cases that rely on empirical research shows that judges make frequent errors in using empirical sources and in applying concepts in statistical analysis. Courts sometimes employ haphazard research methods (such as Internet search engines) and rely on questionable sources (including Wikipedia). Moreover, by attempting to assess empirical research within the technical, legalistic framework of litigation, courts may unduly restrict inquiry into a subject. The weak capacity of courts to assess empirical research raises questions about the legitimacy of rights-based judicial review of legislation in some of its current forms. This chapter will conclude by considering proposals for improving judicial fact-finding capacity in constitutional cases.

[2] *RJR-MacDonald, Inc v Canada* [1994] 1 SCR 311, para 133 (italics added).

[3] *Makhmudov v Russia* App no 35082/04 (2008) 46 EHRR 37, para 65.

[4] *O'Gorman & Young Inc v Hartford Fire Ins Co* 282 US 251, 257 (1930).

[5] See TA Aleinikoff, 'Constitutional Law in the Age of Balancing' (1986) 96 *Yale Law Journal* 943; ET Sullivan and RS Frase, *Proportionality Principles in American Law: Controlling Excessive Government Actions* (Oxford, OUP, 2008) 51–90.

II. The Origins of Balancing Tests in the United States

The connection between proportionality and empirical research can be traced to the origin of balancing tests in constitutional law. The procedural vehicle that parties use to submit empirical evidence regarding the constitutionality of legislation is known both in the United States and elsewhere as a 'Brandeis brief', a term deriving from the US Supreme Court case *Muller v Oregon* (1908).[6] An Oregon statute that prohibited women from working more than 10 hours per day in factories and laundries was challenged on the basis of the freedom of contract, which the Court had earlier held was implied in the 14th Amendment right to due process of law.[7] Louis Brandeis, a Boston lawyer who would later become a justice of the US Supreme Court, filed an amicus brief on behalf of Oregon in defence of the law, which contained only two pages of legal argument and almost 100 pages referencing social science and other factual material.[8] Brandeis advanced factual data and policy arguments regarding the harmful effects of long working hours (on women and their families and communities), mostly by way of quoting medical opinions, academic studies, reports of factory inspectors and bureaus of labour statistics, and other sources. The Court upheld the Oregon law, and Brandeis's brief has been used as a model in many subsequent cases, both in the United States and in other jurisdictions.

Although Brandeis has been hailed as a visionary who made constitutional law responsive to facts,[9] his strategy in *Muller* is better understood as a reaction to the landmark case decided three years earlier, *Lochner v New York* (1905),[10] in which the Supreme Court struck down New York's Bakeshop Act, which limited the hours that bakery employees could work to 60 per week. The Court based its ruling on the 14th Amendment and the right to freedom of contract, which was also the basis of the constitutional challenge in *Muller*. Unlike Brandeis, the attorney for the state of New York did not submit detailed empirical evidence to defend the law being challenged.[11] This contrast has been widely noted, often alongside the claim that Brandeis was the first to use empirical evidence in constitutional litigation. The latter claim, however, is incorrect. The *Lochner* litigation was orchestrated by the New York Master Bakers Association, which hired Henry Weismann to defend Joseph Lochner, the owner of

[6] *Muller v Oregon* 208 US 412 (1908).

[7] *Allgeyer v Louisiana* 165 US 578 (1897).

[8] 'Brief for Defendant in Error, *Muller v Oregon*' in PB Kurland and G Casper (eds), *Landmark Briefs and Arguments of the Supreme Court of the United States Constitutional Law*, vol 16 (Washington, DC, University Publications of America, 1975).

[9] This reputation is based both on the brief in *Muller* and his later judicial career. See eg F Frankfurter, 'Mr. Justice Brandeis and the Constitution' in F Frankfurter (ed), *Mr. Justice Brandeis* (New Haven, Yale University Press, 1932) 52 ('At a time when our constitutional law was becoming dangerously unresponsive to drastic social changes, when sterile clichés instead of facts were deciding cases, [Brandeis] insisted . . . that law must be sensitive to life').

[10] *Lochner v New York* 198 US 45.

[11] See 'Brief for plaintiff in Error, *Muller v Oregon*' (n 8).

a small bakery in Utica, NY, who had been convicted under the Bakeshop Act after one of his employees worked excessive hours.[12] This background of the case is usually overlooked in historical narratives, as is the fact that Weismann filed a brief containing several pages of information regarding working conditions in the baking trade and the causes of ill health and diseases among bakers.[13] Relying on this evidence, Weismann argued that the hours limitation in the Bakeshop Act was unnecessary and did little to promote the health of bakers. The brief included citations to three comparative mortality studies for occupations and professions, one of which found that bakers had a low mortality rate (18th out of 22 occupations surveyed), while two others placed bakers near the middle.[14] In one study the chart score (where a lower number indicates a lower mortality rate) for bakers was 920, which compared favourably to dock workers (1829) and general labourers (1221); bakers were worse off than clergymen (533) but similar to lawyers (810).[15] Weismann also cited articles from medical journals urging improved ventilation and sanitary reforms but not shorter hours – a *Lancet* article suggested that shorter hours would not alleviate health problems.[16] Though the Court did not cite Weismann's brief, it clearly relied on the evidence it contained. Justice Peckham wrote in the majority opinion:

> We think that there can be no fair doubt that the trade of a baker, in and of itself, is not an unhealthy one to that degree which would authorize the legislature to interfere with the right to labor, and with the right of free contract on the part of the individual, either as employer or employee. *In looking through statistics regarding all trades and occupations*, it may be true that the trade of a baker does not appear to be as healthy as some other trades, and is also vastly more healthy than still others.[17]

The content of Weismann's brief has eluded many commentators, and this has contributed to the legend that the Brandeis brief was the first of its kind. One of the few scholars to discuss the brief acknowledged that until reading it he had always regarded Peckham's statistical argument above as a 'flight of fancy'.[18]

The Court assessed the empirical evidence pursuant to an incipient balancing or proportionality test. The Court first rejected any 'labour law' rationale for the Bakeshop Act, holding that the right to freedom of contract prevents the state from limiting working hours on the ground that bakers lack bargaining power in negotiations with employers over desirable working hours.[19] The state was per-

[12] DE Bernstein, 'Lochner v. New York: A Centennial Retrospective' (2005) 83 *Washington University Law Quarterly* 1469, 1487–98.

[13] 'Brief for Plaintiff in Error, *Lochner v New York*' (n 8). Frank Harvey Field was co-counsel with Weismann on the brief.

[14] Ibid.

[15] Ibid.

[16] Ibid.

[17] *Lochner v New York* 198 US 45, 59 (1905) (italics added).

[18] SA Siegel, 'Lochner Era Jurisprudence and the American Constitutional Tradition' (1991) 70 *North Carolina Law Review* 1, n 77.

[19] 'There is no contention that bakers as a class are not equal in intelligence and capacity to men in other trades or manual occupations, or that they are not able to assert their rights and care for themselves without the protecting arm of the state, interfering with their independence of judgment and of action.' *Lochner v New York* 198 US 45, 57 (1905).

mitted to regulate working hours on the basis of the police power to promote health and safety; however, any 'unreasonable, unnecessary, and arbitrary interference with the right of the individual to his personal liberty' would be annulled.[20]

> It is a question of which of two powers or rights shall prevail – the power of the state to legislate or the right of the individual to liberty of person and freedom of contract. The mere assertion that the subject relates, though but in a remote degree, to the public health, does not necessarily render the enactment valid. *The act must have a more direct relation, as a means to an end, and the end itself must be appropriate and legitimate*, before an act can be held to be valid which interferes with the general right of an individual to be free in his person and in his power to contract in relation to his own labor.[21]

Here we find all the key components of the modern proportionality inquiry: (i) scrutiny of the legitimacy of the legislative aim (the Court approved the health and safety aim but rejected the 'labour law' rationale); (ii) a necessity or minimal impairment test regarding the relationship between means and ends of legislation; and (iii) balancing of the public welfare against the 'interference' with the individual right. *Lochner* was possibly the first US Supreme Court case to strike down a law on such a basis.

After noting the mid-level mortality rate of bakers, the Court proceeded to consider other facts in applying the above balancing or proportionality standards, and to justify its use of those standards. The Court observed that in large cities 'there are many buildings into which the sun penetrates for but a short time in each day',[22] which are occupied by the employees of many businesses, and that working prolonged hours in such conditions could be argued to be unhealthy. If a law is valid because it promotes health in any degree whatsoever, the Court reasoned, then it would be possible for a law to prohibit lawyers and bank clerks and other employees from 'contracting to labor for their employers more than eight hours a day'.[23] Thus, in the absence of a necessity or minimal impairment test, no trade or occupation would be safe from the legislature's 'all-pervading power' and 'paternal wisdom'.[24] The Bakeshop Act required proper furnishing of washrooms and set building standards on matters such as drainage and plumbing, ceiling height, and flooring; and it provided for inspections by an official with the power to order alterations. 'Adding to all these requirements', the Court concluded, was unnecessary for the health of bakers; the limitation of working hours was not a 'proper, reasonable and fair provision' but an unjustifiable interference with the right to 'liberty of person and of free contract'.[25] This result, Justice Peckham claimed, was an objective, rational inference from the evidence: 'This is not a question of substituting the judgment of the court for that of the legislature.'[26]

[20] Ibid at 56.
[21] Ibid, 57–58.
[22] Ibid, 59.
[23] Ibid, 60.
[24] Ibid.
[25] Ibid, 62.
[26] Ibid, 56–57.

This language is strikingly similar to that used by modern proponents of proportionality to mark a limit on the scope or intensity of judicial scrutiny.[27]

Brandeis learned the lesson of *Lochner* and shrewdly responded by compiling an extensive record of factual information to defend the law in *Muller*. But he did not invent the technique; he adapted his litigation strategy to the new paradigm of proportionality-based review and consideration of empirical research, a paradigm set in place by *Lochner* itself. The two pages of legal argument in Brandeis's brief focused on *Lochner* and cited its standards regarding minimal impairment of rights and the appropriate relationship between legislative ends and means.[28]

Although the law Brandeis defended in *Muller* survived scrutiny, the US Supreme Court later struck down many other laws concerning economic regulation, working conditions, and related matters, including minimum wage legislation for women in *Adkins v Children's Hospital* (1923),[29] and laws designed to enable workers to join unions without suffering adverse employment consequences.[30] During the '*Lochner* era', which lasted for some 30 years, the Supreme Court and other federal and state courts struck down hundreds of laws, and the case became a byword for excessive judicial activism.[31] Although these cases employed a variety of constitutional doctrines, many of them turned on empirical assessments of the effects of legislation. Justice Brandeis, who was appointed to the Court in 1916, observed (in a 1932 dissenting opinion) that in 'the cases which now come before us there is seldom any dispute as to the *interpretation* of any provision'; the questions are about 'applying' constitutional limitations 'as opposed to what may be accurately called interpreting the Constitution'.[32] This is

> strikingly true of cases under the due process clause when the question is whether a statute is unreasonable, arbitrary, or capricious; [and] of cases under the equal protection clause when the question is whether there is any reasonable basis for the classification made by a statute . . .[33]
>
> These issues resemble, fundamentally, that of reasonable care in negligence cases, the determination of which is ordinarily left to the verdict of the jury. In every such case the decision, in the first instance, is dependent upon the determination of what in legal parlance is called a fact, as distinguished from the declaration of a rule of law. When the underlying fact has been found, the legal result follows inevitably. The circumstance that the decision of that fact is made by a court, instead of by a jury, should not be allowed to obscure its real character.[34]

[27] 'Decisions as to political and social choice are made by the legislature, or by a person assigned the task by a legislature', and 'it is not for the courts to substitute their judgment on the merits of the case for that of the primary decision-maker'. P Craig, 'Unreasonableness and Proportionality in UK Law' in E Ellis, *The Principle of Proportionality in the Laws of Europe* (Oxford, Hart, 1999) 85.

[28] 'Brief for Defendant in Error' (n 8).

[29] *Adkins v Children's Hospital* 261 US 525.

[30] *Adair v United States* 208 US 161 (1908); *Coppage v Kansas* 236 US 1 (1915).

[31] MJ Phillips, *The Lochner Court, Myth and Reality: Substantive Due Process From the 1890s to the 1930s* (Santa Barbara, Praeger, 2001).

[32] *Burnet v Coronado Oil & Gas Co* 285 US 393, 410 (1932) (italics added).

[33] Ibid.

[34] Ibid.

The Supreme Court never explicitly overruled *Lochner*, but it changed its approach to review of economic regulations in the mid-1930s. In *West Coast Hotel Co v Parrish* (1937)[35] the Court overruled *Adkins* and upheld minimum wage legislation for women, and in the following years the Court abandoned the right to freedom of contract as a basis for challenging legislation and applied far less scrutiny to laws on employment and similar subjects.

The Court signalled a new direction in *United States v Carolene Products Co* (1938), which upheld the constitutionality of a consumer-protection law because it had a 'rational basis';[36] this was a minimally searching test that, in general, became the standard for reviewing economic regulations and laws based on the police power to promote health, safety, and public welfare. The Court suggested, however, in the famous footnote 4 of that decision, that it would apply more intensive scrutiny to legislation that 'appears on its face to be within a specific prohibition of the Constitution, such as those of the first ten amendments'.[37] In the ensuing decades the Court adopted a 'strict scrutiny' standard for First Amendment rights to freedom of expression, association, and religion, as well as for claims under the Fourteenth Amendment's Equal Protection Clause when a law made a classification based on race or nationality. The rationale for this approach was stated by the Court in footnote 4:

> prejudice against discrete and insular minorities may be a special condition, which tends seriously to curtail the operation of those political processes ordinarily to be relied upon to protect minorities, and which may call for a correspondingly more searching judicial inquiry.[38]

Thus, after the *Lochner* era, the Court shifted its focus away from economic activity and relationships and toward areas such as privacy; racial equality; and freedom of speech, association, and religion. While the Court developed specialised lines of constitutional doctrine regarding the scope of particular rights and the level of scrutiny with which to apply them, the underlying judicial method that was developed during the *Lochner* era prevailed and remains in operation today. The Court resolves many cases by applying constitutional limitations through balancing tests,[39] and by using empirical evidence to determine the necessity of legislation, the strength of the state's interest in it, and its effects on rights-protected interests of individuals. Felix Frankfurter, writing before his appointment to the Court, described the revolution in judicial technique in the early 20th century as an advance of the modern age and a victory for the scientific method,[40] but erroneously credited its origin to Brandeis's brief in *Muller*:

[35] *West Coast Hotel Co v Parrish* 300 US 379.
[36] *United States v Carolene Products Co* 304 US 144.
[37] Ibid, n 4.
[38] Ibid.
[39] TA Aleinikoff, 'Constitutional Law in the Age of Balancing' (1986) 96 *Yale Law Journal* 943.
[40] F Frankfurter, 'Hours of Labor and Realism in Constitutional Law' (1915) 29 *Harvard Law Review* 353, 363.

> [Previously] courts decided these issues on *a priori* theories, on abstract assumptions, because scientific data were not available or at least had not been made available for the use of courts. But all this time scientific data had been accumulating. Organized observation, investigation, and experimentation produced facts, and science could at last speak with rational if tentative authority. There was a growing body of the world's experience and the validated opinions of those competent to have opinions.
>
> The *Muller* case, in 1908, was the first case presented to our courts on the basis of authoritative data. For the first time the arguments and briefs breathed the air of reality . . . For there can be no denial that the technique of the brief in the *Muller* case has established itself through a series of decisions within the last few years, which have caused not only change in decisions, but the much more vital change of method of approach to constitutional questions.[41]

Like many later commentators, Frankfurter somehow failed to notice that the 'vital change of method' was already accomplished in *Lochner*. Brandeis skilfully elaborated the technique that Weismann had used in *Lochner*, but Weismann has the better claim to inventing it.

In the modern era, the US Supreme Court has considered or directly relied on various kinds of factual information and empirical research in many major cases, including decisions about the constitutionality of abortion law,[42] regulation of obscene and indecent material on the internet,[43] and the death penalty.[44] The Court's most well-known use of social science was in *Brown v Board of Education* (1954),[45] which held that state legislation mandating racial segregation of pupils in public schools violates the Equal Protection Clause of the 14th Amendment. Although the Court did not expressly overrule the 'separate but equal' doctrine adopted in *Plessy v Ferguson* (1896),[46] it held that the doctrine has no place in public education because racially segregated facilities are inherently unequal. This conclusion was based on psychological research showing that segregation generates feelings of inferiority in black schoolchildren that diminish the motivation to learn and inhibit educational and mental development. The Court cited four psychological studies and two books in support of this finding, and suggested that its earlier decision may have been based on flawed or missing empirical data:

[41] Ibid, 364–65 (italics added).

[42] *Roe v Wade* 410 US 113 (1973). In deciding that most state laws on abortion violated the right to privacy, the Court discussed, among other things, medical aspects of pregnancy and abortion, the development of the foetus and the point of viability, and comparative mortality rates for women in childbirth and abortion procedures.

[43] *Reno v American Civil Liberties Union* 521 US 844 (1997). In striking down the Communications Decency Act of 1996, the Court relied on detailed findings on internet technology.

[44] *Gregg v Georgia* 428 US 153 (1976). In a decision to uphold some capital punishment statutes, the Court stated: 'Although some of the studies suggest that the death penalty may not function as a significantly greater deterrent than lesser penalties, there is no convincing empirical evidence either supporting or refuting this view. We may nevertheless assume safely that there are murderers, such as those who act in passion, for whom the threat of death has little or no deterrent effect. But for many others, the death penalty undoubtedly is a significant deterrent.' Ibid, 185–86.

[45] *Brown v Board of Education* 347 US 483.

[46] *Plessy v Ferguson* 163 US 537.

'Whatever may have been the extent of psychological knowledge at the time of *Plessy v Ferguson* this finding is amply supported by modern authority.'[47]

In *Grutter v Bollinger* (2006),[48] the Court upheld the use of affirmative action for minorities in university admissions programmes against a challenge based on the Equal Protection Clause, relying on social science research, expert testimony in the trial court, and amicus briefs from business leaders and military officers, in concluding that such programmes produce beneficial outcomes and that there is a compelling state interest in maintaining them.[49] The Court, however, ventured to predict that in 25 years race-conscious admissions programmes would no longer be necessary because of changed conditions in society.[50] This prediction illustrates the radical dependency of proportionality-based reasoning on factual information. And it suggests that in a future case the Court might strike down, rather than uphold, affirmative action programmes on the basis of updated social science.

III. Proportionality in Europe and Canada

In Europe and Canada the adoption of the proportionality inquiry in constitutional law can be traced to developments distinct from the US history considered in section II, but which sometimes involved similar lines of thought. In Germany proportionality became the standard of review in constitutional rights cases soon after the adoption of the *Grundgesetz* [Basic Law] and creation of the Bundesverfassungsgericht [Federal Constitutional Court] in 1949. Dieter Grimm, a former justice of that court, states that proportionality was first developed by German administrative courts to protect individuals' liberty and property from police measures when laws allowed discretion in the means of enforcement; those courts articulated the now-familiar elements requiring enforcement action to have a legitimate aim and suitable means, employ the least intrusive available means, and strike a proper balance between intrusiveness of the means and the importance of the goal to be achieved.[51] In the 1950s, according to Grimm, the Bundesverfassungsgericht began to transfer this test to constitutional law, but without a fundamental explanation of why rights in the *Grundgesetz* should be applied through proportionality; the 'principle was introduced as if it could be taken for granted'.[52] Something similar could be said of the earlier developments in the United States – *Lochner* and other cases appropriated a doctrine about the appropriate limits to exercise of the police power for use in

[47] *Brown* (n 45) 494 and n 11.

[48] *Grutter v Bollinger* 539 US 306.

[49] Ibid, 330–32.

[50] Ibid, 343.

[51] D Grimm, 'Proportionality in Canadian and German Constitutional Jurisprudence' (2007) 57 *University of Toronto Law Journal* 383, 384–85.

[52] Ibid, 385.

constitutional law, without a full and satisfactory explanation of why the phrase 'due process of law' in the 14th Amendment imposed such substantive limitations on legislative power.[53]

The proportionality inquiry was adopted by the ECtHR in the *Belgian Linguistics Case* (1968)[54] and by the Canadian Supreme Court in *R v Oakes* (1986).[55] In both jurisdictions human rights are formulated in a way that allows rights to be limited,[56] and proportionality is taken to be the appropriate method for determining the justifications for, and legitimate scope of, such limitations.

While the United States has the most extensive history of using empirical research in rights-based judicial review, the practice (together with the use of Brandeis briefs) has tended to follow the adoption of the proportionality tests. For example, when in *Hatton v United Kingdom* (2003) the ECtHR was asked to decide whether a UK ruling permitting night flights at Heathrow airport[57] violated the right of nearby residents to private and home life (Article 8 of the European Convention on Human Rights (ECHR)), the ECtHR considered information about the decibel levels in homes of the noise from planes and the degree to which different levels impair sleep; a statistical study on sleep disturbance and the likelihood of being awakened by aeroplane noise in comparison to other causes; the value of affected homes near Heathrow and the economic feasibility of residents moving elsewhere; economic assessments of the value of night flights at Heathrow to the aviation industry and the UK economy in general; and measures undertaken for the abatement and mitigation of airport noise.[58] The last category included such matters as

> aircraft noise certification to reduce noise at source; the compulsory phasing out of older, noisier jet aircraft; noise preferential routes and minimum climb gradients for aircraft taking off; [and] noise abatement approach procedures (continuous descent and low power/low drag procedures).[59]

The ECtHR, in a divided decision (12–5) by the Grand Chamber, held that the ruling on night flights did not violate Article 8 of the ECHR, because it did not find that UK authorities

[53] See S Legarre, 'The Historical Background of the Police Power' (2006) 9 *University of Pennsylvania Journal of Constitutional Law* 745, especially 785–93, for a discussion of developments in police power jurisprudence and its influence on the constitutional law of the *Lochner* era.

[54] *Case Relating to Certain Aspects of the Laws on the Use of Languages in Education in Belgium*, Series A no 6 (1968), (1979–80) 1 EHRR 252.

[55] *R v Oakes* 1 SCR 103, paras 69–71.

[56] In the European Convention on Human Rights (ECHR), the rights to freedom of speech and private life, as well as other frequently invoked rights, can be limited only as 'necessary in a democratic society' for protecting certain public interests (safety, health, morals, public order) or the rights and freedoms of others. The Canadian Charter of Rights and Freedoms includes a general limitations clause; section 1 guarantees 'the rights and freedoms set out in it subject only to such reasonable limits prescribed by law as can be demonstrably justified in a free and democratic society'.

[57] The ruling was issued by the Secretary of State for Transport pursuant to powers under the Civil Aviation Act 1982.

[58] *Hatton v United Kingdom* App no 36022/97 (2003) 37 EHRR 28.

[59] Ibid, para 74.

> overstepped their margin of appreciation by failing to strike a fair balance between the right of the individuals affected by those regulations to respect for their private life and home and the conflicting interests of others and of the community as a whole.[60]

The Bundesverfassungsgericht and Canadian Supreme Court also regularly rely on empirical research in rights-based judicial review of legislation. In section VI, I will analyse the use of such research in *Chaoulli v Quebec* (2005),[61] which held that a prohibition on private health insurance violates the right to life, and in the recent *Smoking Ban Case* in Germany,[62] which held that certain antismoking laws violate the right to freedom of occupation of the owners of small pubs and other establishments.

IV. Adjudicative and Legislative Facts

Fact-finding is, of course, central to adjudication. There are important differences, however, between reviewing evidence presented in Brandeis briefs and fact-finding in ordinary trials. The American scholar Kenneth Culp Davis introduced the terms 'adjudicative fact' and 'legislative fact' to distinguish two types of information used in judicial decision-making. Adjudicative facts concern the immediate parties in a case, answering the questions 'who did what, where, when, how, and with what motive or intent'.[63] Legislative facts are the general facts about society that inform a court's legislative judgment on questions of law and policy.[64] Davis's distinctions and terminology have (like 'Brandeis brief') been widely adopted by courts and theorists both in the United States and other jurisdictions.

The difference between adjudicative facts and legislative facts does not necessarily turn on the subject matter or complexity of the evidence. Adjudicative facts usually consist in historical information about what a person did or said, the contents of documents, physical characteristics of an object or location, and other discrete facts. But adjudicative facts may also involve expert testimony and evidence on complex scientific and medical issues in areas such as patents, medical malpractice, or forensic use of DNA traces. Legislative facts often pertain to empirical research, but they may consist in general knowledge of a subject such as the stock market (which a judge might rely on in interpreting securities laws). The main conceptual distinction concerns the reason for using the evidence: adjudicative facts relate directly to claims between the parties while legislative facts transcend the instant case and concern the interpretation or constitutional validity of

[60] Ibid, para 129.

[61] *Chaoulli v Quebec* 1 SCR 791.

[62] *Smoking Ban Case* BVerfGE 121, 317.

[63] KC Davis, 'Judicial Notice' (1955) 55 *Columbia Law Review* 945, 952. See also KC Davis, 'Facts in Lawmaking' (1980) 80 *Columbia Law Review* 931.

[64] Ibid.

the law itself.[65] Adjudicative fact-finding is usually retrospective; it concerns past events and their bearing upon the parties in a case. Legislative fact-finding is generally prospective; it anticipates what will happen in the future with regard to the consequences of a law or a contemplated interpretation thereof. When conducting the proportionality inquiry, a court must determine 'what the law will in fact achieve', according to the Canadian Supreme Court.[66] The distinction between adjudicative and legislative facts cannot be marked by a bright line, just as the distinction between questions of law and questions of fact is not clear cut.[67] In some cases it may be unclear whether a judge's reliance on factual information is to inform his understanding of a question of fact in the particular case or a question about the interpretation of a law (or both), but this difficulty need not detain us. Much of the evidence presented in Brandeis briefs and relied on by courts in proportionality tests clearly falls in the category of legislative fact.

Adjudicative facts are admitted to the record in the trial court, through a formal process that is created by law and closely regulated. Legislative facts, on the other hand, need not be admitted into the trial record or undergo any formal scrutiny. Judges regularly seek out legislative facts on their own initiative and conduct their own research,[68] but the extent of this practice is unknown. As Davis explains in relation to the United States:

> How much the Supreme Court goes beyond the record for legislative facts to guide the making of law and policy cannot be accurately ascertained from the opinions just because resort to the practice undoubtedly exceeds specific formal acknowledgments of the practice. But the acknowledgments are numerous enough to show that the practice is a commonplace.[69]

In some cases, evidence of legislative facts and related expert testimony is submitted to the trial court. But in many cases parties submit legislative facts for the first time in appellate briefs, as Brandeis did in *Muller*. In the United States, it is increasingly common for non-parties to submit Brandeis briefs; high-profile, controversial cases can attract dozens of such amicus filings. There are generally no procedural rules regarding whether or how courts should consider amicus briefs and the factual assertions and evidence they contain, or whether the parties have a right to reply to the facts they assert.

V. Institutional Fact-finding Capacities

Judges are not scientists, and they 'inevitably lack the scientific training that might facilitate the evaluation of scientific claims or the evaluation of expert witnesses',

[65] Ibid.

[66] *RJR-MacDonald, Inc v Canada* [1994] 1 SCR 311, para 133.

[67] See TAO Endicott, 'Questions of Law' (1998) 114 *Law Quarterly Review* 292.

[68] Davis, 'Judicial Notice' (n 63) 955–59.

[69] Ibid, 955.

according to US Supreme Court Justice Stephen Breyer.[70] This problem extends to assessing the statistical methods used in social science. David Kaye, co-author of the chapter on statistics in the Reference Manual for Scientific Evidence used by US federal courts, has identified numerous errors in the use of statistics by courts at all levels in the United States, including the US Supreme Court. He shows that judges frequently misapply concepts such as statistical significance and confidence levels, revealing a lack of understanding of research methodology and the technical meaning of terms used to report results.[71] Other scholars have reached similar conclusions and documented widespread mistakes in judicial use of social science and other empirical research.[72]

The difficulties associated with scientific evidence and expert testimony are to some extent unavoidable in adjudicative fact-finding in ordinary private law and criminal cases. While some technical issues can be resolved in specialised tribunals, most disputes in Western legal systems are decided by judges whose professional competence lies in systematic knowledge of the law and legal processes, which is gained through a career and education that leaves little time for mastering the methods of scientific inquiry, or for keeping abreast of scientific developments in various fields. Judges – not scientists – must exercise control over the admission and evaluation of expert testimony on complex factual issues such as the likelihood of matching DNA samples. There has thus been extensive academic discussion of the standards for admitting scientific evidence, the proper role of judges and juries in evaluating such evidence, and ways to improve decision-making in this area.

When a judge relies on empirical research to hold that legislation violates a human right, the decision implies (or claims explicitly) that the legislature failed to make use of the available empirical data or to assess it properly. Thus, in this area, a comparative analysis of institutional capacities is in order. Legislative committees can gather evidence, call witnesses, and initiate studies, all with assistance of scientifically trained staff. Legislatures can use special commissions and inquiries to conduct investigations and in-depth research on specific topics. Some legislatures have established permanent bodies for assistance with fact-finding. The Congressional Research Service, which is one of three in-house research bodies serving the US Congress, has around 700 researchers and a budget of $100 million; annually it responds to about 80,000 specific requests for information from Congress and prepares about 1,000 full-length reports, on topics ranging from terrorism and national security to water resources.[73] The German administration

[70] S Breyer, 'The Interdependence of Science and Law' (1998) 82 Judicature 24, 25–26.

[71] DH Kaye, 'Is Proof of Statistical Significance Significant?' (1986) 61 *Washington Law Review* 1333; DH Kaye, 'Statistical Significance and the Burden of Persuasion' (1983) 46 *Law & Contemporary Problems* 13.

[72] Eg DL Faigman, *Constitutional Fictions: A Unified Theory of Constitutional Facts* (New York, OUP, 2008); DL Faigman, 'Normative Constitutional Fact-Finding: Exploring the Empirical Component of Constitutional Interpretation' (1991) 139 *University of Pennsylvania Law Review* 541; SE Fienberg and ML Straf, 'Statistical Evidence in the US Courts: An Appraisal' (1991) 31 *Journal of the Forensic Science Society* 259; Davis, 'Facts in Lawmaking' (n 63).

[73] Annual Report, Fiscal Year 2007 & Annual Report, Fiscal Year 2002, of the US Congressional Research Service.

and Parliament likewise have extensive resources for empirical research, including the Büro für Technikfolgen-Abschätzung, which advises the Bundestag and its committees on current scientific research and developing technologies.[74] Legislatures may not always fully develop fact-finding resources or use them wisely, and, like any other political process, empirical investigations are subject to misuse or corruption. Nonetheless, legislatures in general have institutional structures and decision-making processes that facilitate broad empirical investigation.

Courts, in contrast, generally lack internal fact-finding resources. Judges may have law clerks and access to library staff, but these individuals usually do not have scientific training. As US Supreme Court Justice Antonin Scalia has observed in oral argument: 'We can't call witnesses and see what the real problems are . . . [W]e have only lawyers before us, we have no witnesses, we have no cross-examination, we have no investigative staff.'[75] Constitutional courts in civil law systems often have original jurisdiction of constitutional complaints, and the Bundesverfassungsgericht, for example, can appoint expert witnesses to testify on scientific and technical subjects. In common law systems it is possible for trial courts to appoint neutral experts to provide testimony on scientific or technical matters, but this is rarely done.[76] Though evidence of legislative facts is sometimes submitted in trial courts, much legislative fact-finding is the product of Brandeis briefs presented on appeal or of appellate judges engaging in research on their own initiative. A state supreme court in the United States has stated that 'when a decision in a case rests upon technical, specialized or scientific knowledge, if we find the record does not make the subject matter sufficiently clear, we will not hesitate to conduct authoritative study on our own', and asserted that most appellate courts do the same.[77]

The discussion thus far has addressed courts' reliance on scholarly publications or the work of established research institutes and government organisations. Courts often rely on less reliable sources for legislative fact-finding: newspaper articles and popular magazines; encyclopedias and other general reference works; books published by popular, commercial presses; and a variety of similar sources.[78] Increasingly, judges cite to sources obtained through Internet search engines – either directly after conducting their own research, or indirectly by relying on information in Brandeis briefs obtained in this way. This can be inferred from, among other things, the growing number of court citations to Wikipedia, the free, online encyclopedia that often tops search results for topics of general interest in Google and other search engines. A recent search of state and federal cases in the United States reveals almost 400 cases that cited Wikipedia between 2004 and 2009.[79] In some of these

[74] K von Beyme, *The Legislator: German Parliament as a Centre of Political Decision-making* (Aldershot, Ashgate, 1998) 23–25.

[75] *Rasul v Bush* 542 US 466 (2004): Transcript of Oral Argument, 46.

[76] Breyer (n 70) 27.

[77] *Samuels v Mladineo* 608 So 2d 1170, 1184–86 (Miss 1992).

[78] Eg *PGA Tour, Inc v Martin* 532 US 661 (2001); *Kerrigan v Commissioner of Public Health* 957 A 2d 407 (Conn 2008); *People v Mar* 52 P 3d 95 (Cal 2002).

[79] A search for 'Wikipedia' on the Westlaw database of all state and federal cases in the United States returned 376 cases on 15 November 2009.

cases courts are responding to the parties' citation of Wikipedia in briefs, and in a few instances the content of Wikipedia entries is related to a material question of fact in the case (for example, parties and witnesses have described their consultation of Wikipedia to explain decisions and actions they took). Many of these citations, however, are for background information related to adjudicative facts or for legislative facts relevant to interpreting statutes or constitutional law.[80] This phenomenon is not confined to the United States. A study in Germany found 294 judgments with citations to Wikipedia,[81] and cases in the European Court of Justice,[82] Canada,[83] and elsewhere have begun to cite to the online encyclopedia.

What is the problem with citing to Wikipedia for legislative facts? After all, it provides quick, free access to a great deal of information on a massive number of subjects. Articles are often written by amateurs with a particular interest in a topic, and the collaborative nature of the enterprise allows others to make corrections or add information. Richard Posner has described it as a convenient and 'terrific resource' that is often recently updated and 'very accurate' (but said he would not rely on it for a 'critical issue').[84] A study published in *Nature* analysed Wikipedia's coverage of science and concluded that its accuracy was close to that of *Encyclopaedia Britannica* (though this claim was vigorously disputed by the latter).[85] Even if the information cited is accurate, however, judicial citations to Wikipedia are unseemly and troubling. Anyone in the world who registers as a user can create new entries, and to edit an entry one does not even need to go through a sign-in process. Contributions may be, and usually are, anonymous, and generally are not overseen by any formal process. The ability of users to correct mistakes may impart a certain degree of reliability for some entries, but the exposure to instantaneous editing can also lead to errors and false claims, whether

[80] In *Bourgeois v Peters* 387 F 3d 1303 (11th Cir 2004), the first US case to cite Wikipedia, the court relied on an entry on the Department of Homeland Security for information about its colour-coded threat level system, in the course of rejecting an argument that the yellow ('elevated') threat level constituted an exceptional circumstance that would justify a police search.

[81] R Zosel, 'Im Namen des Volkes – Gerichte zitieren Wikipedia' in H Rüßmann (ed), *Festschrift für Gerhard Käfer* (Saarbrücken, Juris, 2009).

[82] Eg Case C-275/06 *Productores de Musica de España (Promusicae) v Telefonica de España SAU* [2008] 2 CMLR 17, n 14 (citing Wikipedia on the possibility and difficulty of concealing a computer's IP (internet protocol) address).

[83] Eg *Gauvin c Vallée* [2006] QCCS 3363, n 9.

[84] Posner was interviewed and quoted in Noam Cohen, 'Courts Turn to Wikipedia, but Selectively' *New York Times* (29 January 2007). He said Wikipedia is valuable '[p]artly because it is so convenient, it often has been updated recently and is very accurate', but added that '[i]t wouldn't be right to use it in a critical issue. If the safety of a product is at issue, you wouldn't look it up in Wikipedia'. Ibid.

[85] *Nature* asked academic reviewers to assess and compare 42 pairs of articles from Wikipedia and the online content of Encyclopaedia Britannica and reported this conclusion: 'Only eight serious errors, such as misinterpretations of important concepts, were detected in the pairs of articles reviewed, four from each encyclopaedia. But reviewers also found many factual errors, omissions or misleading statements: 162 and 123 in Wikipedia and Britannica, respectively.' J Giles, 'Special Report: Internet Encyclopaedias Go Head to Head' (2005) 438 *Nature* 900. *Encyclopaedia Britannica* published a corporate response: 'Fatally Flawed: Refuting the Recent Study on Encyclopedic Accuracy by the Journal Nature', at http://corporate.britannica.com/britannica_nature_response.pdf (accessed 19 November 2009). *Nature* replied, in turn, at www.nature.com/nature/britannica/eb_advert_response_final.pdf (accessed 19 November 2009).

intentional or unintentional. Further, the entry cited has no fixed form; its content can change from day to day. This is from the site's own self-description:

> Wikipedia is a work in progress, and many articles contain errors, bias, duplication . . . We encourage readers to help us fix these problems. The great majority of articles are written primarily or solely by individuals who are not subject matter experts, and may lack academic or professional credentials in the area.'[86]

The operators of Wikipedia also acknowledge that its 'radical openness also means that any given article may be, at any given moment, in a bad state: for example, it could be in the middle of a large edit, or a controversial rewrite' and that articles are subject to 'vandalism and insertion of false information.[87]

The underlying problem here is not Wikipedia itself. Rather, the phenomenon of Wikipedia citations demonstrates that many courts are willing to rely on dubious sources, and that legislative fact-finding by courts may be conducted in a haphazard fashion. Judges who are curious about some factual matter relevant to a legal question sometimes do the same thing that many lay persons do when they want information on a topic: they use an Internet search engine.[88] The California Supreme Court, for example, in ruling that defendants cannot be required to wear an electric stun belt while testifying, cited (inter alia) newspaper and magazine articles[89] for information and analysis of the use and medical effects of stun belts, which, according to a dissenting justice, the Court discovered through a search on Google.[90] Information found this way is determined in part by the algorithms that search engines use to generate results; these algorithms are corporate trade secrets, and neither judges nor the public can know exactly how Google, for instance, determines what websites are relevant to a particular search query.[91]

In the US Supreme Court case *PGA Tour, Inc v Martin* (2001),[92] a golfer with a circulatory disorder challenged the Professional Golf Association's rule that players must walk the course, claiming that federal disability legislation required

[86] See 'Wikipedia: Content disclaimer', at http://en.wikipedia.org/wiki/Wikipedia:Content_disclaimer (accessed 17 January 2010).

[87] See 'Wikipedia: About', at http://en.wikipedia.org/wiki/Wikipedia:About (accessed 17 January 2010).

[88] CM Barger, 'On the Internet, Nobody Knows You're a Judge: Appellate Courts' Use of Internet Materials' (2002) 4 *Journal of Appellate Pratice & Process* 417; EG Thornburg, 'The Curious Appellate Judge: Ethical Limits on Independent Research' (2008) 28 *Review of Litigation* 131, 163–65, 198. Cass Sunstein, a Harvard law professor now serving in the Obama administration, told the *New York Times* that he suspects 'that law clerks are using Wikipedia a great deal'. Cohen (n 84).

[89] *People v Mar* (n 78). Publications cited included *The Progressive*, the *Cleveland Plain Dealer*, the *Los Angeles Times*, and the *New York Review of Books*.

[90] Justice Brown stated: 'There is absolutely no evidence in the record bearing on these questions. In the absence of such evidence, we had two choices. We could have deferred to the Legislature, which can make law after hearing from distinguished experts on all sides of controversial issues. Or we could have waited for a case that raised these questions on an adequate record. Instead, the majority, rushing to judgment after conducting an embarrassing Google.com search for information outside the record, has tied the hands of the Legislature, to the likely peril of judges, bailiffs, and ordinary citizens called upon to do their civic duty.' Ibid, 116.

[91] See EB Laidlaw, 'Private Power, Public Interest: An Examination of Search Engine Accountability' (2009) 17 *International Journal of Law and Information Technology* 113, 131–32.

[92] *PGA Tour, Inc v Martin* (n 78).

the PGA to permit him to use a golf cart. The legislation requires 'reasonable modification' unless it would 'fundamentally alter the nature' of the services or facilities to which a complainant seeks access.[93] Thus the Court undertook to decide whether walking the course is part of the nature of golf (or, more precisely, high-level professional golf) and decided that it is not. The Court consulted and relied on *Rules of the Green*, a popular historical book (for the proposition that shot making is the essence of golf); *The Random House International Encyclopedia of Golf* and *Golf Magazine's Encyclopedia of Golf* (describing changes in the methods of transporting clubs over the years); and an article in the *Arizona Republic* about a highly unusual hole-in-one that had recently occurred on the PGA tour, in support of the Court's contention that lucky bounces are also part of the game; hence 'it is impossible to guarantee that all competitors will play under exactly the same conditions or that an individual's ability will be the sole determinant of the outcome'.[94] Frederick Schauer observes that although these sources were central to the Court's decision, none of them were contained in the record, lower court decisions, or the briefs of the parties or amici.[95]

> In other words, the Court locates these sources itself. Seven Justices [ie, those who joined the majority opinion], only one of whom is a serious golfer, with the assistance of approximately twenty-eight law clerks, no more than four or five of whom are likely to be serious golfers, and the library staff of the Supreme Court library, again unlikely to have a large number of serious golfers in their midst, are wandering relatively unguided (by golf expertise) through Lexis, Westlaw, the Internet, and various other sources of nonlegal information in order to decide which of the contingent features of golf are actually essential features of golf.[96]

Despite some misgivings, Schauer argues that this kind of 'muddling through' can be an acceptable way for courts to find legislative facts. He contends that making general factual and policy judgments is an endemic part of the common law process (including statutory interpretation), and that having multi-member appellate courts, assisted by law clerks and library staffs, increases the range of skills and experience represented on the court and reduces the potential for error.[97] Even if this argument is sound with regard to common law development and statutory interpretation, decisions to declare legislation unconstitutional, and thus place the issue beyond the realm of political disagreement, are another matter. Such decisions should not depend on the kind of 'muddling through' exhibited in the Court's fact-finding in *Martin*. Schauer acknowledges that the process in *Martin* is not ideal even for ordinary legal interpretation, and suggests that the growing use of nonlegal information in such cases indicates a need to consider questions about the institutional design of judicial institutions and reforms to improve their fact-finding

[93] Ibid at 682–83.
[94] Ibid at 683–87.
[95] F Schauer, 'The Dilemma of Ignorance: PGA Tour, Inc. v. Casey Martin' (2001) *The Supreme Court Review* 267, 283.
[96] Ibid.
[97] Ibid, 288–89.

capacities.[98] I will consider proposals for reform in the conclusion, but will first review some recent cases in which decisions about whether legislation violates human rights depended on the courts' evaluation of empirical research.

VI. Empirical Research in Recent Case Law

A. United States

In *American Amusement Machine Ass'n v Kendrick*[99] the US Court of Appeals for the 7th Circuit held that an Indianapolis city ordinance limiting access by minors to violent video games violated the right to freedom of speech. The opinion, authored by Judge Richard Posner, is worth considering in detail because Posner in his theoretical work argues for relying on social science in deciding constitutional cases,[100] and he is considered to be, among judges, one of the most skilled in the social sciences. Since the ordinance in this case was a content-based restriction on depictions of violence, Posner inquired whether the city had produced evidence of a compelling (not merely plausible) state interest, which might justify the restriction of speech.[101] He held that the state's legitimate interest is to prevent the harm that minors might inflict on others – or suffer themselves – as a result of playing violent video games; and that the city 'rightly does not rest on "what everyone knows" about the harm inflicted by violent video games', and instead relies on social science evidence.[102]

The city relied primarily on two studies reported in an article by psychologists Craig Anderson and Karen Dill.[103] Posner states:

> The studies do not find that video games have ever caused anyone to commit a violent act, as opposed to feeling aggressive, or have caused the average level of violence to increase anywhere. And they do not suggest that it is the interactive character of the games, as opposed to the violence of the images in them, that is the cause of the aggressive feelings. The studies thus are not evidence that violent video games are any more harmful to the consumer or to the public safety than violent movies or other violent, but passive, entertainments.[104]

Though Posner seems to acknowledge that the studies found a link between violent video games and aggressive feelings, he holds that this link matters only if it is due to the 'interactive character' of games, which distinguishes them from movies

[98] Ibid, 296–97.
[99] *American Amusement Machine Ass'n v Kendrick* 244 F 3d 572 (7th Cir 2001).
[100] RA Posner, 'Against Constitutional Theory' (1998) 73 *New York University Law Review* 1.
[101] *Kendrick* (n 99) 576.
[102] Ibid, 578.
[103] CA Anderson and KE Dill, 'Video Games and Aggressive Thoughts, Feelings, and Behavior in the Laboratory and in Life' (2000) 78 *Journal of Personality and Social Psychology* 772.
[104] *Kendrick* (n 99) 578–79 (italics added).

or other 'passive' entertainment.[105] Contrary to Posner's description of the studies, the authors discuss, in a section titled 'Unique Dangers of Video Games', three reasons why the dangers of violent video games are greater than those for violent movies or television, and the first two directly concern their interactive nature: (i) identification with the aggressor, (ii) active choice of aggressive responses, and (iii) the addictive nature of video games.[106] Posner not only misrepresents the article, he proceeds with a claim that ignores the authors' argument. He states:

> It is highly unlikely that [video games] are more harmful [than movies and television], because 'passive' entertainment aspires to be interactive too and often succeeds. When Dirty Harry or some other avenging hero kills off a string of villains, the audience is expected to identify with him, to revel in his success, to feel their own finger on the trigger. It is conceivable that pushing a button or manipulating a toggle stick engenders an even deeper surge of aggressive joy, but of that there is no evidence at all.[107]

Posner focuses here on identification with a protagonist, but Anderson and Dill contend that video games involve a different kind of interaction, in which the player is the agent who causes the violent scenes through his active choice. They write:

> In a sense, violent video games provide a *complete learning environment for aggression*, with simultaneous exposure to modeling, reinforcement, and rehearsal of behaviors. This combination of learning strategies has been shown to be more powerful than any of these methods used singly (Barton, 1981; Chambers & Ascione, 1987; Loftus & Loftus, 1983).[108]

It is unclear what to make of Posner's claim that the studies do not find that video games have '*caused* anyone to commit a violent act [or] *caused* the average level of violence to increase anywhere',[109] in part because this wording does not track the reported results of the studies, which are summarised in the article abstract:

> Two studies examined violent video game effects on aggression-related variables. Study 1 found that real-life violent video game play was positively related to aggressive behavior and delinquency. The relation was stronger for individuals who are characteristically aggressive and for men. Academic achievement was negatively related to overall amount of time spent playing video games. In Study 2, laboratory exposure to a graphically violent video game increased aggressive thoughts and behavior.[110]

Posner does not question the accuracy of these results. If he thinks that a real-life, observational study such as Study 1 must find a link between violent video game play and actual violent acts in order to support the legislation, then he should

105 Ibid at 579.
106 Anderson and Dill (note 103) 788.
107 *Kendrick* (n 99) 579.
108 Anderson and Dill (note 103) 788 (italics added).
109 Ibid, 578–79 (italics added).
110 Anderson and Dill (n 103) 772.

explain the difference between violent acts and the 'aggressive behaviour' found by the studies. (Must a violent act cause actual physical harm upon another person?) But he does not do this, nor does he explain why evidence of a link to 'aggressive behaviour' is not sufficient to support the state's interest in the welfare of children and others affected by their actions. With regard to a controlled laboratory experiment such as Study 2, it would be unethical to conduct experiments designed to cause subjects of the experiment to commit violent acts that harm another person. Thus, Posner cannot reasonably object to the methodology of Study 2 on the ground that it was limited to finding aggressive thoughts and behaviour.

If Posner's objection is that the statistical analysis in the studies is not robust enough to show causation, then he fails to make his concerns clear. The authors acknowledge that 'causal statements are risky at best' at the current time, since it is possible that aggressive individuals are especially attracted to violent video games, and that more research into the effects of violent video games is needed.[111] In an earlier case, *Tagatz v Marquette University*, Posner repeats the common saying, '[c]orrelation is not causation', but goes on to state, '[c]orrelations can be suggestive of causality; scientific induction *means* inferring causality from correlation'.[112] This proposition, though it passes over some issues, is more sensible than his statements about causation in *Kendrick*. Taken at face value, Posner's claims in *Kendrick* about the failure to show that playing violent video games causes violent acts hold out a difficult (perhaps impossible) standard for finding empirical data to show that the legislation is constitutional.

Several cases since *Kendrick* have held that laws regulating violent video games violate the right to freedom of speech, each one dismissing the social science submitted by the state as insufficient to establish its interest in the law.[113] A number of courts have cited Posner's remarks in *Kendrick* on the failure to show that video games *cause* violence, and some have made more direct, stringent demands regarding proof of causation with regard to violence or psychological harm.[114] The US Court of Appeals for the 8th Circuit held: '[H]aving failed to come forth with *incontrovertible proof of a causal relationship* between the exposure to [video game] violence and subsequent psychological dysfunction, the State has not satisfied its evidentiary burden.'[115] This standard of proof would be more difficult to meet than 'beyond reasonable doubt'; indeed, there are theories in the physical sciences that lack 'incontrovertible proof of a causal relationship'.[116]

[111] Ibid, 782.

[112] *Tagatz v Marquette University* 861 F 2d 1040, 1044 (7th Cir 1988).

[113] *Video Software Dealers Ass'n v Schwarzenegger* 556 F 3d 950 (9th Cir 2009); *Entertainment Software Ass'n v Swanson* 519 F 3d 768 (8th Cir 2008); *Entertainment Software Ass'n v Hatch*, 443 F Supp 2d 1065 (D Minn 2006); *Entertainment Software Ass'n v Granholm* 426 F Supp 2d 646 (ED Mich 2006); *Entertainment Software Ass'n v Blagojevich* 404 F Supp 2d 1051 (ND Ill 2005).

[114] Eg *Blagojevich* (n 113) at 1073–74; *Granholm* (n 113) at 653.

[115] *Swanson* (n 113) (italics added).

[116] See L Smolin, *The Trouble with Physics: The Rise of String Theory, the Fall of a Science, and What Comes Next* (New York, Houghton Mifflin, 2006) 169–71, 237 (discussing theories accepted by many

In the years since *Kendrick*, a number of new studies on violent video games have appeared, and the State of California relied on some of these in defence of a law that prohibited selling certain especially violent video games to unaccompanied minors, which was challenged in *Video Software Dealers Ass'n v Schwarzenegger* (2009).[117] The US Court of Appeals for the 9th Circuit concluded that the evidence 'does not support' the state's interest in preventing psychological harm to minors and struck down the law.[118] The general tenor of the court's approach can be seen in these remarks:

> *Nearly all of the research is based on correlation, not evidence of causation*, and most of the studies suffer from significant, admitted flaws in methodology as they relate to the State's claimed interest. None of the research establishes or suggests a causal link between minors playing violent video games and actual psychological or neurological harm, and *inferences to that effect would not be reasonable*. In fact, *some of the studies caution against inferring causation*. Although we do not require the State to demonstrate a 'scientific certainty,' the State must come forward with more than it has. As a result, the State has not met its burden to demonstrate a compelling interest.[119]

To contrast correlation with causation in this way is to reveal a profound misunderstanding of social science methodology. To the extent that social science can establish a causal relationship, it is inferred (in large part) from correlation. What the court takes to be 'significant, admitted flaws in methodology' are just instances of the technical language that psychologists use to discuss the step-by-step nature of their research. The authors of the studies cited in this case make observations about the limits of individual studies, point out where questions lie for further research, and recite standard cautionary language about drawing causal inferences.[120] This is how such research progresses: it was through a series of repeated, limited studies that researchers established links between smoking and lung cancer.[121] But not all smokers get cancer, and researchers are still exploring why smokers are affected in different ways;[122] thus for some purposes the data show correlation rather than causation. The correlations between smoking and cancer that have been shown in numerous studies may make it reasonable to choose not to smoke on the supposition that there is a causal relationship between smoking and lung cancer. And such studies may lead medical researchers to discover more about the biological mechanisms that cause lung cancer (and how smoking can trigger them); in the meantime, evidence of correlation is valuable even without strict proof of causation.

In another case the state submitted a position statement on entertainment violence jointly issued by six professional organisations (including the American

physicists that have not been verified by experiment).

[117] *Video Software Dealers Ass'n v Schwarzenegger* 556 F 3d 950 (9th Cir 2009).

[118] Ibid, 962–65.

[119] Ibid, 964 (italics added).

[120] Ibid at 963–64. Cf S Nolan and T Heinzen, *Statistics for the Behavioral Sciences* (New York, Worth Publishers, 2008) 206.

[121] J Cornfield et al, 'Smoking and Lung Cancer: Recent Evidence and a Discussion of Some Questions' (2009) 38 *International Journal of Epidemiology* 1175.

[122] Ibid.

Pediatric Association and the American Psychological Association), which the court described as follows:

> The [organisations] have taken the position that violent video games have a 'negative impact' on minors. *The position taken in the joint statement of the medical associations is not based on any scientific study*, but appears to represent the policy or political views of their governing bodies. Of course, this joint statement does not even attempt to describe the 'negative impact' perceived. Once again, this falls far short of the 'substantial evidence' requirement needed to restrict free speech.[123]

A review of the statement shows that the court mischaracterised it and perhaps misunderstood it. The subject is entertainment violence in general; the statement specifically describes negative impacts that may be more severe for video games (based on preliminary studies). The authors state:

> At this time, well over 1000 studies . . . point overwhelmingly to a causal connection between media violence and aggressive behavior in some children. The conclusion of the public health community, based on over 30 years of research, is that viewing entertainment violence can lead to increases in aggressive attitudes, values and behavior, particularly in children . . . The effect of entertainment violence on children is complex and variable. Some children will be affected more than others. But while duration, intensity, and extent of the impact may vary, there are several measurable negative effects of children's exposure to violent entertainment. These effects take several forms.[124]

The statement then claims that exposure to violent entertainment is linked to the following effects on children: (i) seeing violence as an effective way of settling conflicts; (ii) emotional desensitisation towards violence in real life, which decreases the likelihood that one will take action on behalf of victims of violence; (iii) a perception that the world is a violent place, with a resultant increase in self-protective behaviours and a mistrust of others; and (iv) a higher tendency for violent and aggressive behaviour later in life than children who are not so exposed.[125] The statement concludes:

> Although less research has been done on the impact of violent interactive entertainment (video games and other interactive media) on young people, preliminary studies indicate that the negative impact may be significantly more severe than that wrought by television, movies, or music. More study is needed in this area, and we urge that resources and attention be directed to this field.[126]

Contrary to the court's claim that the statement represents policy or political views, the statement explicitly disclaims advocacy of 'restrictions on creative activity' and makes no specific practical recommendations whatsoever (other than to urge more study); it goes no further than its stated aim, which is to give a 'picture of the pathological effects of entertainment violence'.[127] The statement is

[123] *Granholm* (n 113).

[124] See Joint Statement on the Impact of Entertainment Violence on Children, Congressional Public Health Summit (26 July 2000) at www.aap.org/advocacy/releases/jstmtevc.htm (accessed May 2010).

[125] Ibid.

[126] Ibid.

[127] Ibid.

appropriately cautious about the limits of research – '[w]e in no way mean to imply that entertainment violence is the sole, or even necessarily the most important factor contributing to youth aggression, anti-social attitudes and violence' – and mentions family breakdown, peer influence, and availability of weapons as possible contributing factors.[128] By the standards employed in some of the cases discussed above, this would count as an admission that causation has not been proven and serve as grounds for dismissing the studies as without evidentiary value. But in fact the statement shows that the evidence relevant to the question of whether video games are harmful for children is more extensive and complex than is indicated by the cases discussed above.

B. Canada

In *Chaoulli v Quebec*,[129] the Canadian Supreme Court's review of legislative facts played the decisive role in a constitutional challenge to a key component of Canada's public health care system, Medicare, which is directed and partially funded by the federal government and administered by provincial governments. Since the 1960s the federal government has pursued a policy of a single-tier system of national health insurance,[130] in line with which Quebec and five other provinces prohibited private insurance contracts to cover most of the medical services provided by Medicare.[131] Other provinces take measures to discourage such contracts, making them financially unfeasible in general. Canada has consistently rejected a 'two-tier' system in which some people would receive publicly funded care while others would have access to private care through insurance purchased privately (or provided or subsidised by an employer).[132] Jacques Chaoulli, a doctor who was an advocate for the availability of private insurance, and George Zeliotis, a patient who had waited several months for hip replacement surgery, challenged Quebec's prohibition, claiming that it violated the rights to life and liberty in the Canadian Charter of Rights and Freedoms and the Quebec Charter of Human Rights and Freedoms. In a 4–3 decision, the Canadian Supreme Court held that the prohibition was unconstitutional.[133]

The Court[134] found that Quebec's prohibition on private insurance infringed the right to life on the basis of observations about waiting lists and their effects on patient health:

[128] Ibid.

[129] *Chaoulli v Quebec* [2005] 1 SCR 791.

[130] See Canada Health Act, ss 1–13 (establishing criteria provinces must meet in order to receive federal payments for health insurance plans, including public administration, comprehensiveness, universality, and accessibility).

[131] *Chaoulli* (n 129) paras 1, 77.

[132] Ibid, paras 181, 230 (Binnie and LeBel JJ dissenting).

[133] Four justices in the majority rested their decision on the Quebec Charter, while three agreed with respect to the Canadian Charter.

[134] I follow the US convention here in referring to the majority opinion as the opinion of the Court.

> Some patients die as a result of long waits for treatment in the public system when they could have gained prompt access to care in the private sector. Were it not for [Quebec's prohibitions] they could buy private insurance and receive care in the private sector . . . Not only is it common knowledge that health care in Quebec is subject to waiting times, but a number of witnesses acknowledged that the demand for health care is potentially unlimited and that waiting lists are a more or less implicit form of rationing (report by J-L Denis, *Un avenir pour le système public de santé* (1998), at p. 13; report by Y. Brunelle, *Aspects critiques d'un rationnement planifié* (1993), at p. 21). Waiting lists are therefore real and intentional. The witnesses also commented on the consequences of waiting times. Dr. Daniel Doyle, a cardiovascular surgeon, testified that when a person is diagnosed with cardiovascular disease, he or she is [TRANSLATION] 'always sitting on a bomb' and can die at any moment. In such cases, it is inevitable that some patients will die if they have to wait for an operation. Dr. Doyle testified that the risk of mortality rises by 0.45 percent per month. The right to life is therefore affected by the delays that are the necessary result of waiting lists.[135]

The Court was clearly impressed with Doyle's testimony: a concurring opinion also mentioned the phrase 'sitting on a bomb' and added: 'He confirmed, without challenge, that patients die while on waiting lists. Inevitably, where patients have life-threatening conditions, some will die because of undue delay in awaiting surgery.'[136] It is hardly surprising that there was no challenge to this claim, which (as reported) makes no attempt at quantification or contextualisation – we are told only that 'some' will die, not how many. The Court attempts, unconvincingly, to reinforce its conclusion with statistics by citing to Doyle's testimony that the risk of mortality rises by 0.45 per cent per month. The Court does not reference any study on which the testimony is based. Presumably, the claim refers to a study of a group of patients with cardiovascular disease, but there is no information about the age or any other characteristics of this group or the specific nature of the disease (which can include, among other things, congestive heart failure, coronary artery disease, and various post-heart-attack conditions). Moreover, the Court does not state the *absolute* mortality rate of patients with cardiovascular disease. From the information provided, it is impossible to know the meaning and importance of an increase in mortality of 0.45 per cent per month or to be able to compare the mortality rates of patients with cardiovascular disease against other persons of the same age.

Nonetheless, Doyle's testimony is the crucial evidence on which the Court relied to show that Quebec's prohibition on private insurance infringed the right to life; it is the proof given for the Court's general claim that waiting lists cause Canadians to die. The finding that the right to life was infringed did not directly settle the final outcome, but it served to invoke the proportionality test and shift the burden of proof to the government.[137] It remained for the government of Quebec to attempt to prove that this was a justified infringement by providing

[135] *Chaoulli* (n 129) paras 37–40.
[136] Ibid, para 112 (McLachlin CJ concurring).
[137] Ibid, para 60.

evidence that the prohibition on private insurance met the tests of rationality, minimal impairment, and proportionality *stricto sensu*.[138]

Doyle himself, according to the trial court's summary of his testimony, was 'not at all certain the solution lay with private insurance', and he criticised certain practices of US insurance companies with regard to heart patients.[139] Although 2,000 patients were on waiting lists in Quebec in 1992, he said the situation had improved considerably since that time and the government increased facilities in 1997 (the trial was in 1999).[140] He was still concerned about waiting lists, taking the view that 'waiting should not exist in cardiology, that it is often a question of life or death, as cardiac illness is unpredictable'.[141] But he acknowledged that 'waiting lists are everywhere' and observed that the population is growing older and 'it is now necessary to operate on people 85 years old'.[142] He ascribed the waiting lists to various causes, including a lack of nurses and aggressive recruitment of Quebec's cardiovascular physicians, some of whom leave for Ontario or the United States.[143] All of this testimony is from the trial court record. The Supreme Court overlooked it and attempted no detailed analysis of the nature and scope of the problem of waiting lists; neither did the Court discuss evidence and reasons for its belief that the availability of private insurance would alleviate the problems of waiting lists. The Court plucked the figure about the mortality rate increase, and the expression 'sitting on a bomb', from their context and made them the keystone of its finding on infringing the right to life.

The federal policy of promoting a single-tier public health programme, and the decision by Quebec and other provinces to implement that policy by prohibiting private insurance, are two important issues within a web of others, such as funding and taxation, the administrative structure of Medicare and various province-level health providers, and federal–provincial relationships. *Chaoulli* arose in the midst of extensive discussion and political debate about these issues, which was reflected in a major, 400-page report by an independent commission (chaired by Roy Romanow) and by a multi-volume report by the Standing Senate Committee on Social Affairs, Science and Technology (chaired by Michael Kirby). The Romanow Report and the Final Kirby Report (Volume 6: Recommendations and Reform) were issued in 2002, three years after the end of the trial in which Doyle and other experts provided testimony. After discussing alternatives at length, both reports strongly advocated retaining Canada's single-tier public health plan. The Court considered aspects of these reports alongside the evidence presented at trial. Though its judgment was lengthy, its discussion of the general debate over health care reform and its examination of specific issues were severely truncated,

[138] Ibid, paras 45–48.

[139] *Chaoulli v Québec* [2000] RJQ 786, para 47. The quotations in the text above are from the English translation of the judgment of the Superior Court of Quebec in CM Flood et al (eds), *Access to Care, Access to Justice* (Toronto, University of Toronto Press, 2005) App A, 538.

[140] Ibid.

[141] Ibid.

[142] Ibid.

[143] Ibid.

in comparison to the wide-ranging analyses in the Romanow and Kirby reports.[144]

The pivotal question for the Court was whether Quebec's prohibition on private insurance satisfied the 'minimal impairment' step in the proportionality analysis.[145] The government argued that the availability of private insurance would undermine the effectiveness of the public plan in several ways, including the following: (i) popular support for the public plan would diminish because those with insurance would not see a need for it; (ii) the quality of care would decline because influential people would purchase and rely on private insurance rather than press for improvement in the public plan; (iii) many physicians and other health care workers would leave the plan out of a motive for profit; (iv) the increase in for-profit health care would lead to a decline in professionalism and ethical standards among doctors; and (v) physicians would have a financial incentive to keep waiting lists on the public plan long in order to divert patients to the private sector.[146] These and related arguments were advanced at trial by six expert witnesses – leading physicians with academic expertise in public health and administrative experience. The Court noted that these witnesses did not produce studies in the trial court in support of these arguments (though the Court itself was willing to convey Doyle's testimony in conclusory form and cite no study regarding the mortality rate increase); and concluded that their evidence 'carries little weight':[147]

> While it is true that scientific or empirical evidence is not always necessary, witnesses in a case in which the arguments are supposedly based on logic or common sense should be able *to cite specific facts in support of their conclusions.* The human reactions [i.e., the projected consequences of private insurance] described by the experts, many of whom came from outside Quebec, do not appear to me to be very convincing . . . I am of the opinion that the reaction some witnesses described is highly unlikely in the Quebec context.[148]

The witnesses did cite facts; the trial court's summary of their factual and policy reasoning covered several pages.[149] The Supreme Court's judgment not only fails to address adequately the specific arguments of the government's expert witnesses, it focuses narrowly on the evidence presented at trial at this point in its opinion, overlooking a number of studies relevant to those arguments that were among the evidence submitted during the appeal.[150]

The Court proceeds, however, to consider evidence from studies that were not presented at trial regarding various methods of funding public health plans and effects of private insurance options in other countries, including the United Kingdom, Germany, Austria, the Netherlands, Sweden, Australia, and New

[144] The main conclusions and a number of the findings of the reports are summarised in the dissenting opinion by Justice Binnie and Justice LeBel. *Chaoulli* (n 129) paras 173 ff.

[145] Ibid, paras 48, 68.

[146] Ibid, paras 63, 65.

[147] Ibid, para 64.

[148] Ibid, paras 64, 66 (italics added).

[149] *Chaoulli* (n 139) paras 71–122.

[150] See eg Factum of Respondent (mis en cause) Attorney General of Canada, at paras 54 ff, at www.law.utoronto.ca/content_tr.asp?contentId=1109 (accessed 27 April 2010).

Zealand.[151] The Court discusses measures that these countries have taken to prevent private insurance from undermining public health plans, and observes that in some countries only a small percentage of people purchase private insurance: 9 per cent in Germany; 11.5 per cent in the United Kingdom; and in Sweden private insurance accounts for only 2 per cent of total health care expenditure.[152] The Court's message – clearly implied throughout this discussion – is that when private health insurance draws only a small percentage of people and funding, this constitutes evidence of success in maintaining the public health plan. The analysis here thus creates tension – if not outright inconsistency – with the Court's finding that the prohibition on private insurance infringed the right to life. In that earlier part of the opinion, the Court held out private insurance as a way for people to escape waiting lists and receive life-saving health care. Later the Court suggests governments should take measures to limit expansion of private insurance and thereby sustain the effectiveness of public health care.

The Court concludes that a number of means are available to Quebec to protect the integrity of its health care plan, and that the 'choice of prohibiting private insurance contracts is not justified by the evidence'.[153] The Court proceeds to consider questions about its institutional role and the extent to which it should defer to the legislature, and then affirms its own competence:

> Courts do not have to define goals, choose means or come up with ideas. They do not have to create social policies; they just have to understand what the other branches have created. No special expertise is required for such an understanding.' [quoting G Davidov, 'The Paradox of Judicial Deference' (2001) 12 *National Journal of Constitutional Law* 133]. In fact, if a court is satisfied that all the evidence has been presented, there is nothing that would justify it in refusing to perform its role on the ground that it should merely defer to the government' s position . . . The courts have a duty to rise above political debate. They leave it to the legislatures to develop social policy. But when such social policies infringe rights that are protected by the charters, the courts cannot shy away from considering them.[154]

The Court's claim is the same as that of the US Supreme Court in *Lochner*: it is not deciding social policy or substituting its judgment for that of the legislature, it is simply making a determination of whether a constitutional right has been violated on the basis of the available evidence. The Court adds, 'The instant case is a good example of a case in which the courts have all the necessary tools to evaluate the government's measure',[155] but its reasoning and its handling of the evidence strongly suggest that the Court lacks the institutional capacity to decide on the public need for legislation that reflects a key principle in the structure and financing of Canada's public health plan.

[151] Ibid, paras 77–83.
[152] Ibid, paras 78, 80, 81.
[153] Ibid, para 84.
[154] Ibid, paras 87, 89.
[155] *Chaoulli* (n 129) para 96.

C. Germany

In the *Smoking Ban Case*,[156] the *Land* Baden-Württemberg and Berlin (in its law-making capacity as a *Land*) had enacted bans on smoking in public places. Eating and drinking establishments, however, were allowed to set up separate smoking rooms. This exception was extended to discotheques (so long as the separate smoking rooms were limited to adults over 18) in Berlin, but not in Baden-Württemberg. A constitutional complaint was made by the proprietors of two small pubs that did not have sufficient space for a separate smoking room, and by a Baden-Württemberg discotheque owner. The publicans argued that the smoking bans violated their right to occupational freedom (Art 12(1) of the *Grundgesetz*) and right of ownership (Art 14(1) of the *Grundgesetz*) because the prohibition distorted economic competition in favour of larger establishments and had a disproportionate effect on their interests, and the discotheque owner made similar complaints.

The Bundesverfassungsgericht held that the challenged provisions violated the right to occupational freedom, but suspended the effect of its ruling, allowing the legislatures until the end of 2009 to amend the laws. The Court held that it would be constitutionally permissible for legislatures to enact a comprehensive prohibition on smoking in such establishments, as Bavaria had done in 2007. Such a decision would represent an acceptable weighing of the threat to public health from smoking against the fundamental rights at stake.[157] But since lawmakers in this case decided to pursue public health with 'reduced vigour' in order to accommodate the interests of publicans and smokers, they were required to afford equal treatment to all types of establishments and not to impose disproportionate costs on the owners of small pubs or discotheques. The Court held that the measures in question failed to comply with the principles of consistency and proportionality.[158] It arrived at this conclusion after reviewing a considerable amount of empirical evidence, including studies on mortality and other health effects of passive smoking; analyses of the chemical structure of tobacco smoke and the carcinogens it contains, and the ways in which particulates can harm the body; surveys of smoking habits among the German people and attitudes towards smoking; statistical reports on the current and projected impact of the smoking bans on the revenue of different kinds of establishments; and many other matters. This evidence was submitted by public and private bodies, including the Senate Department for Health, Environment and Consumer Protection; the Federal Statistical Office; the German Society of Occupational and Environmental Medicine; the German Cancer Research Center; the German Hotel and Restaurant Association; two anti-smoking advocacy groups; and a group representing the tobacco industry.[159] Some of these groups presented testimony at an oral hearing, and a medical expert

[156] *Smoking Ban Case* (n 62) 317.
[157] Ibid, 333–44.
[158] Ibid, 344.
[159] Ibid, 350–53.

appointed by the Court also testified about the dangers of passive smoking.[160]

Unlike some of the US cases on video games and *Chaoulli*, the Bundesverfassungsgericht does not appear to have made methodological or other obvious errors in assessing empirical research in the *Smoking Ban Case*. But even when courts avoid such errors, there are reasons to question whether the litigation framework is well suited for resolving the kinds of issues presented in these cases. Many of the empirical findings in the *Smoking Ban Case* are, like results of research in social and medical sciences in general, subject to change. These include the health dangers of passive smoking, the smoking habits of the population, and the economic dependency of pubs on smoking patrons. If understanding of these matters is altered due to changed conditions in society or advances in scientific knowledge, needed legislative reforms could be barred or hindered by the constitutional status of the ruling in the *Smoking Ban Case*.

In the US and Canadian cases, the courts imposed stringent burdens of production and proof on the government. Such a mode of inquiry fits comfortably with routine judicial processes, but in rights-based judicial review its effect is to restrict the grounds for legislative action, by disabling the legislature from passing laws without scientific proof of anticipated effects. In *Paris Adult Theatre 1 v Slaton* (1973),[161] which rejected First Amendment protection for obscenity, the US Supreme Court takes a much broader view of the proper reasons for legislation and the required empirical grounding than what was allowed in *Kendrick* and *Chaoulli*. In *Slaton* the Court stated:

> From the beginning of civilized societies, legislators and judges have acted on various unprovable assumptions. Such assumptions underlie much lawful state regulation of commercial and business affairs . . . Likewise, when legislatures and administrators act to protect the physical environment from pollution and to preserve our resources of forests, streams, and parks, they must act on such imponderables as the impact of a new highway near or through an existing park or wilderness area . . . The fact that a congressional directive reflects unprovable assumptions about what is good for the people, including imponderable aesthetic assumptions, is not a sufficient reason to find that statute unconstitutional.[162]

These 'imponderables' have to do with estimating the likelihood of an outcome and placing a value on it, and such matters are in many cases simply not susceptible of empirical proof. The Court continues, asserting that 'common sense' is a valid ground for legislation even in areas that concern fundamental rights:

> If we accept the unprovable assumption that a complete education requires the reading of certain books [which] improve the mind, enrich the human personality, and develop character, can we then say that a state legislature may not act on the corollary assumption that commerce in obscene books, or public exhibitions focused on obscene conduct, have a tendency to exert a corrupting and debasing impact leading to antisocial

[160] Ibid, 353.
[161] *Paris Adult Theatre 1 v Slaton* 413 US 49.
[162] Ibid, 61–62 (internal citations omitted).

> behavior? Mr. Justice Cardozo said that all laws in Western civilization are 'guided by a robust common sense . . .' The sum of experience, including that of the past two decades, affords an ample basis for legislatures to conclude that a sensitive, key relationship of human existence, central to family life, community welfare, and the development of human personality, can be debased and distorted by crass commercial exploitation of sex. Nothing in the Constitution prohibits a State from reaching such a conclusion and acting on it legislatively simply because there is no conclusive evidence or empirical data.[163]

The Court's approach here is surely preferable to demanding social scientific proof of potential harms to society before a legislature can act to prevent them. As Daniel Patrick Moynihan (who was a professor of sociology at Harvard before becoming a New York Senator) stated, social science is concerned to 'predict future events, whereas the purpose of the law is to order them'.[164]

VII. Conclusion

In 1897 Oliver Wendell Holmes wrote: 'For the rational study of the law the black letter man may be the man of the present, but the man of the future is the man of statistics and the master of economics.'[165] The prediction proved accurate for rights-based judicial review of legislation. In *Lochner* the US Supreme Court introduced the proportionality-based, fact-intensive method of judicial review of legislation that now prevails in many constitutional systems worldwide. The cases reviewed in section VI – *Chaoulli v Quebec*, the German *Smoking Ban Case*, and the US cases on violent video games – are all instances of using the proportionality inquiry to resolve a claim that legislation violates a constitutional right, with reliance on empirical research to determine the strength of the state interest in legislation or the degree to which the legislation affects the interests of the claimants.

The revolution in judicial method that *Lochner* marked has not been matched by fundamental changes in the institutional forms of constitutional tribunals and litigation in common law countries, save for the practice of presenting empirical research in 'Brandeis briefs' (which was in fact introduced in *Lochner* itself). Kenneth Davis, the scholar who coined the terms 'adjudicative fact' and 'legislative fact', has proposed that the US Supreme Court should have a dedicated research bureau along the lines of the Congressional Research Service. He notes that the first US Congress (in 1789) 'probably legislated with hardly more facts than were already in the minds of Members'.[166] As industrial economies advanced and society grew more complex, legislatures created new institutional structures

[163] Ibid, 63 (internal citations omitted).
[164] DP Moynihan, 'Social Science and the Courts' (1979) 54 *Public Interest* 12, 16.
[165] OW Holmes, 'The Path of the Law' (1897) 10 *Harvard Law Review* 457.
[166] KC Davis, 'Judicial, Legislative, and Administrative Lawmaking: A Proposed Research Service for the Supreme Court' (1986) 71 *Minnesota Law Review* 1, 5.

to acquire factual information and to assess the growing body of scientific and technological knowledge. Empirical fact-finding is a central aspect of modern lawmaking processes. Since the Supreme Court addresses complex factual questions in applying and interpreting constitutional provisions, Davis argues, it should have a well-resourced research staff with scientific training.[167]

Davis's argument is compelling, and applicable to other constitutional courts. As shown in section V, judges routinely rely on sources of questionable authority and even on non-authoritative sources such as Wikipedia, sometimes discovered haphazardly through Internet search engines. Judges who lack scientific training have difficulty comprehending empirical research in natural, medical, and social sciences; the case reports are replete with errors in assessing statistical analyses and mistakes regarding methodology. We could attempt to improve judicial processes for finding legislative facts through smaller-scale reforms, such as adopting procedural and evidentiary rules to govern the submission of empirical evidence in Brandeis briefs. Justice Breyer encourages greater use of court-appointed experts, but acknowledges that this could impinge on the normal adversarial process of common law litigation and raises a number of questions with no clear answer:

> Will use of an independent expert, in effect, substitute that expert's judgment for that of the court? Will it inappropriately deprive the parties of control over the presentation of the case? Will it improperly intrude on the proper function of the jury? Where is one to find a truly neutral expert? After all, different experts, in total honesty, often can interpret the same data differently. Will the search for the expert create inordinate delay or significantly increase costs? Who will pay the expert?[168]

Judge Henry Friendly proposed that courts first give notice of proposed findings of legislative fact, allowing time for comment by experts and the public (as in some administrative rule-making processes), before relying on those facts in a constitutional decision.[169] All of these proposals are worth exploring, but Davis's idea of a research service may provide the best fit with the fact-specific methods of rights adjudication currently used by constitutional courts. Unless judges have direct access to internal fact-finding resources, it seems that they will continue to rely heavily on Brandeis briefs and their own research efforts, neither of which is an ideal way to establish empirical grounds for constitutional law.

An objection to Davis's proposal is that it would transform constitutional courts into quasi-legislative bodies. If judges can initiate and direct empirical investigations using their own staff, and rely on their results to determine the implications of constitutional rights for a wide range of policy questions, then it would become difficult to distinguish their function from that of legislators. The objection is powerful, but it is also applicable to using the proportionality inquiry

[167] Ibid.
[168] Breyer (n 70) 27.
[169] HJ Friendly, 'The Courts and Social Policy: Substance and Procedure' (1978) 33 *University of Miami Law Review* 21, 37–41.

to determine the validity of legislation. The proportionality inquiry as applied in rights-based judicial review has many of the hallmarks of legislative decision-making, requiring a general assessment of the importance of state aims and an evaluation of the burdens placed on individuals. Moreover, central elements of the proportionality test are empirical in nature, including the inquiry into the efficacy of legislative means, the availability of alternative and equally effective means, and the effects of legislation on society and individuals. Judges are already carrying out their own empirical investigations, but with inferior tools. Such considerations could reasonably lead constitutional framers to decide to withhold from courts the power of judicial review of legislation based on proportionality tests. But if constitutional courts are to have this power, they should also be given institutional capacities that are fit for the task.

Part Three

Absolute Rights: The Example of Human Dignity

11

'Human Dignity Shall Be Inviolable' – Dealing with a Constitutional Taboo

SEBASTIAN UNGER*

According to the Italian philosopher Giorgio Agamben 'the state of exception tends increasingly to appear as the dominant paradigm of government in contemporary politics'.[1] If this finding is correct – and the developments in the fields of life science and biotechnology, as well as the challenges posed by international terrorism, suggest that the legal system is increasingly operating at its boundaries – absolute values providing for a clear and definitive limitation of power gain in importance.[2] Human dignity, which, according to Article 1(1), 1st sentence of the German Constitution (Basic Law) and Article 1, 1st sentence of the Charter of Fundamental Rights of the European Union, is inviolable, seems to be such an absolute value. Against this background, the following considerations analyse the implications of an absolute legal value for a legal system and draw the consequences for its interpretation and application. They do so in four steps. First, they introduce the inviolability of human dignity as the German contribution to the European constitutional tradition. Second, they analyse the operating mode of human dignity as an inviolable and absolute legal value. This leads to a third section, which outlines the implications of such a value for a legal system, a fourth section, which draws the consequences for its interpretation and application, and finally a fifth section, which deals with possible objections and draws a conclusion.

* The author's thanks for valuable comments go to Thomas Burri.

[1] G Agamben, *State of Exception* (Chicago, University of Chicago Press, 2005) 2; cf also S Augsberg, 'Denken vom Ausnahmezustand her: Über die Unzulässigkeit der anormalen Konstruktion und Destruktion des Normativen' in F Arndt et al (eds), *Freiheit – Sicherheit – Öffentlichkeit* (Baden-Baden, Nomos, 2009) 17, 18 f; E Schmidt-Jortzig, 'Zum Streit um die korrekte dogmatische Einordnung und Anwendung von Art. 1 Abs. 1 GG' in J Bröhmer et al (eds), *Internationale Gemeinschaft und Menschenrechte: Festschrift für Georg Ress zum 70. Geburtstag* (Köln, Carl Heymann, 2005) 1569, 1569 f.

[2] Cf with regard to human dignity H Hofmann, 'Die Menschenwürde in Grenzbereichen der Rechtsordnung' in R Pitschas and A Uhle (eds), *Wege gelebter Verfassung in Recht und Politik: Festschrift für Rupert Scholz zum 70. Geburtstag* (Berlin, Duncker & Humblot, 2007) 225; J Isensee, 'Menschenwürde: die säkulare Gesellschaft auf der Suche nach dem Absoluten' (2006) 131 *Archiv des öffentlichen Rechts* 173; K-H Ladeur and I Augsberg, *Die Funktion der Menschenwürde im Verfassungsstaat: Humangenetik – Neurowissenschaft – Medien* (Tübingen, Mohr Siebeck, 2008) 8 f; see generally J Isensee, *Tabu im freiheitlichen Staat: Jenseits und diesseits der Rationalität des Rechts* (Paderborn, Schöningh, 2003) 79.

I. Human Dignity and the European Constitutional Tradition

According to Article 1 of the German Basic Law, human dignity shall be inviolable. To respect and protect it shall be the duty of all state authority. With these two sentences the German Basic Law enters uncharted constitutional territory:[3] neither the classic declarations of human rights promulgated in the American and the French Revolution[4] nor their English predecessors[5] contain a human dignity clause.[6] The same is true for most documents of the European constitutional history. Only three constitutions from the interwar years mention human dignity; however, they do so only in an economic context.[7] It was therefore not until 1948 that the Universal Declaration of Human Rights in Article 1 introduced an explicit commitment to human dignity, stating: 'All human beings are born free and equal in dignity and rights. They are endowed with reason and conscience and should act towards one another in a spirit of brotherhood.'[8] As various documents show, to some extent this clause functioned as a model for the German Basic Law.[9] However, Article 1(1) of the German Basic Law goes beyond it. It not only requires all state authority to respect and protect human dignity but also announces the inviolability of human dignity.[10]

[3] Cf B Pieroth, '§25: Die Grundrechte des Grundgesetzes in der Verfassungstradition' in D Merten and H-J Papier (eds), *Handbuch der Grundrechte in Deutschland und Europa, vol II: Grundrechte in Deutschland: Allgemeine Lehren I* (Heidelberg, CF Müller, 2006) para 59: 'Grundrecht[e] ohne Tradition'; H Dreier, '§1: Grundlagen und Grundzüge staatlichen Verfassungsrechts: Deutschland' in A von Bogdandy, P Cruz Villalón and PM Huber (eds), *Ius Publicum Europaeum, vol I: Grundlagen und Grundzüge staatlichen Verfassungsrechts* (Heidelberg, CF Müller, 2007) para 15: 'kein Vorbild und keine Überlieferung'.

[4] See in particular Virginia Bill of Rights, 12 June 1776, and Déclaration des Droits de l'Homme et du Citoyen, 26 August 1789; for predecessors cf H Dreier, 'Vorbemerkungen' in H Dreier (ed) *Grundgesetz: Kommentar, vol I: Artikel 1–19*, 2nd edn (Tübingen, Mohr Siebeck, 2004) para 5.

[5] See in particular Magna Charta Libertatum, 1215, Petition of Right, 1628, Habeas Corpus Act, 1679, and Bill of Rights, 1689.

[6] H Dreier, 'Art. 1 I' in Dreier (ed) (n 4) para 17; T Geddert-Steinacher, *Menschenwürde als Verfassungsbegriff: Aspekte der Rechtsprechung des Bundesverfassungsgerichts zu Art. 1 Abs. 1 Grundgesetz* (Berlin, Duncker & Humblot, 1990) 38; F Hufen, *Staatsrecht II: Grundrechte*, 2nd edn (Munich, CH Beck, 2009) § 10, para 3; Isensee, 'Menschenwürde' (n 2) 175 f.

[7] P Tiedemann, *Menschenwürde als Rechtsbegriff: Eine philosophische Klärung* (Berlin, Berliner Wissenschafts-Verlag, 2007) 10 f.

[8] T Rensmann, 'Die Menschenwürde als universaler Rechtsbegriff' in C Thies (ed), Der Wert der Mens*chenwürde* (Paderborn, Schöningh, 2009) 75, 75; cf also the preambles of the Universal Declaration of Human Rights, 10 December 1948, the Charter of the United Nations, 26 June 1945, and the United Nations International Covenants on Civil and Political and on Economic, Social and Cultural Rights, 19 December 1966.

[9] See Deutscher Bundestag and Bundesarchiv (eds), *Der Parlamentarische Rat 1948–1949: Akten und Protokolle, vol 5/II: Ausschuß für Grundsatzfragen* (Munich, Boldt im Oldenbourg-Verlag, 1993) 585 f, 592; *vol 9: Plenum* (Munich, Boldt im Oldenbourg-Verlag, 1996) 56, 565 f.

[10] On the evolutionary history of Art 1 para 1 of the German Basic Law see Dreier (n 6) para 21; C Enders, *Die Menschenwürde in der Verfassungsordnung: Zur Dogmatik des Art. 1 GG* (Tübingen, Mohr Siebeck, 1997) 404 f; W Vögele, *Menschenwürde zwischen Recht und Theologie: Begründungen von Menschenrechten in der Perspektive öffentlicher Theologie* (Gütersloh, Christian Kaiser and Gütersloher Verlagshaus, 2000) 274 f.

There are no predecessors to this normative concept of human dignity, and it has been introduced to other constitutions afterwards only in very few cases: although various younger European constitutions contain human dignity clauses, in most countries human dignity is not expressly stated to be inviolable.[11] Only the Finnish constitution and the Polish constitution pursue a similar concept of human dignity. The other constitutions are rather based on a concept of human dignity, which, at least according to the wording, does not absolutely exclude interferences with human dignity if they can only be rationally and proportionally connected to a legitimate objective. Article 54(1) of the Hungarian Constitution, for example, only protects one from being 'arbitrarily' deprived of his right to human dignity, and so apparently does not absolutely exclude restrictions.[12] Other constitutions oblige state authorities to respect, protect or preserve human dignity, but, at least on the face of it, do not prohibit interference with human dignity in any absolute sense.[13] Hence, only with the Charter of Fundamental Rights of the European Union has the German concept of human dignity as an inviolable legal value become an accepted part of the European constitutional tradition. Such acceptance, however, has not come without obstacles: although the introduction of a human dignity clause in the Charter itself met with unanimous approval, the adoption of the inviolability of human dignity in the sense of Article 1(1), 1st sentence of the German Basic Law[14] was highly controversial.[15] In the first draft, Article 1 of the Charter simply stated: 'The dignity of the person must be

[11] For the Italian constitution see P Becchi, 'Menschenwürde: Die italienische verfassungsrechtliche Variante im Unterschied zur deutschen' in G Brudermüller and K Seelmann (eds), *Menschenwürde: Begründung – Konturen – Geschichte* (Würzburg, Königshausen & Neumann, 2008) 107, 110, 112 f; for the Spanish constitution see I Gutiérrez Gutiérrez, 'Die Menschenwürde als europäischer Verfassungsbegriff – Rechtsvergleichender und verfassungsgeschichtlicher Beitrag zur deutschen Debatte um die Menschenwürde' (2006) 89 *Kritische Vierteljahresschrift für Gesetzgebung und Rechtswissenschaft* 384, 385 f, 399 f; cf also C Calliess, 'Die Menschenwürde im Recht der Europäischen Union' in R Gröschner and OW Lembcke (eds), *Das Dogma der Unantastbarkeit: Eine Auseinandersetzung mit dem Absolutheitsanspruch der Würde* (Tübingen, Mohr Siebeck, 2009) 133, 135 f.

[12] Nevertheless, the courts consider human dignity to be unviolable under Art 54 para 1 of the Hungarian constitution, see G Halmai, '§12: Grundlagen und Grundzüge staatlichen Verfassungsrechts: Ungarn' in Bogdandy et al (eds) (n 3) paras 45 f.

[13] Cf Advocate General C Stix-Hackl in Case C-36/02 *Omega Spielhallen- und Automatenaufstellungs-GmbH* [2004] ECR I-9609, para 84: 'As in the aforementioned instruments of international law, however, human dignity seems to appear in the national legal systems of the Member States primarily as a general article of faith or – often in the case-law – as a fundamental evaluation or constitutional principle, rather than as an independent justiciable rule of law. A rule such as that contained in the German Constitution whereby – at least according to the majority viewpoint – respect for and protection of human dignity as embodied in Article 1 of the German Basic Law constitutes not just a "fundamental constitutional principle" but also a separate fundamental right, must therefore be considered the exception.'

[14] S Barriga, *Die Entstehung der Charta der Grundrechte der Europäischen Union: Eine Analyse der Arbeiten im Konvent und kompetenzrechtlicher Fragen* (Baden-Baden, Nomos, 2003) 70; M Borowsky, 'Art. 1' in J Meyer (ed), *Charta der Grundrechte der Europäischen Union*, 2nd edn (Baden-Baden, Nomos, 2006) para 1; W Höfling, 'Art. 1' in PJ Tettinger and K Stern (eds), *Kölner Gemeinschaftskommentar zur Europäischen Grundrechte-Charta* (Munich, CH Beck, 2006) para 2; R Streinz, 'Art. 1 GR-Charta' in R Streinz (ed), *EUV/EGV: Vertrag über die Europäische Union und Vertrag zur Gründung der Europäischen Gemeinschaft* (Munich, CH Beck, 2003) para 1.

[15] Borowsky (n 14) para 14.

respected and protected.'[16] The second draft then replaced this compromise with the current version, reading: 'Human dignity is inviolable. It must be respected and protected.'[17] Thereby the inviolability of human dignity and its operationalisation have gained Europe-wide significance.[18]

II. Human Dignity as an Inviolable and Absolute Legal Value

According to the prevailing opinion, under Article 1(1) of the German Basic Law violations of human dignity cannot be justified under any circumstances.[19] In the clear words of the German Basic Law: 'Human dignity shall be inviolable.'[20] The implications of reading human dignity as an inviolable and absolute legal value become clear by comparing its operating mode to that of 'ordinary' fundamental rights.[21]

A. The Operating Mode of 'Ordinary' Fundamental Rights

Generally speaking and setting aside their human dignity core, 'ordinary' fundamental rights are subject to restrictions, prescribed by law,[22] in the interest of the

[16] Charte 4422/00 Convent 45, 3.

[17] Charte 4470/00 Convent 47, 3; on the evolutionary history of Art 1 of the Charter of Fundamental Rights of the European Union see Borowsky (n 14) paras 6 f.

[18] Cf Calliess (n 11) 164 f.

[19] *Entscheidungen des Bundesverfassungsgerichts* [Decisions of the Federal Constitutional Court] (BVerfGE) 93, 266, 293; BVerfGE 107, 275, 284; BVerfGE 109, 279, 311 f; BVerfGE 115, 118, 153; cf also CD Classen, 'Die Menschenwürde ist – und bleibt – unantastbar' (2009) 62 *Die Öffentliche Verwaltung* 689, 692 f; F Hufen, 'Die Menschenwürde, Art. 1 I GG' (2010) 50 *Juristische Schulung* 1, 9; Isensee, 'Menschenwürde' (n 2) 209 f.

[20] According to the prevailing opinion the same is true for Art 1, 1st sentence of the Charter of Fundamental Rights of the European Union, see Borowsky (n 14) para 40; Höfling (n 14) paras 31 ff; HD Jarass, *Die EU-Grundrechte: Ein Studien- und Handbuch* (Munich, CH Beck, 2005) § 8, para 11; Streinz (n 14) para 6.

[21] Cf Classen (n 19) 693 f; H Dreier, 'Bedeutung und systematische Stellung der Menschenwürde im deutschen Grundgesetz' in K Seelmann (ed), *Menschenwürde als Rechtsbegriff* (Stuttgart, Franz Steiner, 2005) 33, 34 f; W Höfling, 'Unantastbare Grundrechte – ein normlogischer Widerspruch? Zur Dogmatik des Art. 1 Absatz 1 GG' in Gröschner and Lembcke (eds) (n 11) 111, 114 f; Isensee, 'Menschenwürde' (n 2) 175; R Poscher, 'Menschenwürde als Tabu: Die verdeckte Rationalität eines absoluten Rechtsverbots der Folter' in G Beestermöller and H Brunkhorst (eds), *Rückkehr der Folter: Der Rechtsstaat im Zwielicht?* (Munich, CH Beck, 2006) 75, 77; cf also the discussion about the fundamental rights character of Art 1(1) of the German Basic Law: H-G Dederer, 'Die Garantie der Menschenwürde (Art. 1 Abs. 1 GG): Dogmatische Grundfragen auf dem Stand der Wissenschaft' (2009) 57 *Jahrbuch des öffentlichen Rechts der Gegenwart* 89, 89 f; Hufen (n 6) § 10, paras 9 ff; K Stern, 'Die normative Dimension der Menschenwürdegarantie' in M Brenner, PM Huber and M Möstl (eds), *Der Staat des Grundgesetzes – Kontinuität und Wandel: Festschrift für Peter Badura zum siebzigsten Geburtstag* (Tübingen, Mohr Siebeck, 2004) 571, 573 f.

[22] See J Kokott, '§22: Grundrechtliche Schranken und Schrankenschranken' in D Merten and H-J Papier (eds), *Handbuch der Grundrechte in Deutschland und Europa, vol I: Entwicklung und Grundlagen* (Heidelberg, CF Müller, 2004) paras 18 ff; M Sachs, 'Vor Art. 1' in M Sachs (ed), *Grundgesetz: Kommentar*, 5th edn (Munich, CH Beck, 2009) paras 101 f.

common good. However, such restrictions have to be justified. According to the principle of proportionality,[23] restrictions on the exercise of fundamental rights are justified if they are suitable and necessary in order to attain a legitimate objective. Furthermore, they must be proportional to the objective thus pursued. For example, according to recent caselaw, a ban on smoking in pubs as a restriction on the right to conduct a business is justified only if it is suitable and necessary to ensure the safeguarding of public health and, furthermore, is proportional to this objective.[24]

B. The Operating Mode of the Absolute Right to Human Dignity

The operating mode of human dignity is considerably different from that of fundamental rights. The starting point is the widely accepted assumption that a precise definition of human dignity is difficult, if not impossible.[25] Against this background, from its first cases dealing with human dignity the Federal Constitutional Court has not even tried to define human dignity. Instead, it has formulated exemplary scenarios in which human dignity is violated.[26] Although, in later rulings, it has undertaken to contribute to a positive concept of human dignity,[27] the caselaw has always been dominated by such attempts to specify its violation. At the end of this development stands the so-called 'object formula' as a universal concept of human dignity. According to this formula, it contradicts human dignity to make a human being a mere object of the state.[28] Despite criticism,[29] the 'object formula' has dominated the caselaw in human dignity to date. The concept of the 'object formula' can be illustrated by a few sentences from a recent ruling:

[23] See Hufen (n 6) § 9, paras 14 ff; Kokott (n 22) paras 98 ff; Sachs (n 22) para 135.

[24] BVerfGE 121, 317, 344 f.

[25] Isensee, 'Menschenwürde' (n 2) 214. This is certainly one of the reasons for the reluctance to accept human dignity as a legal value; for the English law see D Feldman, 'Human Dignity as a Legal Value – Part 1' (1999) *Public Law* 682, 696 f; D Feldman, 'Human Dignity as a Legal Value – Part 2' (2000) *Public Law* 61, 75 f.

[26] BVerfGE 1, 97, 104; for further specifications see BVerfGE 109, 279, 311 f; cf also G Dürig, 'Der Grundrechtssatz von der Menschenwürde: Entwurf eines praktikablen Wertsystems der Grundrechte aus Art. 1 Abs. I in Verbindung mit Art. 19 Abs. II des Grundgesetzes' (1956) 81 *Archiv des öffentlichen Rechts* 117, 127 f; G Dürig, 'Art. 1 Abs. 1' in T Maunz and G Dürig (eds), *Grundgesetz: Kommentar, vol II: Art. 1–5* (Munich, CH Beck, 1958) paras 28, 34.

[27] Starting with BVerfGE 2, 1, 12; continuing with BVerfGE 5, 85, 204 f; BVerfGE 6, 32, 40; BVerfGE 7, 198, 206; from the recent caselaw see BVerfGE 101, 275, 287; BVerfGE 109, 133, 149 f; BVerfGE 115, 1, 14; BVerfGE 117, 71, 89.

[28] BVerfGE 27, 1, 6. In later rulings the formula has been specified; according to BVerfGE 30, 1, 25 f, a violation of human dignity requires treatment of a human being by public authority which fundamentally calls into question his or her quality as a subject or his or her status as a legal entity by its lack of respect of the value, which is due to every human being for his or her own sake, by virtue of his or her being a person; from the recent caselaw see BVerfGE 109, 279, 312 f; cf also BVerfGE 115, 118, 153; BVerfGE 122, 248, 271; Dürig, 'Menschenwürde' (n 26) 127 f.

[29] Amongst others see M Nettesheim, 'Die Garantie der Menschenwürde zwischen metaphysischer Überhöhung und bloßem Abwägungstopos' (2005) 130 *Archiv des öffentlichen Rechts* 71, 79 f.

> Article 1(1) of the German Basic Law protects the individual human being not only against humiliation, branding, persecution, outlawing and similar actions by third parties or by the state itself . . . [T]he obligation to respect and protect human dignity generally precludes making a human being a mere object of the state . . . What is thus absolutely prohibited is any treatment of a human being by public authority which fundamentally calls into question his or her quality as a subject.[30]

In the 'object formula', the scope of protection, the limitations imposed and their justification in the light of the proportionality test, which are carefully distinguished in fundamental rights dogmatic, converge in a single decision, according to which human dignity is either violated or not.[31] In line with this the proportionality test is irrelevant in the context of human dignity: interferences with human dignity are 'absolutely prohibited' under any circumstances.[32] A balancing of conflicting legal interests, as is characteristic for the application of fundamental rights, does not take place. In the words of the Federal Constitutional Court: 'Human dignity as the basis of all fundamental rights cannot be weighed against any single fundamental right.'[33] This concept of human dignity comes to the fore in recent caselaw of the Federal Constitutional Court: because it is a violation of human dignity, the acoustic surveillance of private homes, which interferes with the core of privacy, is prohibited under any circumstances, even if it can be rationally connected to the prosecution of criminals. A balancing of conflicting interests – in this case, the right to privacy as an emanation of human dignity on the one hand and the efficiency of criminal prosecution on the other hand – does not take place.[34] This illustrates the operating mode of human dignity according to the prevailing opinion: in a system of relative values, human dignity is the only absolute value.[35] This does not only affect Article 1 of the German Basic Law; as the Federal Constitutional Court considers all fundamental rights to be emanations of human dignity,[36] each fundamental right contains an inviolable human dignity core.[37] Furthermore, according to Article 79(3) of the

[30] BVerfGE 115, 118, 153; cf also BVerfGE 109, 133, 149 f; BVerfGE 109, 279, 312 f; BVerfGE 116, 69, 85; BVerfGE 117, 71, 89.

[31] F Wittreck, 'Menschenwürde und Folterverbot – Zum Dogma von der ausnahmslosen Unabwägbarkeit des Art. 1 Abs. 1 GG' (2003) 56 *Die Öffentliche Verwaltung* 873, 874, 877; cf also Dreier (n 21) 34 f; Geddert-Steinacher (n 6) 83: 'Gewährleistungsbereich und Verletzungsgrenze . . . identisch'; Höfling (n 21) 114 f; Hufen (n 6) § 10, para 34.

[32] BVerfGE 107, 275, 284; BVerfGE 115, 118, 153; Wittreck (n 31) 874.

[33] BVerfGE 107, 275, 284; cf also BVerfGE 93, 266, 293; BVerfGE 109, 279, 311 f.

[34] BVerfGE 109, 279, 311 f.

[35] Isensee, 'Menschenwürde' (n 2) 175; cf also Dreier (n 6) para 41: 'Absolutum in einer zutiefst relativistischen Welt'.

[36] BVerfGE 107, 275, 284; cf also BVerfGE 93, 266, 293; BVerfGE 109, 279, 313; see also U Di Fabio, 'Grundrechte als Wertordnung' (2004) 59 *Juristenzeitung* 1, 5 f, 6; U Di Fabio, '§46: Zur Theorie eines grundrechtlichen Wertesystems' in Merten and Papier (eds) (n 3) paras 34, 37; Dreier (n 6) para 162; S Lenz, *Vorbehaltlose Freiheitsrechte: Stellung und Funktion vorbehaltloser Freiheitsrechte in der Verfassungsordnung* (Tübingen, Mohr Siebeck, 2006) 17 f, 71 f; P Tiedemann, 'Vom inflationären Gebrauch der Menschenwürde in der Rechtsprechung des Bundesverfassungsgerichts' (2009) 62 *Die Öffentliche Verwaltung* 606, 613 f.

[37] BVerfGE 109, 279, 313 f; BVerfGE 113, 348, 391 f; BVerfGE 115, 166, 182, 196; Lenz (n 36) 71 f; critically Dreier (n 6) paras 163 ff; Tiedemann (n 36) 613 f.

German Basic Law,[38] Article 1 of the German Basic Law also binds the constitutional legislature in cases of constitutional amendment.[39] Hence, the normative understanding of human dignity as inviolable has far-reaching consequences.[40]

III. The Inviolability of Human Dignity: a Blessing and a Curse

What does the normative understanding of human dignity as inviolable mean for a legal system? An inviolable and absolute legal value is a blessing and a curse at the same time: a blessing, because it reduces complexity by absolutely precluding certain measures and, in doing so, provides for clear guidelines and identity;[41] a curse, because it confronts the operating mode of fundamental rights primarily governed by instrumental rationality [*Zweckrationalität*] with elements of pure value rationality [*Wertrationalität]*.[42] According to German sociologist Max Weber, an action is 'instrumentally rational [*zweckrational*] when the end, the means and the secondary results are all rationally taken into account and weighed'.[43] On the contrary, an action is value rational [*wertrational*] when it is determined by values for their own sake, without regard to the consequences. Therefore, to some extent, value rationality leads to irrationality:

> Value-rational action may thus have various different relations to the instrumentally rational action. From the latter point of view, however, value-rationality is always irrational. Indeed, the more the value to which action is oriented is elevated to the status of an absolute value, the more 'irrational' in this sense the corresponding action is. For, the more unconditionally the actor devotes himself to this value for its own sake . . . the less he is influenced by considerations of the consequences of his action.[44]

[38] 'Amendments to this Basic Law affecting the division of the Federation into Länder, their participation on principle in the legislative process, or the principles laid down in Articles 1 and 20 shall be inadmissible.'

[39] BVerfGE 109, 279, 310 f.

[40] Rensmann (n 8) 85.

[41] Ladeur and Augsberg (n 2) 10: 'Ein deutliches "So Nicht!" bietet eine klare Entscheidungshilfe, die zumindest negative Gewißheit verschafft'; see also Isensee, 'Menschenwürde' (n 2) 198 f; Rensmann (n 8) 77: 'Reflexionsstopp', referring to N Luhmann, *Gibt es in unserer Gesellschaft noch unverzichtbare Normen?* (Heidelberg, CF Müller, 1993) 19.

[42] See Poscher (n 21) 78 f, also with regard to the following considerations.

[43] M Weber, *Economy and Society: An Outline of Interpretive Sociology* (Berkeley, University of California Press, 1978) 26.

[44] Weber (n 43) 26; on Max Weber's concept of rationality see T Raiser, 'Max Weber und die Rationalität des Rechts' (2008) 63 *Juristenzeitung* 853, 854 f; on the rationality of balancing see R Alexy, *Theorie der Grundrechte* 3rd edn (Frankfurt, Suhrkamp, 1996) 296: 'Spiel von Grund und Gegengrund'; Geddert-Steinacher (n 6) 82, n 283; W Höfling, *Offene Grundrechtsinterpretation: Grundrechtsauslegung zwischen amtlichem Interpretationsmonopol und privater Konkretisierungskompetenz* (Berlin, Duncker & Humblot, 1987) 180 f; W Kahl, 'Vom weiten Schutzbereich zum engen Gewährleistungsgehalt: Kritik einer neuen Richtung der deutschen Grundrechtsdogmatik' (2004) 43 *Der Staat* 167, 189 f; S Unger, *Das Verfassungsprinzip der Demokratie: Normstruktur und Norminhalt des grundgesetzlichen*

The distinction between instrumental irrationality and value rationality can be transferred to the operating modes of fundamental rights and human dignity. Whereas the operating mode of fundamental rights allows for a consideration of conflicting objectives as well as consequences (and, in doing so, is in line with the concept of instrumental rationality), the operating mode of human dignity does not (and, in doing so, is based on pure value rationality). As a consequence, public measures or decisions based on the inviolability of human dignity alone are affected by traces of irrationality. This is not a problem as long as public measures or decisions are uncontroversial. It is a problem, however, if public measures or decisions leave the social consensus.[45] With good reason the inviolability of human dignity has therefore been considered a constitutional taboo:[46] Like a taboo it establishes identity by absolutely precluding certain public actions.[47] Like a taboo it contains an absolute und uncontested imperative.[48] Like a taboo, however, it is also affected by traces of irrationality.[49] And finally, like a taboo it only functions as long as its content meets with social consensus.[50] If it does not, public measures or decisions based on it alone, without taking into consideration the objectives and consequences at stake, will be challenged by a strong desire to consider alternatives. In a pluralistic society this will increasingly be the case, especially in international or intercultural contexts.[51] Current examples include the discussion about torturing a hostage taker in order to save the lives of hostages, the debate about downing a hijacked airplane likely to be misused as a weapon against human lives and the whole biotechnological debate, in which the refer-

Demokratieprinzips (Tübingen, Mohr Siebeck, 2008) 137 f; R Zippelius, 'Über die rationale Strukturierung rechtlicher Erwägungen' (1999) 54 *Juristenzeitung* 112, 115 f; critically Lenz (n 36) 233 f.

[45] Cf Dreier (n 21) 35: 'Nur bei durch Konsens und Evidenz gesicherter erdrückender Plausibilität einer Menschenwürdeverletzung läßt sich das Verfahren der "Negativ-Definition" mit Aussicht auf Erfolg praktizieren.'

[46] O Depenheuer, 'Recht und Tabu – ein Problemaufriß' in O Depenheuer (ed), *Recht und Tabu* (Wiesbaden, Westdeutscher Verlag, 2003) 7, 20 f; Dreier (n 21) 35 f; W Höfling, 'Art. 1' in Sachs (ed) (n 22) para 17; Isensee, 'Menschenwürde' (n 2) 179; L Michael and M Morlok, *Grundrechte*, 2nd edn (Baden-Baden, Nomos, 2010) para 131; Poscher (n 21) 79 f; R Poscher, 'Menschenwürde im Staatsnotstand' in P Bahr and HM Heinig (eds), *Menschenwürde in der säkularen Verfassungsordnung: Rechtswissenschaftliche und theologische Perspektiven* (Tübingen, Mohr Siebeck, 2006) 215, 216 f; Rensmann (n 8) 85; critically Ladeur and Augsberg (n 2) 8 f.

[47] Cf T Burri, 'Breaking the Taboo: National Minorities in the EC- and WTO-Trade Regimes' in P Eeckhout and T Tridimas (eds), *Yearbook of European Law 2008* (Oxford, Oxford University Press, 2009) 321, 321; Depenheuer (n 46) 10 f, 18; Isensee, *Tabu im freiheitlichen Staat* (n 2) 79; H Kraft, *Tabu: Magie und soziale Wirklichkeit* (Düsseldorf, Walter, 2004) 177, 211; H Schröder, 'Diagnose Tabu: Zum Stil der temporären Tabuaufhebung in der Arzt-Patienten-Kommunikation' in M Rothe and H Schröder (eds), *Stil, Stilbruch, Tabu: Stilerfahrung nach der Rhetorik: Eine Bilanz* (Berlin, Lit, 2008) 166, 171.

[48] C Enders, 'Die Menschenwürde als Recht auf Rechte – die mißverstandene Botschaft des Bonner Grundgesetzes' in K Seelmann (ed), *Menschenwürde als Rechtsbegriff* (Stuttgart, Franz Steiner, 2005) 49, 56 f; Rensmann (n 8) 77: 'self-evident truth'.

[49] Cf Depenheuer (n 46) 11 f; Rensmann (n 8) 85 f.

[50] Cf Burri (n 47) 321; Rensmann (n 8) 85 f.

[51] M Herdegen, 'Deutungen der Menschenwürde im Staatsrecht' in G Brudermüller and K Seelmann (eds), *Menschenwürde: Begründung – Konturen – Geschichte* (Würzburg, Königshausen & Neumann, 2008) 57, 61 f, 64.

ence to the absolute value of human dignity forecloses a consideration of the objectives pursued by new diagnostic and therapeutic instruments as well as their positive and negative consequences. In an international perspective, the *Omega* case, which concerned the question whether simulated killing action violates human dignity,[52] illustrates that, despite the Charter of Fundamental Rights of the European Union, there is hardly a consistent concept of human dignity even within the European Union.

IV. Consequences for the Interpretation and Application of Human Dignity

What are the consequences of considering human dignity a constitutional taboo for the interpretation and application of human dignity?

A. Human Dignity and Evident Social Consensus

First, any concept of human dignity has to take into account its dependence on an evident social consensus. As the prevailing concept does not allow for a consideration of conflicting interests and, therefore, is affected by traces of irrationality, public measures or decisions based on the inviolability of human dignity alone in the long run will only be accepted if they are not systematically contested.[53]

This is illustrated by the development of the German human dignity approach. On the one hand human dignity has been trivialised and inflated.[54] Examples include the question whether the obligation to wear a robe in court violates human dignity as well as the bans on midget tossing,[55] peepshows,[56] female mud wrestling[57] and simulated killing action,[58] all based on the inviolability of human dignity alone. On the other hand, human dignity has been resorted to in the context of life science and biotechnology, as well as in addressing the challenges posed by international terrorism, as a seemingly simple answer to complex questions.[59]

[52] Case C-36/02 *Omega Spielhallen- und Automatenaufstellungs-GmbH* [2004] ECR I-9609.

[53] Cf Rensmann (n 8) 85 f.

[54] Dreier (n 6) para 47 f; *locus classicus*: 'Art. 1 I GG ist keine "kleine Münze", – etwa im Sinne eines erweiterten Ehrenschutzes oder einer Abwehr von Geschmacklosigkeiten. Genau so schlimm wie seine Nichtbeachtung wäre seine "Abnutzung"', Dürig, 'Menschenwürde' (n 26) 124; cf also Isensee, 'Menschenwürde' (n 2) 187 f; Rensmann (n 8) 88 f.

[55] Verwaltungsgericht Neustadt, 21 May 1992, 7 L 1271/92, (1993) 12 *Neue Zeitschrift für Verwaltungsrecht* 98, 99.

[56] *Entscheidungen des Bundesverwaltungsgerichts* [*Decisions of the Federal Administrative Court*] (BVerwGE) 64, 274, 279.

[57] Bayerischer Verwaltungsgerichtshof, 9 December 1983, 22 CE 83 A.3074 (1984) 115 *Bayerische Verwaltungsblätter* 152, 152.

[58] BVerwGE 115, 189, 198 f.

[59] Dreier (n 6) para 49; Rensmann (n 8) 89 f.

In both cases the objective is to insulate a given standpoint from criticism and constitutional amendment.[60] However, as there are no clear and uncontested answers to the questions raised, there is a strong desire to consider carefully the conflicting interests and the consequences instead of resorting to the binary logic of an absolute value. This desire breaks through in the overt or covert application of the principle of proportionality in the context of human dignity.[61] Thereby the operating mode of human dignity is replaced with the operating mode of fundamental rights. As a consequence, human dignity is no longer an absolute value. Even the Federal Constitutional Court tends to put human dignity in context.[62] Although the Court does not disclose the consideration of conflicting interests, the 'object formula' leaves a wide margin for the covert consideration of the objectives pursued and the interests at stake.[63] This becomes apparent when the Court does not consider preventive detention a violation of human dignity as far as it is necessary due to the dangerousness of the criminal.[64] In this case the balancing of conflicting interests – human dignity on the one hand and public safety on the other – is hidden behind the seemingly binary decision of whether the criminal is made a mere object of the state or not.[65]

Making human dignity overtly or covertly relative[66] can only be avoided by narrowing its scope.[67] In line with the understanding of human dignity as a constitutional taboo its scope has to be narrowed to the uncontested inviolable core of the legal system.[68] Naturally, this means walking a tightrope – law is meant to settle

[60] Isensee, 'Menschenwürde' (n 2) 187.

[61] See K-E Hain, 'Konkretisierung der Menschenwürde durch Abwägung?' (2006) 45 *Der Staat* 189, 191, 206 f; K-E Hain, 'Menschenwürde als Rechtsprinzip' in HJ Sandkühler (ed), *Menschenwürde: Philosophische, theologische und juristische Analysen* (Frankfurt, Peter Lang, 2007) 87, 93 f; cf also Dederer (n 21) 117 f; M Herdegen, 'Art. 1 Abs. 1' in T Maunz and G Dürig, *Grundgesetz: Kommentar, vol I: Art. 1–5* (Munich, CH Beck, 2005) paras 43 ff; Herdegen (n 51) 63 f: 'Wertungs- und Abwägungsgebundenheit des Verletzungsurteils'; M Herdegen, 'Die Garantie der Menschenwürde: absolut und doch differenziert?' in Gröschner and Lembcke (eds) (n 11) 93, 105 f.

[62] Classen (n 19) 690 f.; N Petersen, 'Auf dem Weg zur zweckrationalen Relativität des Menschenwürdeschutzes' (2004) 37 *Kritische Justiz* 316, 324 f.

[63] Classen (n 19) 692 f.; cf also Petersen (n 62) 324 f.

[64] BVerfGE 109, 133, 151 f; BVerfGE 117, 71, 89 f, 94 f; cf also Dederer (n 21) 113 f.

[65] A theoretical reconstruction of this caselaw suggests that human dignity is a principle and a rule at the same time: a principle, because the answer to the question whether human dignity is interfered with is dependent on the balancing of conflicting legal interests; a rule, because any such interference with human dignity is under any circumstances absolutely prohibited; see Alexy (n 44) 95 f: 'Wenn auf der Prinzipienebene die Menschenwürde vorgeht, dann ist auf der Regelebene die Menschenwürde verletzt'; N Teifke, 'Flexibilität der Menschenwürde: Zur Struktur des Art. 1 Abs. 1 GG' in C Bäcker and S Baufeld (eds), *Objektivität und Flexibilität im Recht* (Stuttgart, Franz Steiner, 2005) 142, 143 f. For a similar approach see Herdegen, 'Art. 1 Abs. 1' (n 61) paras 43 f, 69 f. On the detection of covert relativisations of human dignity in the caselaw of the Federal Constitutional Court see Dederer (n 21) 112 f; Geddert-Steinacher (n 6) 84 f; Hain, 'Menschenwürde als Rechtsprinzip' (n 61) 95 f; Herdegen (n 51) 65 f; Michael and Morlok (n 46) para 145; Tiedemann (n 36) 610. Generally, a narrow scope of protection of fundamental rights often derives from a covert balancing of conflicting interests, see Kahl (n 44) 192 f.

[66] For examples see Classen (n 19) 690 f.

[67] Höfling (n 46) para 10; Petersen (n 62) 325.

[68] Cf P Lerche, 'Ausnahmslos und vorbehaltlos gewährleistete Grundrechte' in R Lukes and R Scholz (eds), *Rechtsfragen der Gentechnologie* (Cologne, Carl Heymann, 1986) 99, 100, 110; Michael and

disputes.[69] It fails to do so if in a dispute it is not applicable. However, this is a paradox human dignity shares with a taboo: the moment a taboo becomes subject to discussion and is reflected upon it starts losing its significance.[70] Against this background, the primary instruments to settle conflicts in the field of fundamental rights should be the fundamental rights and not the inviolability of human dignity. Most cases in which human dignity is invoked could easily and more rationally be dealt with on the basis of the fundamental rights, which are tailored to the particular characteristics of different social spheres.[71] To invoke fundamental rights in this broader sense would include refraining from resorting to an inviolable human dignity core embedded in each fundamental right; in doing so, the specific problems connected to the inviolability of human dignity would only be transferred to the single fundamental rights, making each fundamental rights conflict a case of human dignity too.[72] A few examples may illustrate this approach. The preventive detention of a criminal is a problem of Article 2(2), 2nd sentence of the German Basic Law[73] rather than a question of human dignity.[74] Accordingly, the downing of a hijacked airplane likely to be misused as a weapon against human lives is governed by Article 2(2), 1st sentence of the German Basic Law[75] rather than by human dignity.[76] The same is true for large parts of the biotechnological discussion,[77] as well as torture, which – at least *de constitutione lata* – is governed by Article 104(1), 2nd sentence of the German Basic Law.[78] This approach narrows the scope of human dignity to very few cases: in line with the understanding of its inviolability as an answer to the national socialist regime[79]

Morlok (n 46) paras 133, 148; Herdegen, 'Art. 1 Abs. 1' (n 61) paras 41 ff; see also Dreier (n 21) 35: 'Nur bei durch Konsens und Evidenz gesicherter erdrückender Plausibilität einer Menschenwürdeverletzung läßt sich das Verfahren der "Negativ-Definition" mit Aussicht auf Erfolg praktizieren. Der Menschenwürdesatz sichert dergestalt eine allgemein und allseits akzeptierte Tabuzone'; critically Isensee, 'Menschenwürde' (n 2) 196.

[69] B Rüthers, *Rechtstheorie*, 2nd edn (Munich, CH Beck, 2005) § 3, paras 88 f.

[70] Depenheuer (n 46) 10 f.

[71] Hufen (n 19) 9 f; Höfling (n 46) para 65; Tiedemann (n 36) 607 f; with regard to the Bavarian constitution JF Lindner, 'Art. 100' in JF Lindner, M Möstl and HA Wolff (eds), *Verfassung des Freistaates Bayern: Kommentar* (Munich, CH Beck, 2009) para 26.

[72] Dreier (n 6) paras 163 ff; Höfling (n 46) para 66; B Rusteberg, *Der grundrechtliche Gewährleistungsgehalt: Eine veränderte Perspektive auf die Grundrechtsdogmatik durch eine präzise Schutzbereichsbestimmung* (Tübingen, Mohr Siebeck, 2009) 183 f.

[73] 'Freedom of the person shall be inviolable.'

[74] Tiedemann (n 36) 609 f.

[75] 'Every person shall have the right to life and physical integrity.'

[76] Classen (n 19) 696; Tiedemann (n 36) 610 f; in contrast J Kersten, 'Die Tötung von Unbeteiligten: Zum verfassungsrechtlichen Grundkonflikt des §14 III LuftSiG' (2005) 24 *Neue Zeitschrift für Verwaltungsrecht* 661, 662 f; Höfling (n 46) para 22.

[77] Höfling (n 46) para 67.

[78] 'Persons in custody may not be subjected to mental or physical mistreatment.' See also Classen (n 19) 695 f; Rusteberg (n 72) 72.

[79] Pieroth (n 3) para 59; with regard to the constitutions of the German *Länder* see K Stern, *Das Staatsrecht der Bundesrepublik Deutschland, vol V: Die geschichtlichen Grundlagen des deutschen Staatsrechts* (Munich, CH Beck, 2000) 1083 f; with regard to human dignity as a universal concept see Rensmann (n 8) 77.

and the general finding that any constitution reacts to historical experiences,[80] these cases include the totalitarian usurpation of the individual by the state and the total and systematic rejection of minimum humanitarian standards as were characteristic of the Third Reich.[81]

B. Variable Meaning of Human Dignity

Second, as any concept of human dignity has to take into account its dependence on an evident social consensus, human dignity is subject to change.[82] This is obviously true when considered over a period of time and becomes especially clear in the caselaw of the Supreme Court of the United States of America.[83] In *Trop v Dulles* the Court states:

> The basic concept underlying the Eighth Amendment is nothing less than the dignity of man . . . This Court has had little occasion to give precise content to the Eighth Amendment, and, in an enlightened democracy such as ours, this is not surprising. But when the Court was confronted with a punishment of 12 years in irons at hard and painful labor imposed for the crime of falsifying public records, it did not hesitate to declare that the penalty was cruel in its excessiveness and unusual in its character . . . The Court recognized in that case that the words of the Amendment are not precise . . . and that their scope is not static. The Amendment must draw its meaning from the evolving standards of decency that mark the progress of a maturing society.[84]

And referring back to *Trop v Dulles*, the Court in the recent case *Graham v Florida* stresses that although '[c]ommunity consensus . . . is not itself determinative of whether a punishment is cruel and unusual', and thus prohibited by the Eighth Amendment to the United States Constitution, it is nevertheless 'entitled to great weight'.[85] In a similar vein, the Federal Constitutional Court admits that the meaning of the obligation to respect and protect human dignity 'cannot be definitely determined once and for all'.[86]

In addition to this variability over a period of time, human dignity also varies in territorial terms. As the meaning of human dignity is based on an evident social consensus, it is dependent on moral concepts, which differ from region to region.

[80] Dreier (n 3) para 6; F Wittreck, *Die Verwaltung der Dritten Gewalt* (Tübingen, Mohr Siebeck, 2006) 53: 'Erfahrungshorizont'.

[81] Cf Herdegen, 'Art. 1 Abs. 1' (n 61) paras 41 f; Hufen (n 19) 2; Rensmann (n 8) 86 f.

[82] Herdegen, 'Art. 1 Abs. 1' (n 61) para 37; see also E Denninger, 'Embryo und Grundgesetz: Schutz des Lebens und der Menschenwürde vor Nidation und Geburt' (2003) 86 *Kritische Vierteljahresschrift für Gesetzgebung und Rechtswissenschaft* 191, 195 f.

[83] Cf S Kirste, 'Menschenwürde im internationalen Vergleich der Rechtsordnungen' in Gröschner and Lembcke (eds) (n 11) 175, 188 f.

[84] *Trop v Dulles* 356 US 86, 100 f (1958).

[85] *Graham v Florida* 560 US (2010) (slip opinion, at 16; available at www.supremecourt.gov, last visit: 31 May 2010), referring to *Kennedy v Louisiana* 554 US (2008) (slip opinion, at 24; available at www.supremecourt.gov, last visit: 31 May 2010): 'As we have said in other Eighth Amendment cases, objective evidence of contemporary values as it relates to punishment for child rape is entitled to great weight, but it does not end our inquiry.'

[86] BVerfGE 115, 118, 153; see also BVerfGE 45, 187, 229; BVerfGE 96, 375, 399 f.

This casts a light on the perspectives for a Europeanised concept of human dignity. As the *Omega* case[87] shows, the European basis for social consensus is even smaller than within the member states of the European Union. The binary logic of an absolute value is therefore not a suitable matrix for the solution of most problems. Hence, a narrow scope of human dignity, together with a broad scope of fundamental rights, is as important on the European level as it is on the national level. Again, the scope has to be narrowed to the totalitarian usurpation of the individual by the state and the rejection of minimum humanitarian standards.

V. Possible Objections and Conclusion

Against a narrow concept of human dignity it can of course be argued that a narrow scope deprives human dignity of its relevance as a legal value.[88] To a certain extent this is true. However, there is no acceptable alternative.[89] As the application and interpretation of Article 1(1), 1st sentence of the German Basic Law by the Federal Constitutional Court shows, a broad interpretation of human dignity automatically leads to inroads into its absolute quality. Accepting these inroads would mean dismissing human dignity as an absolute legal value and, ultimately, degrading it to just one fundamental right among others.[90] However, a narrow interpretation of human dignity of course does not mean that downing hijacked airplanes or torturing criminals or witnesses is altogether in line with the German Basic Law. It only means that in most of these cases human dignity is not the right matrix to deal with the problem. Instead of allowing for an overt balancing of conflicting interests, as is characteristic for the application of fundamental rights, the broad understanding of human dignity pursued by the Federal Constitutional Court hides the balancing behind the binary and therefore oversimplified logic of human dignity as an absolute legal value.[91]

[87] Case C-36/02 *Omega Spielhallen- und Automatenaufstellungs-GmbH* [2004] ECR I-9609.

[88] See BVerfGE 30, 1, 39 f.

[89] Höfling (n 46) para 10; Petersen (n 62) 325.

[90] Geddert-Steinacher (n 6) 85 f; Petersen (n 62) 320; Tiedemann (n 36) 607; see also Ladeur and Augsberg (n 2) 29.

[91] Cf Tiedemann (n 36) 611.

12

The National Identity of the Member States in Europe and the Jurisprudence of the European Court of Justice: Starting from *Omega*[1]?

JAN KALBHEIM

I. Introduction: European Identity and National Identities of the Member States

A. An Old Problem

Identity is very important for a human being. It offers the answer to the question 'who am I?'. [2] It provides individuals with a set of concepts guiding their behaviour in various situations and on encountering various problems or difficulties. It is based on the roles an individual plays in society and therefore is usually composed of a plurality of identificatory references.[3] The question 'who am I?' can also be applied to a group as 'who are we?'. Therefore, identity may also refer to the collective identity of larger or smaller groups. Groups usually define themselves by referring to some form of agreement on a set of ideas offering orientation when it comes to defining the self and finding internal security, while at the same time distinguishing themselves – not necessarily aggressively – from other groups.[4] As in the case of individual identities, which may be based on (self-)perceptions that may be only partially concurrent with the perception of the outside world, a good deal of this set of ideas consists of fictions or myths, which are used to construct the collective identity[5] with a view to establishing and maintaining

[1] Case C-36/02 *Omega* [2004] ECR I-9609.

[2] E Pache, 'Europäische und nationale Identität: Integration durch Verfassungsrecht? (2002) 120 *DeutschesVerwaltungsblatt* 1154, 1155.

[3] Ibid, 1156.

[4] Ibid, 1155; A von Bogdandy, 'Europäische und nationale Identität: Integration durch Verfassungsrecht?' (2002) 61 *Veröffentlichung der Vereinigung Deutscher Staatsrechtslehrer* 157, 168.

[5] Von Bogdandy (n 4) 169.

control over the group.[6] The precise content may change over time[7] and might be difficult to establish; it is a little like Augustin's difficulties with the concept of time: 'What, then, is time? If no one asks me, I know what it is. If I wish to explain it to him who asks me, I do not know.'[8] Nevertheless, collective identities do exist and effectively fulfil important functions in stabilising groups and supporting decision-making.[9] Therefore, all sorts of groups try to establish and to preserve collective identities, including states and systems of rule like the European Union. Again, collective identities are able to accommodate competing claims to loyalty by leaving gaps which may be filled by other collective identities. The secular state, for example, excludes the field of religion from its claim to loyalty, thereby allowing its members to maintain different religious identities. Or they can collide with other identities if they insist on exclusive claims to loyalty (like the oath of allegiance sworn on taking American citizenship[10]). For the relationship of the European identity and the national identities of the Member States, it is therefore decisive to what extent these identities are competing or complementary.

As early as May 1971, when French President Georges Pompidou and Prime Minister Edward Heath met in Paris, it was the maintenance of the respective national identities of the Member States that was one object of their bilateral talks. In his statement to the House of Commons, the Prime Minister explained:

> We discussed the development of the European Community and the working of its institutions. We agreed in particular that the identity of national states should be maintained in the framework of the developing Community. This means, of course, that, though the European Commission has made and will continue to make a valuable contribution, the Council of Ministers should continue to be the forum in which important decisions are taken, and that the processes of harmonisation should not override essential national interests. We were in agreement that the maintenance and strengthening of the fabric of co-operation in such a Community requires that decisions should in practice be taken by unanimous agreement when vital national interests of any one or more members are at stake.
>
> This is indeed entirely in accordance with the views which I have long held. It provides a clear assurance, just as the history of the Community provides clear evidence, that joining the Community does not entail a loss of national identity or an erosion of essential national sovereignty.[11]

[6] Pache (n 2) 1158.

[7] M Droege, 'Identität und Integration in Europa – der Europäische Verfassungsvertrag als Kulturverfassung' in Y Becker et al (eds), *Die Europäische Verfassung – Verfassungen in Europa* (Baden-Baden, Nomos, 2005) 104, 116.

[8] Augustin, Confessions XI, 14, AC Outler (tr), available at www.ccel.org/ccel/augustine/confessions.xiv.html (last visited 12.10.2012).

[9] Droege (n 7) 112. This is true even if they might not be strictly necessary for the continued existence of a polity, as von Bogdandy (n 4) 173–74 insists.

[10] 'I hereby declare, on oath, that I absolutely and entirely renounce and abjure all allegiance and fidelity to any foreign prince, potentate, state, or sovereignty of whom or which I have heretofore been a subject or citizen . . .'

[11] HC Deb 24 May 1971, vol 818, cols 32 f.

This strongly resembles the contents of the Luxembourg Accords of 29th January 1966, according to which for nearly two decades pleading 'very important interests' was treated as a Member State's veto, which the other Member States would respect.[12] It seems to come from a desire to protect the national identity against claims coming from a European identity.

The first official EC document mentioning the European identity was the Document *On the European Identity* published by the Nine Foreign Ministers on 14 December 1973,[13] in Copenhagen, which was published during a period of severe crisis of the Communities (resulting from the oil crisis and the breakdown of the Bretton Woods system).[14] It defined the European identity with reference to 'the common heritage, interests and special obligations of the Nine' and to the extent to which the nine were 'already acting together in relation to the rest of the world', 'taking into consideration the dynamic nature of European unification' in order to 'achieve a better definition of their relations with other countries and of their responsibilities and the place which they occupy in world affairs'. Its direction was therefore more against the rest of the world than against the Member States and their national identities, suggesting a more supplementary nature of the European identity.

B. Textual Development of the Treaties

The original treaties did not provide for any safeguards for the national identity of the Member States. Obviously the Member States felt no need for an explicit provision as they perceived of themselves as having complete control over the development of the European integration process through their collective decision-making in the council, mostly on the basis of unanimity. But by 1991 it had become clear that this assumption was not fully appropriate. The bold jurisprudence of the European Court of Justice (CJ), forcing the abolition of national rules in the economic field and the extension of the Community's competences by the Court's jurisprudence, and subsequently by the Single European Act and by the Treaty of Maastricht, had strengthened the supranational level. At the same time the latter treaty also strengthened the regional level bringing on the danger of the Member States being wiped out in between those two levels.[15] Therefore the Maastricht

[12] See also P Craig and G de Búrca, *EU Law Text and Materials*, 5th edn (Oxford, OUP, 2011) 8. For a detailed discussion of the Luxembourg accords see R Streinz, *Die Luxemburger Vereinbarung: rechtliche und politische Aspekte der Abstimmungspraxis im Rat der Europäischen Gemeinschaften seit der Luxemburger Vereinbarung vom 29. Januar 1966* (Munich, Florentz, 1984).

[13] Bulletin EC 47/73 (Annex), available at www.cvce.eu/obj/Declaration_on_European_Identity_Copenhagen_14_December_1973-en-02798dc9-9c69-4b7d-b2c9-f03a8db7da32.html (last visited 12.10.2012).

[14] Von Bogdandy (n 4) 164.

[15] See also M Hilf, 'Europäische und nationale Identität der Mitgliedstaaten' in A Randelzhofer et al (eds), *Gedächtnisschrift für Grabitz* (Munich, CH Beck, 1995) 157, 161 f.; A Bleckmann, 'Die Wahrung der "nationalen Identität" im Unions-Vertrag' in (1997) *Juristenzeitung* 265, 265. T Oppermann, 'Nationale Identität und supranationale Homogenität' in A Epiney et al (eds), *Die Herausforderung von*

Treaty for the first time explicitly provided for a duty of the European Union to protect the national identities of its Member States. Article F(1) read 'The Union shall respect the national identities of its Member States, whose systems of government are founded on the principles of democracy.' The Amsterdam Treaty retained that provision, but moved it to form paragraph 3 of Article 6.[16] Article 46 Treaty on European Union (TEU) excluded, nevertheless, Article 6(3) TEU from the jurisdiction of the CJ.

The Constitutional Treaty contained the following provision in Article I-5 CT (Relations between the European Union and the Member States):

> The union shall respect the equality of Member States before the constitution as well as their national identities, inherent in their fundamental structures, political and constitutional, inclusive of regional and local self-government. It shall respect their essential State functions, including ensuring the territorial integrity of the State, maintaining law and order and safeguarding national security.

However, Article I-8 CT provided for a set of EU symbols – symbols which traditionally have been used to focus identification with a state: flag, anthem, motto, currency and Europe day.[17]

The Treaty of Lisbon[18] has abolished the provision on the symbols of the Union and moved the provision concerning the national identities to Article 4(2), replacing the word 'constitution' with the word 'Treaties' and adding a second sentence. It now reads:

> The Union shall respect the equality of Member States before the Treaties as well as their national identities, inherent in their fundamental structures, political and constitutional, inclusive of regional and local self-government. It shall respect their essential State functions, including ensuring the territorial integrity of the State, maintaining law and order and safeguarding national security. In particular, national security remains the sole responsibility of each Member State.

There is, however, no longer any provision comparable to the old Article 46 TEU, which was abolished by the Treaty of Lisbon.

The Treaty of Maastricht also introduced the concept of European identity into the primary law. The preamble to the TEU contained the following provision, which – as far as interests us here – is still part of the TEU as amended by the Treaty of Lisbon:

Grenzen – Festschrift für Bieber (Baden-Baden, Nomos, 2007) 393, 396, calls it a 'defensive concept' [Abwehrbegriff].

[16] It read: 'The Union shall respect the national identities of its Member States.' The second part of the sentence became part of Art 6(1), which read: 'The Union is founded on the principles of liberty, democracy, respect for human rights and fundamental freedoms, and the rule of law, principles which are common to the Member States.'

[17] Even though this only codified the existing symbols used (flag, anthem, Europe day); only the motto is truly new; see C Ohler in R Streinz, C Ohler and C Herrmann (eds), *Die neue Verfassung für Europa* (Munich, CH Beck, 2005) 56.

[18] [2007] OJ C306/1; the most recent publication of the consolidated version of the TEU/TFEU is in [2012] OJ C326/1.

> RESOLVED to implement a common foreign and security policy including the eventual framing of a common defence policy, which might in time lead to a common defence, thereby reinforcing the European identity and its independence in order to promote peace, security and progress in Europe and in the world.[19]

The corresponding treaty provision, which is no longer contained in the TEU as amended by the Treaty of Lisbon, was Article B(1), 2nd indent, by which the European Union set itself the objective 'to assert its identity on the international scene, in particular through the implementation of a common foreign and security policy including the eventual framing of a common defence policy, which might in time lead to a common defence'.[20]

Both provisions see the European identity as directed towards the outside world and thereby remain in the tradition of the Copenhagen declaration. But the Treaty of Nice also introduced into the TEU a rule concerning the enhanced cooperation in the area of Common Foreign and Security Policy (CFSP), which sought to protect the European identity vis-à-vis the Member States: 'Enhanced cooperation in any of the areas referred to in this title shall be aimed at safeguarding the values and serving the interests of the Union as a whole by asserting its identity as a coherent force on the international scene.' However, this provision is no longer contained in the primary law as revised by the Treaty of Lisbon.[21]

C. Positions in the (German) Literature

How are we to interpret Article 6(3) TEU? It is clear that the term 'national identity' cannot be completely under the control of the CJ along the normal line of reasoning concerning the necessarily autonomous construction of the terms used in European legal texts.[22] If the CJ were to define each Member State's identity, that would make the whole concept farcical. Therefore, the Member States are competent to define their own national identity with binding effect on the EU institutions.[23] This obviously creates the danger that the Member States abuse this competence to evade their obligations under European law, endangering the

[19] The wording of this has been revised concerning the common security policy, but has remained unchanged as regards the European identity.

[20] This provision, apart from being renamed Art 2 TEU, was revised by the Treaties of Amsterdam and Nice corresponding to the revisions of the preamble.

[21] Arts 20a to 20e TEU have been replaced by Arts 20 TEU, 326–334 TFEU.

[22] On that normal line of reasoning see Case 17/81 *Pabst & Richarz KG* [1982] ECR 1331, para 18; Case 327/82 *Ekro* [1984] ECR 107, para 13; Case C-287/98 *Linster* [2000] ECR I-6917, para 43; Case C-373/00 *Adolf Truley* [2003] ECR I-1931, para 35; R Streinz, *Europarecht*, 9th edn (Heidelberg, CF Müller, 2012) para 616.

[23] This is generally accepted, see, eg Hilf (n 15) 163; P Lerche, 'Achtung der nationalen Identität (Art F Abs I EU)' in R Scholz (ed), *Ausgewählte Abhandlungen* (Berlin, Duncker & Humblot, 2005) 232, 241 f; A Puttler, 'Article 6 EU' in C Calliess and M Ruffert (eds), *EUV, EGV: das Verfassungsrecht der Europäischen Union mit Europäischer Grundrechtecharta; Kommentar*, 3rd edn (Munich, CH Beck, 2007) para 44; B Beutler, 'Article 6 EU' in H von der Groeben and J Schwarze (eds), *Vertrag über die Europäische Union und Vertrag zur Gründung der Europäischen Gemeinschaft. Kommentar*, vol, 1 6th edn (Baden-Baden, Nomos, 2003) para 201.

creation and maintenance of the internal market.[24] According to the orthodox reading of the treaties this is not permissible.[25] However, there is a consensus that the European identity necessarily needs the national identities as its basis.[26]

Broadly speaking there are two strategies employed to accomplish that task. The first is to downgrade the duty of the European Union flowing from Article 6(3) TEU: the best means is to read the term 'respect' as involving only a duty to take the national identity into consideration when making decisions, but not implying that the national identity could not be overridden.[27] However, the term 'respect' is also used in Article 6(2) TEU, which provides that the European Union shall respect fundamental rights. This section is read to mean that fundamental rights are true barriers to secondary legislation and other activities of EU institutions.[28] It is not particularly convincing to claim that the same term has a substantially different meaning in paragraphs 2 and 3 of Article 6 TEU.

The second strategy is to limit the possible content of national identities.[29] What is fairly common is to reduce Article 6(3) TEU to the protection of the statehood of the Member States,[30] even to the extent that this does not cover sovereign statehood under public international law.[31] Another approach it is to charge the term 'national identity' with Europeanised elements. It is claimed that the 'national identity' has to be understood as the identity of an integrated state which opens up its sovereignty shell to the influence of European law and accords with the essential requirements that Article 6(1) TEU[32] states to be common to the Member States: the principles of liberty, democracy, respect for human rights and fundamental freedoms, and the rule of law.[33]

[24] Representative is R Bieber et al, *Die Europäische Union*, 8th edn (Baden-Baden, Nomos, 2009) § 2 para 58.

[25] The intensity of the fear resulting from that danger might explain the remarkable fact that in his brief commentary on Article 6(3) TEU, one author has a few words put in bold type which contain a proper statement; they read (in translation): 'the Union must preserve, assert and develop its own identity'. M Pechstein, 'Article 6 EUV' in R Streinz (ed), *EUV/EGV*: *Vertrag über die Europäische Union und Vertrag zur Gründung der Europäischen Gemeinschaft. Kommentar* (Munich, CH Beck, 2003) para 25.

[26] See, eg U Haltern, 'Europäischer Kulturkampf. Zur Wahrung "nationaler Identität" im Unionsvertrag' (1998) 37 *Der Staat* 591, 621; Hilf (n 15) 166; Beutler (n 23) para 197 on Article 6 EU; the latter therefore demands (para 201) that the EU shall foster the national identities.

[27] Puttler (n 23) Article 6 EU, para 49; Stumpf, 'Article 6 EUV' in J Schwarze (ed), *EU-Kommentar*, 2nd edn (Baden-Baden, Nomos, 2009) para 40; Bieber et al (n 24) § 2 para 58; Hilf (n 15) 165.

[28] Lerche (n 23) 241.

[29] Here belong also those strategies which try to remove the emotional aspect of identity, see eg Haltern (n 26) 620 and von Bogdandy (n 4) 168–69, who are nevertheless more intent on strengthening the European identity.

[30] Eg T Oppermann et al, *Europarecht*, 4th edn (Munich, CH Beck, 2009) § 6, para 33; Puttler (n 23) para 44 on Article 6 EUV.

[31] Bieber et al (n 24) § 2, para 56.

[32] Now integrated into Art 2, 1st sentence TEU.

[33] Hilf (n 15) 164 f; Haltern (n 26) 619; A Puttler, 'Article I-5' in C Calliess and M Ruffert (eds), *Verfassung der Europäischen Union. Kommentar der Grundlagenbestimmungen* (Munich, CH Beck, 2006); Beutler (n 23) paras 200, 205 on Article 6 EU, who also points out that the post-war project of European integration aimed at avoiding the abusive demarcation which marked the history of national identities.

A third approach is to tie the national identity to readily identifiable core provisions of the constitution.[34] For Germany, reference is made to the so-called 'eternity clause' of Article 79(3) of the Basic Law, which entrenches certain parts of the Basic Law against amendment by Act of Parliament as defining the core of its national identity.[35] A similar approach is to equate the meaning of Article 6(3) TEU with the duty of sincere cooperation of the European Union vis-à-vis the Member States as developed by the CJ,[36] which allows for compensating the removal of Article 6(3) TEU from CJ jurisdiction.[37]

But there are also attempts to broaden the contents of Germany's national identity. It has been argued that the qualification of the central questions concerning broadcasting as a 'cultural' matter is part of the national identity, with the consequence that the European Union must not treat broadcasting as a purely economic matter vis-à-vis Germany.[38] And if one roots national identity in historical experience, Germany's national identity certainly comprises those provisions which explicitly react to the failure of the Weimar Republic and to the dictatorial regime of the Nazis. Such an identity would probably include the free democratic basic order, which includes the principle of defensive democracy. Furthermore, some authors infer from Article 6(3) TEU not only a duty of considering the national identity but of balancing its demands only with the necessities of European integration,[39] or that, taken seriously, Article 6(3) TEU allows the Member States to suspend the applicability of European legislation to protect the national identity if that legislation is ultra vires.[40] One author[41] even tried to use the provision to stem the tide of European integration (like a modern day King Canute?), arguing that this provision guarantees the protection of the sovereign statehood as it existed at the outset of European integration and that it forbids any activities of the European Union working towards the emergence of an overarching European people.

II. The *Omega* case

The CJ has so far only dealt once with an argument based on the national identity of a Member State. This was in the case of *Commission v Luxembourg*,[42] when

[34] This makes sense for Germany, which after the war redefined itself in its western part through (constitutional) law; see also S Korioth, 'Europäische und nationale Identität: Integration durch Verfassungsrecht?' (2002) 62 *Veröffentlichungen der Vereinigung Deutscher Staatsrechtslehrer* (VVDStRL) 117, 124.

[35] See eg, Puttler (n 23) para 48 on Article 6 EU.

[36] Case C-2/88 *Imm Zwartveld* [1990] ECR I-3365, paras 17–18; Case 230/81 *Luxembourg v European Parliament* [1983] ECR 255, para 37.

[37] See eg Hilf (n 15) 165, 168.

[38] Lerche (n 23) 242–43.

[39] Pechstein (n 25) Article 6 EU, para 27; similarly Bieber et al (n 24) § 2, para 59.

[40] K Doehring, 'Die nationale "Identität" der Mitgliedstaaten der Europäischen Union' in O Due et al (eds), *Festschrift Ulrich Everling* (Baden-Baden, Nomos, 1995) 263, 270.

[41] Bleckmann (n 15) 266.

[42] Case C-473/93 *Commission v Luxembourg* [1996] ECR I-3207.

Luxembourg tried to justify a nationality requirement for primary school teachers by pointing out that in order to transmit traditional values and in view of the size of the country and its specific demographic situation, the nationality requirement was an essential condition for preserving Luxembourg's national identity. The Court accepted that that was a legitimate aim but decided it could still be effectively safeguarded in other ways than by a general exclusion of nationals from other Member States.[43] In other words, the Court found the nationality requirement to be disproportionate.

The second reference in the Court's Alphabetical Table of Subject Matter[44] is to the Opinion of AG Poiares Maduro in *Mechaniki*.[45] The Advocate General pointed out that it is true that the European Union is obliged to respect the national identity of the Member States but found that the national provision in question clearly did not comply with the principle of proportionality.[46] To support his general statement, he pointed to two decisions of the Court: *Commission v Luxembourg*, just mentioned, and *Omega*. Even though national identity was not expressly pleaded in *Omega*, it probably was at the back of the minds of the judges.[47]

A. The Facts

The German company Omega operated an installation known as a 'laserdrome' in Bonn. The games organised there involved, inter alia, firing with machine gun-type laser targeting devices at sensory tags installed on jackets worn by other players. The Bonn police authority took the view that 'playing at killing' people and the ensuing trivialisation of violence were contrary to human dignity and consequently prohibited Omega from allowing or tolerating in its laserdrome games which involved simulated homicide.

The administrative complaint and appeals brought against that measure were unsuccessful; the courts accepted the human-dignity-based reasoning of the authority. The court of last instance, the Federal Administrative Court, shared the view of the authority and the lower courts that the game was contrary to human dignity, but wondered whether the fact that Omega used a form of the game developed and marketed by a British company under a franchising agreement meant that the police order was in breach of European law, especially the fundamental freedoms.

[43] Ibid, para 35.

[44] Table alphabétique des matières (vols 1985–2009).

[45] AG Poiares Maduro, Opinion of 8 October 2008, in Case C-213/07 *Mechaniki* [2008] ECR I-9999.

[46] Ibid, paras 31–35; he was careful to insist that respect owed to the constitutional identity of the Member States cannot be understood as an absolute obligation to defer to all national constitutional rules, ibid, para 33.

[47] This impression is supported by the fact that in his contribution on the Basic Law and European integration ('Ein delikater Balanceakt!' *Frankfurter Allgemeine Zeitung* (22 May 2009) B2), CJ President Vassilios Skouris referred to the decision as an example of not levelling the different legal traditions of the Member States but cherishing the relevance of national constitutions.

B. Conclusions of AG Stix-Hackl

The Advocate General considered the case to fall under the provisions on the freedom to provide services and not under the free movement of goods provisions, since the administrative measure restricted the import of goods only in so far as they facilitated participation in the game in question (para 32). She found a restriction of that freedom, which needed justification, and insisted that this justification could not immediately be found in the protection of specific fundamental rights guaranteed by the constitution of a Member State. Rather, an acceptable justification had to be based on grounds acknowledged in Community law, such as the safeguarding of public policy. Therefore, a common conception among the Member States on the matter of protecting public order is not a precondition for such a justification (paras 33, 71). Although she granted that there is hardly any legal principle more difficult to fathom in law than that of human dignity, the Advocate General investigated in detail the content of that concept and referred to the Biotechnology Patents Directive decision of the CJ,[48] in which the Court had acknowledged that respect for human dignity constituted an integral part of the general legal tenets of Community law, both as a constitutional principle of the European Union and as a fundamental right per se (paras 90, 91 n 65). Since it was almost impossible to equate the substance of the guarantee of human dignity under the German Basic Law with that of the guarantee of human dignity as recognised in Community law, the Court should evaluate the national measure, and the justification presented, in the light of Community law (para 93). For the public policy exception, she acknowledged that the Court accepted variation between Member States' assessments as a result of their discretion in determining the requirements of public policy and public security in the light of their national needs, but insisted that Community law nevertheless set strict limits on such assessments, in particular by forbidding discriminatory practices and the pursuit of purely economic ends (paras 96–99). Examining the case itself she found a sufficiently serious threat to fundamental interests of society – human dignity – which was not precluded by a lack of consensus in the Member States. She then concluded that the order constituted a uniformly applicable measure, which was appropriate and necessary, since it only prohibited one variant of the game (paras 100 ff).

C. The Decision of the Court of Justice

The case was decided by the First Chamber, a panel of five judges. Since their inception, chambers of five judges have normally been entrusted with cases which

[48] Case C-377/98 *Netherlands v Council and Parliament* [2001] ECR I-7079.

require the development rather than the simple application of existing case law but which do not call for fundamental decisions to be made.[49]

The Court followed its Advocate General in examining the case purely under the provisions on freedom to provide services. It concentrated its examination of the justification for the restriction of that freedom imposed by the contested order according to what was then Article 46 TEC (Article 52 TFEU) on the ground of public policy, since that was expressly mentioned by the Bonn police authority. It found no indication of any discrimination but insisted that Article 46 TEC was applicable to measures safeguarding public policy independent of the question of discrimination. The Court then reiterated its case law (paras 30–31):

> [T]hat 'the possibility of a Member State relying on a derogation laid down by the Treaty does not prevent judicial review of measures applying that derogation';
>
> that 'the concept of 'public policy' in the Community context, particularly as justification for a derogation from the fundamental principle of the freedom to provide services, must be interpreted strictly, so that its scope cannot be determined unilaterally by each Member State without any control by the Community institutions';
>
> and that 'public policy may be relied on only if there is a genuine and sufficiently serious threat to a fundamental interest of society'; but that 'the specific circumstances which may justify recourse to the concept of public policy may vary from one country to another and from one era to another', so that '[t]he competent national authorities must be allowed a margin of discretion within the limits imposed by the Treaty'.

It then pointed out the importance of fundamental rights in Community law and that the respect for human dignity is a general principle of Community law. Therefore the protection of human dignity is a legitimate objective under Community law irrespective of the status of respect for human dignity in national law. Since both the Community and its Member States are required to respect fundamental rights, protection of those rights is a legitimate interest which, in principle, justifies a restriction of the obligations imposed by Community law, even under a fundamental freedom guaranteed by the treaty. In relation to the still applicable test concerning the utility and the necessity of the measures, the Court held that it is not indispensable in that respect for the restrictive measure issued by the authorities of a Member State to correspond to a conception shared by all Member States regarding the precise way in which the fundamental right or legitimate interest in question is to be protected. It then observed that, according to the referring court, the prohibition on the commercial exploitation of games involving the simulation of acts of violence against persons, in particular the representation of acts of homicide, corresponds to the level of protection of human dignity which the Basic Law seeks to guarantee in Germany and that, by prohibiting only the variant of the game involving 'playing at killing' people, the contested order did not go beyond what is necessary in order to attain the objective pursued

[49] R Schintgen, 'Europäische Gemeinschaftsgerichtsbarkeit' in P Müller-Graff and H Roth (eds), *Die Praxis des Richterberufs* (Berlin, Berlin Verlag, 2000) 101, 113.

by the competent national authorities. It therefore concluded that the contested order justifiably restricted the freedom to provide services.

In reaching its decision, the First Chamber took care to refer to previous decisions, decided between 1974 and 2003, for each legal statement it made. In particular, the most important reasoning in the decision for our question, in paragraph 38, which allows for differences between the Member States, claims that this result 'is apparent from well-established case-law' and cites three decisions, two of which had been handed down by the (Small) Plenary.[50]

III. The (German) Reception of *Omega*

The decision of the CJ had a mixed reception from German commentators. Some regarded it as an appropriate and well-balanced solution which leaves room for the considerations of national and regional peculiarities without delivering the fundamental freedoms into the hands of Member States' concepts of public order.[51] Others welcomed in principle the Court's decision not to impose uniform ideas of public order and the resulting flexibility for the Member States[52] but criticised the Court for not examining for itself whether human dignity was indeed affected.[53] They feared that the Court had given carte blanche to the Member States by allowing for a general prevalence of Member States' concepts of human dignity over the four freedoms,[54] and that there would be no limits to suppressing perceived threats to human dignity.[55]

In addition, *Omega* has been referred to before the Federal Constitutional Court in the proceedings concerning the constitutionality of the German law ratifying the Treaty of Lisbon.[56] Counsel for the complainants adduced that decision to argue that the CJ had prepared the way to reduce human dignity to just one of numerous values to be balanced against one another, thus depriving it of its inviolability and thereby of its character of being *the* supreme value of the German legal

[50] Case C-124/97 *Läärä and Others* [1999] ECR I-6067; Case C-67/98 *Zenatti* [1999] ECR I-7289; both cases were decided by the minimum number (nine) of judges.

[51] F-J Lindner, 'Anmerkung [zu *Omega*]' (2005) 136 *Bayerische Verwaltungsblätter* 206, 208.

[52] J Bröhmer, 'Anmerkung [zu *Omega*]' (2004) 15 *Europäische Zeitschrift für Wirtschaftsrecht* 755, 756; J Schwarze, 'Der Schutz der Grundrechte durch den EuGH' (2005) 58 *Neue Juristische Wochenschrift* 3459, 3461.

[53] Bröhmer (n 52) 757; G Beaucamp, 'Das ordnungsbehördliche Verbot von Laserdromen – europarechtliche, gewerberechtliche und verfassungsrechtliche Probleme' (2005) 120 *Deutsches Verwaltungsblatt* 1174 1176, who both did not share the view expressed by the Federal Administrative Court. Expressly supporting the opposite position that it was not for the CJ to address this question is Ackermann, 'Case Note' (2005) 42 *Common Market Law Review* 1107, 1118.

[54] Bröhmer (n 52) 756 f. The opposite view is held by Ackermann (n 53) 1117, who argues for discretion of the Member States in the whole area of application of human dignity, as long as they do not pursue economic interests under the heading of human dignity.

[55] Beaucamp (n 53) 1179.

[56] BVerfG, 30 June 2009, joined cases 2 BvE 5/08 and 2 BvR 1259/08, BVerfGE 123, 267.

order.[57] This argument was rejected by counsel for the Bundestag, who argued that the Court in *Omega* did not subject the assessment of the Federal Administrative Court and the administrative measure in question to a proportionality test and pointed out that the CJ had stated in *Schmidberger*[58] that 'the prohibition of torture and inhuman or degrading treatment or punishment . . . admit of no restriction'. These rights being derived from the right to human dignity, the right to human dignity itself a fortiori cannot admit of any restriction.[59]

IV. *Omega* in recent case law

Omega is a judgment which is quoted fairly often, according to information available from EurLex. Of the 78 judgments[60] handed down in the fourth quarter of 2004, only three decisions of the Grand Chamber[61] and three decisions of the Second Chamber[62] have been quoted more often than *Omega*, which has been quoted 41 times.

A. References by the Court

The Grand Chamber of the Court has referred to *Omega* eight times.[63] Two references are of particular interest here. In nearly identical terms, the Grand Chamber cited *Omega* to state that the protection of fundamental rights justifies, in principle, the restrictions of the obligations of the Member States under the Treaty, even

[57] A Fisahn, Schriftsatz vom 24. Juni 2008 in den Verfahren vor dem Bundesverfassungsgericht gegen das Zustimmungsgesetz zum Vertrag von Lissabon[submission to the Federal Constitutional Court in the proceedings against the law ratifying the Treaty of Lisbon] at 21–23, at www.jura.uni-bielefeld.de/Lehrstuehle/Fisahn/Veroeffentlichungen_Vortraege/KLagen-end-zusammen.pdf (downloaded 18 May 2009).

[58] Case C-112/00 *Schmidberger* [2003] ECR I-5659; the following quotation is taken from para 80.

[59] F Mayer, Stellungnahme des Deutschen Bundestages vom 22. August 2008 in den Verfahren vor dem Bundesverfassungsgericht gegen das Zustimmungsgesetz zum Vertrag von Lissabon [submissions of the Bundestag in the proceedings before the Federal Constitutional Court against the law ratifying the Treaty of Lisbon], at 108, at www.jura.uni-bielefeld.de/lehrstuehle/mayer/dokumente/Schriftsatz_Lissabon.pdf (downloaded 18 May 2009).

[60] Three judgments by the Plenary, 14 by the Grand Chamber, 26 by the First Chamber, 24 by the Second Chamber, 4 by the Third Chamber, 2 by the Fourth Chamber, 3 by the Fifth Chamber and 2 by the Sixth Chamber.

[61] Joined Cases C-397/01 & 401/01 *Bernhard Pfeiffer and Others v Deutsches Rotes Kreuz* [2004] ECR I-8835 with 105 hits, Case C-210/03 *Swedish Match v Secretary of State for Health* [2004] ECR I-11893 with 61 hits and Case C-442/02 *CaixaBank France v Ministère de l'Économie, des Finances et de l'Industrie* [2004] ECR I-8961 with 43 hits (Eurlex search of 29 May 2012).

[62] Case C-136/02 P *Mag Instrument Inc v OHIM* [2004] ECR I-9165 with 50 hits, Case C-106/03 *Vedial SA v OHIM* [2004] ECR I-9573 with 46 hits and Case C-447/02 *KWS Saat AG v Office for Harmonisation in the Internal Market (Trade Marks and Designs) (OHIM)* [2004] ECR I-10107 with 43 hits.

[63] The Grand Chamber referred to para 33 (fundamental rights are part of European law) once and to paras 25 to 27 (demarcation of the different freedoms) five times.

including the fundamental freedoms, but that the principle of proportionality still applies to the Member States' activities.[64] The First Chamber itself cited its decision five times – twice to bolster its statement that the Member States retain the freedom to determine the requirements of public policy and public security in accordance with their specific national needs but subject to the control of the Court,[65] and once to insist that there must be a genuine and sufficiently serious threat to a fundamental interest of society.[66] The Second Chamber cited *Omega* in two decisions, referring to the supervision by the Court of the Member States relying on the public order exception (para 30) and their margin of appreciation (para 31), the proportionality requirement (para 36) and the possibility of differences between the Member States (paras 37–38).[67] Finally the Third Chamber twice cited *Omega*, referring to the principle of proportionality and the discretion of the Member States in defining the level of protection independently of a conception shared by all Member States.[68] In conclusion it is possible to say that the findings in the *Omega* passages of particular concern in the present context have been confirmed by the CJ.

B. References by AGs

So far, 10 Advocates General have cited *Omega* in 24 opinions. Apart from his opinion in *Mechaniki*, which was discussed earlier, AG Poiares Maduro cited *Omega* in another two opinions to support the statements that relevance of fundamental rights would not remove the national rules from the field of application of the Treaty[69] and that the Member States are allowed a certain amount of discretion in choosing the desired level of protection to be afforded to the public interest at issue.[70] AG Mengozzi cited *Omega* with regard to the discretion of the Member States in defining the concept of public security for its territory[71] and as an example

[64] Case C-438/05 *ITF and SFU v Viking* [2007] ECR I-11767, paras 45–46; Case C-341/05 *Laval un Partneri* [2007] ECR I-10779, paras 93–94.

[65] Case C-33/07 *Jipa* [2008] ECR I-5157, para 23; Case C-319/06 *Commission v Luxembourg* [2008] ECR I-4323, para 50.

[66] Case C-168/04 *Commission v Austria* [2006] ECR I-9041, para 64. The fourth reference is to para 36 of *Omega* (insisting on the proportionality of the national measure) in Case C-257/05 *Commission v Austria* [2006] ECR I-134, para 23; the fifth reference is to para 27 of *Omega* (relating to the delimitation of the fundamental freedoms) in Case C-182/08 *Glaxo Wellcome* [2009] ECR I-8591, para 51.

[67] Case C-208/09 *Sayn-Wittgenstein* [2010] ECR I-13693, paras 86, 87, 90, 91; Case C-137/09 *Josemans* [2010] ECR I-13019, para 69 (to para 36); the latter decision also referred in para 50 to para 26 of *Omega*.

[68] Case C-244/06 *Dynamic Medien Vertriebs GmbH v Avides Media AG* [2008] ECR I-505, paras 42, 44, 49; Case C-227/06 *Commission v Belgium* [2008] ECR I-46, para 61 also referred to para 36 of *Omega*.

[69] AG Poiares Maduro, Opinion of 23 May 2007, in Case 438/05 *ITF and SFU v Viking* [2007] ECR I-10779, para 24, referring to paras 34, 38–40 of *Omega* (n 1); it is interesting to note that the Court in its judgment in that case referred to paras 35–36.

[70] AG Poiares Maduro, Opinion of 13 July 2006, in Case C-434/04 *Ahokainen and Leppik* [2006] ECR I-9171, para 26 referring to paras 32, 37, 39.

[71] AG Mengozzi, Opinion of 13 September 2007, in Case C-244/06 *Dynamic Medien* [2008] ECR I-505, para 81.

of the Court balancing fundamental freedoms and fundamental rights.[72] AG Ruiz-Jarabo Colomer has referred to *Omega* as proof that fundamental rights set limits and even exceptions with regard to mutual recognition.[73] Finally,[74] AG Kokott quoted *Omega* as support for her statement that the Member States may have different but equally legitimate views about the proportionality of measures restricting fundamental freedoms for the benefit of public interests, in particular fundamental rights.[75] In conclusion it is possible to say that the *Omega* judgment has been seized by the AGs as a reference point for attempts to allow for some discretion of the Member States in relation to restricting fundamental freedoms.

C. References by the Parties

As far as it is possible to find out with the help of the publications of the Court, only the Republic of Finland in the case of *Commission v Italy* has cited *Omega* to support its position that the fact that a number of Member States have chosen not to impose an obligation to contract on insurance undertakings does not entail that the Italian measures in question, which imposed such an obligation, are disproportionate.[76] And Finland's citation of *Omega* was ultimately unsuccessful. Thus, it can be said that the Member States have not seized *Omega* as a particular opportunity to justify restrictions of fundamental freedoms, contrary to what some observers expected.[77]

V. Conclusion

Should we believe that *Omega* is a turning point in the jurisprudence of the CJ in relation to the protection of the Member States' competence to define their national identities?

The question referred to the CJ by the Federal Administrative Court in a way brought up Germany's big gun: the protection of human dignity, which is positioned at the top of the Basic Law to mark the turning away from the dictatorial

[72] AG Mengozzi, Opinion of 26 October 2006, in Case C-354/04 P *Gestoras Pro Amnistía* [2007] ECR I-1579, para 176, fn 88.

[73] AG Ruiz-Jarabo Colomer, Opinion of 8 April 2008, in Case C-297/07 *Klaus Bourquain* [2008] ECR I-9425, para 51 referring to paras 34, 37, 38.

[74] The other references – involving also GA Bot, GA Léger, GA Trstenjak, GA Tizzano, GA Mazák and GA Sharpston – concerned the demarcation of the fundamental freedoms, the general relevance of fundamental rights in European law, the necessity to construe the concept of public security strictly and the requirement of a genuine and sufficiently serious threat to a fundamental interest of society.

[75] AG Kokott, Opinion of 8 May 2008, in Case C-73/07 *Stakunnan Markkinapörssi and Satamedia* [2008] ECR I-9831, para 48.

[76] See also AG Mazák, Opinion of 9 September 2008, in Case C-518/06 *Commission v Italy* [2009] ECR I-3491, para 65.

[77] See above at fns 54–55.

Nazi regime. It is simply inconceivable that the CJ could have decided differently by saying that human dignity is a nice thing but either it is not that important compared to the freedom to provide services or the Federal Administrative Court got it wrong in deciding the game in question was contrary to human dignity.

The Court was careful not to accord too much prominence to the *Omega* case. It only assigned the case to a chamber of five judges, not to the Grand Chamber or the full court. The chamber then decided it only on the basis of Articles 55, 46 TEC (now 62, 52 TFEU), without even the slightest reference to Article 6(3) TEU, and was careful to avoid any suggestion of the decision being groundbreaking or even revolutionary. Nevertheless it is the first case which has been referred to within the Court as an example of actually respecting the national identity by allowing the Member State to restrict a fundamental freedom on the basis of a specific aspect of its national identity in the face of conflicting concepts in other Member States. In particular Advocates General have seized on the decision to argue for discretion of the Member States even in the core area of the four freedoms.

Even though the nation and the nation-state are still the primary reference point for political identification,[78] it should not be forgotten that there is a structural tension between European integration and national identity.[79] The mobilisation of the means of production, including people as human resources, aims at the break up of traditional patterns of identification or identity to allow for the efficient allocation of resources. This requires that foreign goods and foreigners are treated as completely acceptable substitutes of national goods and national neighbours. By prohibiting discrimination on grounds of nationality – which is necessary to achieve the creation of the internal market – European law heavily restricts the process of national identity building through differentiation of 'the other'. At the same time, the Court sees as its main task, after the accession of 12 new Member States since 2004, the preservation and strengthening of the primacy and uniform application of European law.[80] It therefore seems unlikely that the CJ will use *Omega* in the foreseeable future as a starting point to seriously extend the discretion of the Member States which would be detrimental to the strengthening of the internal market.

Thus it might be tempting to suggest to the defenders of the nation states against European integration that they follow the maxim of Johann Nestroy: 'The noblest nation is resignation.'

[78] Droege (n 7) 111.

[79] Von Bogdandy (n 4) 185.

[80] T von Danwitz, 'Funktionsbedingungen der Rechtsprechung des Europäischen Gerichtshofes' (2008) 43 *Europarecht* 769, 774.

Part Four

Human Rights and Anti-terrorism Measures

13

Preventive Information Search by the Police as an Anti-terrorism Measure

The German Perspective

FOROUD SHIRVANI

I. The German Terrorist Problem in the 1970s

Terrorism – one of the most serious violations of the values of human dignity, liberty, solidarity and respect for human rights[1] – is not a new phenomenon in the history of the Federal Republic of Germany. The threat of terrorism and the direct attack against the state, its institutions and its legal system were serious problems in the late 1960s and 1970s in this country. The dimension of terrorist crime in that era can be illustrated statistically: between 1967 and 1977, more than 400 terrorist attacks were registered in West Germany.[2] In particular, left-wing terrorism and the activities of the Red Army Faction (RAF) were considered as a pressing danger to the foundation of the state and society.[3] Though it was clear that combating terrorism is one of the main tasks of the public authorities, the relevant question was which instruments and methods to use in order to react to that extraordinary situation.[4] While the country was in a state of emergency, the state had to defend its principles under the rule of law. Thus, the threat of terrorism was a challenge for the federal government and Parliament, which enacted new statutes expanding the scope of instruments available for the security authorities.

[1] See recitals 1 and 2 of the Council Framework Decision of 13 June 2002 on combating terrorism [2002] OJ L164/3.

[2] V Götz, 'Die Sorge für die öffentliche Sicherheit und Ordnung' in KGA Jeserich et al (eds), *Deutsche Verwaltungsgeschichte*, vol 5 (Stuttgart, Deutsche-Verlags Anstalt, 1987) 426, 438.

[3] H Busch et al, *Die Polizei in der Bundesrepublik Deutschland* (Frankfurt, Campus, 1985) 230; H-J Vogel, 'Strafverfahrensrecht und Terrorismus – eine Bilanz' (1978) 31 *Neue Juristische Wochenschrift* 1217, 1218.

[4] M Schröder, 'Staatsrecht an den Grenzen des Rechtsstaates' (1978) 103 *Archiv des Öffentlichen Rechts* 121, 123; E-W Böckenförde, 'Der verdrängte Ausnahmezustand' (1978) 31 *Neue Juristische Wochenschrift* 1881.

A. The Programme for Internal Security in the Federal Republic of Germany

In reaction to the terrorist danger and other kinds of crime, the Federal Minister of the Interior and the Ministers of the Interior of the *Länder* (German states below the federal level) agreed on an agenda titled 'Programme for Internal Security in the Federal Republic of Germany Part I'.[5] Passed in 1972, this programme was aimed at strengthening the police forces and improving the cooperation between the central police authorities and the police organisations of the German Bundesländer. Although the divided responsibility of the federal government and the Bundesländer in the field of internal security was emphasised in the programme, the Ministers proposed an agreement on common standards.[6] These standards were designed to refer to the tasks, the organisation, the equipment and the training of the police forces.[7] Another important aspect of the programme was the development of the Federal Criminal Police Office [*Bundeskriminalamt*, BKA] into an information and communication centre for the entire German police. The BKA would collect and evaluate all the relevant data in the fight against crime and become the centre of the electronic data network.[8] Data collection, data processing and the possibilities of modern technologies were crucial elements in the new police strategy. The data network and the exchange of information were supposed to enhance investigations by the police.[9]

B. Legal Reforms

The concept of internal security was flanked by legal reforms, such as the amendment of the German Basic Law [*Grundgesetz*] in 1972.[10] One of the aspects of this amendment referred to the cooperation between the Federation and the Bundesländer in order to maintain or restore public security. To this end, Article 35(2), 1st sentence of the Basic Law stipulated that a Bundesland could call upon personnel and facilities of the Federal Border Police to assist its police in particularly serious cases where, without such assistance, the police would not be able to fulfil their responsibility.[11] Another aspect of the amendment referred to the cooperation between the Federation and the Bundesländer in different areas of

[5] Beilage Nr 31/1972 zum Gemeinsamen Ministerialblatt.

[6] Ibid, 5.

[7] Ibid, 5.

[8] Ibid, 8.

[9] Busch et al (n 3) 238; H Boldt and M Stolleis, 'Geschichte der Polizei in Deutschland' in H Lisken and E Denninger (eds), *Handbuch des Polizeirechts*, 4th edn (Munich, CH Beck, 2007) A, para 87; Matthias Kötter, *Pfade des Sicherheitsrechts* (Baden-Baden, Nomos, 2008) 114.

[10] Einunddreißigstes Gesetz zur Änderung des Grundgesetzes vom 28. Juni 1972, (1972) *Bundesgesetzblatt I* 1305. See H Hofmann, 'Die Entwicklung des Grundgesetzes von 1949 bis 1990' in J Isensee and P Kirchhof (eds), *Handbuch des Staatrechts*, vol I, 3rd edn (Heidelberg, CF Müller, 2003) § 9, paras 59 ff.

[11] Änderungsgesetz, Art I no 1.

internal security. This cooperation concerned the protection of the constitution and the protection against specific activities on the federal territory which would endanger the external interests of Germany.[12] In a next step, the German Parliament reformed the law regarding the BKA in 1973.[13] This statute expanded the duties of the BKA and underlined its role as the central authority collecting electronically and analysing the database of the police.[14] The main data network established by the Federation and the Bundesländer was called INPOL.[15] Another duty of the BKA was the prosecution of criminal acts against the Federal President of Germany, members of other constitutional bodies or of diplomatic missions where the criminal act could have political motivations and affect the interests of the Federation or its foreign policy.[16]

II. Information Search by the Police after the 9/11 Attacks

A. The Anti-terrorism Packages

Three decades later, the attacks of 11 September 2001 confronted countries with a new kind of threat. In Germany, the legislature enacted several new laws to strengthen the security authorities and expand their power, particularly in the field of information search. To some degree, there are parallels between the procedures following the events in the 1970s and after 11 September 2001. The first measures were two anti-terrorism packages, which the German Parliament passed in 2001 and 2002.[17] The second of these two anti-terrorism packages was particularly extensive and comprised amendments to numerous security statutes. In this context, the legislature pointed out that terrorism had achieved a new international dimension. Thus, it was necessary to recognise potential dangers to internal security and take the necessary measures in order to minimise the risks.[18] Elements of that package were new tasks for the Federal Border Police, the BKA and the Federal Office for the Protection of the Constitution, for example, the use

[12] Ibid, Art I no 2; see Basic Law, Art 73(1) no 10.

[13] Zweites Gesetz zur Änderung des Gesetzes über die Einrichtung eines Bundeskriminalpolizeiamtes (Bundeskriminalamtes) vom 28. Juni 1973 (1973) *Bundesgesetzblatt I* 701.

[14] Änderungsgesetz, Art 1 no 2.

[15] See Götz (n 2) 426, 440.

[16] Änderungsgesetz, Art 1 no 4.

[17] Anti-terrorism package I: Erstes Gesetz zur Änderung des Vereinsgesetzes vom 4. Dezember 2001 (2001) *Bundesgesetzblatt I* 3319; Vierunddreißigstes Strafrechtsänderungsgesetz – § 129b StGB (34. StrÄndG) vom 22. August 2002 (2002) *Bundesgesetzblatt I* 3390. Anti-terrorism package II: Gesetz zur Bekämpfung des internationalen Terrorismus (Terrorismusbekämpfungsgesetz) vom 9. Januar 2002 (2002) *Bundesgesetzblatt I* 361.

[18] Gesetzentwurf der Fraktionen SPD und Bündnis 90/Die Grünen, *Bundestagsdrucksache* 14/7386, 35.

of Federal Border Police personnel in German aircraft to maintain their security,[19] and the authorisation of the BKA to collect data from national or international sources to complete its own database.[20] The Federal Office for the Protection of the Constitution was authorised to obtain information from credit institutions regarding accounts, account holders and streams and investments of money in special cases.[21] These and other amendments of the second anti-terrorism package proved controversial.[22] After the legislative procedure was completed, the critical voices arose very quickly, claiming that the legislature had not considered the different constitutional concerns before the laws came into effect. Critics stressed the legal deficiencies and alleged that the legislature had favoured security interests without achieving a balance between those interests and fundamental rights under the Constitution. The unjustified encroachment on fundamental rights by the government pursuing an intensive concept of prevention was one of the main topics in that debate.

The second anti-terrorism package, however, was not the last measure dealing with security-relevant data in recent years. In 2006 and 2008, the German Parliament approved two other bills in the field of data search and data processing: first, the Act setting up an anti-terrorism database of police authorities and intelligence services[23] and, second, the Act to prevent international terrorist dangers by the BKA.[24]

B. The Anti-terrorism Database

In order to understand the essence of the first Act, which established the anti-terrorism database, it is useful to clarify the difference between the responsibilities

[19] Terrorismusbekämpfungsgesetz, Art 6 no 2.

[20] Ibid, Art 10 no 2.

[21] Ibid, Art 1 no 3.

[22] S Middel, *Innere Sicherheit und präventive Terrorismusbekämpfung* (Baden-Baden, Nomos, 2007) 209 ff; E Denninger, 'Freiheit durch Sicherheit? Anmerkungen zum Terrorismusbekämpfungsgesetz' (2002) 22 *Strafverteidiger* 96 ff; M Nolte, 'Die Anti-Terror-Pakete im Lichte des Verfassungsrechts' (2002) 117 *Deutsches Verwaltungsblatt* 573 ff; M Baldus, 'Nachrichtendienste – Beobachtung völkerverständigungswidriger Bestrebungen' (2002) 35 *Zeitschrift für Rechtspolitik* 400 ff; O Lepsius, 'Liberty, Security, and Terrorism: The Legal Position in Germany' (2004) 5 *German Law Journal* 435 ff.

[23] Gesetz zur Errichtung gemeinsamer Dateien von Polizeibehörden und Nachrichtendiensten des Bundes und der Länder (Gemeinsame-Dateien-Gesetz) vom 22. Dezember 2006 (2006) *Bundesgesetzblatt I* 3409. See also J Stubenrauch, *Gemeinsame Verbunddateien von Polizei und Nachrichtendiensten* (Baden-Baden, Nomos, 2009); KL Lang, *Das Antiterrordateigesetz* (Frankfurt, Peter Lang, 2011); HA Wolff and F Scheffczyk, 'Verfassungsrechtliche Fragen der gemeinsamen Antiterrordatei von Polizei und Nachrichtendiensten' (2008) 40 *Juristische Arbeitsblätter* 81 ff.

[24] Gesetz zur Abwehr von Gefahren des internationalen Terrorismus durch das Bundeskriminalamt vom 25. Dezember 2008 (2008) *Bundesgesetzblatt I* 3083. See also F Roggan, 'Das neue BKA-Gesetz – Zur weiteren Zentralisierung der deutschen Sicherheitsarchitektur' (2009) 62 *Neue Juristische Wochenschrift* 257 ff; HA Wolff, 'Die Grenzverschiebung von polizeilicher und nachrichtendienstlicher Sicherheitsgewährleistung' (2009) 62 *Die Öffentliche Verwaltung* 597 ff; F Shirvani, 'Präventivpolizeiliche Datenerhebung und der Schutz besonderer Vertrauensverhältnisse' (2011) 26 *Zeitschrift für Gesetzgebung* 45 ff.

of the German police on the one hand and the German intelligence services on the other. Traditionally, the police forces seek to prevent concrete, actual dangers to public security and order, whereas the intelligence services are in charge of collecting information in the phase before a dangerous situation occurs, in particular regarding activities against the free democratic basic order.[25] The organisation of the police forces is separate from the organisation of the intelligence services, and until 2006, police and intelligence forces also had separate data networks.[26] The exchange of data was possible, but no joint database existed. With the Act setting up an anti-terrorism database, the legal situation changed. The Act decrees that the BKA, a designated Federal Police agency, the Criminal Police Offices of the Bundesländer, the Offices for the Protection of the Constitution, the Military Counter-Intelligence Service (MAD), the Federal Intelligence Service (BND) and the Customs Crime Office [*Zollkriminalamt*] have to run a joint, standardised central anti-terrorism database.[27] The purpose of this database is to intensify and speed up the data exchange between the participating authorities fighting international terrorism.[28] To this end, the authorities are obliged to store the relevant data in the anti-terrorism database once they obtain information from the police or intelligence services when the data refer to persons who participate in or support a terrorist organisation acting at an international level.[29] Also, data on other persons or groups can be stored in the anti-terrorism database – such as contact persons of terrorism suspects[30] or organisations, groups, foundations or businesses – if it is actually indicated that they are associated with terrorism suspects and information for investigating and fighting international terrorism can be obtained by searching them.[31] The database includes personal data, for instance surname, first name, previous names, divergent spellings of names, sex, date of birth, place of birth, current and previous addresses, special physical features, languages and information on identity documents.[32] With respect to terrorism suspects and special contact persons, the database contains extended basic data such as telephone numbers, e-mail addresses, banking details, safe deposit boxes, marital status, ethnic origin and so on.[33] The participating authorities have access to data stored in the anti-terrorism database pursuant to § 5 of the Act.

[25] See Bundesverfassungsschutzgesetz, § 3 (1) no 1; H Lisken and E Denninger, 'Die Polizei im Verfassungsgefüge' in H Lisken and E Denninger (eds), *Handbuch des Polizeirechts*, 4th edn (Munich, CH Beck, 2007) C, para 114; Wolff and Scheffczyk (n 23) 81.

[26] Wolff and Scheffczyk (n 23) 81, 82.

[27] Antiterrordateigesetz, § 1(1).

[28] Entwurf eines Gesetzes zur Errichtung gemeinsamer Dateien von Polizeibehörden und Nachrichtendiensten des Bundes und der Länder (Gemeinsame-Dateien-Gesetz), *Bundestagsdrucksache* 16/2950, 12.

[29] Antiterrordateigesetz, § 2 sentence 1 no 1(a).

[30] Ibid, § 2 sentence 1 no 2.

[31] Ibid, § 2 sentence 1 no 4.

[32] Ibid, § 3 (1) no 1(a).

[33] Ibid, § 3 (1) no 1(b).

C. Act to Prevent International Terrorist Dangers by the BKA

The second Act mentioned above, the Act to prevent international terrorist dangers by the Federal Criminal Police Office, was a consequence of the reform of the federal structure of Germany in 2006. The amendment to the Basic Law stipulated that the Federation should have exclusive legislative power with respect to the protection by the BKA against the dangers posed by international terrorism when a threat transcends the boundaries of a Bundesland, when the competence of a Bundesland's police authority cannot be perceived, or when the supreme authority of an individual Bundesland requests the assumption of federal responsibility.[34] The new Act refers to the amendment of the Basic Law and lays down the tasks of the BKA.[35] Besides its other responsibilities, the BKA is authorised to prevent dangers and criminal acts in the field of international terrorism. In order to fulfil its duties, the BKA has special powers. The 'BKA-Law' contains traditional police powers such as the right to collect personal data, to verify the identity of a person or to authorise long-term observations.[36] In addition to these traditional instruments, the BKA-Law contains other powers, for instance the right to monitor and record the telecommunication of a suspicious person, provided the BKA obtains a judicial ruling allowing the surveillance.[37] Other instruments include the power to access information technology systems such as personal computers[38] or data screening, which allows the BKA to get access to individual data of special groups from private or public sources in order to compare this data with other databases.[39] Many of these instruments are also components of the police laws of the German Bundesländer. The question of which constitutional requirements apply to these measures is controversial. In recent years, the Federal Constitutional Court of Germany has had to deal with several cases in this field.[40] I will discuss two relevant rulings below.[41]

III. The Preventive Police Strategy

When comparing the situation in the 1970s, when the German state was exposed to left-wing terrorism, with the events after 11 September 2001, we will find

[34] Art 1 no 6 des Gesetzes zur Änderung des Grundgesetzes vom 28. August 2006 (2006) *Bundesgesetzblatt I* 2034; see Art 73 (1) no 9a of the Basic Law.

[35] Bundeskriminalamtsgesetz, § 4a (1).

[36] Ibid, §§ 20b, 20d, 20g (2) no 1.

[37] Ibid, § 20l (1), 1st sentence, no 2, (3).

[38] Ibid, § 20k. See section IV.B below.

[39] Ibid, § 20j. See section IV.A below.

[40] See BVerfGE 100, 313; E 110, 33; E 113, 348; E 115, 320; E 120, 274; E 120, 378; E 125, 260.

[41] See section IV below.

that the state strengthened the powers of the security authorities in both cases, especially in the field of information search and data processing. In contrast with the 1970s, however, the relevance of data search has increased markedly since 11 September 2001. The main reason for this is that extremist and terrorist groups have many opportunities to establish contacts throughout the world and to plan or prepare criminal acts by using modern information technology.[42] Therefore, the police also use information technology to collect data and screen their communication channels. Other differences between the circumstances in the 1970s and the era after 2001 are the features of terrorism. The RAF defined its battle as a revolutionary 'class struggle' and 'counter-violence' against what it perceived as the violence of the state. The targets of their attacks were primarily public representatives and the heads of the economic and 'capitalist system'.[43] Terrorism nowadays is a more internationalised, diffuse and unpredictable phenomenon. It is organised in transnational networks without a command centre.[44] Usually, the prospective planners are known, but often, the real actors and assassins remain undisclosed. Possible targets are not necessarily the government or politicians but a variety of public facilities, for example oil refineries, power plants, trains or airports. Modern terrorism is aware of the vulnerability of advanced societies and uses this fact to its advantage.[45]

In this situation, Germany, similar to other European countries, pursues both an external and an internal policy. The external policy aims at integration of German security institutions into European and international security systems. The European programme is described by Article 67 of the Treaty of the Functioning of the European Union (TFEU). According to this provision the European Union constitutes an area of freedom, security and justice and endeavours to ensure a high level of security through measures to prevent and combat crime.[46] The national policy is the development of a concept that aims at minimising the risks of terrorist threat. The police strategy emphasises being proactive rather than reactive. The focus of the police activities is not the specific, acute danger, but the earlier phase before a dangerous situation occurs. In other words, although the probability of the damage is not clear, the risk of its occurrence will be minimised if important legal interests in a large number of cases can be infringed.[47] Therefore, the security authorities need new instruments because the traditional instruments such as police interrogations or observations are not

[42] BVerfGE 120, 274, 319.

[43] G-J Glaeßner, *Sicherheit in Freiheit* (Opladen, Leske Budrich, 2003) 239 ff; M Petri, *Terrorismus und Staat* (Frankfurt, Peter Lang, 2007) 139 ff.

[44] Glaeßner (n 43) 228.

[45] C Gusy, 'Gewährleistung von Freiheit und Sicherheit im Lichte unterschiedlicher Staat- und Verfassungsverständnisse' (2004) 63 *Veröffentlichungen der Vereinigung der Deutschen Staatsrechtslehrer* 151, 158. W Hoffmann-Riem, 'Freiheit und Sicherheit im Angesicht terroristischer Anschläge' (2002) 35 *Zeitschrift für Rechtspolitik* 497, 498.

[46] See C Calliess, 'Gewährleistung von Freiheit und Sicherheit im Lichte unterschiedlicher Staat- und Verfassungsverständnisse' (2003) 118 *Deutsches Verwaltungsblatt* 1096, 1097.

[47] E Denninger, 'Freiheit durch Sicherheit?' (2002) 35 *Kritische Justiz* 467, 471; Gusy (n 45) 151, 158.

considered to be sufficient to prevent the terrorist threat.[48] These new instruments are meant to minimise the risks and underline the precautionary concept of the police. However, this is not without problems. The main problem of a preventive security concept is that the limits of preventive actions are necessarily blurred. If a danger cannot be localised, many persons can be potentially subjected to police measures.[49] As a result, their fundamental rights could be interfered with. And in exactly those cases, there is a multipolar rather than a bipolar constitutional problem. One of the questions that arises is whether the interference with fundamental rights by these measures is proportionate.

As noted, the Federal Constitutional Court of Germany has had to rule on some of these questions in recent years.[50] I will discuss two of its decisions in order to show the problems mentioned in the field of preventive information search by the police.

IV. Two Rulings of the Federal Constitutional Court regarding Preventive Information Search

A. Information Search by Data Screening

The first ruling concerns a case of data screening conducted in Germany in 2001.[51] Data screening is a special method of tracing that allows the police to access external databases and compare those data with police and other data. A computer, using criminological criteria, screens and separates in several search runs the persons in the database. The persons returned as a result of such screening can then be checked by the police, for instance in individual interviews.[52] After the attacks of 9/11, and due to the fact that several of the terrorists had been living in Germany, the federal police authorities and the BKA carried out data screening. The relevant search criteria were the following: male, age 18 to 40, student or former student, Islamic religious affiliation, country of birth or nationality of certain countries with a majority of Islamic population.[53] In accordance with the request by the police authority of Düsseldorf (North Rhine-Westphalia), the local court issued an order authorising the data screening. All registration offices, including the central register of foreigners and the universities of North Rhine-Westphalia,

[48] Denninger (n 47) 467, 471; C Hillgruber, 'Der Staat des Grundgesetzes – nur 'bedingt abwehrbereit'?' (2007) 62 *Juristenzeitung* 209, 211.

[49] See Calliess (n 46) 1096, 1100.

[50] See section II.C above.

[51] BVerfGE 115, 320.

[52] B Pieroth, B Schlink and M Kniesel, *Polizei- und Ordnungsrecht*, 6th edn (Munich, CH Beck, 2010) § 15, para 50; Middel (n 22) 99 ff.

[53] BVerfGE 115, 320, 323.

had to transmit the requested data to the police.[54] The court justified its decision based on the police law of North Rhine-Westphalia with the threatening situation from September 2001 onwards. It argued that a terrorist attack could be expected because of a likely military strike in the Middle East by the United States.[55] A 28-year-old Muslim student filed two complaints against this decision to the higher courts in North Rhine-Westphalia without success. However, his constitutional complaint to the Federal Constitutional Court in Karlsruhe was successful.[56] The Constitutional Court argued that the student's right to informational self-determination had been violated. Data screening assumed a specific, actual and acute danger for high-value interests, for instance the security of the Federation, individual life or freedom since this preventive measure allowed the transmission of numerous sensitive personal data.[57] The persons subjected to the preventive measures were unsuspicious and had not provoked the police measure by any action,[58] but the screening amounted to an interference of high intensity and could have a stigmatising effect on the persons affected.[59]

This ruling of the Federal Constitutional Court has certainly drawn a line for information searches by data screening. The ruling also accentuates the relevance of the right to informational self-determination in the era of terrorist threat. Nevertheless, some aspects of the ruling were criticised in a dissenting opinion by Judge Evelyn Haas[60] and by academic commentary.[61] One of the important questions is whether data screening can exist as an effective police instrument in the future. If data screening assumes a concrete danger, the police usually know the circumstances in more detail, such as the suspicious persons or the possible localities of the crime, and can take the necessary measures. In this case, data screening is not suitable to prevent the danger because the different procedures of data selection and alignment take too long in order to identify the relevant persons.[62] The other aspect is the supposed high intensity of interference with individual rights. The crucial points are that from the perspective of the individual, the intensity of an anonymous screening and alignment regarding a large amount of data depends on whether his profile is picked up in these searches. The degree of interference with individual rights is not high if his or her data is sorted out in the first search run. For such a person, data screening does not have a stigmatising effect.[63]

[54] BVerfGE 115, 320, 324 f.
[55] BVerfGE 115, 166, 327 ff.
[56] BVerfGE 115, 166, 341 ff.
[57] BVerfGE 115, 166, 346, 348, 349.
[58] BVerfGE 115, 166, 354.
[59] BVerfGE 115, 166, 347, 348, 351.
[60] BVerfGE 115, 166, 371 ff.
[61] See U Volkmann, 'Entscheidungs-Anmerkung' (2006) 61 *Juristenzeitung* 918 ff; Hillgruber (n 48) 209, 212 ff; H-H Trute, 'Rechtsprechungsanalyse. Grenzen des präventionsorientierten Polizeirechts in der Rechtsprechung des Bundesverfassungsgerichts' (2009) 42 *Die Verwaltung* 98 ff.
[62] Volkmann (n 61) 918, 919.
[63] See BVerfGE 115, 166, 373; Hillgruber (n 48) 209, 213.

B. Secret Access to Information Technology Systems

The second judgment of the Federal Constitutional Court to be discussed here deals with a relatively new instrument of information search used by security authorities, the so-called 'secret online search'.[64] The ruling received a lot of attention in 2008 as the media reported on the creation of the 'new fundamental right regarding computers by Karlsruhe', the location of the Federal Constitutional Court. Indeed, Karlsruhe did not use this term and used in a more complex way the 'right to the guarantee of the confidentiality and integrity of information technology systems'. The ruling does not contain a new fundamental right, but a further development in the caselaw of the Federal Constitutional Court within the scope of data protection. The most relevant principles within this scope had been determined already in 1983, when the Court deduced the right to informational self-determination from the constitution. This right confers on the individual the power to determine for himself or herself the disclosure and use of his or her personal data.[65] The Court in 2008 had to decide whether this right or other fundamental rights, in particular the freedom of telecommunication (Article 10 Basic Law) or the right of the inviolability of the home (Article 13 Basic Law), sufficiently protected the individual against the dangers emerging from the use of information technology systems.[66] The Court, scrutinising the provisions of the North Rhine-Westphalia Constitution Protection Act, which regulates secret monitoring of the Internet and secret access to information technology systems by the constitution protection authority, held the protection to be insufficient. It detected a legal loophole in the protection of information technology systems and focused in particular on the possibility of granting third parties access to networks, allowing them to see or even alter existing data.[67] The said right, based on Article 2(1) (protection of personality rights) in conjunction with Article 1(1) (human dignity) of the Basic Law, protects the interest of the user by ensuring that the data that are created, processed and stored by the information technology system remain confidential.[68] This right can be restricted – similar to the right to informational self-determination – under the condition that a statutory basis exists.[69] However, the constitutional requirements of such a legal restriction are high. If the police use the instrument of secret online search in the context of a

[64] BVerfGE 120, 274. See also T Böckenförde, 'Auf dem Weg zur elektronischen Privatsphäre' (2008) 63 *Juristenzeitung* 925 ff; M Kutscha, 'Mehr Schutz von Computerdaten durch ein neues Grundrecht?' (2008) 61 *Neue Juristische Wochenschrift* 1042 ff; M Eifert, 'Informationelle Selbstbestimmung im Internet' (2008) 27 *Neue Zeitschrift für Verwaltungsrecht* 521 ff; A Roßnagel and C Schnabel, 'Das Grundrecht auf Gewährleistung der Vertraulichkeit und Integrität informationstechnischer Systeme und sein Einfluss auf das Privatrecht' (2008) 61 *Neue Juristische Wochenschrift* 3534 ff.

[65] BVerfGE 65, 1.

[66] BVerfGE 120, 274, 306 ff.

[67] BVerfGE 120, 274, 306, 308, 313.

[68] BVerfGE 120, 274, 314.

[69] BVerfGE 120, 274, 315.

preventive goal, certain facts must indicate a danger to an outstanding important legal interest. The state measure cannot be justified if it cannot yet be ascertained with sufficient probability that the danger will arise in the near future.[70] As the person subject to a secret online search does not notice the use of this instrument, he or she cannot challenge the measure in advance by having recourse to the courts. In order to compensate for this deficit, the Constitutional Court placed the secret online search under the precondition of a court order.[71]

V. Conclusion

The debate on preventive information search by the police shows once more an old and well-known dilemma. The duty of the state to protect its citizens against dangers to life and limb has remained current for centuries. Security and freedom are not absolute antipodes; they are in a principally complementary relationship.[72] However, this relationship is not harmonious. The security measures of the government interfere with the freedom of citizens, and not only of those who have committed crimes or caused dangers. From the perspective of the citizens, the measures are a potential threat to their freedom.[73] Such a threat can be the price for a putative high standard of security. At first sight, this price can be high if the government implements the concept of prevention and aims at minimising the risks of terrorism. At second sight, however, the situation is not necessarily hopeless. The preventive state has to accept limits if it intends to keep up its self-image as a guarantor of peace and freedom at the same time. Working out the suitable constitutional concept is primarily the task of the legislature, and secondly the task of the courts. Both cases discussed in this chapter show how complicated this task is, and that this task has not been fulfilled.

[70] BVerfGE 120, 274, 326, 329.
[71] BVerfGE 120, 274, 331, 332.
[72] U Di Fabio, 'Sicherheit in Freiheit' (2008) 61 *Neue Juristische Wochenschrift* 421, 422.
[73] See Hillgruber (n 48) 209, 211.

14

Terrorism, Secrecy and Human Rights

PATRICK BIRKINSHAW

I. Introduction

This chapter will focus on the movement to secret legal 'adjudications' involving terrorist suspects and the difficulties caused to government by the introduction into UK law of the European Convention on Human Rights (ECHR) in 2000 by the Human Rights Act 1998 (HRA).[1] Some of the movement to secret adjudications has been prompted by judicial decisions, but legislation has also introduced such procedures. I will also make some points about secrecy and national security. Outside terrorism, the use of secret trials, legal orders and injunctions to prevent reporting of trials and legal proceedings, and even to prevent the disclosure of the identity of parties seeking such orders or that they have applied for such orders, has caused great disquiet in the United Kingdom.[2] I concentrate on one aspect of judicial secrecy: secret adjudications involving closed procedures to protect national security.

II. The Challenge of Terrorism

The dignified part of British constitutional heritage can be summed up in the rule of law, responsible government and the sovereignty of the Crown in Parliament

[1] See S Turner and SJ Schulhofer, *The Secrecy Problem in Terrorism Trials* (New York, Brennan Centre for Justice at NYU School of Law, 2005). Generally, see C Walker, *Terrorism and the Law* (Oxford, Oxford University Press, 2011) and D Bonner, 'Counter-terrorism and European Human Rights since 9/11: The United Kingdom Experience' (2013) 19(1) *European Public Law* forthcoming.

[2] On the additional phenomenon of anonymisation of litigants' names in cases before the courts, both of which concerned suspected terrorists, *see Guardian News and Media Ltd & Ors, Re HM Treasury v Ahmed & Ors* [2010] UKSC 1 and *Secretary of State for the Home Department v AP* (No 2) [2010] UKSC 26. Letters were used to fill in for names making the court dockets appear like 'alphabet soup', per Lord Roger in *Guardian News*, para 1. *W (Algeria) FC etc v Secretary of State for the Home Department* [2012] UKSC 8 concerns the 'unalterable condition' that a person giving oral or written evidence to the Special Immigration Appeals Commission (SIAC) (see below) on behalf of a suspected terrorist 'that his identity and evidence will forever remain confidential to SIAC and the parties to the appeal', para 6, per Lord Brown.

based on representative democracy. But Britain has long been a military and formerly imperial power in which secrecy was endemic to protect national security, and secrecy influenced the operation of domestic government at all levels. Prerogative powers of the Crown exercised by Ministers played a key role in this culture.

Sustained and serious terrorism was not confined to far-flung outposts of the empire. For 40 recent and continuing years it had a terrible and bloody presence in England, Northern Ireland and Ireland as a result of imperial legacies and Irish Republicanism. Detention without trial and on evidence that could not be tested and Public Interest Immunity certificates (see below), trial without jury (now introduced into England and Wales if there are serious risks of jury tampering), shooting to kill without warnings, torture and inhuman treatment and heavy involvement of the military, intelligence and security services meant maximum secrecy wherever possible. There were egregious miscarriages of justice in murder trials involving suspected terrorists.

The events of 9/11 meant that Irish terrorism became unfashionable, especially in the United States, and was superseded by global terrorism of a fundamentalist nature. In the United Kingdom this occurred at a time after the HRA had come into effect. In the United Kingdom the 'war on terror' had to abide by the rights protected by the ECHR and could no longer be conducted on domestic presumptions of legality and informality. Nonetheless, the governmental response to terrorism has often resulted in legislation being rushed through Parliament with inadequate parliamentary scrutiny.

Recent experience from the United States initially demonstrated that a written constitution, an entrenched bill of rights and a long heritage of freedom of information (FOI) laws could do little to prevent executive excesses in the war on terror.[3] The US Supreme Court, however, ruled first, crucially, that international law could not be removed by executive presumption and only the clearest of statutory provisions could displace the Supreme Court's jurisdiction.[4] Secondly, the Military Commissions Act (MCA) had not removed the right of those detained in Guantanamo to seek habeas corpus before the federal courts, and the inadequate and ineffective procedures in use before the commissions meant the MCA operated as an 'unconstitutional suspension of the writ'.[5] The English case law has moved far beyond discussion of the extent of the ancient writ of habeas corpus as we shall see although discussion continues.

The following is written against a background in which there have been serious and frequent allegations of British complicity in torture overseas of terrorist sus-

[3] P Sands, *Torture Team* (New York, Palgrave Macmillan, 2008); J Mayer, *The Dark Side* (New York, Doubleday, 2008); generally Y Ginbar, *Why Not Torture Terrorists?* (Oxford, OUP, 2008), B Goold and L Lazarus (eds), *Security and Human Rights* (Oxford, Hart Publishing, 2007) and O Gross, 'The Prohibition of Torture and the Limits of the Law' in S Levinson (ed), *Torture. A Collection* (Oxford, OUP, 2004) 229–53.

[4] *Hamdan v Rumsfeld* 548 US 557 (2006).

[5] *Boumediene et al v Bush et al* no 06-1195, 12 June (2008).

pects[6] and in which for the first time the police have commenced inquiries into the involvement of British security and intelligence officials in such practices. The extent of such involvement was to be the subject of a judicial inquiry, which was to take evidence largely in closed sessions and which was to report by 2011. The inquiry was announced by Prime Minister David Cameron[7] and was to be chaired by Sir Peter Gibson. The inquiry was abruptly terminated in January 2012 following criminal investigations in relation to allegations of involvement of British intelligence agents in torture cases in Libya.

III. Secrecy and Human Rights

First of all, although conventions and much of the case law deal with items that are accepted as human rights such as a right to freedom of speech, access to open justice, freedom from torture, inhuman or degrading treatment, protection of private and family life and judicial challenge to detention, I would add one further human right to that list: a right of access to government-held information. The existence of this right as a fundamental right is the subject of ongoing debate.[8] This is relevant for the next point. One of the ubiquitous exemptions or exclusions from access is information protected by national security – it is the same in every country possessing FOI laws. I would not argue for individual rights of access to information which is sensitive on national security grounds excepting special circumstances. I will argue that elected representatives have to be trusted with such information even if that means they have to be security vetted. There are serious problems with current practices for overseeing the security and intelligence services; essential information has been missing in that oversight (see below). I return to this subject in sections VI to IX below.

IV. Human Rights for Whom?

In the first place, human rights for us – those who are defended and protected by the government and its powers. Our right to life and security.[9] But what about our right to know what the government is doing on our behalf? The misuse of intelligence to

[6] Human Rights Watch, *Cruel Britannia: British Complicity in the Torture and Ill-treatment of Terror Suspects in Pakistan* (2009) www.hrw.org/en/reports/2009/11/24/cruel-britannia-0.

[7] HC Deb, 6 July 2010, cols 175–90.

[8] P Birkinshaw, 'Freedom of Information and Openness: Fundamental Human Rights?' (2006) 58 *Administrative Law Reports* 177 and P Birkinshaw in C Hood and D Heald (eds), *Transparency: The Key to Better Governance?* Proceedings of the British Academy 135 (Oxford, OUP, 2006) ch 3.

[9] Committee of Ministers of the Council of Europe, *Guidelines on Human Rights and the Fight against Terrorism*, 11 July 2002.

justify war on Iraq is a well-rehearsed episode. One hundred and sixty-nine UK servicemen and women were killed in Iraq along with thousands of Iraqi civilians. There are allegations that the security service was at fault in the handling of intelligence concerning the 7/7 London bombings despite a largely clean bill of health by the Parliamentary Intelligence and Security Committee (ISC).[10] The CIA was roundly criticised for its role in events prior to 9/11, when they handled intelligence badly. Freedom of information gives rights to know, but in the United Kingdom we cannot ask the services what information they have or request information from them. They are *excluded* from the Freedom of Information Act 2000 (FOIA). Section 23 FOIA protects information from or about the services in the possession of bodies covered by the FOIA by absolute exemption. National security is afforded an exemption which, when properly certified by a minister, is virtually unchallengeable (s 24). 'National security' is often used to cover matters which are not national security concerns but which relate to individual safety, international relations or diplomacy. Important though such matters are, they should not be confused with national security unless the latter feature is truly present.

The law in the shape of the Official Secrets Act 1989 and judicial decisions have given the clandestine activities of the services maximum protection – the services are secret and that means 'secret'. The judgment in *Shayler* stated that emphatically in relation to Art 10 ECHR – security and intelligence officers' secrets must go with them to their graves.[11] Statutory prohibitions on unauthorised disclosure by the officers in absolute terms were not incompatible with Art 10.

But if we do not know ourselves who should know on our behalf? And what should they know? The litigation in English courts concerning the case of *Binyam Mohamed*,[12] which concerned an attempt by Binyam Mohamed to obtain documents from the UK government concerning US intelligence about torture, brought home the serious deficiencies in using existing parliamentary mechanisms to achieve oversight and scrutiny of the services. The most obvious vehicle is the ISC, a special joint committee of Parliament, established under the Intelligence Services Act 1994. Under the Act information is provided to the ISC in various forms, but subject to limitations. The ISC frequently complain about not getting the information they need and as was pointed out in *Binyam Mohamed* it was clear that the 42 documents disclosed as a result of those proceedings (the remaining contested issue concerned non-publication of seven paragraphs from the judgment) were not made available to the ISC in its special investigation into torture allegations and involvement of the security and intelligence services. The

[10] *Review of the Intelligence on the London Terrorist Attacks on 7 July 2005* (Cm 7617, 2009). There were criticisms in the report on information sharing and retrieval by the services.

[11] *R v Shayler* [2002] UKHL 11. The bar is absolute in relation to 'outside' disclosures; 'disclosures' may be made *internally* to designated recipients. Lord Bingham's belief that refusals to publish could be challenged by judicial review must now be seen in the light of *R (A) v B* [2009] UKSC 12 n 13 below.

[12] *R (Binyam Mohamed) v SoS FA* [2009] EWHC 152 (Admin). See A Tomkins, 'National Security and the Due Process of Law' (2011) 64 *Current Legal Problems* 215 and A Kavanagh 'Special Advocates, Control Orders and the Right to a Fair Trial' (2010) 73 *Mod LR* 836. See the Information Tribunal's decision in EA/2011/0049-51 *FCO v All Parliamentary Group on Extraordinary Rendition* (03/05/2012).

court found that ISC reports could not have been made in the terms they were had the ISC possessed the documents. The evidence was that earlier searches had not discovered them. The ISC had not been given full information about the treatment of the torture victims. Members of the ISC are subject to s 1(b) of the Official Secrets Act 1989, and so are under an absolute duty to keep the information they receive in their ISC duties secret. Breach is punishable by the criminal law. Some of the information not given to the Committee is seen by the Secret Intelligence Services Commissioner, and a special tribunal operates with appropriate degrees of secrecy to hear complaints against covert powers exercised by the services, although legal argument is conducted openly. The Supreme Court ruled that the tribunal is the *only* body that can deal with complaints about activities of the services beyond covert powers including preventing publication of a former member's memoirs of service. Proceedings could not be commenced in the High Court under s 7(1)(a) HRA.[13] The Interception Commissioner also supervises interceptions of communications, and both Commissioners are senior judges.

In the decision in *Binyam Mohamed*, the court could not order the disclosure of redacted paragraphs because the US government threatened not to cooperate in future with the UK government on transfer of intelligence. Faced by this threat and its implications for national security, the court felt unable to order disclosure. In further proceedings involving BM, the court ordered the release of the seven contested paragraphs when it believed that a change of government in the United States had led to a less secretive regime and the removal of the threat, although the right to 'control' the documents by the US government was still asserted.[14] However, the documents could not be released pending an appeal by the Secretary of State.[15] The appeal to an unusually powerful Court of Appeal comprising the Lord Chief Justice, the Master of the Rolls and the President of the Queen's Bench Division upheld the decision at first instance. The seven paragraphs were subsequently published.[16] The case disclosed evidence of serious torture. Crucial to the decision on appeal was the fact that information had been published in a federal court in the United States relating to the evidence in question and this publication significantly changed the position. But for this publication in the United States, the decision of the High Court would have been reversed. The court had to revisit its judgment when it published in full a paragraph that was redacted by request of counsel for the Crown in the first judgment. This contained criticism of the approach of some members of the security services to human rights and suppression of evidence.[17]

[13] *R (A) v B* [2009] UKSC 12 upholding the majority in *A v B* [2009] EWCA Civ 24 and reversing the High Court *A v B* [2008] 4 All ER 511. However, this did not prevent actions at common law going to the High Court: *Al Rawi* below notes 33 and 34; and note also *Binyam Mohamed* note 14 below. On vetting cases, see Lord Brown in *Tariq* at para 94, note 34.

[14] *R (Binyam Mohamed) v SoS FA* [2009] EWHC 2549 (Admin). See further *R (Al Sweady) v Secretary of State for Defence* [2009] EWHC 1687 and 2387.

[15] *Binyam Mohamed* (n 14).

[16] *R (Binyam Mohamed) v Secretary of State for Foreign Affairs* [2010] EWCA Civ 65.

[17] Ibid, 158.

The inquiry into alleged British involvement in torture overseas announced by the Prime Minister in July 2010[18] was part of a package to attempt to settle the claims of Binyam Mohamed and others out of court and was accompanied by an announcement that limits were to be set on disclosures of intelligence information in courts by legislation. The government's desire for secret trials has moved on as we shall see below in section IX.

Secondly, the human rights of those subject to executive action are involved. The dilemma concerns secret processes of doing justice and fairness to the 'suspects'. The ECHR has made a huge difference here. But UK judges, and certainly the UK government, have been troubled by the full implications of Strasbourg rulings as we shall see.[19] This balance between secrecy and justice is one of the most sensitive problems facing the law today. How may justice be done when the suspect lacks essential information for his defence or his case but where sight of that information by the suspect may lead to undermining of security operations and the possible deaths of many persons? Before I examine the Special Immigration Appeals Commission (SIAC), which deals with terrorist deportation cases, and control order procedures where these questions have been foremost, I need to say a little about intelligence in security cases.

V. Intelligence and Evidence

Much of the intelligence concerning *suspected* terrorists is not *evidence* that would be usable in civil or criminal cases because it would not *prove* anything. It would also be inadmissible. Furthermore, '[t]here are many limitations to intelligence'.[20] It may be inadmissible as hearsay, intercept evidence or general surveillance material. The procedures about to be discussed allow such 'evidence' to be admitted.

In the case of control orders, for instance those which place severe restrictions on a suspect's free movement, it is material on which the executive (a) has reasonable grounds for suspecting that the individual is or has been involved in terrorism-related activity; and (b) considers that it is necessary, for purposes connected with protecting members of the public from a risk of terrorism, to make a control order imposing obligations on that individual (Prevention of Terrorism Act, s 2(1) 2005). Under the replacement for control orders (see section IX below) the 'reasonable suspicion' is replaced by 'reasonable belief'.

[18] See above text at n 6.

[19] *A and Others v UK* (2009) 49 EHRR 29 remains the leading ECtHR case on Art 6 and suspect terrorism procedures. For the application of *A and Others* to the new procedures replacing control orders, see *BM v Secretary of State for the Home Department* [2012] EWHC 714 Admin, below section IX. On anti-terrorism legislation generally, see C Walker, *Blackstone's Guide to the Anti-Terrorism Legislation*, 2nd edn, Oxford, OUP, 2009).

[20] Cm 7617, paras 14 and 155.

The duty of courts is to see whether that decision is 'obviously flawed'; it is not to establish the truth or falsity of an executive judgement. SIAC (below), which deals with cases of deportation of aliens in the public interest on grounds of national security and which emerged after the EctHR's criticism of existing UK procedures in *Chahal*,[21] has to adopt a robust position in challenging assumptions leading to deportation. It is chaired by a High Court judge, and it is not restricted to an error of law but may decide that executive discretion should have been 'exercised differently'.[22] What it may do by way of challenge was limited by the Law Lords in *Rehman*[23] so that SIAC may not treat 'in the interests of national security' as a jurisdictional fact, which the Secretary of State has to prove on a 'high civil degree of probability'. There are serious questions to be raised about the fairness of its procedures involving Special Advocates (see below).[24] What a subject confronts was well expressed by Lord Bingham in a case involving the Terrorism Act 2000 and the search and seizure powers under ss 44–47:

> In the result, therefore, the House has before it what appear to be considered and informed evaluations of the terrorist threat on one side (based on secret security intelligence) and effectively nothing save a measure of scepticism on the other. There is no basis on which the [Crown's] evidence can be rejected.[25]

By its nature, the use of secret intelligence means that much of this will remain secret and those who use it are unanswerable in any meaningful way to any democratic authority – as the *Binyam Mohamed* case, discussed above, demonstrates. The Law Lords in a momentous decision ruled that evidence obtained by torture overseas by foreign intelligence officers from another party is not admissible in a judicial proceeding in the United Kingdom.[26] The common law found such a prospect abhorrent. Only one Law Lord, Lord Bingham, argued with detailed reference to the ECHR and international law. The Court of Appeal was criticised for treating the issue as a technical rule of evidence and not a constitutional principle – a phrase which neatly sums up the difference of approach in a rights-based culture. But as I have explained elsewhere, the decision will make little or no difference to the way torture evidence is obtained or used; nor will the decision place the suspect in any realistic position to challenge the admissibility of the evidence.[27] The onus is clearly on the suspect to prove that the evidence was obtained by torture to prevent its use.

[21] *Chahal v United Kingdom* App no 22414/93 (1997) 23 EHRR 413.

[22] Special Immigration Appeals Commission Act 1997, s 4(1)(a)(ii).

[23] *Secretary of State v Rehman* [2001] UKHL 47.

[24] *Roberts v Secretary of State for the Home Department* [2005] UKHL 45.

[25] *R (Gillan) v Metropolitan Police Commissioner* [2006] UKHL 12.

[26] *A (FC) v Secretary of State for the Home Department* [2005] UKHL 71. See *Gäfgen v Germany* App no 22978/05 (2008), (2009) 48 EHRR 13, para 99 and *Othman (Abu Qatada) v UK* App no 8139/09, judgment of 17 January 2012. See n 53 below.

[27] See P Birkinshaw, 'English Law and Evidence Obtained by Torture: Vindication of Basic Principle or Judicial Abnegation? Implications of *A* v. *Secretary of State for the Home Department*' in B Clucas, G Johnstone and T Ward (eds), *Torture: Moral Absolutes and Ambiguities* (Baden Baden, Nomos, 2009) on the shortcomings in *A*.

The torture case followed the House of Lords decision in *A v Secretary of State*, where the Law Lords famously ruled that powers of detention of international terrorists in s 23 of the Anti-terrorism, Crime and Security Act 2001 were contrary to Arts 5 and 14 of the ECHR and issued a declaration of incompatibility under the HRA to that effect.[28] The orders derogating from Art 15 of the Convention breached Art 15 because they were disproportionate, discriminatory and irrational. The government had used immigration legislation and deportation to address a problem that also involved suspected terrorists who were British nationals and who were not subject to detention. This was discriminatory. It is the high water mark of 'effective judicial protection' in human rights case law in the United Kingdom in the war on terror. However, the declaration of a state of emergency by the government leading to derogation under Art 15 was, with one dissentient, ruled lawful.

A factor not dealt with by the Law Lords in the detention case, but very much at the heart of what I have to discuss, concerns the nature of the proceedings before SIAC, which heard appeals from detention decisions made by the Secretary of State and the secrecy of their operation. SIAC and Special Advocate procedures were influenced by Canadian practice and have been widely commended by senior judges and eminent lawyers in the United Kingdom.[29]

VI. Special Immigration Appeals Commission (SIAC), Control Orders and Special Advocates

Courts in the United Kingdom, said Lord Bingham in *Shayler*, are not alone in having to ensure that those charged with serious offences of terrorism or serious crime are tried in a fair manner, but in a process that does not compromise disclosure of information which could damage security or endanger informers or the lives of security personnel.[30]

The subjects of secret trials and non-disclosure to a defendant of evidence to be used against him (closed material procedures) have been a pre-eminent feature of the proceedings before SIAC and before courts dealing with 'control orders' to place those suspected of terrorist activities under a form of house arrest (an order renewable every 12 months).[31] The features of secret trials have been extended to

[28] *A v Secretary of State* [2004] UKHL 56. On whether such a declaration constitutes an effective remedy, see *Burden and Burden v United Kingdom* App no 13378/05 (2007) 44 EHRR 51. The Court following earlier case law ruled it did not although it might develop into a binding convention that the UK government *always* accepts such a declaration which might cause the ECtHR to reconsider.

[29] See N Blake, 'Judicial Review of Expulsion Decisions: Reflections on the UK Experience' in D Dyzenhaus (ed), *The Unity of Public Law* (Oxford, Hart Publishing, 2004) 225.

[30] *Shayler* (n 11), para 33.

[31] See Joint Committee on Human Rights (2009–10, HL 64) on annual renewal of control orders.

other procedures,[32] including financial restriction proceedings under the Counter Terrorism Act 2008, Part 6. We shall see that they were originally extended to trials of actions in private law procedure by judicial decision[33] although this decision was subsequently overruled.[34]

SIAC was created by the Special Immigration Appeals Commission Act 1997 in response to the observations in *Chahal*.[35] In *Chahal* a foreign national facing expulsion from the United Kingdom on national security grounds successfully pleaded breaches of Arts 3 (if deported), 5(4) and 13 ECHR. The existing procedures to challenge the decision by the Home Secretary did not allow an effective challenge to be made. The object of the 1997 Act was to provide as effective a remedy as possible for those challenging immigration decisions that involved information which the Secretary of State considered should not be made public because disclosure would be contrary to the public interest. The Act has been amended.[36]

The appeal route for immigration appeals is to the Asylum and Immigration Tribunal (AIT). One ground of appeal is that removal would be incompatible with the appellant's Convention rights. Appeal is precluded to the AIT, however, where the Secretary of State's decision was taken wholly or partly on grounds of national security or wholly or partly in reliance on information which, in the Secretary of State's opinion, should not be made public in the interests of national security, the interests of the relationship between the United Kingdom and any other country, or otherwise in the public interest.

In such a case, an appeal may be made to SIAC. Grounds of appeal include not only breaches of law but, as explained above, that the commission's discretion should be exercised differently. Schedule 1 to the Act provides for the appointment of members to SIAC by the Lord Chancellor. SIAC is deemed to be duly constituted if it consists of three or more members, at least one of whom holds or has held high judicial office, and at least one of whom is, or has been, a legally qualified member of the AIT. Usually SIAC sits in a panel of three, and the third member appointed is a person with experience in security matters. This membership has been commended by senior judges for giving SIAC a firm basis in relevant expertise.[37]

[32] The Proscribed Organisations Appeals Commission; Pathogens Access Appeals Commission; planning inquiries; under s 57 Race Relations Act; Parole Board hearings; judicial review cases; criminal proceedings; the Security Vetting Appeals Panel; and they have been used in Northern Ireland, see n 92 below.

[33] *Al Rawi etc v The Security Service etc* [2009] EWHC 2959 (QB). See *HM Treasury v MJ Ahmed and Others* [2010] UKSC 2.

[34] Both the Court of Appeal and UK Supreme Court allowed *Al Rawi's* appeal holding the Special Advocates could not be used in common law private actions. However, in *Home Office v Tariq* [2011] UKSC 35 Special Advocates could be used in employment vetting cases; no Article 6 ECHR rights were breached.

[35] *Chahal* (n 21).

[36] Eg Nationality, Immigration and Asylum Act 2002. See SIAC and the Special Advocate, HC 323 I & II (04-05), Government Response Cm 6596 (2005); SI 2003/1034 for SIAC's rules of procedure (amended in 2007); for Canadian practices, see paras 71–74 of the judgment of McLachlin CJ in *Charkaoui v Minister of Citizenship and Immigration* [2007] SCC 9.

[37] *RB (Algeria) v Secretary of State for the Home Department* [2009] UKHL 10.

The Lord Chancellor (Minister for Justice) is given the power to make rules under s 5 of the 1997 Act. Under s 5(3) rules may make provision:

> (a) enabling proceedings before the Commission to take place without the appellant being given full particulars of the reasons for the decision which is the subject of the appeal,
> (b) make provision enabling the Commission to hold proceedings in the absence of any person, including the appellant and any legal representative appointed by him, and
>
> ...
>
> (d) make provision enabling the Commission to give the appellant a summary of any evidence taken in his absence
>
> ...
>
> (6) In making rules under this section the Lord Chancellor shall have regard, in particular, to –
> (a) the need to secure that decisions which are the subject of appeals are properly reviewed, and
> (b) the need to secure that information is not disclosed contrary to the public interest.

The Special Immigration Appeals Commission (Procedure) Rules 2003 (SI 2003/1034) and amendments (SI 2007/1285 and 3370) have been made. Rule 4 concerns general duties of SIAC and provides:

> 4(1) When exercising its functions, the Commission shall secure that information is not disclosed contrary to the interests of national security, the international relations of the United Kingdom, the detection and prevention of crime, or in any other circumstances where disclosure is likely to harm the public interest.
> (2) Where these Rules require information not to be disclosed contrary to the public interest, that requirement is to be interpreted in accordance with paragraph (1).
> (3) Subject to paragraphs (1) and (2), the Commission must satisfy itself that the material available to it enables it properly to determine proceedings.

Rule 34 provides for the appointment of Special Advocates, who are security-vetted lawyers.[38] They are appointed by the Attorney General – Rule 35 provides for the manner in which the Special Advocate is to perform his function of representing the interests of an appellant to SIAC. These include cross-examination of witnesses and making submissions to the commission at any hearings from which the appellant and his representatives are excluded. Rule 36 provides that the Special Advocate may communicate with the appellant or his representative up to the time that he is served with 'closed material' but not thereafter unless authorised so to do by SIAC. 'Closed material' is defined by Rule 37(1) to mean material upon which the Secretary of State wishes to rely in any proceedings before the SIAC, but which the Secretary of

[38] See Special Advocates – A Guide at www.attorneygeneral.gov.uk/ABOUTUS/Pages/Special Advocates.aspx.

State objects to disclosing to the appellant or his representative. Such material may only be relied upon if a Special Advocate has been appointed to represent the appellant's interests: Rule 37(2). If the Secretary of State wishes to object to disclosure to the appellant of any material upon which he proposes to rely ('closed material') he must give notice to the Special Advocate (Rule 37) and, after hearing submissions from the Special Advocate and the Secretary of State's counsel, the commission must then decide whether disclosure would be contrary to the public interest and, if it is, uphold the objection. If disclosure is not contrary to the public interest, SIAC will overrule the objection (Rule 38). If the objection is upheld, the closed material is put before the tribunal in a private session from which the appellant and his advisers are excluded (Rule 43) although the Special Advocate will be present. When serving closed material upon the Special Advocate, the Secretary of State must also serve a statement of the material in a form which can be served on the appellant, if and to the extent that it is possible to do so without disclosing information contrary to the public interest. This requirement is found in Rule 37(3)(c).

If SIAC overrules the objection, it may direct the Secretary of State to serve on the appellant all or part of the closed material which he has filed with SIAC but not served on the appellant. Even so, the Secretary of State shall not be required to serve the material if he chooses not to rely upon it in the proceedings.

A wide search is carried out for 'exculpatory material', that is, material that will assist the case of an appellant or weaken the case of the Secretary of State.[39] Exculpatory material is disclosed to the appellant except where this would not be in the public interest, in which case it is disclosed to the Special Advocate. Rule 38 applies to such material.

Section 7 of the 1997 Act confers a right of appeal to the Court of Appeal against a final determination of an appeal made by SIAC in England and Wales 'on any question of law material to that determination'. As we shall see, the House of Lords has interpreted this section very strictly.

In *R (Roberts) v Parole Board*[40] the Law Lords considered the extension of the Special Advocate procedure from national security cases to cases concerning parole hearings before the parole board for prisoners guilty of the most serious of crimes. The board deals with applications for release on 'licence' of life sentence prisoners. Lord Woolf CJ, for the majority approving the extension, said that in cases where Special Advocates were used the task of the court was to decide, looking at the process as a whole, whether a procedure had been adopted which involved 'significant' injustice to the prisoner. The appointment of a Special Advocate 'should not be used as a justification for reducing the rights that the prisoner would otherwise have but only as a way of mitigating the disadvantage he would otherwise suffer if his rights were going to be reduced with or without a

[39] See, however, Baroness Hale in *Secretary of State v AF etc* [2009] UKHL 28.

[40] *R (Roberts) v Parole Board* [2005] UKHL 45; [2005] 2 AC 738, para 83(vii). See now Parole Board Rules SI 2011/2947. See *M v Secretary of State for the Home Department* [2004] EWCA Civ 324 on the assistance of Special Advocates. T Bingham's *The Rule of Law* (London, Allen Lane, 2010) at 106 has an interesting section on events that took place in the *Roberts* case after the Law Lords' majority decision.

Special Advocate'.[41] Their use was consistent with Art 5(4) ECHR depending upon the particular facts of a case. This approach seems *de minimis* to say the least.

There were two powerful dissenting judgments. Lord Bingham believed that denying an applicant information not even disclosed in outline to him or his representatives and which they could not challenge could not meet the fundamental duty of fairness. For Lord Steyn, such a practice was contrary to the rule of law.

In a control order case, *Secretary of State for the Home Department v Abu Rideh*, Ousley J spelt out the scope and limits of Special Advocates:

> 21 . . . In my view, cross-examination by Special Advocates can usually deal with evidential reliability, possible alternative and innocent inferences, internal consistency or contradictions, the significance of pieces of evidence and the strength of the case overall. What they cannot do without instructions or evidence is to provide evidence or explanation which contradicts or explains the closed essential features of the case against him or offer alternative inferences which they are not aware of or lack any support for.[42]

What the controlee cannot do is 'provide the Special Advocate with information or statements to be deployed as the Special Advocate sees fit, which the court and the Secretary of State may never know of' and which might only emerge after allegations in the closed material are disclosed. An essential role of the advocate in adversarial proceedings is therefore denied.

Control orders were introduced under the Prevention of Terrorism Act 2005 and replaced the powers of executive detention under s 23 of the Anti-terrorism, Crime and Security Act 2001 after such powers were ruled a breach of the ECHR by the Law Lords.[43] They basically involve periods of house detention for fixed periods in a day which are continuous, as well as other restrictions on movement and contact.[44] There is an independent reviewer for control orders.[45] The procedures for control orders before courts (civil procedures, not criminal, as the courts have ruled) may also involve the use of a Special Advocate, whose role and limitations have been described above. The procedures are contained in Schedule 1 to the 2005 Act and in the Civil Procedure Rules (CPR) Part 76. For present purposes they operate in a very similar fashion to the SIAC procedures. However, the High Court is the body that deals with judicial aspects of the orders because they involve both British nationals and non-nationals, unlike SIAC. Orders

[41] *Roberts* (n 40) para 67.

[42] *Secretary of State for the Home Department v Abu Rideh* [2008] EWHC 1993.

[43] Following the declarations of incompatibility in *A v Secretary of State* (n 28).

[44] For the relevant ECtHR case law on disclosure to a litigant and Article 6 ECHR see Baroness Hale in *Secretary of State for the Home Department v MB* [2007] UKHL 46, para 62. See also on control orders and the ECHR: *Secretary of State for the Home Department v JJ* [2007] UKHL 45, *Secretary of State for the Home Department v E* [2007] UKHL 47 and *Secretary of State for the Home Department v AP* [2010] UKSC 24.

[45] See Lord Carlisle in his *Fourth Report* (Cm 7642(2009)).

may be of two kinds: derogating (from Art 5 ECHR made by a judge) or non-derogating (in simple terms made by the Secretary of State and subsequently reviewed by the judge). By December 2009, 45 individuals were subject to control orders and seven controlees had absconded. Some of those who have not absconded have generated an extraordinary amount of litigation.[46] By way of added detail Part 79 CPR deals with legislation passed after the 2005 Act and Part 80 concerns the measures replacing control orders under the Terrorism Prevention and Investigation Act 2011.

VII. *MB* and *RB*

MB[47] tackled the question of whether the closed material procedures in which evidence was not given to the defendant or his lawyers but only to the Special Advocate constituted a breach of Art 6 ECHR. Article 6 protects the right to a fair trial before an impartial judge and in open court in the protection of an individual's civil and political rights and against criminal charges. Provision is made for exclusion of the press and public on the familiar grounds, including national security. The Schedule to the 2005 Act (eg (2)(b), 4(3)(d)) and Part 76.2 of the CPR make provision for non-disclosures in the public interest and also anonymity of subjects of the orders. As Lord Bingham expressed the point the case illustrates:

> The problem of reconciling an individual defendant's right to a fair trial with such secrecy as is necessary in a democratic society in the interests of national security or the prevention or investigation of crime is inevitably difficult to resolve in a liberal society governed by the rule of law.[48]

His conclusion was that a fair procedure consistent with Art 6 had not been conducted where essential evidence had been denied. 'The right to a fair hearing is fundamental.'

For Baroness Hale a trial in which evidence had been withheld from parties was not automatically unfair. It depends upon the justification and safeguards. In essence she did not want to rule that the control order procedures were incompatible with the ECHR but there would have to be an examination of

> what steps had been taken to explain the detail of the allegations to the controlled person so that he could anticipate what the material in support might be; what steps had been taken to summarise the closed material in support without revealing names, dates or places; the nature and content of the material withheld; how effectively the Special Advocate had been able to challenge it on behalf of the controlled person; and what

[46] Lord Phillips in *AF* (n 39). R Simcox, *Control Orders: Strengthening National Security* (2010) at www.socialcohesion.co.uk/files/1301651552_1.pdf.

[47] *Secretary of State for the Home Department v MB* [2007] UKHL 46. On judicial treatment of conditions attaching to control orders, see *JJ* (n 44), *E* (n 44) and *AP* (n 44).

[48] *MB* (n 47) para 25.

> difference its disclosure might have made. All of these factors would be relevant to whether the controlled person had been 'given a meaningful opportunity to contest the factual basis' for the order.[49]

She continued by saying that the Secretary of State must give as full as possible an explanation of why she considers that the grounds in section 2(1) are made out. 'The fuller the explanation given, the fuller the instructions that the Special Advocates will be able to take from the client before they see the closed material.' Judges and Special Advocates will have to probe the claim that the closed material should remain closed 'with great care and considerable scepticism' – claims to national security can be exaggerated. Both judge and Special Advocates will have stringently to test the material which remains closed. Material could be redacted or gisted to enable the Special Advocates to seek the client's instructions upon it. 'All must be alive to the possibility that the Special Advocates be given leave to ask specific and carefully tailored questions of the client', although the Special Advocate does not meet the client after the closed material is shown to the advocate. The Secretary of State would have to consent to this. Baroness Hale also relied upon an extra-statutory concession not expressly provided for in CPR 76.24: 'the Special Advocate should be able to call or have called witnesses to rebut the closed material'.[50]

If the judge has no effective option but to confirm an order when crucial evidence has been withheld, that would amount to a breach of Art 6. The solution which the majority adopted was to read paragraph 4(3)(d) of the Schedule to the 2005 Act, and to give it effect 'except where to do so would be incompatible with the right of the controlled person to a fair trial'. This would then bring into play the equivalent of CPR 76.29(7). The Secretary of State may serve the closed material. If pressured, a more flexible approach may be adopted. There is no power to compel production. The court may direct that the matter be withdrawn from consideration by the court where the court considers the material might be of assistance to the controlled person in relation to a matter under consideration. 'If the Secretary of State proceeds with his order it will be quashed if the material is crucial to his decision.' Baroness Hale considered this solution to be Convention compliant, because it requires no derogation and still allows informer and infiltrator evidence and avoids reliance upon torture evidence (although such evidence is inadmissible in UK courts and tribunals, the burden is upon the controllee to establish that torture has been used). Her belief was that Special Advocates are not in themselves always a solution.

SIAC procedures involve similar practices but deal with those subject to deportation orders. In *RB* conjoined appeals concerned questions of deportation of aliens on the grounds of national security and SIAC.[51] The House accepted that a

[49] *MB* (n 47) para 65.
[50] *MB* (n 47) para 66.
[51] *RB* (n 37).

deportation decision does not of itself involve Art 6 rights.[52] Given the serious consequences of deportation it must be questioned whether there should be any difference in quality between Art 13 and Art 6 protection. Article 13 (which is not incorporated under the HRA) requires an effective remedy to protect Convention rights and this, it is submitted, would involve common law fairness and Convention safeguards. Control orders involve Art 6 rights because of serious interference with an individual's civil liberties and potentially rights guaranteed by Arts 8 and 5 – the latter involving the right not to be detained except after judicial process. On the facts of *RB* the applicants' Convention rights were not involved. They were not detained. The ECtHR, however, has subsequently ruled that Art 6 rights were involved because of the likelihood of a risk that evidence obtained by torture against the accused would be used in a trial in Jordan.[53] The case concerned Abu Qatada. The complaints alleged that they were to be deported to countries where they were either likely to be tortured, thereby breaching Art 3, or that they faced the prospect of trials in a country where evidence obtained by torture would be led against them, thereby breaching Art 6. These allegations raised questions of judicial protection in the receiving countries. The basic conclusion of the judgments in *RB* was that SIAC is the guardian of primary fact, and the Court of Appeal could not interfere with its findings of fact in the absence of an error of law. The appeal to the latter on a point of law was similar to a traditional judicial review on the basis of *Wednesbury* unreasonableness, illegality or procedural impropriety. Weighing evidence was not a question of law, one must ask? Although proportionality was accepted as a principle of law, it is quite clear it had no place in the appeal to the Court of Appeal but it would feature in SIAC's considerations on appeal from the Home Secretary. The Court of Appeal had erred in law.

Basically, the Law Lords ruled that SIAC satisfied the requirements of effective legal protection of Convention rights under Art 13 ECHR. The fact that an additional appeal had been provided by Parliament was irrelevant, although SIAC must act fairly. Facts were not to be re-assessed on appeal by the Court of Appeal. SIAC resolved the primary facts and conducted painstaking procedures; its judgment in one case was 136 pages and hearings took place over five days. SIAC's examination of all materials was exhaustive, the Law Lords held. These included memoranda of understanding between the relevant prime ministers and heads of state assuring the United Kingdom that the appellants would not be tortured were the appellants to be returned to the respective countries; there was no independent monitoring of these assurances.[54] Closed evidence had been resorted to and

[52] Ibid, per Lord Hoffmann, para 172, citing *Maaouia v France* (2001) 33 EHRR 1037; Lord Hope, para 222; Lord Brown, para 255. Lord Phillips accepted this but was more circumspect. See *Othman* n 53 below and the views of the ECtHR on Art 5(4) at paras 234–5. Rights under Art 8 or other Arts may be involved depending on the facts.

[53] *Othman (Abu Qatada) v UK* App no 8139/09, judgment of 17 January 2012. No appeal was allowed to the Grand Chamber of the ECtHR.

[54] Anthony Lester QC wrote in *The Guardian* of 20 February 2009 that the UK government had made an agreement with a human rights centre to carry out the monitoring, but the Law Lords said

involved these communications. The full detail of the assurances was not disclosed, but the parts relied on by the UK government were disclosed to the appellants. This evidence did not concern national security but diplomatic and international relations. SIAC had conducted hearings in a fair manner and its use of closed material was lawful. The Law Lords only referred to the evidence in the open case in making their judgments – they refused to view the closed material. The Law Lords' duty is to provide guidance on the development of legal principle and this must be open to all, it was emphasised. There was no need to apply the safety provisions as explained in *MB*. In the case of the evidence in Jordan being obtained through torture, the law in Jordan allowed a defendant to challenge evidence on such grounds but the onus was on the defendant to prove as much. This was consistent with the judgments in *A v Secretary of State* and the inadmissibility of torture evidence.[55] A trial conducted as one might be in Jordan would render a Member State of the Council of Europe in breach of Art 6. But the test was whether there was a flagrant and total denial of a fair trial. The House of Lords, moved by diplomatic sensitivities, did not find this test satisfied. There were no substantial grounds for believing that there was a real risk to the Convention rights of the appellants.

> The issue before SIAC was whether there were reasonable grounds for believing that if Mr Othman were deported to Jordan the criminal trial that he would there face would have defects of such significance as fundamentally to destroy the fairness of his trial or, as SIAC put it, to amount to a total denial of the right to a fair trial. SIAC concluded that the deficiencies that SIAC had identified did not meet that exacting test.[56]

Lord Phillips ruled that SIAC had not erred in law in reaching this conclusion [para 154].

In January 2012 the ECtHR overruled the House of Lords judgment in *RB* holding that the suspect could not be removed to Jordan while there remained a real risk that evidence obtained by torture would be used against him in a trial in Jordan, thereby breaching his Art 6 rights.[57] The ECtHR accepted that diplomatic assurances by Jordan would protect him against torture and a breach of Art 3. The ECtHR also ruled that the SIAC procedures in *RB* involved no breach of Art 13 in conjunction with Art 3. In May 2012 the ECtHR refused an application for an appeal to its Grand Chamber.

there were reservations on the Jordanians' part because of sensitivity about their word being doubted. There was no independent monitoring of the prisoners in Algeria. In *AS and DD v Secretary of State for the Home Department* [2008] EWCA Civ 289 SIAC ruled that a MoA with Libya offered no sufficient guarantee that the claimants would not be tortured and the Court of Appeal rejected the appeal of the Secretary of State. See n 7 above and text.

[55] *A (FC) v Secretary of State* (n 26). See Birkinshaw (n 27). See also *Al-Sirri v Secretary of State for the Home Department* [2009] EWCA Civ 222.

[56] *RB* (n 37) para 153.

[57] *Othman* (n 53) paras 258–287.

VIII. *AF* and *A v UK*

The question to be resolved is to what extent a court in a control order case, or its successor, can rule that there is no breach of Art 6 where essential information is denied to a subject of a control order or its successor? *MB* and *RB* suggest different approaches, but the issues were not identical because Art 6 was clearly engaged in the former whereas the latter was confined to an effective remedy under Art 13 according to the Law Lords. Furthermore, Baroness Hale's 'enigmatic' judgment in *MB* seemed to allow scope for *some* non-disclosure of essential evidence, and it was certainly given different interpretations by different High Court judges.[58] The Court of Appeal in *AF v Secretary of State*[59] had to rule on that question in a control order case, in other words in applying *MB* to specific facts.

In *AF*, before the Court of Appeal, counsel for the Secretary of State had argued that there is 'no room for the principle that there is an irreducible minimum of information, whether in the form of the allegations or the evidence, which must as a matter of law or principle always be given to the controlee himself'. Alternatively, depending upon the details of the particular case, that minimum may be expressed in general terms or, put another way, at a relatively high level of generality.

The majority of the Court of Appeal in *AF* was persuaded by the Lord Carswell dicta in *MF*:

> I do consider, however, that there is a fairly heavy burden on the controlee to establish that there has been a breach of article 6, for the legitimate public interest in withholding material on valid security grounds should be given due weight. The courts should not be too ready to hold that a disadvantage suffered by the controlee through the withholding of material constitutes a breach of article 6.

In all these circumstances the majority's conclusions based on the decisions in *MB* and *AF* were as follows: there are no rigid principles, and the question is for the person or body hearing the case at first instance. The question is whether, taken as a whole, the hearing is fundamentally unfair in the sense that there is significant injustice to the controlee or, put another way, that he is not accorded a substantial measure of procedural justice or the very essence of his right to a fair hearing is impaired. All proper steps should be made to provide the controlee with as much information as possible.[60] Where national security considerations are present, the controlee must be provided with a Special Advocate or Advocates. There is no principle that a hearing will be unfair in the absence of open disclosure to the controlee of an irreducible minimum of an allegation or evidence.

[58] *AF v Secretary of State for the Home Department* [2008] EWHC 453 (Admin); *AN v Secretary of State for the Home Department* [2008] EWHC 372 (Admin); *Secretary of State for the Home Department v AE* [2008] EWHC 132 (Admin).

[59] *AF v Secretary of State* [2008] EWCA Civ 1148.

[60] If necessary by 'gisting' – giving an outline. See n 102 below.

Alternatively, if there is, the irreducible minimum can, depending on the circumstances, be met by disclosure of as little information as was provided in *AF*, 'which is very little indeed'.

The majority therefore ruled that very little information may be given, even of essential allegations, and fairness would not be defeated provided other safeguards were in operation. Special Advocates provided such safeguards in SIAC and control order cases. For Sedley LJ in dissent, Baroness Hale's statement in *MB* 'even though the whole evidential basis . . . is not disclosed' is not intended to mean 'even though none of the evidential basis is disclosed'. As he understood her, she meant 'even though not all of the evidential basis is disclosed'.

Following the Court of Appeal's decision in *AF* was the ECtHR's crucial ruling in *A v UK*.[61] In *A v UK*, which dealt with the ECtHR ruling on the *A* detention case where s 23 of the Anti-terrorism, Crime and Security Act was declared incompatible by the House of Lords (see above), the Strasbourg court ruled that in the case of four of the detainees their detentions had been a breach of Art 5(4) ECHR insofar as their inability to see closed evidence which was *specific* prevented them making an effective challenge against the detention order.[62] The 'open' evidence they saw was merely of a *general* nature. In the case of five other detainees they were allowed to see specific evidence and thereby make an effective challenge before SIAC.

This decision seems to leave little scope for compatibility with Art 6 where vital evidence is not disclosed and the procedure continues to an adverse decision based on that evidence. The House of Lords has now revisited that question.

An appellate committee of nine Law Lords, denoting the special importance of the case, unanimously overruled the Court of Appeal's decision in *AF*.[63] The degree of disclosure required in *A v UK* had not been given and Art 6 had been breached – Arts 5(4) and 6 ECHR require the same standard of protection. Article 6 is owed to everyone, 'even those who are alleged to be the most capable of doing us harm by means of terrorism' said Lord Hope.[64] *A v UK*

> establishes that the controlee must be given sufficient information about the allegations against him to enable him to give effective instructions in relation to those allegations. Provided that this requirement is satisfied there can be a fair trial notwithstanding that the controlee is not provided with the detail or the sources of the evidence forming the basis of the allegations. Where, however, the open material consists purely of general assertions and the case against the controlee is based solely or to a decisive degree on closed materials the requirements of a fair trial will not be satisfied, however cogent the case based on the closed materials may be.[65]

[61] *A v UK* App no 3455/05 [2009] ECHR 301. See on inadequacy of disclosure *AT v Home Secretary* [2012] EWCA Civ 42.

[62] Ibid.

[63] *Secretary of State v AF* (FC) [2009] UKHL 28.

[64] Ibid, para 76.

[65] Ibid, Lord Phillips, para 59.

> If the rule of law is to mean anything, it is in cases such as these that the court must stand by principle. It must insist that the person affected be told what is alleged against him.[66]

> [T]here is no room for an exception where it is thought that the controlled person has no conceivable case to answer. The judge must insist in every case that the controlled person is given sufficient information to enable his Special Advocate effectively to challenge the case that is brought against him. That is the core principle.[67]

The opportunity to make a challenge must be a real one. Although the judgment of Baroness Hale in *MB* was described as 'enigmatic' by Lord Phillips, the Law Lords ruled that the majority of the Court of Appeal in *AF* had correctly interpreted the holding in *MB* so that decision was also inconsistent with the ruling in *A v UK*. The provisions on control orders in the Prevention of Terrorism Act 2005 could be read down as suggested in *MB* so that the House of Lords did not have to issue a declaration of incompatibility in *AF*. Crucially, the Secretary of State conceded this point. Had she not done so, a declaration may have been inevitable. The judgments insisted that *A v UK* did not necessitate disclosing the identity of the source of information or *all* the evidence or presumably the methods involved in obtaining it.

Furthermore, Lord Brown emphasised that *AF* would make no difference to the decision in *RB* which concerned SIAC's procedures and deportation of an alien on national security grounds. 'As was pointed out, the process in those cases was beyond the reach of article 6 and in any event involved no case being made *against* the deportee but rather his case against the state to which it was proposed to deport him'.[68] Surely there is a *case* insofar as the Home Secretary wishes to deport a person because their presence is not conducive to the public interest on the grounds of national security? Finally, there is a clear wish in the judgments that these matters (control orders and successors) will be dealt with conclusively by High Court judges in future who are the 'best judges' of 'closed material issues' with limited grounds of appeal on a point of law to the Court of Appeal.

Some of the judgments expressed the view that the control order regime may wither on the vine because in non-derogating orders the ruling in *AF* will in practice mean that the Secretary of State will have to halt proceedings for orders so as not to compromise national security. However, it may have meant that claims for national security were exaggerated and more information may safely be released. If non-derogating control orders do have to be abandoned, the 2005 Act makes provision for derogating orders. The government would have to derogate from Art 5 ECHR after declaring a state of emergency under Art 15. As will be explained in section IX below, control orders have been abolished and replaced.

Judicial criticism of an absence of a right to make effective challenge to anti-terrorist measures is not restricted to the national courts and the ECtHR. Following

66 Ibid, Lord Hope, para 84.
67 Ibid, para 85.
68 Ibid, para 113. As seen above, n 57, the *Othman* judgment did find a breach of Art 6.

the ECJ decision in *Kadi*,[69] the Court of First Instance in *Othman* annulled a Council Regulation EC 881/2002, which implemented Security Council resolutions naming parties whose assets were to be frozen.[70] The regulation did not allow Othman an effective opportunity to defend himself by challenging the evidence to include his name. These two cases are not only strong vindications of the rule of law. They are also exemplary of the integrity of the EU legal order vis-à-vis the UN Security Council and the shortcomings of executive justice. Similarly, in *HM Treasury v MJ Ahmed*[71] the orders in council implementing the Security Council resolutions into United Kingdom law were ruled unlawful because they breached the claimants' fundamental common law human rights and were ultra vires. The court accepted that because of previous judgments the ECHR did not apply. But the common law of fundamental rights did apply (the ECHR position was changed by subsequent Strasbourg case law in *Al Skeini v UK* [2011] ECHR 1093 and *Al Jeddah v UK* [2011] ECHR 1094). When the Supreme Court refused to suspend the effect of its judgment, the Terrorist Asset Freezing (Temporary Provisions) Act 2010 reversed the effect of the Supreme Court decision to allow orders to be put into effect remedying the defects established by the Supreme Court. This meant the invalid orders were retrospectively validated and still took effect.

IX. Subsequent Developments and the Green Paper *Justice and Security*

The control order regime has now been consigned to history. Under the Terrorism Prevention and Investigation Measures Act 2011 (TPIMA), the UK coalition government removed control orders from the statute book. They were to be replaced by civil preventative measures aimed at protecting the public from risks posed by terrorism where prosecutions cannot take place and deportation is not possible. They are known as terrorism prevention and investigation measures. Under the 2011 Act, measures would be 'less intrusive' and contain increased protection for civil liberties.[72] Details are in TPIMA, s 2 and schedule 1 part 1. The Joint Committee on Human Rights has issued a report[73] and Government Reply[74]. The committee and the government do not agree on the scope of application of *AF (No 3)* and *A v UK* to terrorism prevention and investigation measures. There was to be no power to derogate from Art 5 ECHR as under control orders – a power that was not exercised. However, in the event of a 'very serious terrorist risk' that

[69] Joined Cases C-402 & 415/05 P *Kadi etc v Council and Commission* [2008] ECR I-6351. See Case T-85/09 *Yassin Abdullah Kadi v Commission (No 2)* [2010] ECR II-5177.

[70] Case T-318/01 *Othman v Council EU* [2009] ECR II-1627.

[71] *HM Treasury v MJ Ahmed* [2010] UKSC 2.

[72] Cm 8004 (2011). TPIMA provides that TPIM powers cease after 5 years unless renewed by Order. There is an independent reviewer of the Act who reports annually.

[73] HL 180 and HC 1432 (2010–12).

[74] Cm 8167, and HL 204 and HC 1571 (2010–12).

cannot be managed by other means, an emergency bill was drafted with 'more stringent measures'.[75] Moreover, problems of secrecy and justice are likely to remain, especially as the government published in October 2011 its heavily criticised Green Paper *Justice and Security*.[76] The Administrative Court has also ruled that the standards on fairness set out in the ECtHR in *A v UK* and the House of Lords in *AF (No 3)* (above) also apply to the new measures replacing control orders.[77] The government has chosen to introduce legislation on these measures as announced in the Queen's Speech in May 2012 and not to wait to refine its thoughts in a White Paper.

The 2011 Green Paper, following the Supreme Court's judgment in *Al Rawi* (below), examines the balance to be struck between secrecy of court/tribunal proceedings where sensitive information involving national security is at issue and the government's duty to safeguard national security and the requirements of justice under the rule of law. This is referred to as the twin imperatives of 'justice and security'. The Green Paper is published at a time when the security and intelligence services (SIS) (MI5 and MI6) have featured in 14 cases coming to the House of Lords and Supreme Court since 2001 and many more cases in the lower courts. Before that and for 90 years no case impacting directly on SIS existence reached the House of Lords, the Green Paper claims, although this seems to omit the notorious *Spycatcher* litigation.[78]

The Green Paper outlines 'intelligence successes' in the battle against terrorism. It does not deal with criminal proceedings or with intercept evidence. It will cover civil actions and cases involving measures against terrorist suspects. The Green Paper states that rights to justice and fairness must be protected and that the government is committed to transparency. The use of sensitive evidence before inquests is also examined. Ways to ensure that an investigation into a death can take account of all relevant information and also support the involvement of jurors, family members and other persons are sought.

If the proposals in the Green Paper are taken up, a much reduced role for public interest immunity (PII) is likely in civil cases. No plans to legislate for PII were proposed although the Justice and Security Bill (below) refers to the role of PII applications.

The Green Paper proposes retention and extension of closed material procedures (CMP) under legislation but with suggestions for safeguards. The Supreme Court ruled in *Al Rawi*[79] that the CMP could not be used in private actions under

[75] Enhanced Terrorism Prevention and Investigation Bill at www.homeoffice.gov.uk/publications/about-us/legislation/etpim-bill-docs/etpim-draft-bill?view=Binary.

[76] Cm 8194 (2011). The Green Paper is accompanied by an impact assessment and an equality impact assessment. See the Joint Committee on Human Rights critical reports HL 286 and HC 1777 (2010–12). The Green Paper was criticised by the the Special Advocates themselves: http://adam1cor.files.wordpress.com/2012/01/js-green-paper-sas-response-16-12-11-copy.pdf. The SAs claimed the proposals compared unfavourably with US and Canadian practices. See the government response to the consultation in Cm 8364, MoJ.

[77] *Secretary of State for the Home Department v BM* [2012] EWHC 714 Admin, paras 4 and 21.

[78] *Attorney General v Guardian Newspapers (No 2)* [1988] 3 All ER 545.

[79] *Al Rawi* [2011] UKSC 34.

common law but similar considerations did not preclude their use in employment vetting cases: *Tariq*.[80] The paper seeks advice on ways to facilitate communications between Special Advocates and their representees (those subject to control orders and their replacement) following the service of closed material procedure on the Special Advocate. It wants 'better arrangements' for such communications. Permission for such communications is rarely sought by Special Advocates. A 'Chinese wall' (ie a self-imposed barrier) could possibly exist between government lawyers involved in the case and those within 'an agency' clearing communications so that the former could not view the communications. The Green Paper asks whether control should be within the judicial body.[81]

The Green Paper seeks advice on whether legislation should clarify when the 'gisting' requirement in *AF (No 3)* does not apply and when the disclosure requirements of *AF (No 3)* do not apply. There would, one must emphasise, have to be compliance with Art 6 ECHR in non disclosure. The requirements set out by the EctHR in *A v UK* will have to be maintained. Here it is interesting to observe that the UK government has set out proposals for procedures involving appeals to the EctHR, thereby reducing the number of appeals, and to afford greater leeway to national courts. The Green Paper does not recommend a 'national security court' to deal with sensitive information. It does not recommend increased case management powers for judges nor a more inquisitorial role for the judge, nor a change in remit of the Investigatory Powers Tribunal (established under the Regulation of Investigatory Powers Act 2000). Views are sought on these latter points, however. The Green Paper states that reforms limiting the use of UK courts in *Norwich Pharmacal* cases involving requests for information to be used overseas (against foreign governments) may be made. This was a central issue in *Binyam Mohamed*.[82] The case involved the 'control principle', ie the originator of the intelligence (USA) controls its handling and dissemination. The Green Paper states that since *Binyam Mohamed* the UK government and its foreign government partners 'have less confidence than before that the courts will accept the view of Ministers on the harm to national security that would result from disclosure'.[83]

Finally, the Green Paper seeks suggestions for the reform of oversight of the SIS. It has some interesting points to make about Parliamentary oversight and the introduction of an Inspector General regime. The arrangements for the ISC were

[80] See above (n 34) and below (n 102). On the absence of 'gisting' requirements in *Tariq* see note 104 below. In *Al Rawi*, some of the members of the Supreme Court could see a use for CMP in private actions.

[81] Cases in the past have been struck out where crime investigation methods would be disclosed: *Carnduff v Rock* [2001] EWCA Civ 680, upheld in *Carnduff v UK* App no 18905/02, judgment of 10 February 2004 (unreported).

[82] Above note 12 and *Norwich Pharmacal Co v Customs and Excise Commissioners* [1974] AC 133. *Norwich* established that an innocent party who unwittingly assists wrongdoing by B may be requested by the injured party A to disclose information to A allowing A to identify and pursue legal remedies against B.

[83] Green Paper (n 76) para 1.43.

reviewed in 2007 in the *Governance of Britain* Green Paper.[84] This made a series of reform proposals aimed at bringing the ISC as far as possible into line with other Parliamentary select committees, while maintaining the necessary arrangements for safeguarding sensitive material. These proposals were: an increased role for Parliament in the appointment process for members of the ISC; some hearings of the ISC to be structured to allow unclassified evidence to be heard in open session; providing the Committee with additional support in order to enhance its abilities to conduct investigations; finding alternative, secure accommodation outside the offices of the Cabinet Secretariat; and the ISC Chairman opening debates on its reports in the House, rather than a government minister. All of these proposals have now been implemented with the exception of evidence being heard in open session.

However, there continues to be criticism of the ISC. These criticisms focus on the fact that it is separate and different from other parliamentary committees, that it answers to the prime minister, that it is insufficiently independent, that it does not have sufficient knowledge of the operational work of the Agencies and that the process by which the ISC is appointed, operates and reports is insufficiently transparent.[85]

The 2011 Green Paper favours the ISC becoming a 'statutory committee of Parliament. ISC should be enabled to take evidence from any department or body in the wider intelligence community.'[86] Other proposals include giving Parliament greater powers over membership and the appointment of the chair. Alternative proposals for appointment were considered giving Parliament the final say on the ISC's composition. Suggestions were also made for meetings to be held on the 'Parliamentary estate' rather than the 'Government estate' and to be served by Parliamentary staff rather than Cabinet Office civil servants. Its budget would be funded directly by Parliamentary appropriation.[87] Sessions in public were considered in 2007 but not taken forward 'but both the Government and the current ISC are committed to making this concept work'.[88] The 2011 Green Paper notes that

> Agency Heads have rarely refused an ISC request for information. The Government agrees with the ISC's proposal that the Committee should be given the power to require information from the intelligence Agencies. The Government also agrees with the ISC proposal that this should be subject only to a veto exercisable by the relevant Secretary of State, rather than by the Head of the individual Agency, as now.[89]

Consideration should be given to increasing the statutory remit of the Security and Intelligence Commissioners to monitor the agencies outside their exercise of

[84] Cm 7170 (2007).
[85] Green Paper (n 76) para 3.14.
[86] Ibid, para 3.24.
[87] Ibid, para 3.31.
[88] Ibid, para 3.35.
[89] Ibid, para 3.36.

intrusive powers.[90] This would enhance transparency, cohesion and 'clarity'. The statutory remit would include overseeing the effectiveness of operational policies.

The Justice and Security Bill advancing many of these provisions concerning CMPs and ISC oversight was published in May 2012. As drafted it did not extend to inquests, and it contained some important modifications to the Green Paper. Ministerial applications for CMP in any relevant civil proceedings, meaning *any* civil proceedings, will be considered by a judge. The judge is given no discretion in any cases concerning national security disclosures but to declare that a CMP application may be made. Nothing in the Bill requires a judge to act inconsistently with Art 6 ECHR. Furthermore, the *Norwich Pharmacal* procedure[91] will not apply in cases involving 'sensitive information', ie that held by intelligence bodies or that certified by the Secretary of State whose disclosure would be damaging to national security or international relations. The Bill provides that before making a CMP application, a claim for PII must be considered by the Secretary of State.[92]

X. Criminal Trials and Public Interest Immunity

The 2011 Green Paper does not address criminal trials. The exclusions in SIAC and control order cases are statutory and differ from PII certificates although information is 'closed' on public interest grounds.[93] SIAC and control order proceedings and their replacement involve closed (to one side and the public) procedures. PII is an immunity possessed by (usually) public authorities allowing them to withhold evidence from a trial on the grounds of the public interest. Where it is so withheld, the Crown cannot use the evidence itself in court – although it will be in possession of the evidence. The provenance of PII lies within the realm of Crown prerogative and its principles were largely developed in civil litigation and are subject to judicial determination.[94] Following several critical cases in Strasbourg and breaches of Art 6 ECHR by the courts in England because of the use of PII without safeguards, the House of Lords provided detailed guidance on PII claims in criminal prosecutions.[95] Lord Bingham ruled that:

[90] Ibid, para 3.42. The Intelligence Services Commissioner was invited by the prime minister to monitor the Agencies' compliance with the Consolidated Guidance to Intelligence Officers and Service Personnel on the Detention and Interviewing of Detainees Overseas, and on the Passing and Receipt of Intelligence Relating to Detainees.

[91] *Norwich Pharmacal* (n 82). See the *Government Reply* to the report Cm 8404 (2012). The latter has an appendix listing current closed material procedures. See also the critical legal opinion on the Bill from the Equality and Human Rights Commission at http://www.equalityhumanrights.com/legal-and-policy/parliamentary-briefings/justice-security-bill-with-advice/.

[92] See the House of Lords Constitution Committee HL 18 (2012–13).

[93] Disclosure may be total (to Special Advocate) but restricted only to them; in PII disclosure may be limited but not restricted by reference to parties. See also SI 3085/2008 on financial restrictions under the Counter Terrorism Act 2008.

[94] P Birkinshaw, *Freedom of Information: the Law, the Practice and the Ideal*, 4th edn (Cambridge, CUP, 2010) ch 11.

[95] *R v H* [2004] UKHL 3. See *Edwards and Lewis v UK* (2003) 15 BHRC 189.

> Fairness ordinarily requires that any material held by the prosecution which weakens its case or strengthens that of the defendant, if not relied on as part of its formal case against the defendant, should be disclosed to the defence. Bitter experience has shown that miscarriages of justice may occur where such material is withheld from disclosure. The golden rule is that full disclosure of such material should be made.[96]

Special Advocates had been employed to assist the court in determining claims for PII in criminal trials, but their use should be a last resort and only where 'no other course will adequately meet the overriding requirement of fairness to the defendant'.[97] If material does not weaken the prosecution case or strengthen that of the defendant, there is no requirement to disclose it.[98] When any issue of derogation from the golden rule of full disclosure comes before it, the court must address a series of detailed questions which are set out in Lord Bingham's judgment. These questions must be addressed throughout the duration of the trial.

As shown in *R v H*, the House of Lords has confirmed that where fairness requires 'full disclosure' that should be the 'golden rule' with regard to information which assists the defence or undermines the prosecution. This has been confirmed by *AF*, where the Law Lords noted the strict rules on disclosure in criminal trials. Clearly, abuse of the duties would run the risk of breach of Art 6 under the HRA, but one first has to know that the material exists and what it contains.

A major problem was the non-disclosure of material the prosecution did not intend to use. New procedures covering disclosures were introduced by the Criminal Procedure and Investigations Act 1996, parts I and II, along with a code of practice. These were heavily criticised because too often full and reliable schedules of unused documents were not produced by police disclosure officers.[99] The Criminal Justice Act 2003, part 5, amended the 1996 Act. The Act, together with codes of practice and revised Attorney General's guidelines and a protocol from the judges, *Disclosure: Protocol for the Control and Management of Unused Material in the Crown Court* (20 February 2006), now set out the responsibilities of disclosure officers.[100] The 2003 Act removed the subjective basis for assessing what has to be disclosed to an objective one. There were now to be 'initial' duties of disclosure and 'continuing' duties of disclosure, and the amount of documentation involved will often be voluminous. The UK FOIA is unlikely to be of any use here because of the wide exemptions for criminal investigation materials in ss 30 and 31 FOIA.[101]

[96] *R v H* (n 95), para 14.
[97] Ibid, para 22.
[98] Ibid, para 35.
[99] See M Zander, *Cases and Materials on the English Legal System*, 10th edn (Cambridge, CUP, 2007) 292 f.
[100] *R v K* [2006] EWCA Crim 724. The 1996 and 2003 Acts also changed the law in terms of defence disclosures to the prosecution.
[101] Birkinshaw (n 94).

XI. Conclusion

This chapter has outlined the resort to 'closed material procedures' involving the Special Advocates. It has been shown how the Supreme Court refused to permit the extension of such procedures to common law actions, but not vetting cases before the Employment Tribunal. We have noted the misgivings against the procedure above including the response of the House of Lords to the ECtHR judgment in *A v UK*. How can the fair adjudication of the litigant's civil rights be consistent with the Special Advocate procedure? The first instance judge in *Al Rawi* raised the difficulty on the Crown side where it was sued in contract but, because of PII, it could not use evidence on national security grounds that was essential to its defence. In PII cases, neither side is allowed to use the information, although the Crown will have possession of the information. In the Special Advocate procedure one side (the Crown) does use it, and it is not disclosed to the other side or their lawyers apart from the Special Advocate. In spite of Lord Bingham's judgment in *R v H* that in criminal trials Special Advocates should be a 'last resort', is there a danger that following legislation their use will now become routine in civil actions where national security is raised? Such a development would have serious consequences for 'open justice'. The prospective litigation involving CMPs seems set to be complicated by continuing uncertainties about the content and limits of 'gisting' as illustrated by *Tariq* and the prospect of further tension between the judiciary and the executive on the substance of open justice.

In *Al Rawi et al v Security Service et al*,[102] the Court of Appeal and Supreme Court overruled the High Court judgment that had allowed CMP in a common law action. In simple terms, allowing such a development would undermine the fundamental principle of 'open justice'. A court had no power to replace PII with CMP in civil actions. The Court of Appeal put the matter tersely:

> It would, in our view, be wrong for judges to introduce into ordinary civil trials a procedure which (a) cuts across absolutely fundamental principles (the right to a fair trial and the right to know the reasons for the outcome), initially hard fought for and now well established for over three centuries, (b) is hard, indeed impossible, to reconcile satisfactorily with the current procedural rules, the CPR, (c) is for the legislature to

[102] *Al Rawi et al v Security Service et al* [2010] EWCA Civ 482 and [2011] UKSC 34. In *Tariq v Home Office* [2011] UKSC 35 the Supreme Court ruled that a security vetting case before the Employment Tribunal could resort to Special Advocates without breaching Art 6 ECHR. Furthermore, the Supreme Court set aside the declaration of the Employment Appeal Tribunal, upheld by the Court of Appeal, that there exists an absolute requirement that T or his representatives be provided with sufficient detail of the allegations to allow him to advise his representatives – the 'gisting' requirements. Heavy reliance was placed on the ECtHR judgment *Kennedy v United Kingdom* App no 26839/05 (unreported, BAILII: [2010] ECHR 26839/05) to justify the Art 6 ruling. In *Kennedy* the ECtHR ruled that the Investigating Powers Tribunal's procedures protecting secrecy were Art 6 and 13 compliant on the facts. According to Lord Hope in *Tariq*, '[T]here cannot be an absolute rule that gisting must always be resorted to whatever the circumstances' (para 83). Vetting and surveillance do not attract the same level of protection as liberty and common law rights.

> consider and introduce, as it has done in certain specific classes of case, where it considers it appropriate to do so, (d) complicates a well-established procedure for dealing with the problem in question, namely the PII procedure, and (e) is likely to add to the uncertainty, cost, complication and delay in the initial and interlocutory stages of proceedings, the trial, the judgment, and any appeal.[103]

After the House of Lords rulings in the *A* cases, *MB, AF* and the Supreme Court's decision on *Al Rawi* I detect a movement to sympathy for the executive in other judgments of the now disbanded House of Lords. National security was very much at the heart of one of these cases: *R (Corner House Research) v Director Serious Fraud Office*[104] was widely, and I believe rightly, criticised when the Director of the Serious Fraud Office dropped a prosecution into a corruption and bribery indictment involving BAE systems and a member of the Saudi Arabian royal family. The investigations had led to a Swiss bank account and a threat from Saudi Arabia not to assist in providing terrorist intelligence to the UK authorities. In 2009, criminal proceedings were commenced against BAE Systems Ltd for other allegations of improper book keeping and overseas payments under the Companies Act.[105] The memoranda of understanding concerning torture with foreign states of the type used in *RB* have been criticised extra-judicially by Lord Steyn.[106] And in *R (Bancoult) v Secretary of State for Foreign Affairs*,[107] the House of Lords ruled by majority (overruling the Court of Appeal) that there was no legitimate expectation induced by a promise from HM Government to allow the British Indian Ocean Territory (BIOT) Islanders to return to their homes because the land was required for a US military base. The majority judgments were poorly reasoned in a variety of respects.[108] Even in *Binyam Mohamed*, Lord Neuberger made clear, with the support of Sir Anthony May, that the disclosure of the relevant information in US litigation made a vital difference to the national security claims for non-disclosure in the English courts. As was so often stated in *Spycatcher*, the 'cat was out of the bag!' While the 'control principle', ie the original possessor of the intelligence has the last say on disclosure when it is in the hands of another state, is not a rule of law, it is a constraining influence on judicial attitudes.[109]

[103] *Al Rawi* [2010] EWCA Civ 482 at para 70.

[104] *R (Corner House Research) v Director Serious Fraud Office* [2008] UKHL 60.

[105] See International Development Committee (HC 847, 2010–12) I and II and Government Response HC 848.

[106] Lord Steyn, 'Civil Liberties in Modern Britain' [2009] *Public Law* 228. See the ECtHR in *Othman* at note 53.

[107] *R (Bancoult) v Secretary of State for Foreign Affairs* [2008] UKHL 61.

[108] M Elliott and A Perreau-Sausinne, 'Pyrrhic Public Law: Bancoult and the Sources, Status and Content of Common Law Limitations on Prerogative Power' [2009] *Public Law* 697.

[109] See Lord Neuberger, *Binyam Mohamed* (n 11), paras 186–191. See also para 182 on the limits of public interest disclosures. At para 51 Lord Judge LCJ stated: 'The enormous concentration on the redacted paragraphs may have led us to overlook that this litigation has endorsed the application of public interest immunity and the maintenance of confidentiality over secret information. The Divisional Court has in effect upheld and applied PII principles to a vast body of material . . . It is clear that the crucial importance of the confidentiality principle was recognised by the Divisional Court and in overwhelmingly large measure applied by it. This litigation therefore demonstrates that the courts in the UK treat the confidentiality principle with the importance it requires, and have endorsed it in this litigation.'

The cases show a complex picture. The courts have ruled that while torture and executive detention without charge and trial are heinous practices, there has been a far greater sensitivity to the context of judgments which involve questions of international relations, diplomacy, national security and disclosure in deportation cases. To criticise other countries (Islamic) for not being up to the standards of the ECHR may be seen as displaying arrogance and a lack of sensitivity to 'less advanced standards of justice'. But some of these UK cases leave a deep, indelible stain of injustice. It will raise questions in the minds of those who cherish the rule of law about our commitment to the rule of law when the going gets tough. The British opt-out from the full effect of the EU Charter of Fundamental Rights reveals how deep-seated the anti-rights culture of our governments is. As I write, it is not clear how safe the Human Rights Act will be under a Conservative dominated Government – a party with traditional hostilities to the concept of human rights. David Cameron's thinking on a replacement for the Human Rights Act by a 'domestic' bill of rights is confused and otiose although it will now have to take into account Liberal Democrat views. The committee appointed to examine the proposed case for a bill of rights is evenly split.

I do not believe the disclosure cases fall under this category of executive sympathy because the judgments of the ECtHR at Strasbourg left UK courts with no alternative where ECHR rights are engaged. The judgments present painfully difficult dilemmas. But I believe the last word has still to be spoken on the approaches taken by national courts and the ECtHR on this issue. The intention of the government to legislate on the detail of the 2011 Green Paper was explained above. Any legislation running counter to *A v UK* and *AF (No 3)* is likely to be subject to judicial declarations of incompatibility. Control order cases may well have gone, but the problems associated with the Special Advocate procedures have not been removed and look likely to intensify.

My last comment, ironically perhaps, is that I do not share the scepticism of those who argue that the British judges have either not been strengthened by the HRA, or if they have, then that is a bad thing. The 'information' cases that I have examined have shown a real development and improvement in terms of protection under the law. We know far more now than we did about the 'three wise men' procedure used until 1997 in cases of national security deportation. Of course, the ideal of the rule of law will forever be frustrated by the actuality; it needs no ghost come from the grave to tell us that. Law is a richly woven but never ending tapestry. The English courts have come a long way since they could say that natural justice must take a back seat in questions of national security and absolve themselves of any oversight.[110] The words of Lord Denning in *McIlkenny v CC West Midlands*[111] following a civil action by the Irishmen accused of murdering 21 victims in the notorious Birmingham pub bombings in 1974 are worth recalling. The Irishmen claimed they had been beaten up by the police and prison officers and

[110] Lord Denning, *Hosenball* [1977] 3 All ER 452 and more recently *Cheblak* [1991] 2 All ER 319.
[111] *McIlkenny v CC West Midlands* [1980] 2 All ER 227, 240.

their confessions had been extracted under such treatment. Their appearance in court after the bombings suggested serious physical abuse. The action was struck out by the Court of Appeal. Success for the convicted terrorists was 'such an appalling vista' it could not be allowed to proceed. The whole system on which the convictions had been built would be seen to be gravely deficient. 'The case shows what a civilised country we are' continued Lord Denning.[112] Eleven years later the convictions were quashed for being 'unsafe and unsatisfactory'.

[112] See Lord Hope in *RB* (n 37).

INDEX

www.ingramcontent.com/pod-product-compliance
Ingram Content Group UK Ltd.
Pitfield, Milton Keynes, MK11 3LW, UK
UKHW020220041026
15470UKWH00012B/841

9 781849 461245